MARKET-BASED MANAGEMENT

Strategies for Growing Customer Value and Profitability

Third
Edition

MARKET-BASED MANAGEMENT

Strategies for Growing Customer Value and Profitability

Roger J. Best

Emeritus Professor of Marketing
University of Oregon

UPPER SADDLE RIVER, NEW JERSEY 07458

Library of Congress Cataloging-in-Publication Data information is available.

Senior Editor: Bruce Kaplan
Editor-in-Chief: Jeff Shelstad
Assistant Editor: Melissa Pellerano
Editorial Assistant: Danielle Rose Serra
Marketing Manager: Michelle O'Brien
Marketing Assistant: Amanda Fisher
Managing Editor (Production): John Roberts
Production Editor: Renata Butera
Production Assistant: Joe DeProspero
Permissions Coordinator: Suzanne Grappi
Associate Director, Manufacturing: Vincent Scelta
Production Manager: Arnold Vila
Manufacturing Buyer: Michelle Klein
Cover Design: Bruce Kenselaar
Cover Illustration: Rob Colvin/SIS, Inc.
Composition: Carlisle Communications
Full-Service Project Management: Carlisle Communications
Printer/Binder: Hamilton

Credits and acknowledgments borrowed from other sources and reproduced, with permission, in this textbook appear on page 393.

Pearson Education LTD.
Pearson Education Australia PTY, Limited
Pearson Education Singapore, Pte. Ltd
Pearson Education North Asia Ltd
Pearson Education, Canada, Ltd
Pearson Educación de Mexico, S.A. de C.V.
Pearson Education–Japan
Pearson Education Malaysia, Pte. Ltd

Prentice Hall

10 9 8 7 6 5 4 3 2 1
ISBN 0-13-008218-X

To Mike, a great friend and
always there when we
needed you.

Brief Table of Contents

Contents

PART III   MARKETING MIX STRATEGIES   165

CHAPTER 7   Product Positioning and Brand Strategies   167

CHAPTER 16 Profit Impact of Market-Based Management   368

Preface

Based on positive feedback from students, professors, and those working in the field of marketing, I was encouraged to pursue a third edition of *Market-Based Management*. The strength of the book remains its focus on market orientation and the processes and tools for building marketing strategies that deliver superior levels of customer value and profitability. A differentiating feature of this book is its focus on marketing profitability, and the role marketing strategies play in building the profits of a business. The best way to accomplish this is with a market-driven strategy that attracts, satisfies, and retains target customers with a value that is superior to competing products or services.

The third edition builds on this theme in several ways. A special effort was made to include more coverage of Customer Relationship Management, E-Marketing Strategies, and Brand Management Strategies. In addition, Application Problems at the end of each chapter have been revised. However, the feature that will greatly enhance the third edition the most is the online, interactive spreadsheets that can be used to analyze the application problems. This will give students the opportunity to solve real-world marketing problems online as well as experiment with the interactive spreadsheets to further develop marketing insights. For instructors, the application problems and interactive spreadsheets can be used to create additional assignments.

Market-based management is intuitively easy but deceptively difficult. The reason students and professionals like this book is because it is readable, and because it presents the tools and processes needed to actually build a market-driven strategy. The concepts, by themselves, are important and are the backbone of market-based management. However, they are of limited value if they cannot be applied in a way that delivers superior customer value and profitability. Those in marketing need to take a greater level of responsibility for managing profits and the external performance metrics of a business. This is an important benefit of this book. It is my hope that this book will help you in your understanding of, commitment to, and practice of market-based management.

Roger J. Best
Emeritus Professor of Marketing
University of Oregon

About the Author

Dr. Best is an Emeritus Professor of Marketing at the University of Oregon. He earned a Bachelor of Science in Electrical Engineering from California State Polytechnic University in 1968. Following graduation, he joined the General Electric Company where he worked in both engineering and product management. While at GE, he received a patent for a product he developed. Dr. Best completed his MBA at California State University, Hayward in 1972 and received his Ph.D. from the University of Oregon in 1975. He taught at the University of Arizona from 1975 to 1980 and the University of Oregon from 1980 to 2000.

Over the past twenty-five years, he has published over fifty articles and won numerous teaching awards. In 1998 he received the *American Marketing Association Distinguished Teaching in Marketing* award. In 1988, the *Academy of Marketing Science* voted an article on marketing productivity by Dr. Best and co-authors the Outstanding Article of the Year. He is a co-author of *Consumer Behavior: Implications for Marketing Strategy* (8th ed.). Dr. Best has also developed the **Marketing Excellence Survey** (*www.MESurvey.com*), a benchmarking tool for assessing a manager's marketing knowledge and market attitudes based on a worldwide database of over 15,000 managers and **MarkProf** (*www.MarkProf.com*), an online marketing profitability tool to help marketing managers assess the profit impact of marketing strategies.

Over the past twenty years, Dr. Roger J. Best has been active in working with a variety of companies in both marketing strategy consulting and management education. These companies include General Electric, Dow Chemical, Dow Corning, DuPont, Eastman Kodak, MediaOne, Lucas Industries, Tektronix, ESCO, Pacific Western Pipe, James Hardie Industries, Sprint, and US West. Dr. Best has also taught many executive management education programs at INSEAD, in Fontainebleau, France.

Acknowledgments

A book such as this is an assimilation of knowledge from many sources. It is an integration of perspectives intended for a particular audience. An author's added value is in the focus, integration, and presentation, but the basic knowledge is derived from many sources. I would like to acknowledge specific individuals whose knowledge contributed to the writing of this book.

Second, I would like to acknowledge the individual feedback I received from the following reviewers:

- Torsten Ringberg, University of Wisconsin–Milwaukee
- Glen Christensen, Penn State University–University Park
- Ron Goldsmith, Florida State University
- Douglas Lincoln, Boise State University
- Robert McMurrian , University of Tampa
- Steve Kopp, University of Arkansas–Fayetteville

Their thoughtful reviews and suggestions for improvement are greatly appreciated and will enhance this third edition.

Finally, I would like to thank managers from 3M, Dow Chemical, Dow Corning, and Sprint for their comments and encouragement. Also, the third edition would not have been possible without the support of Dr. Bruce Cooley. His participation and contributions were critical to every aspect of the third edition and are greatly appreciated. I also owe a special thanks to my editor, Bruce Kaplan, who stayed on me to finish the third edition, and my wife Robin, who endured my ups and downs in writing the third edition.

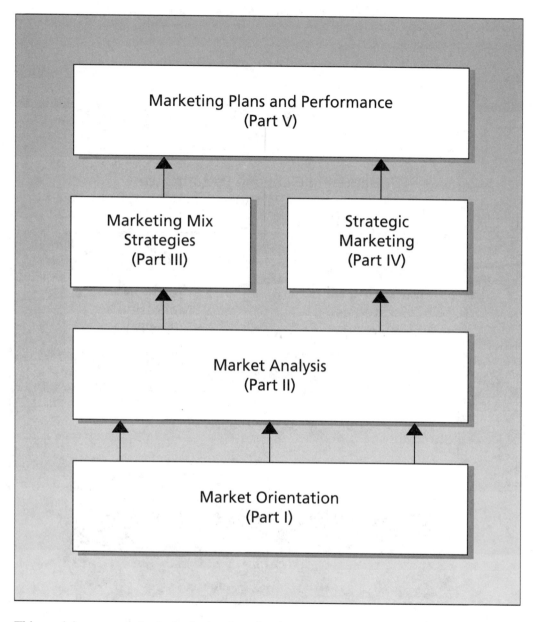

Marketing Plans and Performance
(Part V)

Marketing Mix
Strategies
(Part III)

Strategic
Marketing
(Part IV)

Market Analysis
(Part II)

Market Orientation
(Part I)

This model represents both the logic of market-based management and organization of this book. Market orientation (part I) is the bedrock of market-based management and fosters a market analysis (part II) built around customer needs, market trends and competition.

A commitment to market orientation and on-going market analysis gives rise to the development of focused marketing mix strategies (part III) and strategic marketing (part IV), long run market strategies. Marketing plans and performance (part V) are the culmination of this process.

Successful implementation of this process is designed to create and deliver higher levels of customer value that enhance customer satisfaction and contribute to higher levels of profitability.

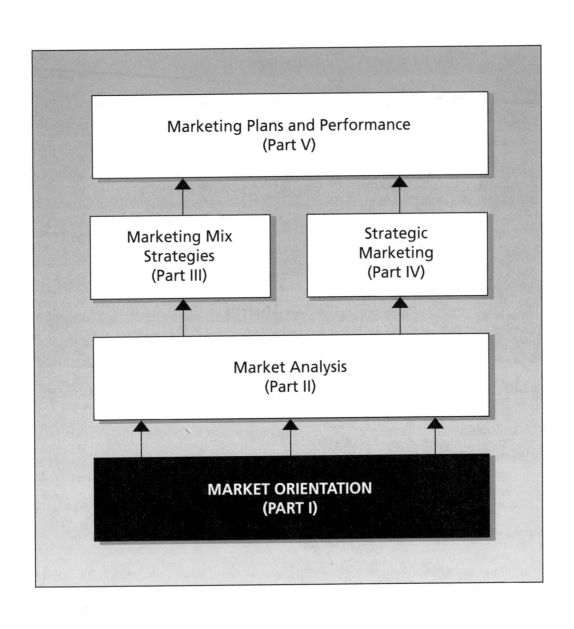

PART

I MARKET ORIENTATION

Marketing isn't somebody's responsibility;
marketing is everybody's responsibility.
—Jack Welch, CEO 1981–2001
General Electric Co.

A market-based business has a strong market orientation that cuts across the functions and employees of an organization. While those in marketing have the primary responsibility to lead marketing excellence, in a market-based business, all members of the organization have a strong market orientation. This means all members of the organization are sensitive to customers' needs, aware of competitors' moves, and work well across organizational boundaries toward a timely market-based customer solution. The payoff—market-based businesses with a strong market orientation are more profitable.

The purpose of part I is to make explicit the connectivity between market orientation, customer satisfaction, market-based management, and profitability. In chapter 1, we examine the fundamental components of market orientation and how each is related to customer satisfaction and retention. From this perspective, we will demonstrate the profit impact of a lifetime customer as well as the high cost of customer dissatisfaction. While a strong market orientation enhances a business's chances for long-run survival, short-run profits can also be increased with marketing efforts to increase customer satisfaction and retention.

A strong market orientation does not occur by mere proclamation. To attain a strong market orientation, a business needs to adopt a market-based management philosophy. This means implementing a process for tracking market performance and restructuring an organization around markets rather than products or factories and creating an employee culture that is responsive to customers and changing market conditions. Market-based management also requires businesses to measure profits at the market level and to track external, market-based performance metrics. These topics, and their relation to marketing strategies and profitable growth, are discussed in chapter 2.

1 | MARKET ORIENTATION AND PERFORMANCE

In today's globally competitive world, customers expect more, have more choices, and are less brand-loyal. Businesses such as IBM, Sears, and General Motors at one time seemed invincible in terms of their market domination. However, in each case, these companies have had to restructure (reengineer) their organizations to address changing customer needs and emerging competitive forces. In the long run, every business is at risk for survival. Although companies such as Dell Computer, Microsoft, and Wal-Mart were business heroes of the nineties, there is no guarantee that these same companies will continue to dominate over the next decade. The only thing that is constant. . . is *change*.

- Customers will continue to *change* in needs, demographics, lifestyle, and consumption behavior.
- Competitors will *change* as new technologies emerge and barriers to foreign competition shift.
- The environment in which businesses operate will continue to *change* as economic, political, social, and technological forces shift.

The companies that *survive* and *grow* will be the ones that *understand change* and are out in front leading, often creating, change. Others, slow to comprehend change, will follow with reactive strategies, while still others will disappear, not knowing that change has even occurred.

LONG-RUN AND SHORT-RUN BENEFITS

A sports reporter once asked Wayne Gretzky what made him a great hockey player. Gretzky's response was, "I skate to where the puck is going, not to where it is." In other words, Wayne Gretzky has a tremendous instinct for change. He is able to position himself as change is occurring in such a way that he can either score a goal or assist in scoring a goal. Businesses that can sense the direction of change, and position themselves to lead in the change, prosper and grow. Those that wait to read about it in the *Wall Street Journal* are hopelessly behind the play of the game and, at best, can only skate to catch up.

Businesses that are able to skate to where the puck is going have a strong (external) market orientation. They are constantly in tune with customers' needs, competitors' strategies, changing environmental conditions, and emerging technologies, and they seek ways to continuously improve the solution they bring to target customers. This process enables them to move with—and often lead—change.

One of the benefits of a strong market orientation is long-run survival. Western cultures have long been criticized for being extremely short-term in perspective. Consequently, long-run survival of a business may not be a strong management motive in developing a strong market orientation. Managers are often judged on the last quarter's results and not on what they are doing to ensure the long-run survival of the business. Likewise, shareholders can be more interested in immediate earnings than in the long-run survival of a business.

Although the long-run benefits of a strong market orientation are crucial to business survival and the economic health of a nation, the purpose of this chapter is to demonstrate the *short-run* benefits of a strong market orientation. Businesses with a strong market orientation not only outperform their competition in delivering higher levels of customer satisfaction, they also deliver higher profits in the short run. Businesses driven by a strong market orientation create greater customer value and, ultimately, greater shareholder value. But perhaps the best way to understand the marketing logic that links market orientation to customer and shareholder value is to examine the sequence of events that evolves when a business has little or no market orientation.

How to Underwhelm Customers and Shareholders

Businesses with a weak market orientation underwhelm both customers and shareholders. A business with a weak market orientation has only a superficial or poor understanding of customer needs and competition. Moving clockwise from the top in Figure 1-1, this poor understanding translates into an unfocused competitive position and a "me-too" customer value.[1] Customers are easily attracted to competitors who offer equal or greater customer value, which leads to high levels of customer turnover

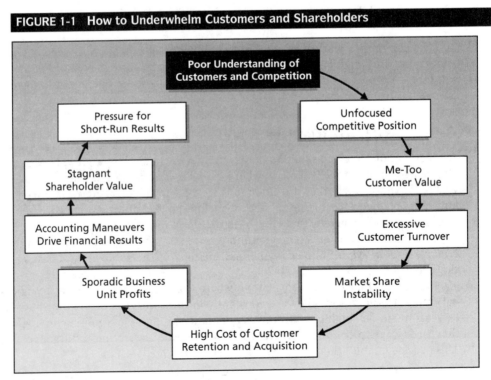

FIGURE 1-1 How to Underwhelm Customers and Shareholders

and market share instability. Efforts to hold off customer switching are expensive, as is the cost of acquiring new customers to replace lost customers.

The combination of market share instability and higher marketing costs results in sporadic business profits. In response, short-term sales tactics and accounting maneuvers are used to achieve short-run financial results. However, investors and Wall Street analysts are able to see through this facade, and shareholder value generally stagnates. Perhaps even worse, as shown in the scenario described in Figure 1-1, management is now under even greater pressure to produce short-run results. This means that there is not the time, the inclination, or the motivation to understand customer needs and to unravel competitors' strategies, and the circular performance displayed in Figure 1-1 continues.

Market Orientation and Customer Satisfaction

Contrary to the scenario presented in Figure 1-1, a market-oriented business has three management characteristics that make it unique:[2]

- **Customer Focus**: An obsession with understanding customer needs and delivering customer satisfaction.
- **Competitor Orientation**: Continuous recognition of competitors' sources of advantage, competitive position, and marketing strategies.
- **Team Approach**: Cross-functional teams dedicated to developing and delivering customer solutions.

A strong *customer focus* enables a business to stay in close contact with customer needs and satisfaction. Marketing strategies in these businesses are built around customer needs and other sources of customer satisfaction. The strength of a business's market orientation also relies on how well it *understands key competitors* and evolving competitive forces. This aspect of market orientation enables a business to track its relative competitiveness in such areas as pricing, product quality and availability, service quality, and customer satisfaction. Businesses with a strong market orientation also work well as a team *across functions*, thereby leveraging cross-functional skills and business activities that affect customer response and satisfaction.

The real benefit of a strong market orientation and higher levels of customer satisfaction is a higher level of customer retention.[3] Keeping good customers should be the *first priority* of market-based management. As shown in Figure 1-2, a business with a strong market orientation is in the best position to develop and implement strategies

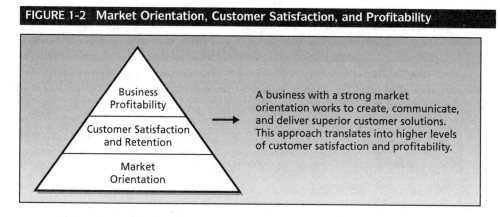

FIGURE 1-2 Market Orientation, Customer Satisfaction, and Profitability

Business Profitability

Customer Satisfaction and Retention

Market Orientation

A business with a strong market orientation works to create, communicate, and deliver superior customer solutions. This approach translates into higher levels of customer satisfaction and profitability.

that deliver high levels of customer satisfaction and retention. In turn, customer satisfaction and retention drive customer revenue and the cost of doing business. Ultimately, they are key forces in shaping the profitability of a business.

Customer Satisfaction: A Key Market Performance Metric

While a market-based business will have several external metrics to track market performance, an essential performance metric is customer satisfaction. There are many marketing strategies that can be developed to attract customers, but it is the business that completely satisfies customers that gets to keep them. This viewpoint may sound philanthropic to those who do not accept the whole concept of market orientation and market-based management. We will demonstrate in this chapter the tremendous leverage a business can create in growing profits from a base of very satisfied customers and proactive management of dissatisfied customers.

There are many ways to measure customer satisfaction. However, one common measure of customer satisfaction can be derived from customers' ratings of their overall satisfaction on a seven-point scale that ranges from 0 (very dissatisfied) to 6 (very satisfied), as shown below.

0	1	2	3	4	5	6
Very Dissatisfied	Moderately Dissatisfied	Slightly Dissatisfied	Neutral (Neither)	Slightly Satisfied	Moderately Satisfied	Very Satisfied

When this method of measuring customer satisfaction is applied to a sample of customers, we can compute an overall measure of customer satisfaction. Assume, for example, that an interview with 100 Xerox copier customers produced an average score of 4.32. An overall average of 4.32 does not tell us much and is not likely to get management's attention. To increase the sensitivity of this measure, we need to index it in a more meaningful way. By dividing the average score by the maximum score of 6 (very satisfied) and multiplying by 100, we can create an index that varies from 0 to 100. When this index is used, the overall average of 4.32 translates to a score of 72, where 100 would be the maximum. Management can quickly discern that the business has achieved a 72 level of customer satisfaction, whereas a 100 would be equivalent to 100 percent very satisfied customers.

Is an overall customer satisfaction score of 72 a good level of performance? That depends on what the business's overall score was in earlier measurements, its target objective, and the overall score given to a leading competitor. Let's assume that an overall score of 72 is an improvement over earlier average scores and that the average score of a leading competitor is 62. Those numbers would lead many businesses to feel pretty good about their level of performance and perhaps become complacent in their pursuit of customer satisfaction. Also, efforts to increase customer satisfaction cost time and money, and many managers may argue that the incremental benefit is not sufficient to justify the cost. That argument would *not* apply at Xerox, where customer satisfaction is a top corporate performance metric and priority.[4] To really understand customer satisfaction and to leverage its profit potential, we need to expand our view of customer satisfaction.

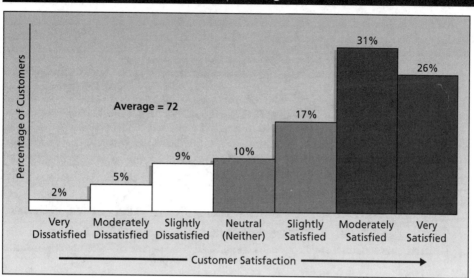

FIGURE 1-3   Customer Satisfaction: A Wide-Angle View

A Wide-Angle View of Customer Satisfaction

An average customer satisfaction score of 72 (where 100 is the maximum) may be viewed as acceptable, and even very good. However, *managing to the average* masks our understanding of customer satisfaction and opportunities for increased profits.[5]

If we expand our view of customer satisfaction by reporting the percentage for each category on our customer satisfaction scale, a more meaningful set of insights emerges. The average customer satisfaction score of 72 was derived from 74 percent who reported varying degrees of satisfaction, 10 percent who were indifferent or neutral, and 16 percent who reported varying degrees of dissatisfaction, as illustrated in Figure 1-3. The 10 percent who were neutral in their customer satisfaction are certainly vulnerable to competitor moves, but it is the 16 percent categorized as dissatisfied who are very serious candidates to exit as customers. Thus, our immediate concern should be our dissatisfied customers.

Customer Dissatisfaction and Customer Exit

Dissatisfied customers often do not complain to a manufacturer, but they do walk and they *do* talk.[6] Well-documented studies show that out of 100 dissatisfied customers, only 4 will complain to a business.[7] Of the 96 dissatisfied customers who do not complain, 91 will exit as customers, as shown in Figure 1-4. While market position is quietly eroded by exiting customers, attracting new customers is made more difficult because each dissatisfied customer will tell 8 to 10 other people of his or her dissatisfaction.

The market impact is enormous. For example, assume that a business has captured 10 percent of a 2-million-customer market, or 200,000 customers. If 15 percent of those 200,000 customers were dissatisfied, this business would have 30,000 dissatisfied customers. The statistics presented in Figure 1-4 would indicate that the business would lose 92 percent of those dissatisfied customers——27,600 customers—each year. This

FIGURE 1-4   Customer Dissatisfaction and Customer Exit

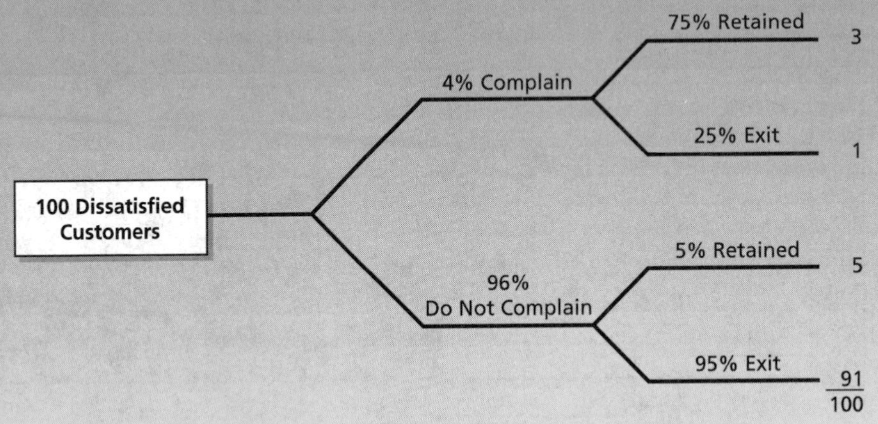

Each of the 100 dissatisfied customers tells 8 to 10 other people of his or her dissatisfaction. This communication chain makes both retention of existing customers and acquisition of new customers very difficult.

percentage translates to a 1.4 point reduction in market share. To hold a 10 percent share of the market (customers), the business would have to attract 27,600 new customers. This, of course, is a very expensive way to hold market share.

But the situation is much worse.[8] Many dissatisfied customers become "terrorists;" they vent their dissatisfaction by telling others about it. Recall that each dissatisfied customer tells 8 to 10 other people. This means that the 30,000 dissatisfied customers will communicate their dissatisfaction to approximately a quarter of a million other individuals. These may not all be potential customers, but this level of negative word-of-mouth communication makes new customer attraction much more difficult and more expensive.[9]

This kind of market behavior has led some businesses to develop programs to encourage dissatisfied customers to complain. For example, Domino's Pizza instituted a program in which their strategy was simply to encourage dissatisfied customers to complain rather than just leave.[10] Figure 1-5 illustrates that their efforts succeeded in getting 20 percent of their dissatisfied customers to complain. For those who complain, Domino's can resolve 80 percent of the problems in twenty-four hours. When complaints can be resolved quickly, 95 percent of those customers can be retained. When complaints cannot be resolved within twenty-four hours, the customer retention rate falls to 46 percent.

Not surprisingly, if customers do not complain, the odds of retention drop below 40 percent. Thus, while it may seem odd at first, one of the jobs of market-based management is not only to track customer satisfaction but also to *encourage dissatisfied customers to complain.* Only with the specific details of a customer complaint and the source of dissatisfaction can a business take corrective action.[11]

Companies such as AT&T proactively address potential customer dissatisfaction by encouraging customer complaints through full-page ads with toll-free telephone numbers. Their proactive marketing efforts have two important effects. First, their

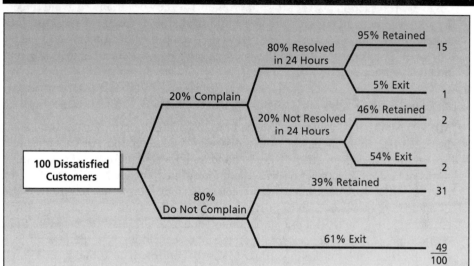

FIGURE 1-5   Efforts to Encourage Customer Complaints and Manage Customer Dissatisfaction

proactive services address problems as they occur, greatly reducing potential customer dissatisfaction and exit. Second, communicating their proactive services reinforces customer satisfaction by communicating the importance of their efforts to provide maximum customer satisfaction.[12]

Customer Satisfaction and Profitability

Customer satisfaction is an excellent market-based performance metric and barometer of future revenues and profits, as stated below.

> Customer satisfaction is a forward-looking indicator of business success that measures how well customers will respond to the company in the future. Other measures of market performance, such as sales and market share, are backward-looking measures of success. They tell how well the firm has done in the past, not how well it will do in the future.[13]

Thus, customer satisfaction is a good leading indicator of future operating performance. A business may have produced excellent financial results while underwhelming and disappointing a growing number of its customers. Because customers cannot always immediately switch to alternative solutions, customer dissatisfaction often precedes customer exit and reductions in sales and profitability. Thus, for many businesses, quarterly measures of customer satisfaction provide an excellent leading indicator of future performance. If customer satisfaction is on the decline, an early warning signal is given, providing the opportunity to correct a problem before real damage is done. Of course, if a business does not track customer satisfaction, it forgoes the opportunity to correct problems before declines in sales and profits result.

For example, a dissatisfied FedEx customer can move quickly to an alternative provider of overnight mail. That fact has led FedEx to develop a service quality index for every transaction in order to spot problems as they occur and to avoid the potential loss of customers. In the long run, it is more profitable to keep existing customers than to continually have to work to attract and develop new customers to replace exiting ones. FedEx has demonstrated that gains in customer satisfaction, driven by improvements in service quality, provide gains in revenue and lower cost.

Profit Impact of Customer Dissatisfaction

MBNA America is a Delaware-based credit card company that, in the early 1990s, became frustrated with customer dissatisfaction and defection. All 300 employees were brought together in an effort to understand and develop methods of delivering greater levels of customer satisfaction with the intent of keeping each and every customer. At the time, MBNA America had a 90 percent customer retention rate. After several years of dedicating themselves to improved customer satisfaction and retention, they raised customer retention to 95 percent. That may seem like a small difference, but the impact on their profits was a *sixteen-fold* increase, and their industry ranking went from 38th to 4th.[14] Thus, their marketing efforts to satisfy and retain customers paid off in higher levels of profitability.

As demonstrated, most dissatisfied customers do not complain; they just walk away. To hold market share in a mature market, a business must replace those lost customers. Let's examine a business that is in a mature market with 200,000 customers and has a 75 percent rate of customer retention. Each year this business loses 50,000 customers and, to hold a customer base of 200,000, must replace those customers with 50,000 new customers. However, before we look at the profit impact of this level of customer satisfaction and retention, let's look at how this business got to a level of 75 percent customer retention. A closer look at customer satisfaction, complaint behavior, and customer retention enables us to build the *Customer Retention Tree* in Figure 1-6. As shown, the business is operating at a 70 percent level of customer satisfaction. Of the 30 percent who are dissatisfied, 24.9 percent are lost. Furthermore, the majority of dissatisfied customers who are lost do not complain to the business about the source of their dissatisfaction.

The customer profitability profile shown in Figure 1-7 reflects the information presented in Figure 1-6. It shows the average annual revenue, margin, and marketing expense per customer for retained customers, lost customers, and new customers. As shown, retained customers are the profit driver of this business, producing 80 percent of the sales revenue and 89 percent of the total contribution.

Lost customers are generally dissatisfied or neutral customers. Because they are not with the business for the whole year or are in the process of reducing their purchases from the business, the annual revenue per customer is much lower. However, retaining dissatisfied customers is also expensive because they require the business to expend extra resources in an attempt to keep them. These extra efforts often mean extra work for the sales force, price concessions, adjustments to inventory or terms of sale, and more customer service. The net result of losing dissatisfied customers in this example is a negative *net marketing contribution* of $2.5 million per year. The net marketing contribution shown in Figure 1-7 is the total revenue received from customers less variable

FIGURE 1-6   Customer Retention Tree

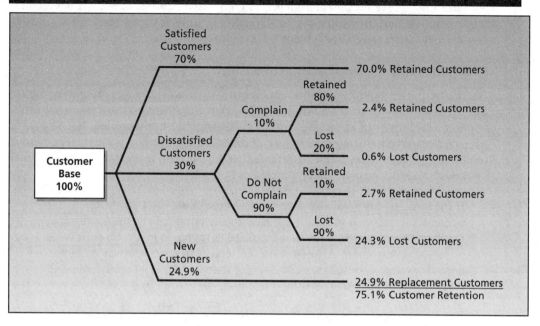

costs of producing those revenues less direct marketing expenses needed to serve this level of customer volume. This concept will be discussed in detail in chapter 2.

New customers are also less profitable. Advertising and sales promotion dollars have to be spent to generate sales leads and produce trial purchases. This raises the marketing expenses associated with attracting, qualifying, and serving new customers. New customers also generally buy less because they are in the evaluation stage and

FIGURE 1-7   Profit Impact of 75 Percent Customer Retention

Customer Performance	*Retained Customers*	*Lost Customers*	*New Customers*	*Overall Performance*
Number of Customers	150,000	50,000	50,000	250,000
Revenue per Customer	$800	$200	$400	
Sales Revenue (millions)	$120.0	$ 10.0	$ 20.0	$150.0
Variable Cost per Customer	$400	$150	$300	
Margin per Customer	$400	$ 50	$100	
Total Contribution (millions)	$ 60.0	$ 2.5	$ 5.0	$ 67.5
Marketing Expense per Customer	$ 60	$100	$300	
Total Marketing Expense (millions)	$ 9.0	$ 5.0	$ 15.0	$ 29.0
Net Marketing Contribution (millions)	$ 51.0	−$ 2.5	−$ 10.0	$ 38.5
Operating Expenses (millions)				$ 30.0
Net Profit before Taxes (millions)				$ 8.5
Return on Sales				5.67%

have not yet fully committed themselves to the business or its products. This lowers both the annual revenue and margin produced by each new customer. The net result in this example is that the business actually loses $10 million in net marketing contribution each year in its efforts to replace lost customers.

Profit Impact of Customer Retention

For the business situation presented in Figure 1-7, overall sales revenues of $150 million produce a net profit of $8.5 million, a 5.67 percent return on sales. But what would be the profit impact of improved customer satisfaction? Let's assume that $1 million were dedicated to reducing the number of dissatisfied customers so that 80 percent of the business's customers could be retained each year. The marketing logic and profit impact of this strategy can be summarized as follows:

> If the business can retain 80 percent of its customers each year instead of 75 percent, the business will reduce the cost associated with customer dissatisfaction and exit and will not have to spend as much on marketing efforts to attract new customers. Also, because retained customers produce a higher annual revenue and margin per customer than do lost or new customers, the total profits of the business should increase.

This effort would produce only a slight increase in sales revenues, as shown in Figure 1-8. However, there would be a tremendous improvement in marketing efficiency and profitability. Because retained customers are more profitable than new customers, the overall total contribution derived from retained customers would increase from $60 million to $64 million. The overall marketing expenses would go up because of the $1 million that were added to the business's marketing budget to achieve an 80 percent customer retention. The net result would be a $3 million improvement in net marketing contribution derived from retained customers.

FIGURE 1-8 Profit Impact of 5 Percent Improvement in Customer Retention

Customer Performance	Retained Customers	Lost Customers	New Customers	Overall Performance
Number of Customers	160,000	40,000	40,000	240,000
Revenue per Customer	$800	$200	$400	
Sales Revenue (millions)	$128.0	$ 8.0	$ 16.0	$152.0
Variable Cost per Customer	$400	$150	$300	
Margin per Customer	$400	$ 50	$100	
Total Contribution (millions)	$ 64.0	$ 2.0	$ 4.0	$ 70.0
Marketing Expense per Customer	$ 62.5	$100	$300	
Total Marketing Expense (millions)	$ 10.0	$ 4.0	$ 12.0	$ 26.0
Net Marketing Contribution (millions)	$ 54.0	−$ 2.0	−$ 8.0	$ 44.0
Operating Expenses (millions)				$ 30.0
Net Profit before Taxes (millions)				$ 14.0
Return on Sales				9.2%

More important, the net loss of managing dissatisfied customers who exit and the net loss associated with attracting new customers would be reduced by a total of $2.5 million in this example. The cumulative impact of increased customer satisfaction and retention is an increase of net profits from $8.5 to $14 million. This incremental gain in net profits is derived from a larger number of retained customers, the reduced cost of serving dissatisfied customers, and reduced expenses associated with acquiring new customers to maintain the same customer base. This is a 64 percent increase in net profits with essentially *no change in market share or sales revenue.*

One can readily see the enormous potential for increased profits and cash flow that centers around customer satisfaction and retention. For each additional customer that is retained, net profits increase. Inefficient costs associated with serving dissatisfied customers and the cost of acquiring new customers to replace them are reduced. Thus, there is tremendous financial leverage in satisfying and retaining customers.

Customer Satisfaction and Customer Retention

The relationship between customer satisfaction and customer retention is intuitively easy to discern. However, different competitive conditions modify this relationship.[15] For example, in less competitive markets, customers are more easily retained even with poor levels of customer satisfaction because there are few substitutes or switching costs are high. In markets where there are relatively few choices, such as phone service, water companies, or hospitals, customers may stay even when dissatisfied. In these types of markets, where choice is limited or switching costs are very high, higher levels of customer retention are achievable at relatively lower levels of customer satisfaction.

However, in highly competitive markets with many choices and low customer switching costs, even relatively high levels of customer satisfaction may not insure against customer defection. Grocery store, restaurant, and bank customers can switch quickly if not completely satisfied. While the time between purchase events is longer, personal computer, automobile, and consumer electronics customers can also easily move to another brand if not completely satisfied. In these markets, customer retention is much more difficult. And, as a result, it takes higher levels of customer satisfaction to retain customers from one purchase to the next.

Customer Retention and Customer Life Expectancy

Customer satisfaction and retention are important linkages to a market-based strategy and profitability. The ultimate objective of any given marketing strategy should be to attract, satisfy, and retain target customers. If a business can accomplish this objective with a competitive advantage in attractive markets, the business will produce above-average profits.

The customer is a critical component in the profitability equation but is completely overlooked in any financial analysis or annual reports. Customers are a *marketing asset* that businesses have yet to quantify in their accounting systems. Yet, the business that can attract, satisfy, and keep customers over their lifetime of purchases is in a powerful position to deliver superior levels of profitability. Businesses that lack a market orientation look at customers as *individual purchase transactions.* A market-based business looks at customers as *lifetime partners.* The *New York Times* tracks its customer retention and the retention rates of competing newspapers by length of subscription.[16]

FIGURE 1-9 Customer Life Expectancy and Customer Retention

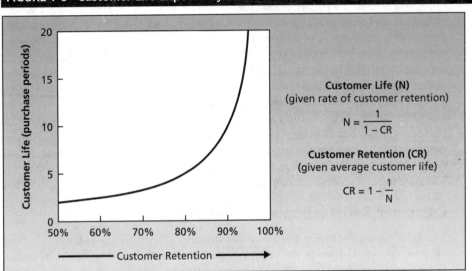

Among *Mature Subscribers*, those who have had subscriptions longer than twenty-four months, the *New York Times* has a retention rate of 94 percent. Their closest competitor has an 80 percent retention rate.

The higher the rate of customer retention, the greater the profit impact for a given business. In the short run, we showed this to be true on the basis of increased profits from retained customers, reduced losses from lost customers, and a lower cost of attracting new customers in order to maintain a certain customer base. However, there is also a longer-term profit impact of higher levels of customer retention because a higher rate of retention lengthens the life of a customer relationship.

A business that has a 50 percent rate of customer retention has a fifty-fifty chance of retaining a customer from one year to the next. This fact translates into an average customer life of two years, as shown in Figure 1-9. The average life expectancy of a customer is equal to one divided by one minus the rate of customer retention. Therefore, as customer retention increases, the customer's life expectancy increases. But, more important, customer life expectancy increases exponentially with customer retention, as illustrated in Figure 1-9.

For example, the average level of customer retention among health care providers is 80 percent.[17] This translates into an average customer life of five years. If a health care provider could manage to increase its customer retention to 90 percent, that increase would produce an average customer life of 10 years. Thus, the life expectancy of a customer grows exponentially as a business moves to higher levels of customer retention.

The Lifetime Value of a Customer

The Cadillac division of General Motors estimates that a Cadillac customer will spend approximately $350,000 over a lifetime on automotive purchases and maintenance. If Cadillac loses that customer early in this customer life cycle, it forgoes hundreds of thousands of dollars in future cash flow. And, to replace that lost customer, Cadillac has

FIGURE 1-10   Customer Lifetime Value

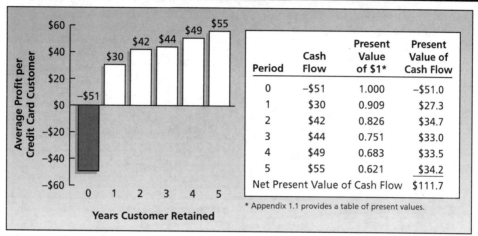

Period	Cash Flow	Present Value of $1*	Present Value of Cash Flow
0	–$51	1.000	–$51.0
1	$30	0.909	$27.3
2	$42	0.826	$34.7
3	$44	0.751	$33.0
4	$49	0.683	$33.5
5	$55	0.621	$34.2
Net Present Value of Cash Flow			$111.7

* Appendix 1.1 provides a table of present values.

to attract and develop a new customer, which is an expensive process. Thus, the cost of marketing efforts to ensure customer satisfaction is small in comparison with both the current and future benefits of customer purchases, as well as the cost of replacing customers if they become dissatisfied and leave. In general, it costs five times more to replace a customer than it costs to keep a customer.

Figure 1-10 illustrates the average profit per credit card customer generated over a five-year period. Acquiring and setting up accounts for new credit card customers nets an annual loss of $51 per customer. Newly acquired credit card customers are also slow to use their new cards; they produce an average profit of $30 the first year, $42 the second year, and $44 the third year. By year five, the average profit obtained from a credit card customer is $55. Thus, the lifetime value of a credit card customer continues to grow. Of course, if a credit card company loses a customer after year four because of customer dissatisfaction, the process of replacing him or her is expensive. This cost in the first year following customer exit is $106 ($55 in lost profit from the exiting customer and the $51 loss associated with attracting a new customer to replace that customer).

In this example, the average customer life is five years. Working backward, we can estimate the customer retention to be 80 percent, as shown below.

$$\frac{\text{Customer}}{\text{Retention}} = 1 - \frac{1}{N} = 1 - \frac{1}{5} = 0.80 \text{ (or 80\%)}$$

To estimate the lifetime value of a customer at this rate of customer retention, we need to compute the *net present value* of the customer cash flow shown in Figure 1-10. The initial $51 that it cost to acquire this customer is gone immediately. However, it takes a year to achieve the first year's revenue of $30. The present value of $30 received a year in the future is less than $30 received immediately. In this example, the business has a discount rate of 10 percent. Therefore, the present value of $1 received after one year is $0.909 (the rate at which $1 is discounted for one year at 10 percent). Thus, $30 to be received one year later is $27.27 ($30 − 0.909). This discounting is performed for each year's receipts, and the values are totaled to arrive at the net present

FIGURE 1-11   Net Present Value of Online Customers

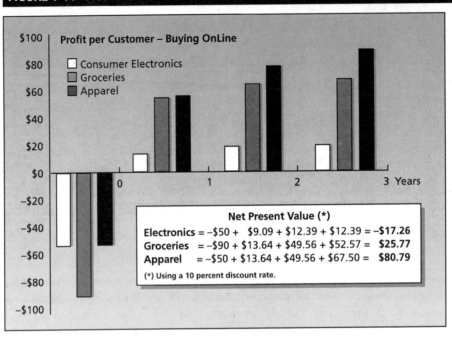

value of this cash flow. When each year's cash flow is properly discounted, the net present value of the sum of these cash flows is equal to $111.70. This is what this customer is worth in today's dollars. If customer life expectancy were only three years, the customer value (net present value) would be considerably smaller. The longer the rate of customer retention the longer the average customer life expectancy and the greater the customer value.

To better understand this concept let's look at the customer value (net present value) over a three-year period for online shoppers for consumer electronics, groceries, and apparel[18] as illustrated in Figure 1-11. The cost of acquiring a grocery customer is almost twice the cost of acquiring a consumer-electronics customer. After three years, the online consumer-electronics customer has a negative net present value of -$17.26. The average online grocery customer produces a net present value of $25.77 in three years. The average online apparel customer is even more profitable, producing a net present value of $80.79 in three years.

CUSTOMER RELATIONSHIP MANAGEMENT

While we have shown customer satisfaction and retention to have a positive impact on profitability, a business can have customers it *wants to keep* as well as customers it should *strive to abandon*.[19] Likewise, with the acquisition of new customers there are customers the business *should pursue* and customers the business *should avoid*. This is part of a process called *Customer Relationship Management* (CRM) which is addressed in greater detail in Chapter 5.

Managing Customer Retention

To manage customer relationships effectively with regard to retention, it is useful to classify customers on the basis of customer loyalty and profitability.[20] Not all customers are the same. Some may be loyal and profitable, others profitable but not loyal, some loyal but not profitable, and others neither loyal nor profitable. The job of *Customer Relationship Management* is to manage these differences in an effort to obtain higher levels of loyalty and profitability.

The most profitable customers are *Core Customers*.[21] They make up the majority of a businesse's profits and are loyal customers as presented below. The primary objective of Customer Relationship Management is to understand the needs of these customers and strive to build programs that deliver superior levels of customer satisfaction.

- **Core Customers** (Profitable and Loyal) – These customers are the key source of a businesse's profits.
- **At-Risk Customers** (Profitable but Not Loyal) – These are profitable customers who could leave the business due to declining customer satisfaction or weakening customer value.
- **Non-profit Customers** (Not Profitable but Loyal) – These customers are satisfied and retained but can not be served profitably by the business.
- **Spinners** (Not Profitable and Not Loyal) – These are price shoppers who are acquired and exit quickly.

At-Risk Customers are profitable but not loyal. These customers are vulnerable to competitors' efforts to lure them away. An effort to build loyalty among these customers is important to retain them and the profits they produce. Managing customer retention also requires management of *Non-profit Customers*. These customers are satisfied and loyal customers but do not produce positive net present value.[22] Often these customers buy infrequently or in amounts that do not cover the cost of serving them. These customers need to be managed to produce an acceptable net present value.

Spinners are "revolving door" customers who enter, purchase and exit. Often these customers are attracted by sales promotions. It is best to avoid these customers altogether when possible. AT&T found that it had 1.7 million customers who were *spinners*, customers who switched telephone carriers an average of three times per year.[23] Even worse, one telephone carrier estimated that 3 percent of its customers sign up, use the company's services, and move on without paying their bills.

Managing New Customer Acquisition

Charles Lillis, former CEO of MediaOne, once said *"I will know when our businesses have done a good job of market segmentation when they can tell me who we should not sell to."*

Acquiring customers is a tricky process that requires careful Customer Relationship Management. It is common to think of every new customer as beneficial to the business. When the phone rings and someone wants to buy, it takes a rare individual to say "no." However, the acquisition of new customers can result in *Non-profit Customers* who are loyal but not profitable, or *Spinners* who buy once and exit. This results in an even higher loss given the cost of customer acquisition with little or no offsetting income. Thus, it is important to understand the differences between target customers and non-target customers as described below.

- **Target Customers** (Good Profit Potential) – These are customers who match the *Core Customer* profile based on customer needs and buying behavior.
- **Non-Target Customers** (Poor Profit Potential) – These are customers who match the profile of *Non-profit Customers* or *Spinners*.

A customer profile of who is *not* a good target customer is just as valuable as a profile of who *is* a good target customer. A new customer acquisition process that can identify *Non-profit Customers* or *Spinners* and avoid them can lower the total cost of acquisition and raise customer retention rates. To the degree a business can attract *Target Customers* and avoid *Non-target Customers*, the business can reduce the overall cost of new customer acquisition and contribute to higher rates of customer retention.

Managing New Customers

Every new customer has the potential to develop into a highly profitable *Core Customer*. *First Time Customers* need to be managed differently. They lack any experience with the business and need above-average service to acclimate them to the business' products and services as described below. How they are managed greatly influences their level of profitability and loyalty.

New customers may also be *Win-back Customers*. These are customers who switched to a competing alternative because they were "mismanaged." These *Win-back Customers* need special attention that addresses the dissatisfaction that caused them to leave in the first place. If the customer relationship management program is working effectively, both types of new customers can evolve to the level of a *Core Customer*.

- **First-Time Customers** (Good Profit Potential) – These customers have no prior purchase experience but match the *Core Customer* target customer profile.
- **Win-Back Customers** (Good Profit Potential) – These previous customers were profitable but were lured away to a competing product and have been won back by the business.

Managing Customer Exit

Every business loses customers at one time or another. However, customers are lost for different reasons. Some are *Core Customers* that a business would like to win back. These were *Mismanaged Customers* who left the business due to dissatisfaction and/or low loyalty as described below. Lost customers can also include *Abandoned Customers* who were unprofitable and successfully abandoned.

- **Mismanaged Customers** (Profitable but Left) – These are *At-risk Customers* who were once *Core Customers* the business lost but would like to gain back.
- **Abandoned Customers** (Not Profitable and Left) – These customers never should have been customers due to a poor fit with the business and poor profitability (i.e. *Spinners* and *Non-profit Customers*).

Customer Relationship Management is an important aspect of managing customer retention and profitability.[24] Careful management of all customer relationships starts with identifying target customers to retain and acquire, as well as how to manage new customers and abandon unprofitable customers. Each customer relationship has an impact on overall retention levels and profitability. Successful CRM involves managing all customers' relationships to avoid *Spinners* and *Non-profit Customers* while minimizing the loss of *At-risk Customers* and retaining the profitable, loyal *Core Customers*.

BUILDING A MARKET ORIENTATION

Businesses with a strong market orientation are in the best position to develop responsive marketing strategies that deliver high levels of customer satisfaction and retention. But how does a business build a strong market orientation? Why do some businesses have a strong market orientation while others cannot seem to develop one? There are three fundamental forces that drive the degree to which a business has a market orientation:

- **Marketing Knowledge:** The degree to which managers and employees have been educated and trained in the area of marketing directly affects the market orientation of a business.
- **Marketing Leadership:** The market orientation of a business starts at the top. If the senior management and key marketing managers of a business do not have a strong market orientation, it is difficult for a business to establish any level of marketing excellence.
- **Employee Satisfaction:** If employees are unhappy in their jobs and uninformed as to how they affect customers, the business's market orientation will never achieve even minimal effectiveness regardless of senior management speeches and market-based statements of mission and philosophy.

Market Orientation and Marketing Knowledge

The extent to which a manager has a strong market orientation is directly related to their level of marketing knowledge:[24] the higher one's level of marketing knowledge, the stronger that individual's marketing orientation as shown in Figure 1-12. This

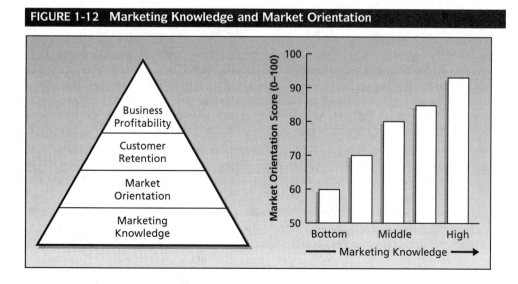

FIGURE 1-12 Marketing Knowledge and Market Orientation

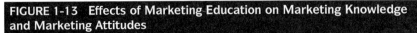

FIGURE 1-13 Effects of Marketing Education on Marketing Knowledge and Marketing Attitudes

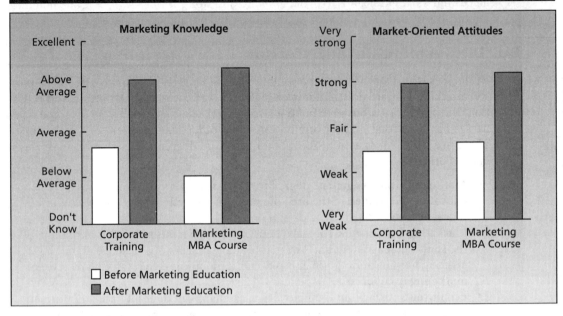

graphic was built from a database of 15,000 managers from over sixty countries.[25] Further analysis of these data also found that marketing knowledge and market orientation are strongly correlated to marketing education, marketing experience, and participation in marketing training programs. Businesses that build a strong market orientation also have higher levels of customer retention and profitability.

Marketing excellence requires more than words. Businesses seeking to build a strong marketing orientation need to invest in building marketing knowledge. Measures of marketing knowledge and marketing attitudes *before and after* corporate marketing education programs demonstrate that meaningful improvements in marketing knowledge can be obtained as illustrated in Figure 1-13. This has training implications for businesses wanting to build their marketing knowledge in pursuit of marketing excellence.

MBA marketing education can also make a difference. Measures of marketing knowledge and marketing attitudes before and after a first year MBA marketing course for over 1,000 MBAs at Northwestern University, Penn State University, and the University of Oregon demonstrated a significant gain in marketing knowledge and attitudes. This has obvious recruiting and hiring implications for companies interested in building marketing excellence.

While formal marketing education and training are absolutely essential for those in marketing and higher-level positions of leadership, market orientation is also fundamental to every employee of the organization. For example, Disney spends four days training personnel who clean their theme parks.[26] They train what they call the "popcorn people" to be information guides because they are the first to be asked where something is located. These "popcorn people" are also trained to treat customers as guests and to consider themselves on stage. Naturally, the individual marketing orientation of these employees plays a key role in creating a Disney company market orientation that delivers high levels of customer satisfaction.

Market Orientation and Marketing Leadership

A marketing orientation audit of a mid-sized high-tech company involved assessing marketing attitudes and practices at several layers of the business's management hierarchy. The following comments were given in response to the question "How often do you see customers?"

> **Company CEO:**   I really don't have too much time for that. I have many financial issues, administrative tasks, and many meetings. So I leave it to my vice president of marketing.
>
> **Vice President of Marketing:**   Well, I have a rather considerable staff and many responsibilities with regard to marketing plans and day-to-day decisions regarding our sales force and advertising. So I really don't have the time. But we have a very highly trained sales force, and they are talking to customers all the time.
>
> **Sales Force:**   Sure, we are in continuous contact with our customers and we bring back new ideas all the time. But nobody in management has the time to listen.

Obviously, this business lacks marketing leadership at the top. To build a strong market orientation, all levels of management, and senior management in particular, need to have a strong customer focus. Market orientation and marketing leadership start at the top.

For example, IBM's top 470 executives are personally responsible for more than 1,300 customer accounts.[27] In addition, IBM gives frontline employees the authority, without prior management approval, to spend up to $5,000 per complaint to solve problems for a customer on the spot. Nordstrom has created a market-based culture in which every customer interaction is an opportunity to build customer satisfaction.[28] This initiative is led from the top and permeates all levels of the Nordstrom management hierarchy. Starbucks senior management believes that the first four hours of new employee training are the most important in shaping an employee's market orientation. To the degree that management fails to communicate its customer orientation during this training, it will have failed to shape Starbucks' market orientation.

Every marketing decision implicitly or explicitly sends a message to employees relative to management's commitment to a market orientation. The actions and words of senior and middle management set the tone of a business's market orientation. Their market orientation and leadership are essential in building a market-based business culture. A top management decision to unjustifiably raise customer prices in order to meet short-term profit objectives sends a clear signal of the business's lack of commitment to a market orientation. Thus, consistent market-based leadership is a requirement for building a market-oriented business culture.

Market Orientation and Employee Satisfaction

Think about calling a business with a complaint and interacting with a person who hates their job and the company they work for. What kind of reception do you think you will get? Employee satisfaction is a key factor in delivering customer satisfaction.[29] As shown

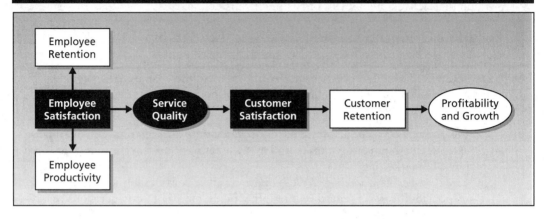

FIGURE 1-14 Employee Satisfaction is a Key Driver of Service Quality and Customer Satisfaction

in Figure 1-14, employee satisfaction affects customer service, which in turn influences customer satisfaction and retention. And, as we have already shown, higher levels of customer satisfaction contribute to higher levels of customer retention and profitability.

Sears found that in all of its many stores, there was a high correlation between customer satisfaction, employee satisfaction, and store profitability.[30] NCR found that, among 12 manufacturing operations, higher levels of employee job satisfaction corresponded with higher levels of customer satisfaction.[31] Thus, building a strong market orientation requires a healthy business environment in which employees enjoy their jobs and working for the organization.

Summary

The strength of a business's market orientation is directly related to its ability to develop market-based strategies that deliver high levels of customer satisfaction. For years, many observers would have considered that statement to be a nice academic philosophy that had little to do with a company that was in business to make a profit. Today, however, there is considerable evidence that businesses that operate with higher levels of customer satisfaction are more profitable. They are more profitable because they are able to retain a high percentage of customers, have less rework as a result of poor product or service quality, and need to spend less time and money attracting new customers to replace lost customers.

Thus, businesses with a strong market orientation are able to deliver higher levels of both customer satisfaction and profitability.

As is true of most concepts, the words come much more easily than the results. There are three critical components to achieving a strong market orientation:

- A business must have strong individual market orientation among all its managers and employees. A business's market orientation is only as strong as the collective sum of all the individual market orientations of its managers and employees.
- Market-oriented businesses have a strong customer commitment and Customer Relationship Management

Program. Not all retained, new or lost customers are the same in profitability and loyalty. Customer differences need to be managed effectively in order to achieve high levels of customer retention and profitability.

- The ultimate goal of a strong market orientation is to develop and implement marketing strategies that attract, satisfy, and retain target market customers. Formal measures of customer satisfaction, dissatisfaction, and retention play an important role in achieving a strong market orientation.

A business with a strong market focus is in a position to develop marketing strategies that are responsive to customer needs and competitive forces. By delivering higher levels of customer satisfaction and value, these businesses are able to retain a higher proportion of their customers. Having higher customer satisfaction and retention lowers the cost of serving customers and acquiring new ones. Perhaps more important, it creates the opportunity to keep customers throughout their customer life cycle. Keeping customers contributes to both current and future profits, enabling a business to invest in other market opportunities. In the end, a strong market orientation rewards customers, employees, and shareholders.

Market-Based Logic and Strategic Thinking

1. What is a market orientation? How would a business with a strong market orientation differ from one with a weak market orientation?
2. How are a strong market orientation and commitment to understanding customer needs related to shareholder value?
3. Why are customer satisfaction and customer retention important drivers of profitability?
4. Why are average measures of customer satisfaction misleading indicators of market-based performance?
5. How does the mix of customers who are satisfied, neutral, and dissatisfied affect a business's net profits?
6. Using the Customer Retention Tree in Figure 1-6, determine how customer retention would change if the business increased its percentage of satisfied customers from 70 to 80 percent.
7. Why do high levels of customer dissatisfaction make attracting new customers more difficult?
8. How do high levels of customer dissatisfaction increase the cost of marketing and hence lower net profits?
9. Why are satisfied customers crucial to a business's net profits?
10. If the average customer life of a credit card (see Figure 1-10) were extended one year, what would be the level of customer retention required? Also, if the profit obtained in the sixth year is the same as that in the fifth year, what is the net gain in customer value (net present value)?
11. How does customer selection affect customer retention?
12. Why is marketing education an important element in building a strong market orientation?
13. What role does employee training play in building market orientation? Why is a market orientation important at all levels of an organization?
14. What role does marketing leadership play in building the market orientation of a business?
15. How can the senior management of an organization destroy a business's market orientation?
16. How does employee satisfaction impact customer satisfaction? Why is it difficult to build customer satisfaction when employee satisfaction is low?

APPLICATION PROBLEM: AIRCOMM

AirComm is a wireless communication service with five million customers and annual sales of $1.9 billion. Though profitable, AirComm has never measured its customer satisfaction. To better understand customer satisfaction, usage, and what customers do when they are dissatisfied, AirComm conducted a comprehensive study of 1,000 customers, the key results of which are outlined below.

CUSTOMER SATISFACTION

- Sixty-seven percent of AirComm's customers are satisfied and 33 percent are dissatisfied.
- Satisfied customers produce an average revenue of $400 per year and an average margin of $250.
- Dissatisfied customers who are retained produce an average revenue of $300 per year and an average margin of $150.
- Dissatisfied customers who discontinue their service produce an average $200 in revenue per year and an average margin of $100.

CUSTOMER COMPLAINT BEHAVIOR

- Only 5 percent of AirComm's dissatisfied customers complain to AirComm about dissatisfaction. Of these, 90 percent are retained and 10 percent discontinue their service.
- Ninety-five percent of AirComm's dissatisfied customers do not complain. Of these, 20 percent are retained as customers and 80 percent discontinue their service.

NEW CUSTOMERS

- New customers generate an average revenue of $150 and an average margin of $50 the first year.

- AirComm actively seeks new customers to maintain its customer base of five million in an increasingly competitive market.

MARKETING COSTS

- The average marketing cost for retaining a satisfied customer is $50.
- The average marketing cost of managing a dissatisfied customer is $100.
- The average marketing cost to attract a new customer is $250.

Questions

For access to interactive software to answer the questions below, go to www.RogerJBest.com or www.prenhall.com/Best.

1. How does customer retention, sales revenues, and marketing profits change if customer satisfaction is improved to 75 percent?

2. How would revenues, margins, and marketing expenses change if the percentage of dissatisfied customers who complained increased from 5 percent to 25 percent (assume the customer satisfaction stayed at 67 percent)?

3. What level of customer satisfaction would be needed to achieve an 90 percent customer retention assuming all other customer characteristics stayed the same? How would profits change if this level of customer satisfaction were obtained?

4. What would be the value of a customer if the customer life improved from 4 to 5 years?

Notes

1. Bradley Gale, *Managing Customer Value* (New York: Free Press, 1994), chapter 2.
2. Ajay K. Kohli and Bernard J. Jaworski, "Market Orientation: The Construct, Research Propositions, and Managerial Implications," *Journal of Marketing* 54 (April 1995):1–18; Bernard J. Jaworski and Ajay K. Kohli, "Market Orientation: Antecedents and Consequences," *Journal of Marketing* 57 (July 1993):53–70; Ajay K. Kohli, Bernard J. Jaworski, and Ajith Kumar, "Markor: A Measure of Market Orientation," *Journal of Marketing* 30 (November 1993):467–77; John C. Narver and Stanley F. Slater, "The Effect of a Market Orientation on Business Profitability," *Journal of Marketing* 54 (October 1990):20–35; and Stanley F. Slater and John C. Narver, "Does Competitive Environment Moderate the Market Orientation-Performance Relationship," *Journal of Marketing* 58 (January 1994):46–55.
3. Frederick F. Reichheld and W. Earl Sasser Jr., "Zero Defections: Quality Comes to Services," *Harvard Business Review* (September–October 1990):106–11; and Frederick F. Reichheld, "Loyalty-Based Management," *Harvard Business Review* (March–April 1993):64–73.
4. M. Menezes and J. Serbin, "Xerox Corporation: The Customer Satisfaction Program," Harvard Business School Publishing.
5. Patrick Byrne, "Only 10% of Companies Satisfy Customers," *Transportation and Distribution* (December 1993); and Tom Eck, "Are Customers Happy? Don't Assume," *Positive Impact* (July l992):3.
6. Valarie Zeithaml, A. Parasuraman, and Leonard Berry, *Delivering Quality Service* (New York: Free Press, 1990), chapter 1; and John Goodman, Ted Mama, and Liz Brigham, "Customer Service: Costly Nuisance or Lower Cost Profit Strategy?" *Journal of Bank Retailing* (Fall 1986):12.
7. TARP, "Consumer Complaint Handling in America: An Update Study," White House Office of Consumer Affairs, Washington, DC, 1986; TARP, "Consumer Complaint Handling in America, Final Report," U.S. Office of Consumer Affairs, Washington, DC, 1979; and Kathy Rhoades, "The Importance of Customer Complaints," *Protect Yourself* (January 1988):15–18.
8. J. Singh, "Consumer Complaint Intentions and Behavior," *Journal of Marketing* (January 1988):93–107; Jack Dart and Kim Freeman, "Dissatisfaction Response Styles Among Clients of Professional Accounting," *Journal of Business Research* 29 (January 1994):75–81.
9. A.M. McGahan and Panlcaj Ghemawat, "Competition to Retain Customers," *Marketing Science* 13 (Spring 1994):165–176; Mark H. McCormack, "One Disappointed Customer Is One Too Many," *Positive Impact* 4 (September 1993):7–8, Jeffery Gitomer, "Customer Complaints Can Breed Sales If Handled Correctly," *Positive Impact* 5 (February 1994):10–11; Financial Services Report, "Most Popular Trends in Retention—Appealing to Your 'Best' Customers," *Positive Impact*, 5 (May 1994):24; and Sreekanth Sampathkumaran, "Migration Analysis Helps Stop Customer Attrition," *Marketing News* 28 (August 1994):18–19.
10. T. Lucia, "Domino's Theory—Only Service Succeeds," *Positive Impact* (February 1992):6–7.
11. Bernice Johnston, *Real World Customer Service—What to Really Say When the Customer Complains* (Small Business Source Books, 1996).
12. See the following articles in *Positive Impact*: Debbie Mitchell Price, "More Than Ever, It Pays to Keep the Customer Satisfied," 3 (February 1992):7–8; Rosalie Robles Crowe, "Customer Satisfaction Paramount," 5 (April 1994):7–8; Rod Riggs, "More-Than-Satisfied Customer Now the Goal," 5 (January 1994):4–5; Peter Larson, "Customer Loyalty Is a Commodity Worth Fighting For," 4 (November 1993):4; and Julie Bonnin, "L.L. Bean Keeps Its Customers Returning," 5 (January 1993):7–8.

13. Steven Schnaars, *Marketing Strategy* (New York: Free Press, 1998):186–205.

14. Reichheld and Sasser, "Zero Defections: Quality Comes to Services," 106–111; and Reichheld, "Loyalty-Based Management," 64–73.

15. Thomas Jones and W. Earl Sasser Jr., "Why Satisfied Customers Defect," *Harvard Business Review* (November–December 1995):88–89.

16. Frederick Reichheld and Phil Schefter, "E-Loyalty: Your Secret Weapon on the Web," *Harvard Business Review* (July–August 2000):105–113.

17. Roberta Clarke, "Addressing Voluntary Disenrollment," *CDR Healthcare Resources* (1997):10–12.

18. Michael Johnson and Anders Gustafsson, *Improving Customer Satisfaction, Loyalty, and Profit* (New York: Jossey-Bass, Inc., 2000).

19. Paul Nunes and Brian Johnson, "Are Some Customers More Equal than Others," *Harvard Business Review* (November 2001):37–50.

20. Jill Griffin and Michael Lowenstein, *Customer Winback* (Jossey-Bass, 2001).

21. Melinda Nykamp, *The Customer Differential* (AMACOM, 2001).

22. Werner Reinartz and V. Kumar, "On the Profitability of Long-Life Customers in a Noncontractual Setting: An Empirical Investigation and Implications for Marketing," *Journal of Marketing* (October 2000):17–35.

23. Steve Schriver, "Customer Loyalty—Going, Going . . . ," *American Demographics* (September 1997):20–23.

24. Roger Best, "Determining the Marketing IQ of Your Management Team," *Drive Marketing Excellence* (November 1994), New York: Institute for International Research. Roger Best and JoDee Nice, "Building Marketing Excellence", Marketing Excellence Survey, 2001, 1–13.

26. Mary Connelly, "Chrysler Adopts Disney Mindset for Customers," *Automotive News* (February 1992).

27. Robert Hiebeler, Thomas Kelly, and Charles Ketteman, *Best Practices: Building Your Business with Customer-Focused Solutions* (New York: Simon and Schuster, 1998):167–200.

28. Rosalind Bentley, "The Name Nordstrom—Aim to Keep Customer Happy Is Legendary," *Positive Impact* (July 1992):5.

29. Jack W. Wiley, "Customer Satisfaction and Employee Opinions: A Supportive Work Environment and Its Financial Costs," *Human Resource Planning* 14 (1991):117–23; Anita Bruzzese, "Happy Employees Make Happy Customers," *Positive Impact* 4 (November 1993):8–9; Jim Cathcart, "Fill the Needs of Employees to Better Serve Customers," *Positive Impact* 5 (November 1994):7–8; and Peter Lawson, "Studies Link Customer–Employee Satisfaction," *Positive Impact* 3 (March 1992):11–12.

30. Anthony Rucei, Steven Kirin, and Richard Quinn, "The Employee—Customer Profit Chain at Sears," *Harvard Business Review* (January–February 1998):82–97.

31. Leonard A. Schlesinger and Jeffery Zomitsky, "Job Satisfaction, Service Capability, and Customer Satisfaction: An Examination of Linkages and Management Implications," *Human Resource Planning* 14 (1991):141–49.

Appendix 1.1

PRESENT VALUE TABLE

Period (N)	DR=8%	DR=9%	DR=10%	DR=11%	DR=12%	DR=13%	DR=14%	DR=15%
0	1.000	1.000	1.000	1.000	1.000	1.000	1.000	1.000
1	0.926	0.917	0.909	0.901	0.893	0.885	0.887	0.870
2	0.857	0.842	0.826	0.812	0.797	0.783	0.769	0.756
3	0.794	0.772	0.751	0.731	0.712	0.693	0.675	0.658
4	0.735	0.708	0.683	0.659	0.636	0.613	0.592	0.572
5	0.681	0.650	0.621	0.593	0.567	0.543	0.519	0.497
6	0.630	0.596	0.564	0.535	0.507	0.480	0.456	0.432
7	0.583	0.547	0.513	0.482	0.452	0.425	0.400	0.376
8	0.540	0.502	0.467	0.434	0.404	0.376	0.351	0.327
9	0.500	0.460	0.424	0.391	0.361	0.333	0.308	0.284
10	0.463	0.422	0.386	0.352	0.322	0.295	0.270	0.247
11	0.429	0.388	0.350	0.317	0.287	0.261	0.237	0.215
12	0.397	0.356	0.319	0.286	0.257	0.231	0.208	0.187
13	0.368	0.326	0.290	0.258	0.229	0.204	0.182	0.163
14	0.340	0.299	0.263	0.232	0.205	0.181	0.160	0.141
15	0.315	0.275	0.239	0.209	0.183	0.160	0.140	0.123
16	0.292	0.252	0.218	0.188	0.163	0.141	0.123	0.107
17	0.270	0.231	0.198	0.170	0.146	0.125	0.108	0.093
18	0.250	0.212	0.180	0.153	0.130	0.111	0.095	0.081
19	0.232	0.194	0.164	0.138	0.116	0.098	0.083	0.070
20	0.215	0.178	0.149	0.124	0.104	0.087	0.073	0.061

Present Value Formula

$$PV = \frac{1}{(1 + DR)^N}$$

PV = Present Value of $1.00
N = Number of periods before the $1.00 will be received
DR = Discount Rate (cost of borrowing or desired rate of return)

Example I: N = 5 periods and Discount Rate (DR) = 10%

$$PV = \frac{1}{(1 + 0.10)^5} = \frac{1}{1.611} = 0.621 \ (\$1.00 \text{ received in 5 years is worth } \$0.621 \text{ today})$$

Example II: N = 2.33 periods and Discount Rate (DR) = 10%

$$PV = \frac{1}{(1 + 0.10)^{2.33}} = \frac{1}{1.249} = 0.801 \ (\$1.00 \text{ received in 2.33 years is worth } \$0.801 \text{ today})$$

2 | MARKET-BASED PERFORMANCE

CommTech is a $454 million business that manufactures a wide range of imaging and data transmission products for medical, industrial, and business-to-business markets. Five years ago, a new management team was put in place after several years of disappointing performance. The new management team reorganized the business and designed programs to lower unit costs, control overhead expenses, and facilitate better management of assets. In addition, the new management team put in place an extensive sales training program that enabled the sales force to improve its sales productivity from $1.4 million to $2.2 million per salesperson.

The results were sensational! In five years, the new management team almost doubled sales and more than tripled net profits. As shown in Figure 2-1, CommTech's return on sales grew from 6.3 percent to 12.1 percent, and its return on assets increased from 11.3 percent to 26.7 percent. On the basis of this information

- How would you rate CommTech's performance over the last five years?
- What aspects of CommTech's performance were most impressive?
- Should CommTech follow the same strategy for the next five years?

MARKET VERSUS FINANCIAL PERFORMANCE

Most of us would be quick to conclude that CommTech's performance over the last five years was outstanding. Who would not like to have run a business in which the sales almost doubled and the profits more than tripled over a five-year period?

FIGURE 2-1 CommTech's Five-Year Financial Performance						
Performance (millions)	*Base Year*	*1*	*2*	*3*	*4*	*5*
Sales Revenues	$254	$293	$318	$387	$431	$454
Cost of Goods Sold	$183	$210	$230	$283	$314	$331
Gross Profit	$ 71	$ 83	$ 88	$104	$117	$123
Marketing and Sales Expense	18	23	24	26	27	28
Other Operating Expense	37	38	38	41	40	40
Net Profit (before taxes)	**$16**	**$22**	**$26**	**$37**	**$50**	**$55**
Return on Sales	6.3%	7.5%	8.2%	9.6%	11.6%	12.1%
Assets (millions)	$141	$162	$167	$194	$205	$206
Return on Assets	11.3%	13.6%	15.6%	19.1%	24.4%	26.7%

Despite those impressive increases, it is probably a mistake to evaluate CommTech's performance in such rosy terms when all the criteria used to arrive at this judgment are *financial* measures of performance. Sales revenues, net profits, return on sales, assets as a percentage of sales, and return on assets are all excellent measures of internal financial performance. These measures, however, do not provide an *external or market-based view* of performance. As a result, we do not know how CommTech has performed relative to external benchmarks such as market growth, competitive prices, relative product and service quality, and satisfying and retaining customers. Therefore, following the same strategy for the next five years may or may not be the best strategy for achieving profitable growth.

Using traditional methods of tracking performance, most would judge CommTech to be a real success story. But it can be demonstrated that, in reality, its efforts represent a cumulative loss to the corporation and its shareholders of $122 million in net income and cash flow over the five-year period. This difference in performance is due largely to a lack of market-based performance metrics and an overreliance on traditional financial measures as a guide to strategic thinking and performance evaluation.

To complement a business's internal financial performance, a business needs a parallel set of external metrics to track market-based performance.[1] Although these measures may not have the additive elegance of financial accounting, individually and collectively they provide a different and more strategic view of business performance. In Figure 2-2 is a set of market-based performance metrics that paints a different picture of CommTech's performance over the past five years.

One can readily see several strategic flaws in CommTech's market-based performance. First, CommTech sales, while showing impressive growth, were increasing at a rate less than the market growth rate. This analysis shows that CommTech was actually losing market share over the past five years. New product sales, product quality, and service quality each eroded *relative to competition*. Declines in relative product and service quality do not necessarily mean that CommTech's actual product or service quality declined.

FIGURE 2-2 CommTech's Five-Year Market-Based Performance

Performance Metric	Base Year	1	2	3	4	5
Market Growth (dollars)	18.3%	18.3%	18.3%	18.3%	18.3%	18.3%
CommTech Sales Growth	12.8%	17.8%	13.3%	24.9%	18.2%	7.7%
Market Share	20.3%	18.3%	17.5%	16.2%	14.4%	13.0%
Customer Retention	88.2%	87.1%	85.0%	82.2%	80.9%	80.0%
New Customers	11.7%	12.9%	14.9%	24.1%	22.5%	29.2%
Dissatisfied Customers	13.6%	14.3%	16.1%	17.3%	18.9%	19.6%
Relative Product Quality (*)	119	120	117	120	109	107
Relative Service Quality (*)	100	100	95	93	89	87
Relative New Product Sales (*)	108	108	103	99	95	93

(*) Relative index where 100 is equal to competition, greater than 100 ahead of competition and below 100 behind competition

In many instances, the competition simply moved ahead in delivering a higher level of product and service quality. On a relative basis, the competition's more rapid progress caused CommTech to lose ground to competitors in these areas.

Declines in quality, along with declines in relative new product sales, made it more difficult to hold customers as customer satisfaction declined and the percentage of dissatisfied customers grew. The net results were an eroding market-based performance, high levels of customer turnover, and a steady decline in market share.

A Market-Based Strategy

What would have been the impact of a strategy to hold market share? To hold a 20 percent share in a growing market, the marketing budget and product R&D would have needed to keep pace with market demand and the competition. At this level of investment and a 20 percent market share, the results presented in Figure 2-3 would have been plausible.

Although the market-based strategy to hold share would have delivered approximately the same return on assets as the internally driven strategy, it would have produced an additional $122 million in net profit (before taxes). Thus, over the five-year period, the business gave up $122 million in cash to the bottom line. Furthermore, CommTech's lost income will be even greater over the next five years, even if share erosion is halted and market growth completely subsides. If the market continues to grow, and market share continues to erode, CommTech's lost profit opportunity could easily approach $500 million over the next five years.

Market-Based Performance

It is clear from the CommTech business situation that market-based management has the potential to dramatically improve profits. The foundation of market-based performance is built around a commitment to market performance metrics, marketing profitability, and a strong market orientation as outlined below.

> *Market Performance Metrics:*   External measures of market performance
> *Marketing Profitability:*   Profitability measure of a marketing strategy
> *Market Orientation:*   Behaviors and systems used to achieve market orientation

FIGURE 2-3   Market-Based Strategy to Hold a 20 Percent Market Share

Performance (millions)	Base Year	1	2	3	4	5
Sales Revenues	$254	$312	$363	$477	$596	$697
Cost of Goods Sold	$183	$216	$251	$339	$415	$484
Gross Profit	$ 71	$ 96	$112	$138	$181	$213
Marketing and Sales Expense	18	24	27	32	41	50
Other Operating Expense	37	41	45	52	59	66
Net Profit (before taxes)	$ 16	$ 31	$ 40	$ 54	$ 81	$ 97
Return on Sales	6.3%	9.9%	11.0%	11.3%	13.6%	13.9%
Assets (millions)	$141	$172	$196	$253	$310	$355
Return on Assets	11.3%	18.0%	20.4%	21.3%	26.1%	27.3%
Lost Income (before taxes)*	$ 0	$ 9	$ 14	$ 17	$ 31	$ 42

*Difference in Net Profits in Figures 2-3 and 2-1

Market-Based Performance Metrics are a powerful complement to conventional measures of financial performance. A metric to index **Marketing Profitability** would allow marketing managers to understand, track, and manage the profit impact of a marketing strategy.[2] Finally, **Market Orientation** provides a company-wide infrastructure that is sensitive to customer needs and competitors' actions, and committed to working as a team to develop and implement market-driven strategies. Each of these elements of market-based performance is critical in taking a business to a higher level of marketing effectiveness and profitability.

MARKET-BASED PERFORMANCE METRICS

The CommTech situation underscores the importance of market-based performance metrics. Most business systems are set up to track revenues, costs, factory overhead, accounts receivable, operating expenses, and profits. Yet a business's customers are its most important asset and the only significant source of positive cash flow. Giving up customers in a period of growth simply means that the business has to work harder and spend more in order to replace each lost customer.

Internal Versus External Performance Metrics

To be successful, a business needs both internal and external performance metrics.[3] As presented in Figure 2-4, internal measures are critical for tracking unit costs, expenses, asset utilization, employee and capital productivity, and overall measures of profitability. Market-based performance metrics are equally important for providing an external view of the business's market-based performance. While CPA firms have done an excellent job in developing procedures for internal measures of a business's performance, the next frontier for either CPA firms or market research firms will be the development of standardized procedures for external measures of a business's market-based performance. With both sets of performance metrics, managers as well as financial analysts and shareholders will be in a much better position to evaluate a business's marketing effectiveness and business performance.

FIGURE 2-4   Internal and External Measures of Performance Metrics

Internal Performance Metrics	External Performance Metrics
Unit Cost	Market Share
Manufacturing Overhead	Relative Share
Marketing Expenses	Customer Satisfaction
R&D Expense	Market Coverage
Sales/Employee	Product Awareness
Inventory Turn	Relative Quality
Days Accounts Receivable	Relative Price
Return on Sales	Customer Preferences
Asset Turnover	Relative New Product Sales
ROI and ROE	Response Time to Problems

In-Process Versus End-Result Performance Metrics

The primary purpose of market metrics is to maintain an ongoing measure of market performance. And, because many market metrics precede financial performance, they are critical to strategy implementation and financial performance. However, not all market metrics are leading indicators of business performance. There are *in-process market metrics* and *end-result market metrics*.[4] Both are important, but in-process market metrics are particularly important because they are also leading indicators of financial performance. End-result metrics correspond more closely to financial performance.

Product awareness, intention to purchase, product trial, and customer satisfaction and dissatisfaction, along with customer perceptions of relative product quality, service quality, and customer value, all serve as in-process market metrics. Changes in each, positive or negative, generally precede actual changes in customer purchase behavior. As a result, these in-process measures of customer thinking and attitude are important leading indicators of future purchase behavior and, hence, of revenue and profit performance.

For example, perhaps customers are satisfied, but their perceptions of the value they derive from your product, relative to competing alternatives, are steadily diminishing. You may well have done nothing wrong to dissatisfy customers; the competition may have simply improved in delivering customer value based upon a combination of total benefits in comparison to total cost. However, the net effect is that customer perceptions of the value derived from your product have diminished. This change in customer perceptions, in turn, opens the door to competitors' products that your customer may be inclined to try or purchase. With an early warning signal, a market-based business can take corrective action before customers switch their purchase to a competitor. Without in-process market metrics, problems may go undetected and unresolved until after declines in financial performance.

End-result market metrics include market share, customer retention, revenue per customer, and others, as outlined in Figure 2-5. End-result market metrics are likely to occur at the end of a financial performance period. However, each provides a different set of performance diagnostics and insights.

FIGURE 2-5   Internal vs. External and In-Process vs. End-Result Performance Metrics

Measurement Perspective	*Time of Measurement*	
	In-Process Metrics	*End-Result Metrics*
Internal (in-company)	Product Defects Late Deliveries Billing Errors Accounts Receivable Inventory Turnover	Net Profit/Earnings Return on Sales Margin per Unit Return on Assets Asset Turnover
External (in-market)	Customer Satisfaction Relative Product Quality Relative Service Quality Intentions to Purchase Product Awareness	Market Share Customer Retention Relative New Product Sales Revenue per Customer Market Growth Rate

For example, let's assume that sales revenues are increasing and are ahead of forecast, and financial performance is also better than expected. Most businesses would feel pretty good about their performance. However, if end-result performance metrics show that the business is losing market share in a growing market, and poor customer retention is masked by new customer growth, there should be cause for concern. Without end-result market metrics, the business has only an internal perspective of end-result performance.

MARKETING PROFITABILITY

Although market-based performance metrics are essential to understanding external performance, it is also important that a business be managed to grow and to protect profits and shareholder value. Consider, for example, the Santa Fe Sportswear Company. The company's sales of $125 million were built around five product lines. The company was profitable overall, but two of the product lines had not performed well. In response, the senior management team of Santa Fe Sportswear met to review its product line performance. In preparation for the senior management review, the finance manager prepared the product line profitability summary presented in Figure 2-6.

Using this information, the finance manager argued the following:

> We are wasting resources on the Casual Shorts and Knitted Sweaters product lines. One makes no money and the other loses money. I recommend we drop both product lines and refocus our efforts on the profitable product lines.

Would this be a good decision? How should the marketing manager present her interpretation of the profit performance of the Casual Shorts and Knitted Sweaters product lines? What is needed is a measure of marketing profitability to help us gauge the degree to which a marketing strategy contributes to a business's profits.

But, what is marketing profitability? How is it measured? How is it managed? And, how would it help us understand the profitability of the Casual Shorts product line?

Measuring Marketing Profitability

To create a measure of marketing profitability, we need to examine more closely the elements of profitability and determine which come under the influence of the marketing function. To do this, we need to systematically break down the elements of profitability and marketing strategy to better understand how they interact.[5] The best method is to start with a very broad definition of net profit and then break down

FIGURE 2-6 Santa Fe Sportswear Product Line Profitability						
Santa Fe Sportswear Performance (millions)	*Khaki Pants*	*Wind Breakers*	*Classic Polo*	*Casual Shorts*	*Knitted Sweaters*	*Company Total*
Sales Revenues	$60.0	$25.0	$15.0	$10.0	$15.0	**$125**
Cost of Goods Sold	$37.5	$16.0	$ 7.5	$ 8.0	$11.0	**$ 80**
Gross Profit	$22.5	$ 9.0	$ 7.5	$ 2.0	$ 4.0	**$ 45**
Operating Expenses	$17.0	$ 7.0	$ 4.0	$ 3.0	$ 4.0	**$ 35**
Net Profit (before taxes)	$ 5.5	$ 2.0	$ 3.5	($ 1.0)	$ 0.0	**$ 10**

the profit equation into a definition that encompasses a market-level measure of profitability. Thus, in its most basic terms, a business's net profit is simply revenues minus expenses:

$$\text{Net Profits (before taxes)} = \text{Revenues} - \text{Expenses}$$

The Casual Shorts product line produces $10 million in sales revenues as shown below. The cost of goods sold is $8 million. Various expenses that make up the cost of goods sold are summarized in Figure 2-7. After deducting operating expenses of $3 million, net profit before taxes is -$1 million. From the finance manager's perspective, eliminating this product line would improve profits by $1 million.

$$
\begin{aligned}
\text{Profits (Casual Shorts)} = &\quad \text{Sales} \qquad \text{Cost of} \qquad \text{Operating} \\
&\text{Revenues} - \text{Goods Sold} - \text{Expenses} \\
= &\ \textbf{\$10 million} \ - \textbf{\$8 million} - \textbf{\$3 million} \\
= &\ \mathbf{-\$1\ million}
\end{aligned}
$$

However, to understand marketing profitability and how it contributes to a business's profits we need to isolate marketing and sales expense. When this is done, as shown below, we can see that the Casual Shorts product line produces $1 million in net marketing contribution.

FIGURE 2-7   Cost of Goods Sold, Marketing Expenses and Operating Expenses

Cost of Goods Sold − The total cost of producing a product that varies with volume sold

Variable Cost	Includes purchase materials, direct labor, packaging, transportation costs and any other costs associated with making and shipping a product.
Manufacturing Overhead	This is an allocated cost based on use of the fixed manufacturing plant, equipment and other fixed expenses needed to run the production operation.

Marketing and Sales Expense* − A direct expense that varies with a marketing strategy

Marketing Management	Expenses associated with marketing management and resources needed to support this function.
Sales, Service, and Support	Expenses associated with the sales force, customer service and technical and administrative support services.
Advertising and Promotion	All expenses associated with the marketing communications budget.

Operating Expenses − Indirect expenses that do not vary with the marketing strategy

Research and Development	Expenses for developing new products and/or improving old products.
Corporate Overhead	Overhead expenses for corporate staff, legal council, professional services, corporate advertising, and the salaries of senior management and their staff.

* Marketing & Sales Expenses are traditionally a part of Sales, General & Administration (SG&A) in most annual reports.

$$\begin{array}{llllll}
\text{Profits} & & & & \text{Marketing} & \text{Other} \\
\text{(Casual Shorts)} = & \text{Sales} & \text{Cost of} & - & \text{\& Sales} & - & \text{Operating} \\
& \text{Revenues} & - & \text{Goods Sold} & \text{Expenses} & \text{Expenses} \\
-\$1\text{ million} & = \$10\text{ million} & - & \$8\text{ million} & - & \$1\text{ million} & - & \$2\text{ million}
\end{array}$$

$$\begin{array}{lll}
-\$1\text{ million} & = \$1\text{ million} & - & \$2\text{ million} \\
& \textbf{Net Marketing} & \textbf{Operating} \\
& \textbf{Contribution} & \textbf{Expenses}
\end{array}$$

The $1 million in Net Marketing Contribution from the Casual Shorts product line is a measure of Marketing Profitability. If the Casual Shorts product line were eliminated, Santa Fe Sportswear would reduce its overall profits by the $1 million marketing profit produced by the Casual Shorts product line. The marketing and sales expenses associated with the Casual Shorts product line would eventually go to zero since there would be no purpose for these expenses. However, $2 million of operating expenses were allocated to the Casual Shorts product line. If the Casual Shorts product line were eliminated, the $2 million would have to be re-allocated to the other product lines. To make effective market-based decisions, we need to separate marketing and sales expenses from overall fixed operating expenses.[6] Net Marketing Contribution does this, capturing the actual profitability of a product line without including any allocated overhead not directly related to the product line itself.

NET MARKETING CONTRIBUTION

With this measure of marketing profits we can now better understand how marketing strategies contribute to the overall profits of a business as shown in Figure 2-8.

Profits = [All Product-Line Net Marketing Contributions (NMC)] − Operating Expenses

$$\begin{array}{l}
= [\text{NMC}(1) + \text{NMC}(2) + \text{NMC}(3) + \text{NMC}(4) + \text{NMC}(5)] - \text{Operating Expenses} \\
= [\ \$15.5\ +\ \$6.0\ +\ \$5.5\ +\ \$1.0\ +\ \$2.0] - \$20 \\
= \$10\text{ million}
\end{array}$$

If we combine revenues, variable expenses, and marketing expenses, we can create a measure of marketing profitability. However, to manage profit at the market level, we

FIGURE 2-8 Product Line − Net Marketing Contribution

Santa Fe Sportswear Performance (millions)	Khaki Pants	Wind Breakers	Classic Polo	Casual Shorts	Knitted Sweaters	Company Total
Sales Revenues	$60.0	$25.0	$15.0	$10.0	$15.0	$125
Cost of Goods Sold	$37.5	$16.0	$ 7.5	$ 8.0	$11.0	$ 80
Gross Profit	$22.5	$ 9.0	$ 7.5	$ 2.0	$ 4.0	$ 45
Marketing & Sales Expenses	$ 7.0	$ 3.0	$ 2.0	$ 1.0	$ 2.0	$ 15
Net Marketing Contribution	$15.5	$ 6.0	$ 5.5	$ 1.0	$ 2.0	$ 30
Operating Expenses	$10.0	$ 4.0	$ 2.0	$ 2.0	$ 2.0	$ 20
Net Profit (before taxes)	$ 5.5	$ 2.0	$ 3.5	($ 1.0)	$ 0.0	$ 10

need to rewrite the net profit equation based on how we break down revenues and variable and fixed expenses as they are related to the profit impact of marketing strategies. Because the volume portion of revenues and that of variable expenses are the same, we can express net profit in *marketing terms* in the following way:

The portion bracketed as *Net Marketing Contribution* is our measure of marketing profitability. These are the components of profitability that are largely under the control of the marketing function. Operating expenses are generally not under the control of the marketing function. Thus, we can rewrite the net profit of a business as shown, where marketing controls the Net Marketing Contribution (NMC) component of net profit:

Net Profit (before taxes) = Net Marketing Contribution − Operating Expenses

From this perspective, a marketing strategy produces a net marketing contribution.[7] This net marketing contribution has to cover the business's operating expenses and more in order for the business to make a profit.

Using net marketing contribution as a measure of profitability, the marketing manager can more readily evaluate the profit impact of a marketing strategy. Each product or market should be managed to produce a *positive* net marketing contribution. In this way, marketing decisions can be evaluated with respect not only to revenue and share gains but also to how they will affect profits by the level of net marketing contribution they produce.

Recognizing net marketing contribution as the measure of marketing profitability, we need to reexamine Santa Fe Sportswear's product line profitability. For example, Santa Fe Sportswear's marketing strategy for Khaki Pants currently produces a net marketing contribution of $15.5 million, as shown in Figure 2-8. This level of marketing profitability is the result of a 12.5 percent share of a twelve million unit market demand, a price of $40 per unit, a variable cost of $25 per unit, and marketing expenses of $7 million.

$$
\begin{aligned}
\text{NMC} \atop (P1) &= \left[{\text{Market} \atop \text{Demand}} \times {\text{Market} \atop \text{Share}} \times \left({\text{Price} \atop \text{per Unit}} - {\text{Variable Cost} \atop \text{per Unit}} \right) \right] - {\text{Marketing} \atop \text{Expenses}} \\
&= [12 \text{ million} \times 0.125 \times (\$40 - \$25)] - \$7 \text{ million} \\
&= [1.5 \text{ million} \times \$15 \text{ per unit}] - \$7 \text{ million} \\
&= \$22.5 \text{ million} - \$7 \text{ million} \\
&= \$15.5 \text{ million}
\end{aligned}
$$

To demonstrate how the profit impact of a marketing strategy can be assessed, assume that the marketing manager of Santa Fe Sportswear's Khaki Pants line proposed to cut prices by 10 percent in order to grow share from 12.5 to 15 percent. This marketing strategy would produce 300,000 more units in sales volume, but at a lower margin ($15 vs. $11). The net result of this marketing strategy would be a decrease in net marketing contribution from $15.5 million to $12.8 million and, therefore, a decrease in net profits of the same amount.

$$
\begin{aligned}
\text{NMC (Khaki Pants)} &= [12 \text{ million} \times 0.15 \times (\$36 - \$25)] - \$7 \text{ million} \\
&= [1.8 \text{ million} \times \$11 \text{ per unit}] - \$7 \text{ million} \\
&= \$19.8 \text{ million} - \$7 \text{ million} \\
&= \$12.8 \text{ million}
\end{aligned}
$$

FIGURE 2-9 Santa Fe Sportswear Product Line Marketing Profitability						
Santa Fe Sportswear Performance (millions)	*Khaki Pants*	*Wind Breakers*	*Classic Polo*	*Casual Shorts*	*Knitted Sweaters*	*Company Total*
Market Demand (units)	12	10	15	20	5	**62**
Market Share	12.5%	5.0%	3.3%	2.0%	4.0%	**5.0%**
Unit Volume	1.5	0.5	0.50	0.40	0.20	**3.1**
Average Price per Unit	$40	$50	$30	$25	$75	**$220**
Sales Revenues	$60	$25	$15	$10	$15	**$125**
Cost per Unit	$25.0	$32	$15	$20	$55	**$ 40.32**
Average Margin per Unit	$15	$18	$15	$ 5	$20	**$ 14.52**
Gross Profit	$22.5	$ 9.0	$ 7.5	$ 2.0	$ 4.0	**$ 45.0**
Marketing and Sales Expenses	$ 7	$ 3	$ 2	$ 1	$ 2	**$ 15**
Net Marketing Contribution	**$15.5**	**$ 6.0**	**$ 5.5**	**$ 1.0**	**$ 2.0**	**$ 30.0**
Operating Expenses	$10	$ 4	$ 2	$ 2	$ 2	**$ 20**
Net Profit (before taxes)	**$ 5.5**	**$ 2.0**	**$ 3.5**	**($ 1)**	**$ 0**	**$ 10**

Net Marketing Contribution and Business Unit Profitability

When a business has several product lines, it produces several sources of net marketing contribution. The sum of the net marketing contributions of all these product lines is the only source of cash flow produced by the business; everything else is expense, as shown:

$$\underset{\text{NMCs from all served markets}}{\underbrace{\begin{array}{c}\text{Net Profit}\\\text{(before taxes)}\end{array} = \begin{array}{c}\text{NMC}\\\text{Product (1)}\end{array} + \begin{array}{c}\text{NMC}\\\text{Product (2)}\end{array} + \cdots + \begin{array}{c}\text{NMC}\\\text{Product (n)}\end{array}}} - \begin{array}{c}\text{Operating}\\\text{Expenses}\end{array}$$

Now, let's return to the question raised earlier: Would eliminating the Casual Shorts and Knitted Sweaters product lines be a good idea? And would such a decision improve the net profits of Santa Fe Sportswear?

First, Figure 2-9 presents a market-based view of Santa Fe Sportswear's product line profitability and overall company net profits (before taxes). As shown, each product line produces a positive net marketing contribution. Thus, each product line is making a positive contribution to operating expenses and net profit (before taxes). If we assume that the operating expenses of the business would not change with the elimination of the Casual Shorts and Knitted Sweaters product lines, the business would actually reduce the net profits before taxes by the amount of the net marketing contribution these two product lines were producing. Eliminating the Casual Shorts and Knitted Sweaters would reduce sales by $25 million, and net profits would fall from $10 million to $7 million:

$$\begin{array}{c}\text{Net Profit}\\\text{(before taxes)}\end{array} = \begin{array}{c}\text{NMC}\\\text{(Khaki Pants)}\end{array} + \begin{array}{c}\text{NMC}\\\text{(Wind Breakers)}\end{array} + \begin{array}{c}\text{NMC}\\\text{(Classic Polo)}\end{array} - \begin{array}{c}\text{Operating}\\\text{Expenses}\end{array}$$

$$= \textbf{\$15.5 million} + \textbf{\$6.0 million} + \textbf{\$5.5 million} - \textbf{\$20 million}$$
$$= \textbf{\$7.0 million}$$

FIGURE 2-10   Santa Fe Sportswear: Product Line Marketing Profitability

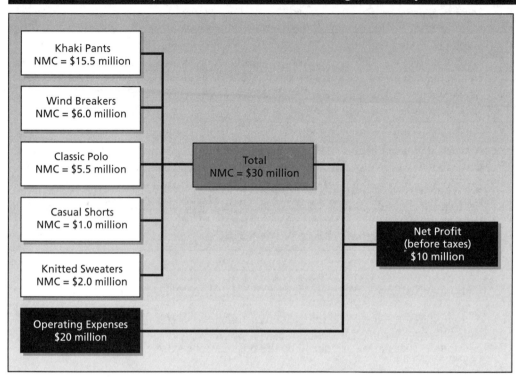

Another way for the marketing manager to demonstrate how each product line contributes to overall net profits is presented in Figure 2-10. As shown, each product line is producing a positive net marketing contribution. As a result, each makes a contribution toward covering operating expenses and producing net profit. Eliminating any of these products without a commensurate reduction in operating expenses would result in a reduction in net profits.

MARKET-BASED MARKETING PROFITABILITY

Accounting systems are generally built around producing something. Revenues and costs are directly associated with the production of something, whether it be a product or a service. Costs that are not directly related to production are allocated to products or services using some agreed-upon accounting rules that have nothing to do with satisfying customers or making money. To develop marketing strategies that satisfy customers and grow profits, we need to extend the accounting unit of analysis to better assist the marketing function in managing marketing profitability. To accomplish this, we need an alternative way to track a business's revenues, variable costs, fixed expenses, and net profits.

It is convenient to report performance by product, but there are several reasons we should also track performance by markets and customers. Regardless of the technical or psychological appeal of a business's products or services, cash flow is produced only when a customer buys a business's product or service. There are many products and ser-

FIGURE 2-11   Santa Fe Sportswear − Market-Based Marketing Profitability

Santa Fe Sportswear Performance (millions)	Traditional Buyer	Fashion Buyer	Trend Setters	Company Total
Market Demand (customers)	6.8	6.0	8.0	**20.8**
Market Share	9.0%	3.5%	6.0%	**6.26%**
Customer Volume	0.612	0.21	0.480	**1.302**
Revenue per Unit	$90	$145	$65	**$ 90**
Sales Revenues	$55	$ 30	$31	**$125**
Average Cost per Customer	$55	$ 90	$40	**$ 55**
Average Margin per Customer	$35	$ 55	$25	**$ 35**
Gross Profit	$21	$ 12	$12	**$ 45**
Marketing and Sales Expenses	$ 6	$ 4.5	$ 4.5	**$ 15.0**
Net Marketing Contribution	**$15.4**	**$ 7.1**	**$ 7.5**	**$ 30.0**
Operating Expenses	$ 8.0	$ 6.0	$ 6.0	**$ 20.0**
Net Profit (before taxes)	**$ 7.4**	**$ 1.1**	**$ 1.5**	**$ 10.0**

vices a business may produce, but there are only a finite number of actual and potential customers in any given market. The objective of a marketing strategy should be to attract, satisfy, and retain target customers in a way that grows the profits of the business.

Using customers and the market segments they belong to as the accounting units, we can create a more insightful understanding of market-based profitability and ways to grow it. But, let's first see what a market-based profitability statement would look like.

In Figure 2-11, we have rebuilt the performance of Santa Fe Sportswear around the three markets served. One can quickly observe that product-based and market-based approaches produce the same total revenue, total contribution, net marketing contribution, and net profits. However, each presents a different insight into market-based management. Both are important and meaningful. The product-based accounting statement (Figure 2-9) helps us understand product unit volume, product price, and unit margin for products. Market-based accounting (Figure 2-11) helps us understand customer demand, customer share, customer volume, revenue per customer, and variable cost per customer. In both cases, we have units of analysis producing net losses (or no net gain). In Figure 2-9, it is Casual Shorts and Knitted Sweaters, and in Figure 2-11 it is Trend Setters. However, each produced a positive net marketing contribution and, thus, contributed to covering operating expenses and producing net profit.

MARKET-BASED STRATEGIES AND PROFITABLE GROWTH

Recognizing the product or customer as the unit of analysis, we can evaluate different aspects of net marketing contribution in order to gain a better insight into the development of marketing strategies designed to grow profitability.[8] As shown in Figure 2-12, each element of the net marketing contribution equation offers the potential to create a marketing strategy that will affect profits. In each case, the net marketing contribution of a proposed strategy must exceed the current net marketing contribution in order to grow the net profits of the business. In light of this fact, there are a limited number of

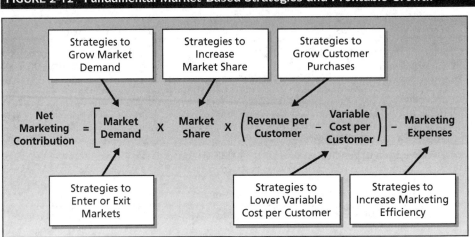

FIGURE 2-12   Fundamental Market-Based Strategies and Profitable Growth

fundamental marketing strategies that a business can consider in order to grow net marketing contribution.

Consider, for example, Santa Fe Sportswear's performance among Traditional Buyers, as presented in Figure 2-12. As shown below, Traditional Buyer currently produces a net marketing contribution of $15.4 million. This is derived from a 9 percent share of a market demand of 6.8 million customers, revenues of $90 per customer, variable costs of $55 per customer, and marketing expenses of $6 million.

$$= [6.8 \text{ million customers} \times 0.09 \times (\$90 - \$55)] - \$6 \text{ million}$$
$$= [612{,}000 \text{ customers} \times \$35] - \$6 \text{ million}$$
$$= \$21.4 \text{ million} - \$6 \text{ million}$$
$$= \textbf{\$15.4 million}$$

Marketing strategies to grow marketing profitability are many. In the remainder of this section, we will discuss the market-based strategies suggested in Figure 2-12 and assess how selected strategies in each area might affect the profits of Santa Fe Sportswear.

Strategies to Grow Market Demand

In many markets, a large part of the marketing challenge is to bring more customers into the market. If you think about the Sony Walkman, cellular telephones, and personal computers, you realize that a good portion of the profitable growth comes from new customers. Thus, marketing strategies to attract more customers and grow market demand offer one way to grow the net profits of a business. If a business is able to hold or grow share while attracting new customers to the market, there is a potential to grow profits. Profits will grow, however, only when the net marketing contribution produced by the proposed marketing strategy exceeds the current net marketing contribution.

For example, the Santa Fe Sportswear's Traditional Buyer marketing manager believes that segment demand could be grown from 6.8 million customers to 8.0 million customers with a 50 percent increase in marketing effort. If this increase could be achieved, and Santa Fe Sportswear were able to maintain a 9 percent share, volume would increase by 108,000 customers. But would this proposed strategy improve Traditional Buyer's marketing profitability and increase the business's overall profitability?

We can see from the following calculations that this would be a worthwhile marketing strategy. Net marketing contribution would increase by $0.8 million (from $15.4 to $16.2 million). The gain of 108,000 new customers would produce enough additional total contribution to cover the additional $3 million in marketing expenses required.

$$
\begin{aligned}
\text{NMC (Traditional Buyer)} &= [8.0 \text{ million customers} \times 0.09 \times (\$90 - \$55)] - \$9 \text{ million} \\
&= [720,000 \text{ customers} \times \$35 \text{ per unit}] - \$9 \text{ million} \\
&= \$25.2 \text{ million} - \$9 \text{ million} \\
&= \textbf{\$16.2 million}
\end{aligned}
$$

In some instances a business may actually take lower net marketing contributions in the short run in order to build demand and future net marketing contributions. However, the discounted cash flow from the long-term strategy has to exceed that of the current strategy in order for this approach to be viable.

Strategies to Increase Market Share

Perhaps the most common marketing strategy to grow revenue and profits is market share penetration. For any served market, a strategy is developed to grow the business's share of its served market. The same rules apply; a market penetration strategy is likely to cost money, margin, or both, and the net marketing contribution of the penetration strategy needs to exceed the current net marketing contribution for the business to improve profitability. For example, in Traditional Buyer, Santa Fe Sportswear could consider a strategy to increase its market share from 9 to 11 percent by lowering its prices 10 percent. As the following shows, the overall 136,000 customer gain would not be sufficient to offset the lower margin that would result from a 10 percent price decrease. The net result is a projected decrease in net marketing contribution from $15.4 million to $13.45 million.

$$
\begin{aligned}
\text{NMC (Traditional Buyer)} &= [6.8 \text{ million customers} \times 0.11 \times (\$81 - \$55)] - \$6 \text{ million} \\
&= [748,000 \text{ customers} \times \$26 \text{ per customer}] - \$6 \text{ million} \\
&= \$19.45 \text{ million} - \$6 \text{ million} \\
&= \textbf{\$13.45 million}
\end{aligned}
$$

Strategies to Increase Revenue per Customer

In a mature market with a strong share position, a business may not find it feasible or profitable to grow market demand or market share. However, the business's customers still remain its best strategic asset, and an examination of customer needs might reveal new products and services to better serve those needs and grow revenues. To evaluate the overall profit impact of such a marketing strategy, a business would have to project what higher prices could be attained and what increases in the average cost per unit would be required.

Also to be considered are potential additional marketing expenses, such as the additional advertising dollars that would be necessary to make existing customers aware of product or service improvements. Thus, it is important to examine all aspects of the strategy to ensure that a strategy to increase price per unit leads to an increase in net marketing contribution.

To illustrate the profit impact of a strategy to build revenue per customer, let us consider that, in Traditional Buyer, a major product line improvement would be able to raise average revenue per customer from $90 to $100. However, this improvement would also raise the average variable cost per customer by $5 because of increased materials costs. In addition, another $2 million in marketing expense will be needed to introduce the improved product line and to communicate its benefits. As shown below, this marketing strategy would produce an incremental gain of $1.1 million in net marketing contribution when compared with the current net marketing contribution of $15.4 million.

$$
\begin{aligned}
\text{NMC (Traditional Buyer)} &= [6.8 \text{ million customers} \times 0.09 \times (\$100 - \$60)] - \$8 \text{ million} \\
&= [612{,}000 \text{ customers} \times \$40 \text{ per customer}] - \$8 \text{ million} \\
&= \$24.5 \text{ million} - \$8 \text{ million} \\
&= \mathbf{\$16.5 \ million}
\end{aligned}
$$

Strategies to Lower Variable Cost

Another way to grow net profits is by lowering the variable cost per unit. For example, perhaps the transportation costs and sales commissions could be lowered with a new distribution strategy for a given market or market segment. This strategy would lower variable expenses per unit and increase margin per unit, but the business has to be concerned about the level of customer satisfaction that will be delivered by this alternative distribution system. If customer satisfaction lessens, so will customer retention. And, in the long run, net profits will erode even though the business has achieved a lower variable cost and higher margin per unit. Thus, a successful marketing strategy must hold or increase customer satisfaction while growing net profits through increases in net marketing contribution.

Continuing with the Santa Fe Sportswear example, Traditional Buyer's management is evaluating a new customer order entry and billing system that would improve customer satisfaction and lower the variable cost of serving a customer by $5 per customer. However, this new system will add $1 million per year in fixed marketing expense. This system would improve customer satisfaction and lower variable costs, but would it improve profitability? As shown below, the proposed order entry and billing system would improve the net marketing contribution by $2.1 million, improving both customer satisfaction and profitability.

$$
\begin{aligned}
\text{NMC (Traditional Buyer)} &= [6.8 \text{ million customers} \times 0.09 \times (\$90 - \$50)] - \$7 \text{ million} \\
&= [612{,}000 \text{ customers} \times \$40 \text{ per customer}] - \$7 \text{ million} \\
&= \$24.5 \text{ million} - \$7 \text{ million} \\
&= \mathbf{\$17.5 \ million}
\end{aligned}
$$

Strategies to Increase Market Efficiency

Another way to improve the profitability of a marketing strategy is to lower fixed marketing expenses: that is, to be more efficient in the use of marketing expenses to achieve a particular performance objective. The more focused a business is with respect to target customers, the fewer marketing dollars it has to expend in order to achieve a desired marketing objective. Likewise, alternative forms of distribution affect the fixed marketing expenses needed. For example, a business short on financial resources may elect to use a distributor rather than incur the fixed cost of direct selling and distribution.

Santa Fe Sportswear currently uses a direct sales force in Traditional Buyer and, as we have seen, spends $6 million in marketing expenses to obtain a market share of 9 percent. The business is considering shifting to manufacturers' representatives as a way to lower marketing expenses. The reps would be paid a 10 percent sales commission, and the business could reduce its marketing expenses by $2 million. As shown below, the 10 percent sales commission would be too costly in terms of reduced margin. As a result, the business is better off with its current marketing strategy because the current net marketing contribution ($15.4 million) is greater than the net marketing contribution of the projected marketing strategy.

$$
\begin{aligned}
\text{NMC (Traditional Buyer)} &= [6.8 \text{ million customers} \times 0.09 \times (\$90 - \$9 - \$55)] - \$4 \text{ million} \\
&= [612{,}000 \text{ customers} \times \$26 \text{ per unit}] - \$4 \text{ million} \\
&= \$15.9 \text{ million} - \$4 \text{ million} \\
&= \mathbf{\$11.9 \text{ million}}
\end{aligned}
$$

MARKETING PRODUCTIVITY

Recognizing net marketing contribution as the measure of marketing profitability, a manager can readily evaluate the profit impact of marketing strategies, as has been illustrated. In addition, we can evaluate the efficiency of the marketing budget used to produce a given level of marketing profitability (net marketing contribution) by creating the following measure of marketing productivity.

$$
\text{Market Productivity} = \frac{\text{Net Marketing Contribution}}{\text{Marketing Budget}}
$$

The ratio of net marketing contribution to marketing budget (marketing and sales expenses) provides a measure of how efficient a given marketing budget is in producing marketing profits. For example, Santa Fe Sportswear produces an overall net marketing contribution of $30 million with a marketing budget of $15 million. This is a market productivity ratio of 2.0, which means that each dollar of marketing budget produces $2 of net marketing contribution:

$$
\begin{aligned}
\text{Marketing Profitability} &= \frac{\text{Net Marketing Contribution}}{\text{Marketing \& Sales Expenses}} \\
&= \frac{\$30 \text{ million}}{\$15 \text{ million}} \\
&= \mathbf{2.0}
\end{aligned}
$$

We can also assess the marketing productivity of each segment served by Santa Fe Sportswear. Using the net marketing contribution and marketing expenses reported in Figure 2-11, we can see that each segment strategy is producing a good level of net marketing contribution for each dollar of marketing budget. Traditional Buyers produce the largest sales revenue, and the marketing strategy used in this segment is the most efficient in producing marketing profits. And, while Trend Setters are reported to produce an overall loss of $1 million, the marketing strategy developed for Trend Setters is profitable and produces $1.70 of marketing profits for each dollar of marketing budget.

Marketing Performance Metric	Traditional Buyer	Fashion Buyer	Trend Setter	Company Total
Net Marketing Contribution	$15.4 million	$7.1 million	$7.5 million	$30 million
Marketing & Sales Expenses	$6.0 million	$4.5 million	$4.5 million	$15 million
Marketing Productivity	2.6	1.6	1.7	2.0

This market-based performance metric helps managers evaluate the relative efficiency with which they are growing net marketing contribution. It may be that two marketing strategies yield an equivalent net marketing contribution, but one is more efficient because it has a higher marketing productivity. Put simply, one strategy can produce the same level of marketing profitability (net marketing contribution) but for fewer dollars of marketing budget. This, of course, is an advantage to any business, since those extra dollars can be used for other purposes.

Another benefit of this marketing metric is that it can be used in comparisons with other companies or benchmark businesses. Figure 2-13 presents the marketing productivity of five competing computer manufacturers. In this case Dell Computer produced the highest level of marketing productivity. While Compaq's sales revenues and percent gross profits were higher than Dell, Dell had much lower marketing and sales expenses as a percentage of sales. Gateway's marketing productivity is much lower because of its lower margins and high marketing and sales expenses when measured as a percentage of sales. HP and IBM sell a wider range of products and services, making comparisons of HP and IBM with the other three a little more difficult. Nevertheless, both HP and IBM are below the level of marketing productivity achieved by Dell Computer in 2001.

FIGURE 2-13 Marketing Productivity for Five Computer Companies in 2001					
Performance (millions)	*Dell*	*Compaq*	*Gateway*	*HP*	*IBM*
Sales Revenues	$31,888	$33,548	$6,099	$45,226	$85,900
Cost of Goods Sold	$25,445	$26,436	$5,261	$36,935	$54,084
Gross Profit	$ 6,443	$ 7,112	$ 838	$ 8,291	$31,816
Gross Profit (% sales)	20.2%	21.2%	13.7%	18.3%	37.0%
Marketing & Sales Expenses	$ 3,193	$ 5,336	$2,022	$ 5,134	$17,197
Marketing & Sales Exp (% sales)	10.0%	15.9%	33.2%	11.4%	20.0%
Net Marketing Contribution	$ 3,250	$ 1,776	($1,184)	$ 3,157	$14,619
Marketing Productivity	1.02	0.33	−0.59	0.61	0.85

MARKET ORIENTATION

Businesses with a strong market orientation have different behaviors, systems and measurements. Their commitment to a market orientation leads them to use market metrics in an effort to achieve desired levels of profit performance.[9] Underlying a strong market orientation are three distinct areas of commitment—customer orientation, competitor orientation, and working as an integrated team. Each of these areas of market orientation leads to behaviors, systems and measurements that differentiate an externally focused, market-based business from an internally focused product business.[10] Each of these core areas of market orientation is discussed in the following section, along with measures that have been developed for assessing a business's level of commitment to each area of market orientation.[11]

MARKET ORIENTATION	MARKET METRICS	PROFIT METRICS
(Behaviors)	(Measurements)	(Performance)

Customer Orientation

Lexus has a strong market orientation. At its core is a management and employee culture built around a strong customer orientation. Each year every employee must call a Lexus owner to discuss their satisfaction with their Lexus. The Lexus marketing team conducts personal interviews with Lexus owners at their homes to better understand their customers and customer lifestyles. A new Lexus model will have many design changes before it is finalized based on customer evaluations of the new car design and related features. This level of customer commitment pays off as year after year Lexus is rated number one in customer satisfaction among luxury cars in the JD Powers Customer Satisfaction Survey.

The customer orientation of a business can be assessed based on the degree to which a business engages in the following customer-oriented behaviors. Rate each of the statements below on a 1 to 7 scale where 1 equals **not at all** and 7 equals **extensively.** The higher the average score, the higher a business's customer orientation.

_____ We constantly monitor our level of commitment and orientation to serving our customers.

_____ Our business objectives are driven primarily by customer satisfaction.

_____ Our strategy for competitive advantage is based on our understanding of customer needs.

_____ Our business strategies are driven by our beliefs about how we can create greater value for customers.

_____ We measure customer satisfaction systematically and frequently.

_____ We give close attention to after-sales service.

Customer Orientation (average score)

Each of these behaviors is part of the FedEx culture and overall business operations. At FedEx, these measurements and behaviors are not part of an annual survey. They are at work everyday and in some instances, a part of every customer shipment.

Competitor Orientation

Competitor orientation is difficult for most companies—even those with a strong customer orientation. It is simply more difficult to obtain good competitor intelligence. Often in situations where good competitor intelligence is available, either it is not used, it is discredited, or even distorted. During World War II, Winston Churchill set up an office outside his chain of command whose only job was to provide him with the unvarnished truth. Without a competitor orientation it is difficult to develop and implement successful marketing strategies, even when a business has a good understanding of customer needs. To be successful, a business needs to understand both customers and competitors.[12]

General Electric is known for having a strong competitor orientation. Managers focus on markets where they can create a superior value relative to competition and strive to build a sustainable competitive advantage. This involves more than words, however. At GE, there are courses taught on competitor analysis and behaviors, much like those outlined below, ingrained in GE management. Being number one in a market means you need to benchmark the top competitors in a market and accurately calibrate your competitive position relative to these top competitors. This has allowed GE to achieve a market share leadership position in most of the markets they elect to serve and to achieve above average profits.

The following behaviors have been successfully used to gauge the level of a business's competitor orientation. Using statements and a scale that ranges from 1 **not at all** to 7 **extensively** one can assess the level of a business's competitor orientation. The higher the average score, the stronger the business's competitor orientation.

_____ We rapidly respond to competitive actions that threaten us.

_____ Our salespeople regularly share information within our organization
          concerning competitors' strategies.

_____ Top management regularly discusses competitors' strengths and strategies.

_____ We target customers where we have an opportunity for competitive advantage.

[   ]   **Competitor Orientation** (average score)

Team Approach

David Packard once said, "marketing is too important to leave to the marketers." He did not mean that those in marketing are incompetent. What was intended was that all aspects of the organization need to be involved in understanding customer needs and competitors' positions, and working across the organization as a team to build superior customer solutions.

This leadership attitude helped Hewlett-Packard build a market-oriented company that relies heavily on a team approach. Rapid change in HP's business environment demands quick responses to ensure growth and survival. Cross-functional teams leverage a variety of skills, enhance communication across departments, and allow a market-based customer solution to evolve faster and at a lower cost. A business with a strong team approach will re-engineer its organization to better facilitate development and delivery of market-based customer solutions.[13]

A business can evaluate its level of Team Approach using the following statements and a scale that ranges from 1 **not at all** to 7 **extensively**. Naturally, the higher the average score, the stronger the business's commitment to a Team Approach in building a market-based management culture.

_____ All of our business functions (e.g., marketing/sales, manufacturing, engineering,
          R&D, finance, etc.) are integrated in serving the needs of our target markets.

_____ All of our business functions and departments are responsive to each other's needs and requests.

_____ Our top managers from very function regularly visit our current and prospective customers.

_____ We freely communicate information about our successful and unsuccessful customer experiences across all business functions.

Team Approach (average score)

An overall average of the average scores for customer orientation, competitor orientation, and team approach provides a measure of a business's market orientation. Using this measure of market orientation, businesses with higher overall average scores have been shown to be more profitable than businesses with lower overall average scores.

Summary

A market-based business engages in three important distinguishing practices:

- It tracks market-based measures of performance.
- It measures marketing profits by product, market, or both.
- It organizes around markets rather than products.

Without an external set of market-based performance metrics, a business will never know its market performance. For CommTech, an overreliance on traditional measures of internal performance cost the business and its shareholders $122 million in net profits. Thus, an important step in becoming a market-based business is the development of a key set of external market-based measures of performance. These external market metrics can include in-process metrics, which typically precede financial performance measurement, and end-result market metrics, which are more likely to coincide with financial performance measurement.

To develop and implement marketing strategies that are going to increase customer satisfaction and grow profits, a business needs to be able to measure the profitability of a marketing decision. This means understanding the revenues that result from serving a target market of customers and all the costs associated with serving that market. A common problem often arises here in most accounting systems: the need to allocate overhead costs. This has the potential to distort profitability and can lead to decisions that actually reduce profitability. To grow profits, a business needs to grow net marketing contribution. Allocating overhead costs will distort net marketing contribution. If the accountants persist in allocating cost, simply ask that costs be allocated after the net marketing contribution has been computed so that market-level profitability can be clearly observed.

With market-based management, the focus is on the customer. How much revenue does a customer produce? What are the costs of acquiring customers? What are the costs of serving those customers after they have been acquired? What is the net marketing contribution per customer in different segments of the market? Measures of marketing profitability and marketing productivity help us evaluate the profit impact and spending efficiency of a marketing strategy.

Businesses with a strong market orientation have a commitment to understanding customers and competitors and working as a team in building value-added customer solutions. These market-focused businesses with distinctly different behaviors, systems and measurements go beyond traditional internal performance metrics. Businesses with a stronger market orientation achieve higher levels of customer retention and have to be more profitable.

APPLICATION PROBLEM: DELL COMPUTER

The worldwide market demand for personal computers grew from 117 million units in 1999 to 132 million in 2001 as shown in the figure below. The market is projected to grow to 161 million units by 2003 and 216 million units by 2006.

Dell Computer was number 2 in market share until it became the global market share leader in 2001.

In 2001 Dell's market share of 14.2 percent translated into $33.88 billion in sales and $2.77 billion in operating income.

Performance (millions)	1999	2000	2001	2003	2006
PC Market Demand	117	129	132	161	216
Market Share	8.7%	11.2%	14.2%		
Unit Volume	10.14	14.45	18.74		
Sales Revenues	$18,243	$25,265	$31,888		
Cost of Goods Sold	$14,137	$20,047	$25,445		
Gross Profit	$ 4,106	$ 5,218	$ 6,443		
Marketing & Sales Expense	$ 1,788	$ 2,387	$ 3,193		
R&D and Other Expenses	$274.00	$379.00	$478.00		
Operating Income	$ 2,044	$ 2,452	$ 2,772		

For access to interactive software to answer the following questions below, go to www.RogerJBest.com or www.prenhall.com/best.

Questions

1. How will Dell unit volume change if Dell can grow market share to 15 by 2003 and 18 percent by 2006?

2. Estimate average price and average unit cost for 2003 and 2006. Then evaluate projected gross profits.

3. Estimate the Marketing and Sales Expenses (as a % sales) for 2003 and 2006 given market share objectives. Then evaluate projected Net Marketing Contribution and Marketing Productivity for 2003 and 2006.

4. Using the previous assumptions, estimate the operating income for 2003 and 2006 when assuming R&D and other operating expenses will remain at 1.5 percent of sales.

Market-Based Logic and Strategic Thinking

1. Why are market-based measures of performance critical to achieving profitable growth?
2. How do market-based measures of performance differ from internal measures of performance? Why are both necessary?

3. Why does a business need both internal (financial) measures of performance and external (market-based) measures of performance?
4. What roles do market-based measures of performance play in achieving profitable growth?
5. Why are performance metrics important?
6. What is the fundamental difference between a market performance metric and a financial performance metric?
7. Why are in-process metrics an important part of a successful marketing strategy? What is the relationship between in-process metrics and end-result metrics?
8. What are some of the fundamental differences between product-based accounting and customer-based accounting?
9. How does net marketing contribution enable a business to better understand the profit impact of a marketing strategy?
10. What is the difference between a variable cost and a fixed expense?
11. Why are marketing expenses considered semi variable expenses and cost of goods a variable expense?
12. How can treatment of operating expenses distort interpretations of profitability?
13. How can one assess the profit impact of a specific marketing strategy?
14. Under what conditions would you expect operating expenses to change with changes in marketing strategies?
15. What fundamental marketing strategies can a business pursue to grow marketing profits?
16. Explain how any given marketing strategy might affect different components of net marketing contribution.
17. Why would a business want to measure its profitability by market segment?
18. What does a marketing productivity of 0.5 mean? What does it mean when a competitor with approximately the same market share has a marketing productivity of 1.0?
19. Why would a business with a strong customer orientation be more profitable than a business with a weak customer orientation?
20. How would a strong competitor orientation contribute to a higher level of profits?
21. Why would a team approach be an important element of market orientation?

Notes

1. Bradley Gale, "Tracking Competitive Position Drives Shareholder Value," *Global Management* (1992):367–71.
2. Yuxin Chen, James Hess, Ronald Wilcox, and Z. John Zhang, "Accounting Profits Versus Marketing Profits: A Relevant Metric for Category Management," *Marketing Science*, 18, No. 3 (1999):208–229.
3. Robert Kaplan and David Norton, "The Balanced Scorecard—Measures That Drive Performance," *Harvard Business Review* (January–February 1992):71–79; and Robert Eccles, "The Performance Measurement Manifesto," *Harvard Business Review* (January–February 1991):131–37.
4. George Cressman, "Choosing the Right Metric," *Drive Marketing Excellence* (November 1994), New York: Institute for International Research.
5. John Shank and Vijay Govindarajan, *Strategic Cost Analysis* (New York: Irwin, 1989):99–112.
6. John Shank and Vijay Govindarajan, "The Perils of Cost Allocation Based on Production Volumes," *Accounting Horizons* 4 (1988):71–79; and John Shank and Vijay Govindarajan, "Making Strategy Explicit in Cost Analysis: A Case Study," *Sloan Marketing Review* (Spring 1988):15–30.
7. Michael Morris and Gene Morris, *Market-Oriented Pricing* (New York: NTC Business Books, 1990):99–100; and Don Schultz, "Spreadsheet Approach to Measuring ROI for MCI," *Marketing News* 28 (February 1994):12.
8. William Christopher, "Marketing Achievement Reporting: A Profitability Approach," *Industrial Marketing*

Management (New York: Elsevier North Holland, Inc. 1977):149–62; Patrick Dunne and Harry Wolk, "Marketing Cost Analysis: A Modularized Contribution," *Journal of Marketing* (July 1977):83–94; Stanley Shapiro and V. H. Kirpalard, *Marketing Effectiveness: Insights from Accounting and Finance* (Needham Heights, MA: Allyn and Bacon, 1984):377–424; and Jean-Claude Larreche and Hubert Gatignon, *MARKSTRAT* (New York: Scientific Press, 1990):22–23.

9. John Narver and Stanley Slater, "The Effect of Market Orientation on Business Profitability," *Journal of Marketing* 54 (October 1990):20–35.

10. Theodore Levitt, "Marketing Myopia," *Harvard Business Review* (July–August 1968):45–56.

11. Bryan Lukas and O.C. Ferrell, "The Effect of Market Orientation on Product Innovation," *Journal of the Academy of Marketing Sciences*, 28, No. 2, 239–247; Hubert Gatignon and Jean-Marc Xuereb, "Strategic Orientation of the Firm and New Product-Performance," *Journal of Marketing Research* (February 1997):77–90; Judy Siguaw, Gene Brown, and Robert Winding II, "The Influence of Market Orientation of the Firm on Sales Force Behavior," *Journal of Marketing Research* (February 1994):106–116.

12. George Day, "Aligning the Organization to the Market," in *Reflections on the Future of Marketing,* ed. D. Lehmann and Katherine Tocz (Cambridge, MA: Marketing Science Institute, 1994):67–96; George Day, "The Capability of Market-Driven Organizations," *Journal of Marketing* (January 1994):37–52; and John Workman Jr., Christian Hornburg, and Kjell Graner, "Marketing Organization: An Interactive Framework of Dimensions and Determinants," *Journal of Marketing* (July 1988):21–41.

13. Frederick Webster, *Market-Driven Management* (New York: Free Press 1994): Chapter 8; Harvard Business School Press, 1993).

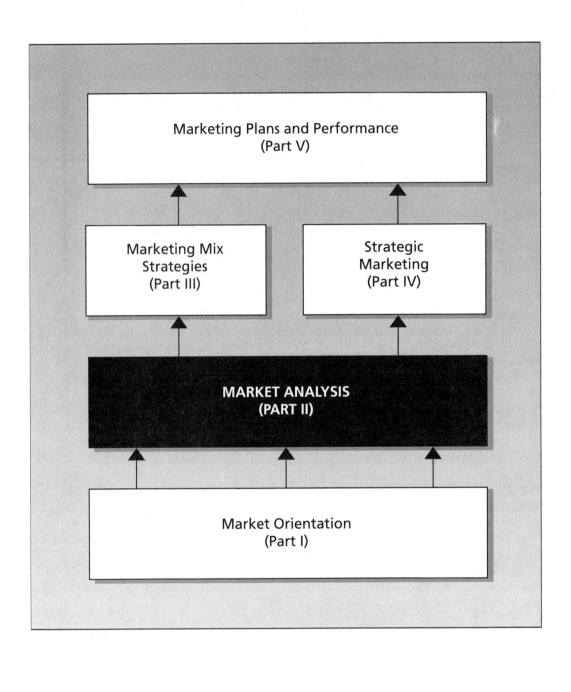

PART

II | MARKET ANALYSIS

*"The customer is always right, but we get
to pick who is a customer."*
—ANONYMOUS

Market analysis is an essential input to the development of market-based management strategies that deliver superior levels of customer satisfaction and profitability. The continuous pursuit of customer needs, ongoing monitoring of competitors' moves and capabilities, and tracking of market-based performance are the core competencies of market-focused business.

Part II includes four chapters that are built around the fundamental inputs of market analysis: market demand, customer analysis, market segmentation, and competitor analysis. Chapter 3 focuses on market definition, market potential, market demand, and market growth opportunities. However, markets do not buy products; customers buy products. Chapter 4 covers customer analysis and the discovery of benefits that deliver a superior value.

Because customers in any market differ in many ways, rarely can one marketing strategy adequately serve all their needs. Chapter 5 addresses needs-based market segmentation and the development of segment strategies. Finally, Chapter 6 focuses on competitor analysis, competitive position, and sources of competitive advantage.

CHAPTER

3 | MARKET POTENTIAL, DEMAND, AND MARKET SHARE

At any point in time, the overall demand for a product or service is finite. That is, there is a fixed number of customers who buy at a certain rate of purchase; thus, there is a certain level of market demand, whether for fast food, personal computers, or automobiles. At any point in time, there are *existing* customers who make up current market demand and *potential* customers who provide the opportunity for growing market demand.

Potential customers help us define the level of future market demand. In mature markets, the market potential (maximum number of customers) is close to the market demand (existing number of customers). In emerging or growing markets, market demand will grow as more customers enter the market. However, for a business to achieve a desired level of performance in a market, it needs to obtain a desired share of that market. To manage performance over time, a business needs to understand

- The market's existing level of demand and potential demand.
- The rate of replacement purchase and new customer purchase.
- The business's market share and potential market share.

With a good understanding of these dimensions of performance, a business can assess the market's current and future volume. This chapter explains the factors that shape market demand, the forces that influence market growth, and the parameters of marketing strategy that yield a certain level of market share and unit volume.

MARKET DEFINITION

The cola wars of the 1980s lured soft drink manufacturers into a limited vision and, hence, a limited definition of their markets. Strategies to hold share and grow market demand in an intensely competitive market blurred their market vision. Though there is nothing inherently wrong with a narrow product–market focus, a pure product–market focus limits a business's view of other market opportunities and competitive threats. Many observers would agree that this limited focus was the only choice these manufacturers had because the loss of one market share point in the soft drink market is worth almost $600 million in retail sales. Losing one share point in this market has to hurt profits because marketing and overhead expenses are not likely to go down in the midst of a battle to hold market share. Thus, their aggressive moves to hold share could be legitimately defended.

57

FIGURE 3-1   Strategic Market Definition of the Beverage Market

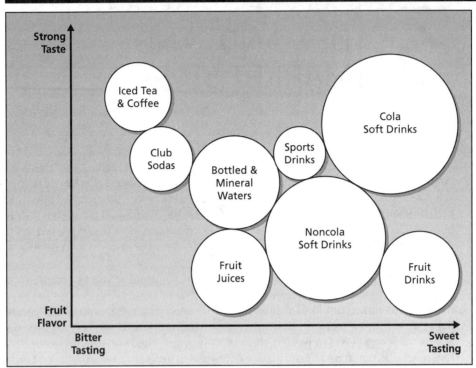

The battle to hold share in the soft drink market, however, represents only one portion of the battlefield. Adjacent to this battlefield is a whole new set of competitive threats that have emerged over the last twenty-five years. As illustrated in Figure 3-1, these new product markets include mineral waters, sports drinks, fruit juices, fruit drinks, and specialty tea and coffee products.

Because of their focus on the soft drink market, soft drink manufacturers were late to react to these new forms of competition. Yet where did the consumers of Perrier, Gatorade, Snapple, Ocean Spray, and New York Express Iced Coffee come from? Many came from the soft drink market into these new product–markets while others were drawn away from alcoholic beverages and hot-served coffees and teas. Collectively, these substitute products produce $30 billion in annual retail sales, approximately half that of the soft drink market. In response to these new market opportunities, Coca-Cola and Pepsi have aggressively entered these markets. They are working to better position themselves to gain share as these markets continue to grow at twice the rate of the soft drink market.

Market Vision

Perhaps the biggest threat to business survival and a major cause of missed market opportunities is the lack of a broad market vision: that is, being unable to see the broader picture of customers, market demand, and the forces that shape unserved market demand.[1] Theodore Levitt's timeless perspective on marketing myopia applies today as well as it did when he first wrote on the subject more than forty years ago: "A myopic vision of the potential markets a business might serve translates into a narrow product-focused market definition."[2]

Individuals with a broad market vision usually see the world differently. Their view of market demand goes beyond a view of existing products and customers and enables them to see more clearly untapped or emerging market opportunities that most cannot see or others conclude are too small or foolish. With unrestricted market vision, these businesses moved quickly to control their own destinies.[3]

Strategic Market Definition

The first step in understanding market demand is to develop a broad vision of what the market is. A market definition that is limited to a particular product focus maintains the status quo. A business with a narrow market focus sees only the *articulated needs* of served customers.[4] A broad market vision encourages discovery of *unarticulated needs* and uncovers new *unserved* opportunities. For Fred Smith, founder of Federal Express, a broad market focus meant a vision of overnight mail, new choices for customers, and a profitable business opportunity that bankers, professors, and industry experts could not envision and said would not work. For Phil Knight, founder of Nike, it meant a market vision for running and sports footwear as well as sports clothing. And, for Bill Gates, cofounder of Microsoft, it meant a market vision of people using computers in a variety of ways.

To avoid a narrow market definition and, hence, its potential to restrict discovery of new market opportunities, a business needs a broad *strategic market definition*. This includes a broader definition of all product–markets that are potential substitutes for the product–markets currently served by the business. For example, the market definition for soft drinks could be limited to the soft drink product domain and not include important substitute product–markets. A broader strategic market definition would include all relevant substitute products. The degree of substitutability in a broad strategic market definition is represented by the distance between markets.[5] The closer one market is to another, the greater the likelihood that customers will substitute one product for another.

A broad strategic market definition enables managers to see a broader set of customer needs and potential new market opportunities. This ability, of course, provides a wider range of market-based strategies as management assesses which markets it would like to participate in, recognizing its own core competencies and capabilities. Thus, a broad strategic market definition provides three key benefits to a market-based business:

- It opens the window of opportunity to a broader set of customer needs.
- It provides better understanding of potential substitutes and competitive threats.
- It helps a business better understand fundamental customer needs.

Vertical Versus Horizontal Market Opportunities

With a broader market vision, a business is able to see more opportunities for growth. These broader market opportunities often exist in adjacent *vertical* and *horizontal* markets. Vertical markets represent market opportunities along the vertical market's

FIGURE 3-2 Vertical and Horizontal Markets and Growth Opportunities

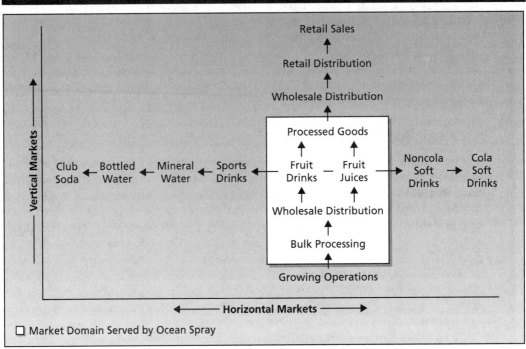

☐ Market Domain Served by Ocean Spray

"value chain." A business can either *forward* or *backward integrate* to expand its market domain and opportunity for growth.[6] A manufacturer who takes over the retail sale of its products is expanding its vertical market domain and opportunity to grow. Horizontal market opportunities exist in substitute product markets. For soft drink manufacturers, the various markets shown in Figure 3-1 represent horizontal market opportunities. However, companies without a broad market vision rarely take such opportunities seriously.

Nevertheless, adjacent vertical and horizontal markets offer potential growth opportunities that require consideration for any business seeking growth. For example, as illustrated in Figure 3-2, Ocean Spray has expanded its vertical market domain from bulk-processing capabilities to vertically integrate into processed goods that initially included cranberries and fruit juice. Changing customer needs also created a horizontal market opportunity, and, in response, Ocean Spray developed a line of fruit drinks. The combination of both vertical and horizontal market expansion has contributed significantly to the overall growth of Ocean Spray.

Served Market Definition

With a broad market definition, a business is now in a position to better define the market domains in which it will elect to compete. Recall that the primary determinant of market vision is the *fundamental customer need* we are serving. This fundamental customer need has a tremendous impact on how the business defines its market and the size of the market it will develop and serve. A *served market* is defined as the market in which a business competes for target customers.[7] It includes both the business's and its competitors' customers.

For example, the served market for Lexus is much different from that for Tercel, though both are Toyota products. Each has a separate and distinct set of customers and competitors that make up unique served markets. The automotive market, while broadly defined as a transportation market, is made up of many smaller served markets based on the unique needs of customers for price and car benefits. Likewise, a broad market definition of the beer market has enabled Anheuser-Busch to create several served market definitions. As the beer market matured, it fragmented into many new market opportunities along with new types of customers and competitors. It required a broad market vision and more than one served market definition to effectively manage penetration of these new market opportunities.

MARKET POTENTIAL

Once a served market definition has been established, a business is in a better position to understand several important aspects of market demand. The first, and most crucial, is how many customers make up the maximum potential for this market definition.[8] This perspective creates a sharp contrast between a product-focused and a market-based business.

> A product-focused business is interested in product volume, whereas a market-based business is interested in how many customers make up a market.

Product volume and sales revenues can vary with customer behavior and competitive strategies. However, the potential number of customers within a market domain is a finite number of great strategic significance because it places the true upper limit on the number of consumption units.

For example, what is the market potential for disposable diapers? The number of babies between newborn and two years of age might be a reasonable estimate of the maximum number of consuming units. But, do all households with children in this age bracket purchase disposable diapers? No! Some cannot afford them; others oppose them because of their negative environmental impact; still others may simply prefer the advantages they see in cloth diapers. Thus, the number of consuming units is almost always less than the maximum market potential (maximum number of customers).

Untapped Market Opportunities

Many new markets and most global markets are well below their full market potential. That is, there are large numbers of possible customers who have not yet entered the market. For example, the market potential (maximum number) for personal computers is estimated to be 250 million per year. At this time there will be an estimated installed base of one billion personal computers. In 2001, the level of market penetration (131.5 million PCs) was slightly over 50 percent, as illustrated in Figure 3-3. But, one could ask, why will it take so long for this market to reach its full market potential? There are five major forces that can restrict a market from reaching its full potential, as illustrated in Figure 3-4.

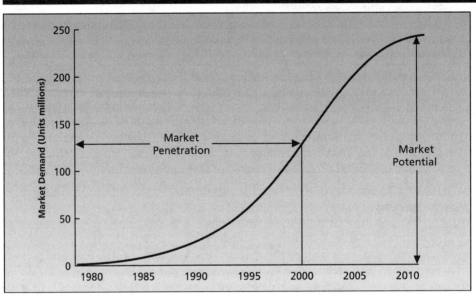

FIGURE 3-3   Personal Computer Market Development

Awareness

This does not mean just *product awareness* but *complete comprehension of benefits.* If potential customers are unaware of a product, or do not fully or accurately understand its benefits, then they will not be fully informed and they will be unable to discern the product's potential value to them. For the personal computer, most potential customers in a worldwide market would be aware of the product, but many may not fully comprehend the benefits. Because the product is complex and experiential, many of the benefits are understood only after a period of use.

Availability

A second force that restricts market demand is lack of *availability.* Personal computers can be readily purchased by many people, but services to support them might not be available in many geographic markets. For most mature markets, product availability is not a significant force that restricts market demand. However, lack of availability of products that may be in short supply, or difficult to make available, or lack of services to support their use, can be an important source of reduced market demand.

Ability to Use

The inability to use a product can also restrict expansion of a market to its full potential. People in many parts of the world would benefit from the use of a personal computer, but if you do not have electricity, you cannot use one even when the product is available. Perhaps more important, the ability to use a personal computer requires a certain level of specialized education. In response to this need, businesses such as Apple Computer and Microsoft have funded educational programs that should contribute to the market development of the personal computer market.

FIGURE 3-4   Maximum Market Potential and Current Market Demand

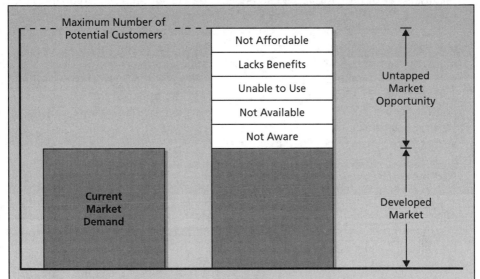

Forces that limit market demand

- *Awareness:* These potential customers would buy the product if they knew it was available and accurately understood its benefits.
- *Availability:* Potential customers are aware, able to buy, and have the desire to buy, but this product or service is not available in their geographic market.
- *Ability to Use:* Although the product is affordable and attractive, customers are not able to use it because of the use environment in which they operate. These customers lack the knowledge, other resources, and/or requirements to make the product or service workable.
- *Benefit Deficiency:* The key benefits of the product or service are not important (or are even unattractive) to a subset of potential customers.
- *Affordability:* Regardless of product attractiveness or perceived benefits, the cost is simply too high for some consumers.

Benefit Deficiency

For some consumers, the benefits of a given type of product are not attractive or compelling enough for them to enter the market. For others, such as those consumers who oppose disposable diapers for environmental reasons, the benefit proposition is simply deficient and not strong enough to stimulate purchase even if the product is available and affordable and a proper use situation exists. Because consumers have a wide range of product and lifestyle needs, it may be difficult to accommodate all the needs and desired benefits in any given market. So there is a practical limit that may restrict any market from reaching its maximum market potential. For example, many older people may not see a benefit in owning a personal computer. However, with the expansion of e-mail and Internet home shopping, this growing segment of the population could become an important source of new customer growth that would contribute to further development of the PC market.

Affordability

Finally, many of the products some people take for granted are simply not affordable for others. While the benefits are known and attractive, the product is too expensive given the income available to many potential customers. Once again, businesses with narrowly focused product orientation will never see beyond their current customer market. As a result, they will never challenge their engineers and production managers with the task of building a lower-cost version of their products. The largest portion of new customer purchases in the PC market is in the under-$1,000 segment. This price point triggered the entry of a new group of buyers based on affordability. As low-end PC prices approach the price of low-end televisions and VCRs, the PC will continue to attract price-sensitive buyers into the market.

Market Development Index

The real benefit of a broader market definition is in knowing both the overall potential of a market and the forces that currently restrict market demand. If we create a ratio of maximum market potential to current market demand, we can index the opportunity for market development.

$$\text{Market Development Index} = \frac{\text{Current Market Demand}}{\text{Maximum Market Demand}} \times 100$$

A market development index (MDI) of less than 33 would suggest that there is considerable growth potential. As shown in Figure 3-3, the personal computer market is in its first half of market development. Although price declines for personal computers have contributed to market development, this market's maximum market potential probably will not be reached for many years.

The first third of the market potential can generally be served with higher prices and basic benefits. To bring more customers into the market, businesses have to lower prices, offer a wider range of product alternatives, and expand distribution to increase availability. When the market development index is between 33 and 67, development of the market is based on addressing benefit deficiencies and price reductions that bring more customers into the market at a more affordable price.

When the market development index goes above 67, there still exists considerable opportunity for growth. However, the task will be more difficult as the business faces the more difficult causes that restrict full market development. These forces are likely to include affordability, benefit deficiency, and inability to use. Overcoming these hurdles requires real market-based, customer-focused solutions. Though a tougher marketing task, developing this untapped portion of customers provides a more differentiated position and one that competitors may find hard to copy. Thus, while the challenge may be greater, the rewards of market ownership could also be greater.

Market Potential and Market Growth

Recognizing that every market has some upper limit (its market potential), marketing people are intrigued by the question of how fast the market will grow as it expands to its full potential. Shown in Figure 3-5 are the market growth curves for several products. The upper limit in each case represents the market potential for each product–market. The rate at which customers enter a market is a market-specific phenomenon based on

FIGURE 3-5   Market Penetration and Market Development Index

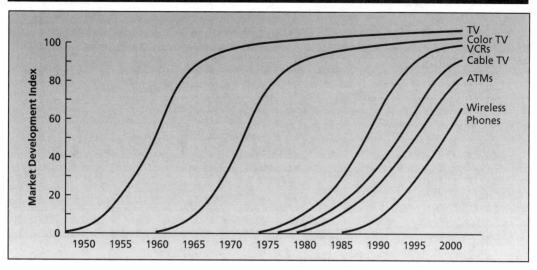

product attractiveness, customer characteristics, and marketing efforts.[9] However, the early pattern established by the rate of customer entry into a market provides sufficient information to accurately project the market growth rate in most instances.[10]

There are three fundamental forces that capture the shape of the market growth curve and hence the rate of market growth:

- **Market Potential:** The maximum number of customers who can enter the market given a specific served market definition.
- **Market Penetration:** The total number of customers who have entered that market at a specific point in time.
- **Rate of Entry:** The rate at which new customers enter the market.

The combination of these three forces defines the shape and individual parameters of a market's customer attraction and growth. However, some markets grow faster and reach their full potential much faster than others. But why? Why do some product–markets grow at a fast rate and others at a comparatively slow rate? The next section addresses these questions as well as marketing strategies that can be developed to accelerate market growth.

Rate of Market Development

New markets depend on finding new customers. Most potential customers are not going to be the first to buy a new product. New products are often higher priced, more complex, and less accepted by mainstream society than are established products. As a result, there are a variety of risks associated with being among the first buyers of a new product or technology.

Emerging markets are initially relatively small and made up of *innovators* and *early adopters,* as shown in Figure 3-6. In general, the customers who make up the *early market* possess more knowledge, are less price-sensitive and more benefit-driven, and

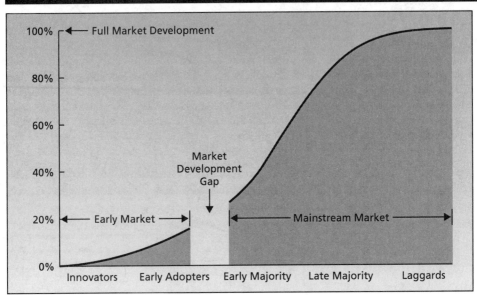

FIGURE 3-6   Customer Adoption and Market Development

are less dependent upon what others do or think than are most people. These *lead customers* are critical. If they cannot be attracted, satisfied, and retained, the market is likely to die because the mainstream market will not buy if the lead customers do not. The first job in successfully developing a new product market is to identify lead customers and penetrate the early market.

However, for a new market to move from the *early market* to the *mainstream market* requires the development of *complete solutions*.[11] Although customers in the early market are willing to struggle to make new products workable, those in the mainstream market are less willing to put up with less-than-complete solutions; they want a 100 percent solution. Thus, to successfully reach the mainstream market, a business needs to create a complete solution, one that has all the necessary features, functions, and supporting products and services.[12]

Unfortunately, there is one more problem. The mainstream market is made up of many segments, each with a different view of what it considers a complete solution.[13] To successfully reach the mainstream market, a business must carefully identify its target customers and focus on the delivery of what those target customers consider a complete solution. And, just as there are lead customers in the early market, there are *lead segments* in the mainstream market. As a result, further success in the mainstream market is partially dependent on the influence of one segment over another. The more quickly businesses address the complete solution needed to close the *market development gap* shown in Figure 3-6, the faster the market growth.

Accelerating Market Growth

Developing and delivering a complete solution requires more than further product development. The rate at which the mainstream market adopts a new product is also dependent upon customer characteristics, product positioning, and market influences.

FIGURE 3-7 Forces That Affect the Rate of Mainstream Market Growth		
	Slows Market Development	*Accelerates Market Development*
Customer Influences		
Felt Need	Low — — — — — — —	High
Perceived Risk	High — — — — — — —	Low
Innovativeness	Low — — — — — — —	High
Decision-Making Unit	Group — — — — — — —	Individual
Product Influences		
Relative Advantage	Minimal — · — — — — — —	Substantial
Relative Cost	High — — — — — — —	Low
Complexity	Extensive — — — — — — —	Minimal
Ease of Use	Difficult — — — — — — —	Easy
Market Influences		
Observability	Do Not See — — — — — — —	Easily Seen
Trialability	Cannot Try — — — — — — —	Easy to Try
Marketing Effort	Minimal — — — — — — —	Extensive

Given adequate product awareness and availability, there are eleven forces that act to accelerate or slow customer attraction and the rate of market growth.[14]

Customer Influences

As shown in Figure 3-7, there are four customer characteristics that affect the rate at which customers enter a market. When the *felt need* for the product is low, customer attraction will be slow. For years, many customers simply did not feel a strong need to have a microwave oven, and the lack of a felt need slowed the rate at which customers entered this product–market. Also, many customers perceived a safety risk with microwave ovens, and this perception also slowed market growth. Customer perceptions of risk can include a variety of *perceived risk* factors such as perceived safety, social, and economic risk.

A third customer factor is the degree to which the market is made up of *innovative* customers. Younger people tend to be innovative and likely to try new things, whereas many older people are conservative and slow to try new products. The demographics and lifestyles of target customers can play a key role in the rate of new customer attraction. Finally, the nature of the *decision-making unit* influences the rate of new customer market entry. Group decisions, whether in a business or in a family, slow the rate of customer entry. Individual decision-making units are less likely to be inhibited by others and are freer to make decisions quickly. Collectively, when all the customer characteristics line up on the positive side, they provide an accelerating effect on the rate at which customers enter a given product–market.

Product Influences

The strength of a product's positioning (relative benefits) also plays a key role in the rate of market growth. The stronger the *relative advantage* and the lower the *relative cost,* the greater the customer value created by the product and the faster the rate of customer market entry. However, this is the point at which many businesses stop. They do not follow through and examine more closely the *perceived complexity* and *ease of use* perceived by potential customers. If the product is not compatible with the way things are normally done, or it is difficult to use, customers may be reluctant to try or purchase the product.

When first introduced, the microwave oven, while expensive, had some attractive benefits. However, many people did not buy a microwave oven because they thought they were too complex and hard to use because they required a different way of cooking. Likewise for many high-tech products: the relative advantages are enormous, but the perceived complexity and the difficulty in using them can be deterrents in attracting customers and growing market demand.

Market Influences

If a product does not offer a complete solution, potential customers are reluctant to enter a market. To accelerate customer market entry, a business needs to ensure that all related products and services are available to create a complete solution. Mainstream customers want "plug-in" solutions that are easy to use. In addition, the market demand for products that are *easily observed,* such as a Walkman, color TV, or fashionable sunglasses, grows faster than for products that are less observable, such as household cleaners, insurance programs, or bed sheets. Also, the easier it is to try a product without buying, the faster its rate of market penetration. The Walkman is both *observable* and *easy to try.* Insurance programs are difficult to observe and cannot be tried without purchasing the product. Finally, the more extensive the *marketing effort* supporting the product, the faster the rate of market development.

MARKET DEMAND

Based on the rate of market development, at any point in time, the market demand for a product is made up of the number of customers in the market and the amount they purchase. Because some customers are new to the market while others have been in the market for some time, their purchase amounts may differ. Thus, we can decompose market demand in any given period into existing and new customers and their respective purchase behaviors.

$$\text{Market Demand} = \left(\text{Existing Customers} \times \text{Purchase Amount} \right) + \left(\text{New Customers} \times \text{Purchase Amount} \right)$$

The cellular phone market attracts approximately five million new customers each year. The customer base is expected to be approximately sixty-five million by the year 2000. However, new customers typically consume at a lower rate than existing customers. In fact, each year the average customer purchase amount goes down as more low-use customers enter the market. As shown below, this combination of new and existing customers produces an estimated usage of twenty-five billion minutes per year.

$$\text{Market Demand} = \left(\frac{60 \text{ Million}}{\text{Customers}} \times \frac{400 \text{ Minutes}}{\text{per Year}} \right) + \left(\frac{5 \text{ Million}}{\text{Customers}} \times \frac{200 \text{ Minutes}}{\text{per Year}} \right)$$

$$= 25 \text{ Billion Minutes per Year}$$

FIGURE 3-8 Market Demand for Personal Computers

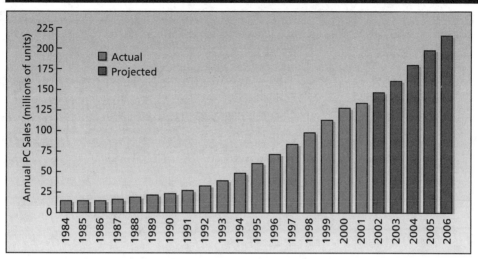

The market demand for Personal Computers (PCs) in any given year is a little more complex. First, existing customers repurchase at an average rate of every four to five years. As shown below, in 2000 the market demand was made up of almost half replacement purchases from 1995 and 1996 and half new-customer purchases.

$$\begin{array}{ccc}
\textbf{Market Demand} & \textbf{Replacement Purchases} & \textbf{New Customer Purchases} \\
\text{(year 2000)} = & \text{(average of 1995 and 1996)} + & \text{(Entering Market in 2000)} \\
= & 64.5 \text{ million} + & 64 \text{ million} \\
= & 128.5 \text{ million} &
\end{array}$$

In 2005 market demand is derived from the average units sold to existing customers in 2000 and 2001. This is estimated to an average of 130 million units. These units become replacement purchases in 2005. Using this estimate of replacement purchases and projected market demand in 2005 shown in Figure 3-8, we can estimate the number of new-customer purchases by computing the difference between the projected volume to be sold and the projected replacement purchases. This is estimated to be sixty-seven million new-customer purchases. When combined the market demand in 2005 will be almost 80 percent of the estimated market potential of 250 million units per year. As the PC market demand approaches its market potential, the number of new customers will diminish until the market demand is almost entirely replacement purchases.

$$\begin{array}{ccc}
\textbf{Market Demand (2005)} = & \textbf{Replacement Purchases} & \textbf{New Customer Purchases} \\
& \text{(average of 2000 and 2001)} + & \text{(entering the market in 2005)} \\
197 \text{ million units} = & 130 \text{ million units} + & 67 \text{ million units}
\end{array}$$

Using the combination of the number of existing customers, their rate of repurchase, and new unit sales, one can create the market demand forecast shown in Figure 3-8.

FIGURE 3-9   Profit Life Cycle and Components of Marketing Profitability

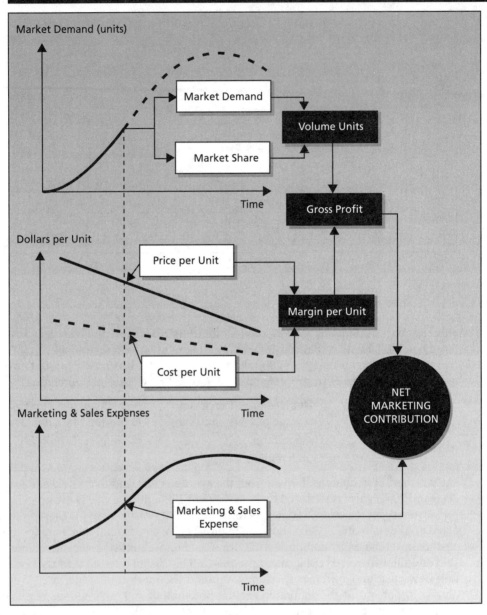

PRODUCT LIFE CYCLE

In Figure 3-8 we can clearly see the introductory and growth stages of a product life cycle. As the market demand approaches the market potential, growth will slow. Eventually the market will become a mature market with little or no growth, as shown in Figure 3-9. This is critical since the volume in any given year of the product life cycle is derived from a combination of market demand and market share. When market

FIGURE 3-10   **Product Life Cycle and Marketing Profitability**

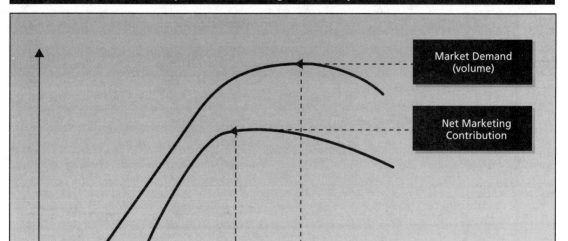

demand ceases to grow, gains in volume can only be achieved with gains in market share. When a market enters the decline phase of the product life cycle, declining volumes are inevitable.

In addition to changes in volume over the product life cycle, there are important changes in the average selling price and average cost per unit. As shown in Figure 3-9, prices, unit costs, and margins per unit decline over the product life cycle. In general, market demand and volume are increasing faster than margins are decreasing. This allows gross profit to grow during the growth stage of the product life cycle.

While a business's volume is the result of market demand and market share, a business has to spend money on marketing and sales to achieve a market share. In the early stages of the product life cycle the marketing and sales expense is greater than the gross profit because volumes are very small. This results in a negative net marketing contribution, as shown in Figure 3-10. As the business moves into the growth stage it is able to reach a breakeven net marketing contribution (gross profit equals marketing and sales expenses). Beyond that point, net market contributions grow and normally peak in the late growth stage of the product life cycle.

As a market matures, the combination of flat market demand, lower margins, and high marketing and sales expenses results in a lower net marketing contribution as shown in Figure 3-10. In the decline stage, marketing profits will continue to decline

FIGURE 3-11   Intel Product Life Cycles

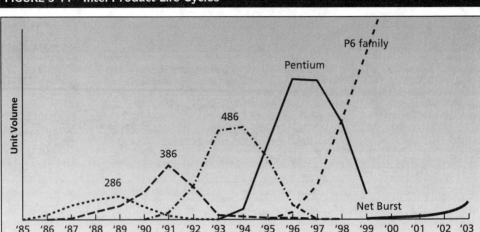

with decreases in market demand despite efforts to milk the product for profits while reducing marketing and sales expenditures.

As markets evolve, they are supported by an evolution of products that also go through a life cycle. Shown in Figure 3-11 is the PC market demand over the product life for six generations of Intel products. In each case there was an emerging market period followed by a period of rapid growth. Growth in this case was driven by both *new customers* entering the market and *expanding purchase amounts by existing customers.* In this example, the growth phase was followed by a very short mature market period and then a stage of rapid decline in market demand.

All of these product life cycles had very similar durations (less than ten years), and each subsequent product achieved a higher level of life cycle demand. Furthermore, there was an overlap between product life cycles. This type of market growth and product life cycle behavior is typical of many high-tech product markets. However, many more mature markets, such as the automotive, commercial aircraft, and housing markets, have much longer product life cycles. Growth in these markets is largely dependent on increases in the population and favorable economic factors that affect customer purchase behavior.

MARKET SHARE AND SHARE POTENTIAL

The potential of a market, its growth rate, and the shape of the product life cycle provide key insights into current and future market demand. A business needs to translate this information into a sales forecast of unit volume. Somebody has to decide how much to produce and how big a manufacturing operation to build. A business's estimate of sales volume can have a dramatic impact on profitability. If the unit volume forecast is correct, and a plant with the right level of capacity is built, total production volume will be near plant capacity, and the best production economies will be achieved. On the other hand, if a business overbuilds capacity, manufacturing overheads will be higher, and lower overall profits will result. And, if the business under-

FIGURE 3-12 Share Development Tree

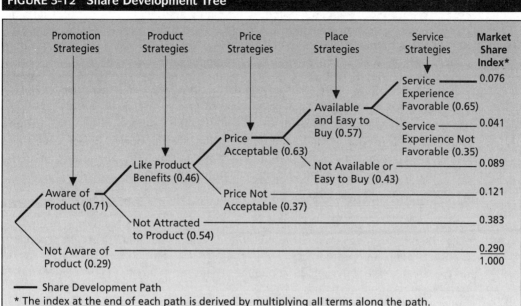

*The Market Share Index is derived by multiplying all terms along a given path.

builds capacity because of poor sales planning, it will forgo a great deal of potential profit due to lost customer sales.

A first step in developing a good estimate of sales is to develop a good estimate of market demand. The market demand sets an upper limit on sales. If a business had a 100 percent market share, then its sales would equal the total market demand. Following this logic, a business's sales are equal to the product of its market share and market demand, as shown here:

$$\text{Volume (units)} = \text{Market Demand (units)} \times \text{Market Share}$$

As an example, Kodak film sales are approximately 400 million rolls of film per year, a 67 percent share of a 600 million roll American film market. Next year's sales depend on two factors: what will the total market demand be? And what will Kodak's share of that demand be? If this is a mature market, the demand will not change drastically. And, depending on competitive conditions, share change could also be minimum. However, for growth markets with considerable competitor entry, both market demand and market share can change dramatically from one year to another.

Share Development Tree

Although market share estimation can involve a complex set of mathematical propositions, there is a simple marketing logic that provides a reasonable estimate of what a business's market share should be. Market share can be estimated from the combination of a set of hierarchical market share effects, as shown in Figure 3-12. Each step along the *Share Development Path* indicates how customer response influences market share.[15] Because there are many other factors that can affect actual market share, the market share index is simply an indicator of what market share *should* be, given certain expected levels of market performance. Each step along the Share Development Path and its impact on share is explained in the remainder of this section.

As shown in Figure 3-12, an index of market share can be created from a combination of market share effects. The Share Development Path traces a hierarchy of market share effects that leads to a particular level of indexed market penetration. Perhaps more important is that the overall share index is the interaction between effects. Should one perform poorly, the overall index will perform poorly. Further, each share effect is derived from a particular component of what we call the "marketing mix." The marketing mix for a given group of target customers includes:

$$\text{Market Share} = \text{Promotion} \times \text{Product} \times \text{Price} \times \text{Place} \times \text{Service}$$

- **Promotion** strategies intend to create awareness of a product and its benefits.
- **Product** positioning strategies build around benefits designed to create product attractiveness and preferences.
- **Price** strategies are designed to enhance intentions to buy based on a price that creates an attractive customer value.
- **Place** strategies ensure that there is adequate availability and service to facilitate purchase.
- **Service** strategies are intended to enhance customer satisfaction and retain customers.

As shown in Figure 3-12, each of these marketing mix factors creates a different impact on target customer response and share development. In managing market share, a business must develop a successful strategy for each element of the marketing mix.

Product Awareness

The first share effect in the Share Development Tree is product *awareness*: the percentage of the market that is aware of the product. For very mature products such as Coca-Cola, Kodak film, or Ford cars, product awareness is not an issue because virtually all target market customers know about the company's product. However, if a business has low awareness, then its market share is limited by a marketing communications problem.

In the early 1980s, Hewlett-Packard began to think about products such as computers and printers for the consumer market. HP had already established its name to some degree with HP calculators, so it thought awareness would not be an issue. However, a survey of U.S. households in the early 1980s showed that less than 10 percent had any awareness of Hewlett-Packard.

Awareness is a particular problem for many industrial and commercial businesses. They rely mostly on specialized advertising, trade shows, sales promotions, and sales calls to communicate their product awareness and positioning. Consumer goods manufacturers are able to better utilize a variety of mass media and in-store merchandising techniques to build awareness of their products. Nevertheless, the first marketing challenge in building market share, whether as a consumer goods business or as a manufacturer of capital equipment, is to build a broad base of product awareness among target market customers.

Product Attractiveness

Even if target customers are aware of a product, the product needs to be *attractive* to target customers. That is, target customers have to have favorable attitudes and interest in the product and the benefits it offers at a particular price. If customers are indifferent or negative, the purchase path is short-circuited and market share is dramatically reduced, as illustrated in Figure 3-12. When this is the case, there is very little chance of gaining market share from these customers. In the example presented in Figure 3-12, 71 percent of the target market customers are aware of the product, but only 46 percent of these customers prefer it (find it attractive). As a result, a significant portion of the business's share potential is lost.

This marketing problem is most likely a product positioning problem. Well-positioned products with attractive benefits and price are likely to be in the customer's choice set; products that are not well positioned are simply not considered in a purchase decision. Of course, if there are very few close substitutes, then it is easier to capture a higher percentage of favorable predispositions. For IBM in the personal computer market, the product differentiation between IBM and competitors decreased and the number of competitors increased throughout the late 1980s and into the 1990s. As a result, it was difficult to hold a dominant position as the most favored personal computer manufacturer. The percentage of customers preferring IBM over other personal computers declined, as did IBM's market share.

Price Acceptable

If a large percentage of customers is favorably attracted to a product, we would expect many to also have high *intentions to buy* the product. However, owing to economic constraints, customers are not always able to switch or to buy immediately. Understanding why these customers have low intentions to buy when interested in a product could uncover a creative marketing solution that would help grow share. In the example shown in Figure 3-12, 63 percent of the customers who are aware of the product and are attracted to it also intend to purchase. Those customers who do not intend to purchase cost the business another 12 percent of its potential market share. To stimulate intentions to purchase, a business may have to give the customers extra incentives to purchase its product. This is where sales promotion programs can be a valuable marketing tool to offset high price barriers and to stimulate trial usage. Once customers have tried the product, we would hope that they would be able to more fully comprehend the product's benefits. In addition, buy-back programs and customer financing could provide customer solutions when attractiveness is high but intentions to buy are low.

Product Availability

A fourth share management factor in building market share is product *availability*. If potentially interested customers seek a product and cannot find it at their preferred point of purchase, there is a loss of potential market share. As shown in Figure 3-12, the lack of product availability results in an 8.9 percent reduction in potential market share. If a business could succeed in building its availability to customers intending to buy from 57 percent to 70 percent, it could increase its overall market share index from 7.6 percent to 9.3 percent.

Service Experience

Finally, while the Share Development Path shown in Figure 3-12 takes a customer to the point of purchase, a bad service experience can negate the entire marketing effort. Most banks and grocery stores have high awareness, the same products, similar prices and convenient locations, so service is often the determining factor in customer purchase. Most customer dissatisfaction occurs as a result of poor customer service. As shown in Figure 3-12, only 65 percent of the potential customers who could buy this product had a positive service experience. Increasing this market metric to 80 percent would improve the company's market share index from 7.6 percent to 9.4 percent.

Market Share Index

If we follow the Share Development Path from awareness to product preference, intention to purchase, product availability, and actual purchase, we can create a *Market Share Index.* The Market Share Index is the product of these five share performance factors along the Share Development Path shown in Figure 3-12. In the example, a Market Share Index of 0.076 is derived as follows:

$$\begin{matrix} \text{Market} \\ \text{Share} \\ \text{Index} \end{matrix} = \begin{matrix} \text{Product} \\ \text{Awareness} \end{matrix} \times \begin{matrix} \text{Product} \\ \text{Preference} \end{matrix} \times \begin{matrix} \text{Intention} \\ \text{to Buy} \end{matrix} \times \begin{matrix} \text{Product} \\ \text{Availability} \end{matrix} \times \begin{matrix} \text{Product} \\ \text{Purchase} \end{matrix}$$

$$= 0.71 \times 0.46 \times 0.63 \times 0.57 \times 0.65$$

$$= 0.076 \ (7.6\%)$$

Although a business's actual market share may be slightly higher or lower, this market share index is a reasonable approximation. It provides us three important benefits:

- It helps identify important sources of lost market share opportunity.
- It provides a mechanism to assess the market share change when a certain level of improvement is directed in a key area of poor performance.
- It enables us to estimate what might be a reasonable market share potential, given reasonable levels of performance in each area along the purchase path.

Share Potential and Market Share Management

Summarized in Figure 3-13 are the marketing performance gaps between actual customer response and *desired* customer response along the Share Development Path. For each area of performance, the performance gap highlights the degree to which

FIGURE 3-13 Current versus Potential Market Share Index

Share Performance Factor	*Current Response*	*Desired Response*	*Performance Gap**
Product Awareness	0.71	0.80	−0.09
Product Attractiveness	0.46	0.60	−0.14
Price Acceptable	0.63	0.80	−0.17
Product Availability	0.57	0.70	−0.13
Service Experience	0.65	0.75	−0.10
Market Share Index	**0.076**	**0.202**	**−0.126**

*Performance Gap = Current Response − Desired Response

market share is lost along the purchase path. On the basis of the performance gaps shown in Figure 3-13, a business could estimate the share and revenue loss due to below-expected levels of share performance. For example, assume that a business serves a $500 million market and has a 7.6 percent market share index based on the actual response in each area of performance shown in Figure 3-12. If the business could improve product awareness from 71 percent to 80 percent, it should increase its market share and revenue. We cannot determine the exact extent of the impact on share, but a reasonable estimate can be made based on the planned improvement, as shown:

$$\frac{\text{Market Share Index}}{\text{(current awareness)}} = \mathbf{0.71} \times 0.46 \times 0.63 \times 0.57 \times 0.65 = 0.076 \; (7.6\%)$$

$$\frac{\text{Market Share Index}}{\text{(improved awareness)}} = \mathbf{0.80} \times 0.46 \times 0.63 \times 0.57 \times 0.65 = 0.085 \; (8.5\%)$$

This is an estimated increase of 0.9 percent market share. And 0.9 percent of a $500 million market is $4.5 million in incremental gain in sales revenue. If the business focused instead on the performance gap created by product availability, increasing actual availability from 57 to 70 percent, it could improve its market share index by 1.7 percent, as shown:

$$\frac{\text{Market Share Index}}{\text{(improved availability)}} = 0.71 \times 0.46 \times 0.63 \times \mathbf{0.70} \times 0.65 = 0.093 \; (9.3\%)$$

This level of share impact would increase sales revenue by $8.5 million. Of course, in each case, management must assess the cost of marketing efforts needed to affect the level of these changes in order to assess the profit impact (change in net marketing contribution).

Market Share Potential

Establishing a *desired level of response* at each step along the Share Development Path provides a basis for estimating a business's market share potential. For example, in Figure 3-13, if we compute the market share index on the basis of desired response, we can estimate our share potential as shown below.

$$\frac{\text{Market Share Index}}{\text{(potential)}} = 0.80 \times 0.60 \times 0.80 \times 0.70 \times 0.75 = 0.202 \; (20.2\%)$$

This means that if the business achieves the desired level of performance at each step along the customer purchase path, it should achieve a share index considerably greater than the current share index. In this way, a business can assess its actual share relative to its share potential and can assess the degree to which further growth can be achieved with market share gains.

Share Development Index

Having determined its market share potential, a business is now in the position to assess its opportunity for market share development. In our example, the business's current market share index should have been 7.6 percent. However, owing to a variety of other factors, the actual market share was only 6.3 percent. Furthermore, we estimated that the business's market share index potential would be 20.2 percent if the

FIGURE 3-14   Market Development–Share Development Matrix

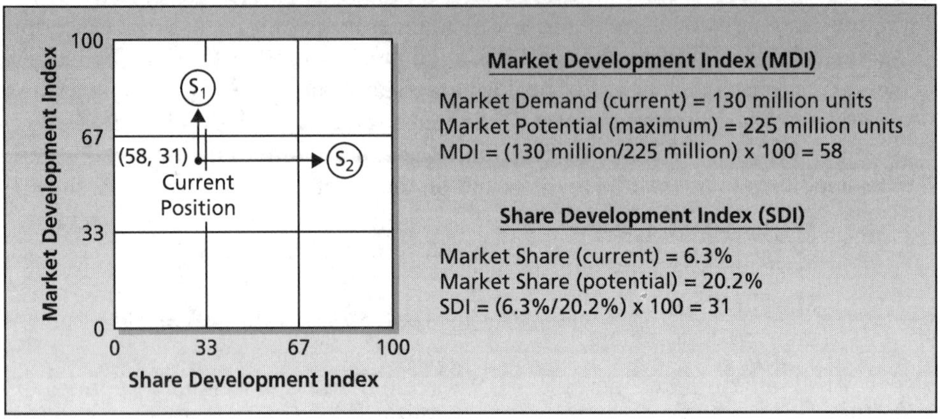

Market Development Index (MDI)

Market Demand (current) = 130 million units
Market Potential (maximum) = 225 million units
MDI = (130 million/225 million) x 100 = 58

Share Development Index (SDI)

Market Share (current) = 6.3%
Market Share (potential) = 20.2%
SDI = (6.3%/20.2%) x 100 = 31

business achieved the desired level of customer response along the Share Development Path. A ratio of actual market share to potential market share provides a Share Development Index (SDI), as shown:

$$SDI = \frac{\text{Actual Market Share}}{\text{Potential Market Share}} \times 100$$

$$= \frac{6.3\%}{20.2\%} \times 100 = 31$$

In this case, the Share Development Index is 31. That is, the business has achieved only 31 percent of its potential market share performance given full effectiveness of its delivered marketing strategy at each step along the Share Development Path.

If we combine the Market Development Index presented earlier with the Share Development Index, we are able to create an important planning matrix that can help uncover opportunities for growth as illustrated in Figure 3-14. On the vertical axis is the Market Development Index, the degree to which the market has been developed. On the horizontal axis is the Share Development Index, the business's level of market share development. When combined, this graphic provides a way to evaluate growth opportunities. Depending on the situation, the business may find one of several strategies to aid it in its development of marketing strategies that will contribute to profitable growth. As illustrated in Figure 3-14, further growth could be achieved with either market or share development.

Summary

A critical first step in any marketing strategy is to determine the size of the market. A business with a narrow product focus will see only the products it sells. Therefore, it is important to start this process with a broad, strategic view of the market that encompasses a wide range of substitute products.

From a broad market vision, a business can begin to see more of its markets, as well as adjacent markets that might serve as new opportunities for growth.

With a broader market definition, a business can begin to understand the maximum potential of the market it intends to serve. In some instances the market may be underdeveloped and well below its maximum potential demand. When this is the case, it is important to determine the sources of lost market demand. That is, what is preventing customers from entering the market? Factors such as a lack of awareness, preferences, price, availability, and service contribute to lost market opportunity. A Market Development Index helps quantify when efforts should be made with respect to market development.

Market demand over time is an important aspect of market planning and strategy development. For many markets, today's market demand is made up of both new customers and existing customers making replacement purchases. Based on the rate at which new customers come into the market, the time it takes for all potential customers to enter the market, and the rate of product replacement, a unique market demand occurs over time. The rate at which a market approaches its full potential is a function of target customer characteristics, product positioning, and marketing effort. Each of these factors can be influenced by the marketing strategies developed by a firm and its competitors.

Over time market demand emerges from small volumes in the introductory stages to rapidly accelerating growth in volume. During this stage of the product life cycle prices and margins decline while marketing expenses increase. However, the combination of volume, margins and marketing expenses produces increasing net marketing contribution throughout the fast growth phase of the product life cycle. As growth slows net marketing contributions typically peak and start to modestly decline as the product life cycle enters a mature stage with little or no market growth.

The demand for a business's products is also based on the share of market it can extract from a given level of market demand. Market share is simply the proportion of sales a business can obtain from the total market demand at any given point in time, but a business needs to know if its share performance is at, above, or below what it should expect. Five marketing mix factors (promotion, product, price, place, and service) are used to create an index of market share response. The Market Share Index helps a business understand its share potential.

Combining the Market Development Index with a Share Development Index allows us to better discover sales volume and opportunities to grow sales volume. For a given segment or geographic market we can determine what our best opportunities for sales growth are. In instances where the market is fully developed and we have achieved the full potential of our market share performance, defensive strategies can be developed.

Market-Based Logic and Strategic Thinking

1. How does a product-focused market definition differ from a broad, strategic market definition?
2. What are some of the benefits of a broad, strategic market definition?
3. Why is market vision an important element of market demand?
4. What is the difference between vertical and horizontal market opportunities?
5. Why is it important to establish the maximum potential for market demand?
6. What would be the maximum market potential for disposable diapers?
7. What forces would restrict today's market demand for disposable diapers from reaching the maximum market demand?
8. What factors help accelerate market growth? How can a business affect these factors to accelerate market growth?
9. How does a Market Development Index help a business in its market planning?

APPLICATION PROBLEM: PERSONAL COMPUTER INDUSTRY

MARKET DEMAND AND MARKET POTENTIAL

The personal computer industry emerged in 1975 with sales of 50,000 units and grew slowly for the next 15 years to a market demand of 24 million units per year in 1990. By 1990, the market demand of 24 million was slightly less than 10 percent of an estimated market potential of 250 million units. By 2000, the market demand had grown to 128 million units per year, roughly 50 percent of the PC market potential. Somewhere between 2005 and 2010 the PC market demand will reach its full market potential of 250 million units per year.

AVERAGE SELLING PRICE AND MARGINS

In 1990 the Average Selling Price was almost $3000 per unit. The average Margin was 45 percent of sales and Marketing and Sales Expenses were close to 25 percent of sales on average. By 2000, the Average Selling Price had eroded by $1000 to slightly under $2000 per unit. Margins also dropped by almost half, from 45 percent of the Average Selling Price to 22 percent of the Average Selling Price. This trend is projected to continue to 2005 as shown in the following figure.

MARKETING AND SALES EXPENSES

In 1990 the industry's average Marketing and Sales Expenses were approximately 25 percent of sales. Based on total industry revenues of $71.3 billion, 1990 Marketing and Sales Expenses were $17.8 billion. By 2000, the Marketing and Sales Expenses had dropped to approximately 15 percent of sales, which translates to $37.2 billion. Shown in the following figure is the estimated Marketing and Sales Expenses as a percent of sales for 2005.

Performance (millions)	1990	1995	2000	2005*	2010
Market Demand	24	58	128	197	250
Sales	$71,300	$156,000	$248,000	$330,000	
Average Selling Price	$ 2,971	$ 2,690	$ 1,938	$ 1,675	
% Margin	45%	30%	22.0%	18%	
Gross Profit	$32,085	$ 46,800	$ 54,560	$ 59,400	
% Marketing and Sales Expense	25%	20%	15%	12%	
Marketing and Sales Expense	$17,825	$ 31,200	$ 37,200	$ 39,600	

* Industry estimate.

For access to interactive software to answer the questions below go to www.RogerJBest.com or www.prenhall.com/best.

1. How will the stage of the Product Life Cycle and Market Development Index change between 2000 and 2005?

2. Estimate the average PC price and % margin for 2010 to estimate the project margin per unit in 2005.

3. Estimate the 5% Marketing & Sales Expenses for 2010 and evaluate the Marketing & Sales Expense Trend over the product life cycle.

4. Estimate the Net Marketing Contribution for 2010 based on previous estimates and evaluate Marketing Profitability (net marketing contribution) over the Product Life Cycle.

10. What are the ways a business could affect the rate of market development?
11. Why is it important to decompose market demand into replacement and new purchases?
12. Why do volumes, prices and margins vary over the product life cycle?
13. In Figure 3-9 why is the net marketing contribution negative in the introductory stage of the product life cycle?
14. Why does the net marketing contribution peak during the late growth stage of the product life cycle?
15. What performance factors underlie market share performance?
16. How would a business use an index of its current and potential market share?
17. What are the advantages of computing a Market Share Index?
18. Why might a business's actual market share be different from its Market Share Index for a given target market?
19. How could the Market Development−Share Development matrix be used to develop international marketing strategies?

Notes

1. Noel Tichy and Stratford Sherman, *Control Your Destiny or Someone Else Will* (New York: Harper Business, 1993); and Richard Ott, "The Prerequisite of Demand Creation," in *Creating Demand* (Burr Ridge, IL: Business One Irwin, 1992): 3–10.

2. Theodore Levitt, "Marketing Myopia," *Harvard Business Review* (July–August 1960):45–56.

3. Jerry Porras and James Collins, "Successful Habits of Visionary Companies," *Built to Last* (New York: Harper Collins, 1994); and Burt Nanus, *Visionary Leadership* (San Francisco: Jossey-Bass, 1992).

4. Gary Hamel and C. K. Prahalad, *Competing for the Future* (Cambridge, MA: Harvard Business School Press, 1994): 103.

5. R. E. Bucklin and V. Srinivasan, "Determining Interbrand Substitutability through Survey Measurement of Consumer Preference Structures," *Journal of Marketing Research* (February 1991):58–71; "Car Makers Use Image Map As Tool to Position Products," *Wall Street Journal* (March 22, 1984):33; and "Mapping the Dessert Category," *Marketing News* (May 14, 1982):3.

6. Michael Porter, *Competitive Advantage* (New York: Free Press, 1985): 37; and Jeffrey Rayport and John Sviokla, "Exploiting the Virtual Value Chain," *Harvard Business Review* (November–December 1995):75–85.

7. Derek Abell and John Hanunond, *Strategic Market Planning* (Upper Saddle River, NJ: Prentice Hall, 1979), 185–86.

8. Philip Kotler, *Marketing Management,* 7th ed. (Upper Saddle River, NJ: Prentice Hall, 1991): 240–60.

9. Roger Calantorte, Anthony di Benedetto, and Sriraman Bhoovaraghavan, "Examining the Relationship between the Degree of Innovation and New Product Success," *Journal of Business Research* 30 (June 1994):143–48; and Fareena Sultan, John Farley, and Donald Lehmann, "A Meta-Analysis of Applications of Diffusion Models," *Journal of Marketing Research* (February 1990):70–77.

10. Frank Bass, Trichy Krishonan, and Dipak Jain, "Why the Bass Model Fits without Decision Variables," *Marketing Science* 13 (Summer 1994):203–23.

11. Geoffrey Moore, *Inside the Tornado* (New York: Harper Collins, 1985): 11–26.

12. William Davidson, *Marketing High Technology* (New York: Free Press, 1986).

13. John Naisbitt, *Global Paradox: The Bigger the World Economy, the More Powerful Its Smallest Players* (New York: Morrow, 1994).

14. Delbert Hawkins, Roger Best, and Kenneth Coney, *Consumer Behavior—Implications for Marketing Strategy,* 8th ed. (New York: Irwin, 2001: 250–251

15. Doug Schaffer, "Competing Based on the Customer's Hierarchy of Needs," *National Productivity Review* (Summer 1995).

4 | CUSTOMER ANALYSIS AND VALUE CREATION

In developing a customer strategy for the Lexus, the Lexus marketing team starts with current customers. They conduct in-depth interviews with current customers, many in the homes of the customers, to determine their likes and dislikes as well as their lifestyles. From this customer input and comparisons with competing luxury cars, the Lexus team identifies product improvements that range from more leg room to better fuel economy to a longer coat hook (customers complained that the conventional coat hook was not long enough to carry dry cleaning). They believe that product improvements that enhance product benefits are critical to delivering a superior customer value. To further build customer value, the Lexus marketing team seeks to also find a price that enhances customer value, as illustrated in Figure 4-1.

DISCOVERING CUSTOMER BENEFITS

The Lexus marketing team does more than just survey target customers. They try to understand all aspects of the customers' product usage, lifestyles, and demographics. Gathering this information requires more than a survey of customer perceptions and preferences. To discover customer benefits, one needs to understand the total customer environment, not simply the product features customers like or do not like. What we really need to find out is *what the customers want but cannot get from the products they purchase.*

A Day in the Life of a Customer

One way to better understand customer needs is to become the customer.[1] Although customers' descriptions of their needs are important, customers do not always reveal (or think of) the frustrations they encounter in the purchase, use, and disposal of a product when asked. For example, to better understand how customers used their car trunks, Honda employees videotaped people loading groceries. Different cars, different consumers, and different grocery bags all affected how much car owners had to struggle to get the bags into their car trunk. Some arranged their plastic bags to keep them from tipping over; others paused to rest a bag on the edge of the trunk wall and then had to lift the lid again after it partly closed. Watching the videos, Honda engineers put themselves in the customers' shoes. They could see and feel users' experiences and envision better trunk designs.

FIGURE 4-1 Lexus's Customer Value Creation Process

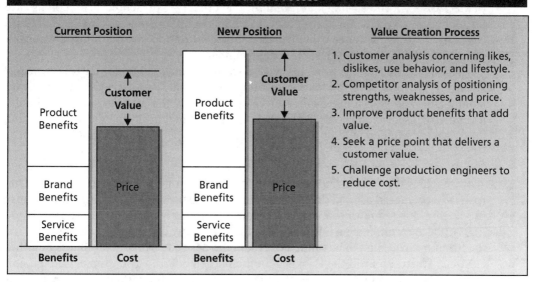

Empathic Design Process

Videotaping customer product use is one form of the *Empathic Design Process.*[2] This is an observational approach to understanding customer needs and discovering customer problems and frustrations that arise when acquiring, using and disposing of a product. Intuit, the maker of the personal-finance software Quicken, has a *Follow Me Home* program. Product developers gain permission from first-time buyers to observe their initial experience with the software in their own homes. In this way, they learn what other software applications are running on the customer's system and how that software can interfere with or complement Quicken. Product developers can also see what other data files the customer refers to and accesses and whether they are on paper or in electronic form. From in-home observations, Intuit designers discovered that many small-business owners were using Quicken to keep their books; that discovery led to a whole new product line.

Although actual observation might be preferred, it may not be possible to observe customers in many consumer, business, or industrial markets. As an alternative, one could develop two *hypothetical videos.*[3] Video I requires a customer to describe the product he or she wants to buy and, in a sequence of scenes, the *process* he or she goes through in the acquisition, installation, use, maintenance, and disposal of this product. It is particularly important to note the parts of each scene that create customer problems or frustrations. Remember that Video I is not product-specific; it is a *narrative of the process* the customer goes through in acquiring and using the product of interest. Video I describes a typical day in the life of a business's customer.

Video II requires the customer to *redescribe* the scenes of Video I with improvements they would *desire* in each scene. This video provides the opportunity to discover new customer benefits. For example, a marketing team from the Weyerhaeuser Corporation visited a large furniture maker to better determine what they wanted when they purchased particleboard. The furniture maker made it clear that what they wanted was a *low price with reliable quality.* Weyerhaeuser presented a compelling case for higher quality, but the customer was not swayed. Weyerhaeuser was left with no basis for creating customer value because they could not compete on price against a competitor that had a considerable cost advantage.

This is where most businesses would stop in their analysis of customer needs. However, Weyerhaeuser put together a multifunctional team to revisit the furniture manufacturer to gain a more complete picture of how the manufacturer purchased, inventoried, used, and processed particleboard in making furniture (Video I). This time they wanted to understand the customer process in using the product, not just product-specific purchase criteria.

By focusing on the *process* of using a product, and not just the *product,* Weyerhaeuser discovered important customer frustrations in using particleboard. One frustration centered around the grit found in most particleboard. More grit led to more production downtime to sharpen saw blades and more expense due to shorter blade life. Grit also resulted in an unsatisfactory finish in many instances. When this occurred the furniture piece had to be sanded to obtain the desired level of smoothness. Another customer frustration was the thickness of the particleboard. The customer had to laminate pieces of particleboard to get the thickness required for certain furniture. The following summarizes the customer frustrations and their association cost uncovered in customer visits used to create a hypothetical Video I.

Video I—The Current Process

Customer Use Process	Customer Frustration	Cost to Customer
Cut the particleboard	Saw blades wear out quickly from excess grit	Production downtime Saw blade sharpening/replacement
Build furniture	Need to use thicker pieces	Lamination process to glue pieces
Produce finished product	Desired finish not achieved	Requires sanding for desired finish

In the ideal situation in this example the solution was pretty obvious. The customer wanted particleboard with less grit and available in thicker pieces. Less grit would significantly lower the associated cost of saw blades and sanding. Thicker pieces would eliminate the lamination process. The combined benefits of this customer solution would significantly reduce the furniture manufacturer's costs as the following summarizes.

Video II—The Desired Process

Customer Process	Ideal Solution	Benefit to Customer
Cut particleboard to size	Saw blades last longer	Less production downtime Lower saw blade expenses
Build furniture	Buy thicker pieces	Eliminate lamination process
Produce finished product	Smoother finish	Less sanding required for finish

With these customer insights, Weyerhaeuser responded with thicker, cleaner (less grit) particleboard. Although more expensive per unit, the new product saved the customer money; thicker pieces of particleboard eliminated the laminating process, and

FIGURE 4-2   Weyerhaeuser Value-Added Customer Benefits

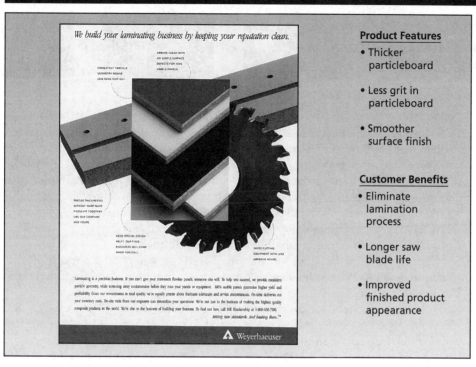

less grit reduced tool wear, each providing significant savings. These product features translated into meaningful customer benefits, as presented in Figure 4-2.

Lead User Solutions

Not all customers use products the same. Some may be new users and lack experience with the product. Others may be occasional users and have a limited base of experience. Observing or probing these customers for sources of dissatisfaction or opportunities for improvement most often will result in limited insight. However, for most products there are *lead users,* customers who are more knowledgeable users and who often extend the application of the product to solve other problems or achieve a more complete customer solution.

Studying lead user behavior can provide valuable insights into how the product can be improved and the process of using the product made easier. A deeper understanding of lead user needs and desired solutions can lead to significant incremental improvements in products and customer value. For example, lead users of cell or wireless phones devised ways to extend the capabilities of the phone beyond its intended application by using them to access the Internet—a technology that is spawning new products and new companies.

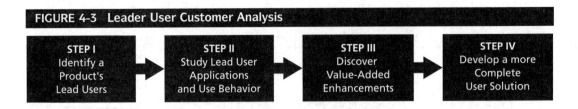

FIGURE 4-3 Leader User Customer Analysis

STEP I	STEP II	STEP III	STEP IV
Identify a Product's Lead Users	Study Lead User Applications and Use Behavior	Discover Value-Added Enhancements	Develop a more Complete User Solution

Identifying lead users of a product is Step I in the process of uncovering lead user solutions as outlined in Figure 4-3 above.[4] Discovering how lead users use the product to solve their own problems (Step II) opens the door to uncovering new insights into how a product is used or enhanced by lead users to create a more complete customer solution. With these insights a business can better understand how they can add value-added features, functions and services (Step III). Step IV involves engineering products based on these insights to enhance existing products or develop completely new products which offer more complete customer solutions.

In applying this process 3M identified lead users in museum-transportation. The need to carefully pack valuable and often very delicate museum pieces led these users to develop many innovative packing solutions. By studying how these lead users adapted conventional packing material for museum pieces, 3M was able to develop a new line of off-the-shelf packaging materials.[5] Furthermore, 3M has found that refining or building off "lead user" applications of existing products produces eight times more revenue than new products generated by more conventional analysis of existing customer needs.[6]

Staple Yourself to an Order

Another way to expand a business's insight into how products are acquired and used is the process of following the steps a customer takes in purchasing a product. By taking a detailed look at the customer order process, a business can discover problems and sources of frustration in the customer buying process. This day in the life of a customer process is called *"staple yourself to an order."*[7]

This customer analysis process, outlined in Figure 4-4, involves tracking the customer order process from the early stages of order planning to the resolution of claims when after-purchase problems arise. Each step of the customer order cycle presents potential customer problems and frustrations we have all experienced. The earlier these problems occur in the cycle, the less likely a customer is to buy from a business. Problems or frustrations that occur later in the process hurt the chances of repurchase and, hence, lower customer retention.

One way to operationalize this process is to ask, what are the worst things we could do to a customer at each stage of the customer order cycle? On the basis of the level of customer frustration these problems create, and the frequency with which they occur, a market-based business would identify the opportunities to build customer value by improving the customer buying process. While product-oriented competitors are focused on product features and price, a market-based business focusing on product benefits and the customer order cycle can develop important sources of customer value competitors will never see.

FIGURE 4-4 Stages in the Customer Order Cycle and Opportunities to Build Values	
Stage in the Customer Order Cycle	*Potential Problems, Customer Frustrations, and Opportunities to Build Value*
Order Planning	Customers do not recognize your solution in solving a problem
Order Development	Insufficient or incorrect information on your solution
Order Evaluation	Misperceptions or incomplete information limit fair evaluation
Order Placement	Difficulties in placing order with your business
Order Entry	Order recorded or priced incorrectly
Order Processing	Order in process but customer not aware of order status and delivery
Order Delivery	Product delivered late or damaged; wrong product delivered
Customer Invoice	Bill has errors, no one to contact, and calls lead to voice mail hell
After-Sale Services	Problems after purchase with no one to call; calls not returned
Product Usage	Inadequate instructions; no hot line offered
Product Problems	Product does not work and must be returned at customer's expense
Returns and Claims	Customer has to fight to get warranty claim resolved

Customer Benefits and Customer Value

Weyerhaeuser's, Intuit's, and Honda's efforts to create increased customer benefits went beyond product-specific thinking. They each engaged in an analysis of the customer situation and the various problems customers encountered. With a deeper understanding of the use situation, they were able to engineer customer solutions that went beyond those provided by currently available products.[8] Had Weyerhaeuser focused only on the product features and not on the customer needs, they would not have discovered their customer solution. Or, if Intuit had only sold the product but had not sought to understand how it was used, they would not have discovered new products.

All customers have problems that require solutions. The more help a business's product or service provides to customers, the more value it adds to a customer solution. A business should view itself as a *provider of solutions* rather than a *seller of products and services*. To accomplish this requires a much broader view of your customers' underlying problems that go beyond products or services. A business that goes beyond selling products to building customer solutions will be in the best position to discover new opportunities to add more value.[9]

Customers are willing to pay more for products and services that add value. To do this requires a more comprehensive understanding of customer needs and use situations. This provides a business with a better opportunity to create customer benefits that add value for customers. However, the overall value derived from customer benefits needs to exceed the costs of acquiring those benefits:

$$\text{Customer Value} = \text{Customer Benefits} - \text{Cost of Purchase}$$

Creating attractive benefits at a very high cost could result in negative customer value. Thus, a business needs to be sensitive to both the benefits it creates in response to customer needs and the total cost of acquiring those benefits. In the following sections, we will examine several ways in which a business can create customer benefits and deliver a greater value to target customers.

ECONOMIC BENEFITS AND VALUE CREATION

To deliver a customer value that creates a superior *economic value* requires that the customer achieve a *net economic gain*. For example, Weyerhaeuser created an economic value for furniture manufacturers even though the cost of the purchased product was higher than the cost of competing products. The savings created by eliminating the need for lamination to make thicker furniture legs and the reduced cost of saw blade wear more than offset the higher price of the new, improved product. Thus, the customer value created was greater than that of competitors' products, and it was measurable in actual savings (economic value).

There are six primary sources of economic value creation, as outlined in Figure 4-5. The price paid for a product or service stands out as the most obvious cost of purchase to most customers. As a result, a business with a lower price and the same quality can easily communicate its economic value to target customers. Because customers may not look beyond a product's price, other sources of economic value may go unnoticed. However, other sources of value creation can include costs associated with acquisition, usage, maintenance, ownership, and disposal of a product. Discovering these value creation opportunities is marketing's job and one of the key benefits of spending a day in the life of a customer.

Low Price

Quite often, price or terms of payment can destroy customer value. Regardless of benefits and potential economic value, the product may simply be unaffordable, or the price may be too high relative to the benefits provided. For example, DuPont found that for more expensive blood analyzers, large hospitals could justify a high price based

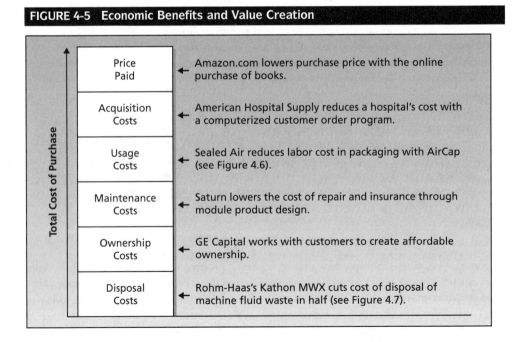

FIGURE 4-5   Economic Benefits and Value Creation

on overall benefits. Smaller hospitals simply did not have the volume of blood chemistry work to justify purchasing a higher-priced, more sophisticated blood analyzer. As DuPont rolled out subsequent new product improvements, they met resistance from large hospitals that wanted to buy the newer products but could not economically justify the purchase because the existing product worked well and was still relatively new. This situation led to a strategy in which DuPont bought back the old blood analyzers from the large hospitals, refurbished them, and then resold them to smaller hospitals. In this way, DuPont created an affordable combination of benefits and price for both large and small hospitals.

Acquisition Costs

With respect to acquisition costs, American Hospital Supply found that one-half of every dollar spent by hospitals on pharmaceuticals, chemicals, and hospital equipment went to the acquisition and inventory of such products. As identified in Figure 4-5, acquisition costs are a part of the total cost of purchase. By putting computers in hospitals to streamline order entry, logistics, and inventory procedures, American Hospital Supply created an economic value for hospital customers, saving them a significant portion of their acquisition and inventory costs. American Hospital Supply won a large share of this market by creating an economic value that was real and measurable by hospital customers.

Usage Costs

The cost associated with using a product is an obvious area of potential value creation and the one that enabled Weyerhaeuser to deliver a greater economic value even with a higher price. The same is true for a manufacturer's telecommunications switch, as shown in Figure 4-6. The customer's current telecommunications switch had a total (life cycle) cost of purchase of $1,000. The purchase price was only $300, but an additional $200 was spent for installation and start-up, as well as $500 in usage and other

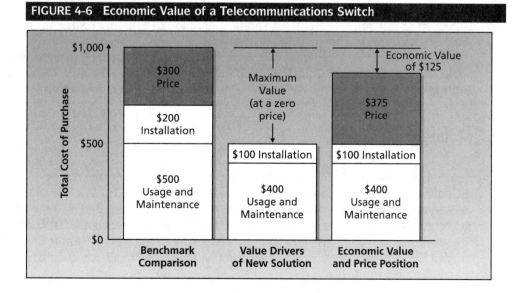

FIGURE 4-6   Economic Value of a Telecommunications Switch

FIGURE 4-7   Lower Labor and Freight Costs Drive AirCap's Economic Value

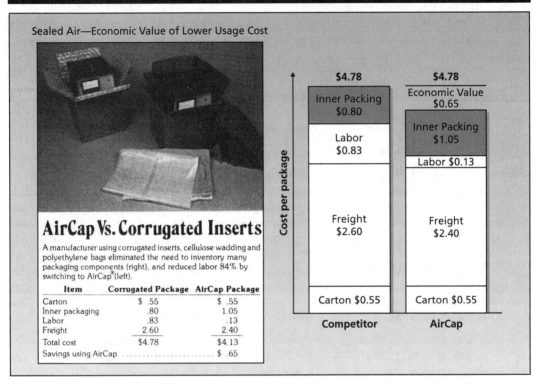

Sealed Air—Economic Value of Lower Usage Cost

AirCap Vs. Corrugated Inserts

A manufacturer using corrugated inserts, cellulose wadding and polyethylene bags eliminated the need to inventory many packaging components (right), and reduced labor 84% by switching to AirCap®(left).

Item	Corrugated Package	AirCap Package
Carton	$ .55	$ .55
Inner packaging	.80	1.05
Labor	.83	.13
Freight	2.60	2.40
Total cost	$4.78	$4.13
Savings using AirCap	....	$ .65

postpurchase costs. The business's new product offered customers a solution that could cut the start-up costs in half and reduce the usage cost by $100. As shown in Figure 4-6, this solution created an economic value of $500. However, the product had to be priced in a way that created economic value for both customers and the business. In response, the business set its price at $375, $75 more than the existing customer solution of $300. However, at this price, it created a solution that added $125 per switch to the customer's bottom line.[9, 10]

A second example is presented in Figure 4-7. Sealed Air's AirCap provided an economic value of $0.65 even though its price was $0.25 higher than the price of the competition's product. The $0.65 economic value was made possible by reduced costs of labor and freight relative to those for the competing product.

Maintenance Costs

The cost of repair and maintenance can be expensive for both customers and businesses. The cost of repair for products under warranty is generally the responsibility of the business that sold the product. After warranty, repair and normal maintenance are costs to the customer. As presented in Figure 4-5, General Motors designed the Saturn to be easily repaired in the event of an accident. This design saves both customers and insurers potentially millions of dollars. The savings are so significant over the life of the car that the customer's cost of insurance for a Saturn can be hundreds of dollars lower than for a comparable car.

A second example is Loctite's Quick Metal. Quick Metal can be applied to worn or cracked machine parts during routine maintenance to prevent an extended shutdown. Quick Metal's value proposition, "Keep the machinery running until the new part arrives," tells customers how Quick Metal can create an important savings (economic value) for them.

Ownership Costs

Some products are simply more expensive to own than others. These products often have purchase prices that require financing or higher insurance costs or both. General Electric, many years ago, developed GE Capital to create affordable ownership with GE financing. GE Capital has been very successful and is today a large business, serving both GE and non-GE customers.

Ownership also has the risk of dissatisfaction: what happens after a product warranty expires? Copiers, for example, have potentially high ownership cost if the product goes bad. As a response to this risk, Xerox created a customer satisfaction program that guarantees product performance for an extended period of time.

Disposal Costs

The way products are disposed of offers another important source of economic value creation. FP International (FPI) manufactures styrene packaging materials from waste styrene packaging that it picks up from its customers. FPI then sells its recycled styrene packaging back to the customer at a premium price. Because FPI lowers the total cost of the product by solving the customer's disposal problem, it is able to charge a higher price for its product.

A second example is described in Figure 4-8. Kathon MWX is a product that creates a significant economic value for machine shop owners by extending the life of metal-working fluids. The net result is a significant reduction in the cost of disposing of these fluids.

PRICE-PERFORMANCE AND VALUE CREATION

While economic value provides a powerful basis for creating a cost-based customer value, there are aspects of product performance that are more difficult to quantify in the total cost of purchase. Performance can also include product features and functions that do not save money but enhance usage and, in that way, create customer value. For example, a car has cost-based value drivers in its fuel economy, maintenance requirements, insurance, and resale value. A car also offers safety, reliability, design, and other features such as front-wheel drive, luggage racks, and comfort. Although these latter components of customer value are difficult to quantify with respect to the total cost of owning a car, they can be evaluated with respect to performance. *Consumer Reports* provides one way to rate the performance of consumer products.

Relative Performance

The overall performance rating for fifteen toasters based on the *Consumer Reports'* evaluations of eight product features[11] is shown in Figure 4-8. On a scale that ranged from zero to 100, the overall performance of the toasters listed ranged from a low of 55

FIGURE 4-8 Lower Cost of Disposal is the Value Driver

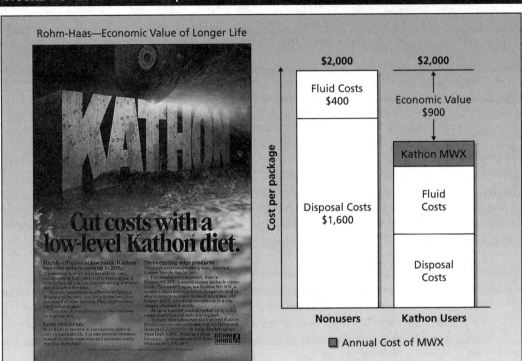

Rohm-Haas—Economic Value of Longer Life

to a high of 88, with an average performance of 69. We can create a relative measure of performance by dividing the overall rating of each toaster by the overall average. This measure of product performance will help us more readily assess performance around a benchmark average of 100, as shown below.

$$\frac{\text{Relative}}{\text{Performance}} = \frac{\text{Product Performance}}{\text{Average Performance}} \times 100$$

When each toaster's *Consumer Reports* rating is divided by the average of all ratings (69) and multiplied by 100, we have a measure of relative performance in which the average performance is equal to 100. Now we can readily assess performance as it varies from a low of 80 to a high of 128, where 100 is average. Sunbeam, for example has a relative performance of 119. This means that Sunbeam's overall performance is 19 percent better than the average of the fifteen toasters evaluated, as illustrated below.

$$\frac{\text{Relative}}{\text{Performance}} = \frac{82}{69} \times 100 = 119$$

Relative Price

To acquire Sunbeam's above-average relative performance requires paying a certain amount of money. Their price is reported as $28, but it is difficult to readily infer the attractiveness of this price in absolute dollars. Thus, a measure of relative price is also

FIGURE 4-9   Toaster Relative Price-Performance and Relative Value

Number and Name of Toaster	Overall Performance	Relative Performance	Toaster Price	Relative Price	Relative Value
1 Cuisinart CPT-60	88	128	$70	215	−87
2 Sunbeam	82	119	28	85	33
3 KitchenAid	81	117	77	237	−120
4 Black & Decker	77	112	25	77	35
5 Cuisinart CPT-30	75	109	40	123	−14
6 Breadman	74	107	35	108	−1
7 Proctor-Silex 22425	72	104	15	46	58
8 Krups	70	101	32	98	3
9 Oster	65	94	45	138	−44
10 Toastmaster B1021	63	91	16	49	42
11 Proctor-Silex 22415	60	87	35	108	−21
12 Toastmaster B1035	58	84	21	65	19
13 Betty Crocker	58	84	25	77	7
14 Proctor-Silex 22205	57	83	11	34	49
15 Rival	55	80	13	40	40
Average	69.0	100.0	$32.50	100.0	0

important in understanding value creation. For the fifteen toasters evaluated, the overall average price was $33. When the average price is used as a performance benchmark, Sunbeam's relative price is 85, as shown below.

$$\text{Relative Price} = \frac{\text{Product Price}}{\text{Average Price}} \times 100$$

$$\text{Relative Price (Sunbeam)} = \frac{\$28}{\$33} \times 100 = 85$$

This means that the price of Sunbeam's toaster is 15 percent lower than the average price of the fifteen toasters evaluated. As shown in Figure 4-9, the relative price of the fifteen toasters ranged from a low of 34 to a high of 237. At the lowest price, a customer could buy a toaster 67 percent below the average price, and at the high end a customer would pay 137 percent more than the average price. Thus, the Sunbeam relative price, although attractive, is not the lowest relative price of the 15 toasters considered.

Customer Value

With measures of relative performance and relative price, we can readily identify products that are above or below average in performance or price. However, to infer customer value we need to compute the difference in these two relative measures, as shown below for Sunbeam.

$$\text{Customer Value} = \text{Relative Performance} - \text{Relative Price}$$
$$\text{Customer Value (Sunbeam)} = 119 - 86 = 33$$

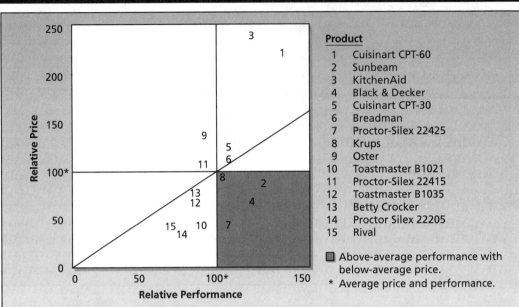

FIGURE 4-10 Price-Performance Value Map

Product

1 Cuisinart CPT-60
2 Sunbeam
3 KitchenAid
4 Black & Decker
5 Cuisinart CPT-30
6 Breadman
7 Proctor-Silex 22425
8 Krups
9 Oster
10 Toastmaster B1021
11 Proctor-Silex 22415
12 Toastmaster B1035
13 Betty Crocker
14 Proctor Silex 22205
15 Rival

■ Above-average performance with below-average price.
* Average price and performance.

In this example, Sunbeam has a positive customer value of 33. A customer value of zero would mean that the relative performance was offset by the relative price. This offset could occur for a product with above- or below-average performance. For example, the Breadman toaster has an above-average relative performance (107) that is almost entirely offset by an above-average relative price (108). The net difference is a customer value of −1.

Using this measure of customer value, we can assess the value of different combinations of performance and price. As shown in Figure 4-9, the customer value for these fifteen toasters ranges from a low of −119 to a high of +58. To better understand this range of customer value we need to examine these results a little further.

Value Map

A graph of relative performance versus relative price allows us to create a *value map,* as illustrated in Figure 4-10. As shown, all the toasters to the right of the diagonal line have positive customer values. However, four of the nine toasters that stand out as having above-average performance have below-average price. For these four brands, customer value is created with very attractive prices. Thus, price-sensitive customers might find alternative 7 the most attractive value, because it has both a low relative price and slightly above-average relative performance. A performance-oriented customer would probably find Sunbeam (alternative 2) particularly attractive, because it offers above-average performance with a lower-than-average price.

Alternatives 1 and 3 may seem to be overpriced relative to performance. This method of inferring customer value, however, does not take into account the perceived status or reputation of a brand, which can also be an important source of value creation and one that we can include in a measure of customer value.

FIGURE 4-11 Measuring Perceived Product Benefits						
Customer Determined Product Benefits	*Relative Importance*	*Business Rating*	*A*	*Competitor B*	*C*	*Relative Advantage*
Machine Up-Time	40	8	7	5	6	27
Print Speed	30	9	8	5	5	20
Image Quality	20	7	7	7	6	0
Ease of Use	10	4	6	7	6	− 10
	100					37

Relative Product Benefits =100 + 37 =137

PERCEIVED BENEFITS AND VALUE CREATION

Economic value and price-performance relative value provide an excellent measure of customer value. However, our evaluation of products often needs to go beyond economic and price-performance measures of customer values. Customer *perceptions* of service quality, brand reputation, and costs other than price also affect customer value. This next section examines how we can utilize customer perceptions of a broader range of benefits and costs to infer the level of customer value for a business's products or services.

Product Benefits

Value creation is logically affected by perceptions of product benefits. These perceived benefits are not easily translated from economic benefits or objectively rated measures of product performance. Yet, it is customer perceptions of product benefits that drive purchase behavior.[12] We need a method for measuring customer perceptions of product benefits and the relative value derived from them when compared with a competitive benchmark.[13]

Shown in Figure 4-11 are four product benefits sought in the purchase and use of a commercial copier. Each product benefit is weighted with respect to relative importance. For instance, in this example, *Machine Up/Time* is weighted twice as important as *Image Quality,* four times as important as *Ease of Use,* and so on. To determine the degree to which a relative advantage in delivering these product benefits is created by a business, the business needs to evaluate each customer benefit relative to competing products. In this case, three competitors were used to benchmark the business's perceived performance and overall relative advantage.

The ratings shown for the business and each competitor are ratings of perceived machine up time that range from zero (disastrous) to 10 (outstanding). If the business outperforms a competitor by more than one point, it receives a portion of the importance allocated to that customer benefit. For example, in Figure 4-11, competitor A is rated only one point lower than the business, whereas competitors B and C are rated more than one point lower. As shown below, the business derives no perceived advantage over competitor A and, hence, gets zero points. However, because the business is perceived to be better than competitors B and C (by more than one point), it receives the forty points attached to perceived machine up-time from each competitor. When these three perceived performance impacts are averaged, an overall relative advantage of 27 is obtained:

$$\frac{\text{Machine}}{\text{Up-Time}} = \frac{0 + 40 + 40}{3} = \frac{80}{3} = 27$$

For *print speed,* the business also outperformed two of the competitors by more than one point and, therefore, received two-thirds of the relative importance allocated to print speed. However, the business achieved no relative advantage in *image quality* and was hurt by being rated more than one point below each of the three competitors with respect to *ease of use.*

When the relative advantage is added up for all four product benefits, this business produces an overall relative advantage of 37. This means that, on the basis of perceived ratings of product benefits relative to the competition, the business produces 37 percent greater benefits. When this overall relative advantage is added to a base index of 100, a relative product benefit index of 137 is produced.

Service Benefits

For many markets (or segments), product differentiation may be minimal, because competitors are able to emulate the best features of each other's products. When this is the case, service quality can be a crucial source of differentiation and competitive advantage.[14] To measure a business's perceived service benefits, we can use the same approach we used for perceived product benefits.

Shown in Figure 4-12 is a measure of perceived service benefits for the same business as that evaluated in Figure 4-11. In this case, the business is roughly equal to two and behind one of its benchmark competitors with respect to *repair time.* This position detracts from its overall perceived service benefits because 60 percent of the importance is attached to this aspect of service benefits. With respect to *response to problems,* the business roughly matches competitor A and competitor B, and outperforms competitor C. The net result is a slight relative advantage. However, there is an excellent opportunity to move ahead of fairly average competitor performance, as illustrated:

$$\frac{\text{Response to}}{\text{Problems}} = \frac{0 + 0 + 30}{3} = \frac{30}{3} = 10$$

With respect to *quality of service,* the business failed to capture any relative advantage. Overall, the business produced a service benefit index of 90. This implies that the business is 10 percent less attractive than its competitors in delivering service benefits to target customers.

FIGURE 4-12   Measuring Perceived Service Benefits

Customer Determined Service Benefits	*Relative Importance*	*Business Rating*	*A*	*Competitor B*	*C*	*Relative Advantage*
Repair Time	60	5	7	6	5	−20
Response Time to Problems	30	5	5	6	2	10
Quality of Service	10	7	7	6	8	0
	100					−10

Relative Service Benefits = 100 − 10 = 90

FIGURE 4-13 Measuring a Business's Brand or Company Benefits						
Customer Determined Company Benefits	*Relative Importance*	*Business Rating*	*A*	*Competitor B*	*C*	*Relative Advantage*
Customer Commitment	60	8	7	6	4	40
Reputation for Quality	40	9	8	9	8	0
	100					40

Relative Service Benefits =100 + 40 =140

Company or Brand Benefits

A third source of customer benefit is a business's brand or company reputation. Whether a brand such as Lexus or Perrier, or a company such as Nordstrom or Hewlett-Packard, the company or brand name itself provides potential benefit to some customers. For Lexus and Perrier, the name adds social status to the product. This is an intangible benefit that could be of great importance to many customers. For Nordstrom, the reputation for customer service creates an added company benefit that goes beyond actual customer service. For HP, its reputation for innovation is valued by many customers and creates a customer benefit that is neither product- nor service-specific.

To measure a business's perceived brand or company benefits, we can use the same method we used for measuring perceived product or service benefits. As shown in Figure 4-13, the company benefits for this copier company were driven by two factors: *customer commitment* and *reputation for quality*. In this case, the business leads two benchmark competitors in customer commitment and has no relative advantage in reputation for quality. The net result of these customer perceptions is an overall index of 140 with respect to company benefits.

Overall Customer Benefits

To arrive at an overall measure of perceived customer benefits, we need a way to combine these three key sources of customer benefits. Combining them requires weighing the relative importance of each of these major sources of customer benefit. In this example, the majority of the weight was given to product benefits (0.60), and smaller amounts to service (0.30) and company (0.10) benefits, as illustrated in Figure 4-14.

When the relative index for each area of benefit is weighed by the proportions shown, an overall index of perceived benefits can be obtained. In this case, the overall perceived benefit score of 123 can be interpreted to mean that the business is 23 percent ahead of the competition in delivering perceived customer benefits. But has the

FIGURE 4-14 Measuring Overall Perceived Customer Benefits			
Customer Determined Benefits	*Relative Importance*	*Relative Advantage*	*Overall Benefits*
Product Benefits	0.60	137	82
Service Benefits	0.30	90	27
Company Benefits	0.10	140	14
	1.00		123

Overall Relative Benefits = 100 − 123

FIGURE 4-15 Measuring the Total Costs of Purchase				
Customer Determined Cost of Purchase	*Relative Importance*	*Competitive Position*	*Cost Multiplier*	*Overall Cost of Purchase*
Purchase Price	40	15%	1.15	46
Service and Repair	30	10%	1.10	33
Toner	20	0%	1.00	20
Paper	10	−20%	0.80	8
	100			107

Overall Relative Cost of Purchase = 107

business created a superior customer value? We don't know. The level of perceived customer value cannot be determined until we also determine the perceived cost of acquiring these benefits.

Perceived Cost of Purchase

Before we can determine the overall level of value created for customers, we need to determine the perceived cost of purchase. The first step is very similar to computing overall perceived benefits. We have to first determine the cost components considered by the customer in a purchase decision and the relative importance of each component. In Figure 4-15, there are four sources of cost to be considered in the customer's total cost of purchase. The purchase price carries the majority of the relative importance. Other factors, such as service and repairs, toner, and paper are also significant cost components of the customer's total perceived cost of purchase.

In this case, the business is perceived to be 15 percent higher in purchase price, and, as a result, the competitive position multiplier is 1.15 (a constant of 1 plus the relative position). By simply multiplying the relative importance for price (40) by the competitive position multiplier (1.15), we can index the overall perceived position of the business on purchase price as 46. Note that a positive competitive position multiplier increases the total cost of purchase, whereas a negative position reduces the total cost of purchase.

The business's competitive position with respect to service and repair is perceived to be higher than the competitors', which increases the perceived total cost of purchase. However, the business is perceived to be less expensive with regard to the cost of paper, which decreases the perceived total cost of purchase. Because there is no perceived difference in the cost of toner between this business and its competitors, the cost multiplier is 1.00 and the relative weight of 20 translates to a value of 20 for the overall perceived position on this factor.

The sum of these four areas of perceived cost produces an index of overall perceived cost of purchase, which in this case is 107. This can be interpreted to mean that the business is perceived to be 7 percent more expensive to do business with than its competitors; the difference can be traced back to its higher prices and higher service and repair costs, despite a lower cost of paper.

Perceived Customer Value

Once customers' perceptions of overall benefits and total cost of purchase have been obtained, a business can evaluate the degree of value it creates for its customers.

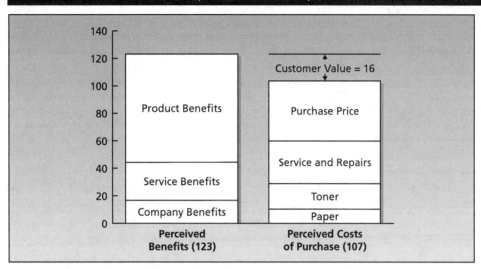

FIGURE 4-16   Perceived Benefits, Costs of Purchase, and Customer Value

Shown in Figure 4-16 is the customer value created by the copier company. Each area of perceived benefit and perceived cost is graphed using the results presented in Figures 4-14 and 4-15. The difference between the overall customer benefits (123) and the total cost of purchase (107) creates an index of perceived customer value score of 16. This means that the business has been able to create a superior customer value while commanding a 15 percent price premium. If a business wanted to further improve its perceived customer value without lowering price, it could strive to improve key weaknesses in areas of importance to customers. Ease of use, repair time, and service and repair are all areas that detract from customer value. To the degree that these areas could be improved, the business could improve the value it creates for customers while maintaining a price premium.

EMOTIONAL BENEFITS AND VALUE CREATION

So far, we have looked at customer benefits that could be described largely as *rational* benefits. The rational appeal of an automobile includes gas economy, maintenance cost, insurance, resale value, size, and price. Less tangible rational benefits might include quality of repair service, friendliness of service personnel, and manufacturer reputation. For many customers there are also *emotional* benefits that are tied to psychological needs that are more personal in nature.[15] The same can be true in many business-to-business purchases, in which emotional benefits could be tied to security, reputation, or friendship. Thus, to be complete in our understanding of customer benefits and value creation, we need to also understand sources of emotional customer benefits and how they contribute to customer value.

Emotional Benefits and Psychological Value

Each of us has both physical and psychological needs. Physical needs such as hunger, thirst, sleep, and safety generally come first. But as those needs are met, our psychological needs

FIGURE 4-17 Brand Personality and Personality Traits						
Brand Personality	*Personality Trait*	*Not at All Descriptive*				*Extremely Descriptive*
Sincerity	Down-to-earth	—	—	—	—	—
	Honest	—	—	—	—	—
	Wholesome	—	—	—	—	—
	Cheerful	—	—	—	—	—
Excitement	Daring	—	—	—	—	—
	Spirited	—	—	—	—	—
	Imaginative	—	—	—	—	—
	Up-to-date	—	—	—	—	—
Competence	Reliable	—	—	—	—	—
	Intelligent	—	—	—	—	—
	Successful	—	—	—	—	—
Sophistication	Upper-class	—	—	—	—	—
	Charming	—	—	—	—	—
Ruggedness	Outdoorsy	—	—	—	—	—
	Tough	—	—	—	—	—

such as the need for warm relationships, affiliation, status, recognition, respect, fun, enjoyment, excitement, and self-fulfillment become more important to us. Because many products have personalities with psychological meanings, our psychological needs can be served with the purchase of products that offer a set of emotional benefits that are consistent with those needs. As shown below, our psychological needs will draw us to products with a brand personality that satisfies our psychological needs. To the degree that a product's brand personality delivers desired emotional benefits, our psychological needs can be fulfilled.

Psychological Needs → Brand Personality → Emotional Benefits

As an example, a consumer with a need to be seen as rugged, tough, and self-sufficient might be attracted to a Chevy truck and the advertising that positions the Chevy truck as strong, independent, and rugged. On the other hand, consumers with a need for status, recognition, sophistication, and respect might be attracted to a Mercedes. Thus, for products that project a "brand personality" there is the opportunity to create customer value through the delivery of emotional benefits.

Brand Personality and Value Creation

In a comprehensive study of human personality and brand personality, five dominant brand personalities were identified,[16] as presented in Figure 4-17. As you look over the five dominant brand personalities and their related personality traits, ask yourself which of the five would best describe the following brands or companies: Nike, Gateway Computer, Lexus, Timberland, and Hewlett-Packard.

Most people would align Nike with excitement. Nike's brand personality has been carefully honed to exemplify daring, spirit, imagination, and being ahead of the crowd (up-to-date). Gateway Computer, on the other hand, projects an image of being down-to-earth, honest, and wholesome, which translates into sincerity. Timberland footwear has a brand personality that projects ruggedness. Lexus seeks to project sophistication. Hewlett-Packard products project an image of competence built around intelligence, success, and reliability.

In each case, consumers with psychological needs that match well with the brand personality of a product will be drawn to that product. This conclusion assumes that other product benefits, service benefits, and price needs are adequately met. To the degree that the brand delivers these emotional benefits, it will contribute to the overall value a customer derives from the purchase of one product over another.

For example, what if Nike had used John Wooden (a famous college basketball coach) instead of Michael Jordan to endorse Nike Air basketball shoes (later named Air Jordan)? The personality of the Nike brand would be very different, and the emotional benefits created by the product would be considerably less for the target customers. Products have personalities. The spokesperson and ad copy used to promote a product help create the product's brand personality and emotional benefits.

TRANSACTION VALUE

A customer buying a refrigerator would be interested in *product features* such as size, storage configuration, color, freezer capacity, and operating efficiency, as well as the *costs and benefits* associated with the price paid, delivery, terms of payment, return policy and warranty. In contrast, a channel intermediary is less interested in end-user customer benefits and more interested in the value created by the sales transaction. Whether a Kool-Aid stand or Wal-Mart, the basic purpose of a channel intermediary is to connect producers with consumers. To accomplish this channel, intermediaries must invest in space to provide products, marketing resources to promote products, and people to facilitate customer transactions. Value for the channel intermediary is derived from a combination of (1) profitable use of space, (2) inventory turnover (the rate at which merchandise in that space is sold) and (3) the marketing expenses needed to promote the merchandise held in that space.

Space Value

In Figure 4-18 let's assume that a channel intermediary has 5,000 square feet of space (each square is 100 square feet). The four gray squares amount to 400 square feet that an intermediary such as Home Depot has allocated to the sale of major appliances. The first aspect of managing value in this situation is to know how much potential value the intermediary can obtain from 400 square feet of major appliances. Let's assume that for major appliances the average margin per square foot is $25. This means that space is worth $10,000 if customers bought the entire inventory of major appliances in that space.

$$\textbf{Space Value} = \textbf{Margin} \text{ per Square Foot} \times \textbf{Inventory} \text{ (square feet)}$$
$$= \textbf{\$25} \text{ per square foot} \times \textbf{400} \text{ square feet}$$
$$= \textbf{\$10,000}$$

If the channel intermediary had the option of placing another line of merchandise in the same 400 square feet at $30, that space has a value of $12,000. All things being equal, the alternative at $30 per square foot offers a better space value.

FIGURE 4-18 Intermediaries Use Space to Connect Manufacturers with Customers

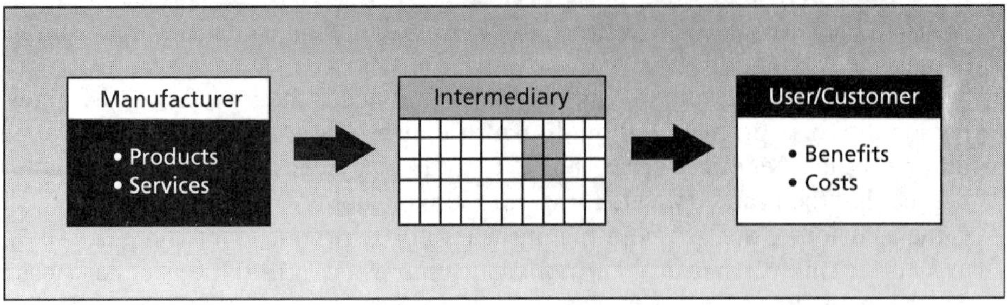

However, overall value to the intermediary depends on the rate at which this inventory sells and the marketing expenses associated with selling it. It may be that merchandise with a higher margin per square foot does not sell as fast as the lower margin merchandise. Or, perhaps the higher margin merchandise requires more marketing expenses to attract and serve customers. Thus, the overall transaction value has to take into account all these factors.

Transaction Value

The $10,000 of profit potential for the intermediaries' space will be converted into gross profit based on the rate at which the intermediary can sell the major appliance inventory. If the inventory can be sold five times per year, then 400 square feet of space allocated to major appliances can produce $50,000 in gross profit per year. For this level of sales transaction to occur, the intermediary has to invest in marketing. Marketing expenses typically include displays, advertising, product literature, sales training, and promotional samples when applicable. For major appliances let's assume that the channel intermediary spends $10,000 per year marketing its major appliances. The net result is a transaction value of $40,000 that the channel intermediary derived from the use of 400 square feet of space.

$$
\begin{aligned}
\text{Transaction Value} &= \frac{\text{Margin per}}{\text{square foot}} \times \frac{\text{Inventory}}{\text{square feet}} \times \frac{\text{Inventory}}{\text{Turnover}} - \frac{\text{Marketing}}{\text{Expenses}} \\
&= \frac{\$25 \text{ per}}{\text{square foot}} \times \frac{400}{\text{square feet}} \times \frac{5 \text{ Turns}}{\text{per year}} - \$10,000 \\
&= \$50,000 - \$10,000 \\
&= \$40,000
\end{aligned}
$$

Thus, the transaction value for an intermediary is going to vary based upon margins, efficient use of space, inventory turnover, and marketing expenses. Each of these areas of transaction value can be affected by the manufacturer's product, market demand, margins and marketing policies.

For example, Home Depot wanted to sell large appliances but did not want to carry a large inventory of different sizes and colors of various large appliances. Carrying this type of inventory is very expensive in terms of retail floor space, ware-

FIGURE 4-19 The Silent Floor: Customer Value Creation across the Supply Chain

Building-Products Retailer	Contractor Home Builder	Home Owner End-User Customer
Transaction Value....... is created with a value-added product with higher margins and higher inventory turnover due to strong demand	**Economic Value**....... comes from superior labor savings, fewer callbacks, product warranty, and code approval	**Perceived Value**....... is derived functionally and emotionally from a floor that does not squeak or rattle the glasses when crossing the room

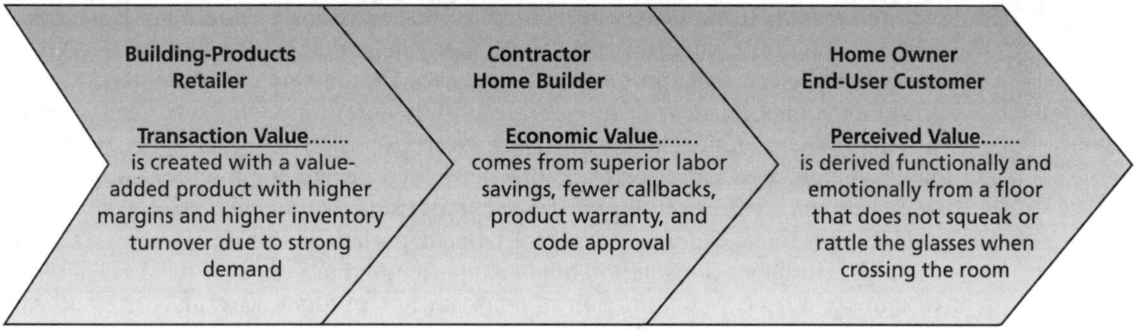

house space, and financing costs. To create an attractive transaction value, GE offered to hold the inventory and take over the responsibility of delivering the appliances from GE warehouses. Home Depot would keep a few floor models for display, and GE would operate a computer kiosk in the Home Depot store from which customers could make color and size selections. The net result was less space allocated to the sale of major appliances, less investment in inventory, no delivery expense, and reduced marketing expenses at the point of sale. Each of these contributed to a tremendous increase in transaction value for Home Depot while GE benefited by gaining access to the millions of consumers who shop at Home Depot.

Value Creation Across the Supply Chain

In many markets the supply chain involves more than one intermediary. For most building products the supply chain includes a channel intermediary, builder, and owner. As shown in Figure 4-19, each of these is a customer with different needs and unique ways of determining customer value.

The Silent Floor is a building product that creates different types of customer value across the supply chain. *The Silent Floor* is a partially assembled flooring system that will not squeak or bounce when someone walks across it. In focus-group interviews home owners indicated they would pay more for a floor that didn't bounce or squeak. While the product could be developed to achieve success for these consumers, the manufacturer also had to address the needs of the other customers in the value chain shown in Figure 4-19.

The value drivers that influenced retailers and builders were less focused on the product itself and more on the process of selling and using it. For building-product retailers *transaction value* was derived from margin per square foot, inventory requirements, inventory turnover, and marketing expenses. Value for contractors and home builders was created by the *economic* value derived from lower installation costs, fewer callbacks for rework, a manufacturer's product warranty that limited liability, and a code-approved product that accelerated the completion process. As shown in Figure 4-19, *The Silent Floor* created an attractive customer value for each of these different types of customers in the supply chain.

IDENTIFYING VALUE DRIVERS

We have shown that there are several ways to create customer value, but it can be challenging to determine which aspects of customer value are the key value drivers. Asking customers directly is one approach, but when asked in this way, customers tend to think everything is important. We can more accurately determine what a customer values when they make product choices involving several alternative product-price configurations. In the process of making trade-offs between different combinations of price and benefits we can create a set of preference curves using *conjoint analysis.*[17]

Using *The Silent Floor* as an example, nine hypothetical flooring systems were created from four dimensions of potential value presented in Figure 4-20.[18] Each alternative shows a different combination of labor savings, product warranty, price and callbacks. In this case, home builders would be asked to rank these nine alternatives in order of preference as a purchase alternative. Shown in Figure 4-20 are the preferences curves derived from a conjoint analysis of the rank order preferences also shown in Figure 4-20.

In this example the preference curves represent how the home builder values the different performance features and price for a flooring system. The higher the number on each preference curve, the more important that level of performance was in creating

---

FIGURE 4-20   Home Builder's Trade-Off Analysis for Flooring Nine Systems

Flooring System – A	Flooring System – B	Flooring System – C
Labor Savings.............None	Labor Savings.............None	Labor Savings.............None
Product Warranty.......5 years	Product Warranty.......10 years	Product Warranty.......None
Delivered Price..........Competitive	Delivered Price..........+20%	Delivered Price..........+40%
Customer Callbacks....None	Customer Callbacks....Frequent	Customer Callbacks....Some
Customer Ranking: 5	**Customer Ranking: 6**	**Customer Ranking: 8**

Flooring System – D	Flooring System – E	Flooring System – F
Labor Savings.............20%	Labor Savings.............20%	Labor Savings.............20%
Product Warranty.......10 years	Product Warranty.......10 years	Product Warranty.......5 years
Delivered Price..........Competitive	Delivered Price..........+20%	Delivered Price..........+40%
Customer Callbacks....Some	Customer Callbacks....None	Customer Callbacks....Frequent
Customer Ranking: 1	**Customer Ranking: 7**	**Customer Ranking: 9**

Flooring System – G	Flooring System – H	Flooring System – I
Labor Savings.............40%	Labor Savings.............40%	Labor Savings.............40%
Product Warranty.......None	Product Warranty.......5 years	Product Warranty.......10 years
Delivered Price..........Competitive	Delivered Price..........+20%	Delivered Price..........+40%
Customer Callbacks....Frequent	Customer Callbacks....Some	Customer Callbacks....None
Customer Ranking: 3	**Customer Ranking: 2**	**Customer Ranking: 4**

Builder's Preference Ranking: D, H, G, I, A, B, E, C, F
Conjoint Analysis used in this ranking to create the preferences curves below.
(See Appendix 4.1 for details)

customer value.[19] A 40 percent labor savings (1.00) is considerably more important than a 20 percent labor savings (0.33). The larger the range from low to high on a performance feature or price, the more important that aspect of value was to the customer when ranking the alternatives. The percentages shown in the preference curves represent the importance of each performance feature and price. In this example price accounted for 34 percent of the overall influence in preferences ranking influence, while the other 65 percent was influenced by the three performance features. Labor savings was the most important performance feature at 28 percent, while warranty and callbacks each accounted for 19 percent in the ranking of these alternative flooring systems.

To determine the value driver of any flooring system we need to build a *customer-value index* (CVI) for a specific flooring system. This can be done by using the preferences curves shown in Figure 4-21. For example, the conventional flooring system has a CVI of 1.67. This score is derived from the performance and price of this flooring system and how the home builder valued the performance features and price as shown

FIGURE 4-21   Home Builder's Trade-Off Analysis for Flooring Systems

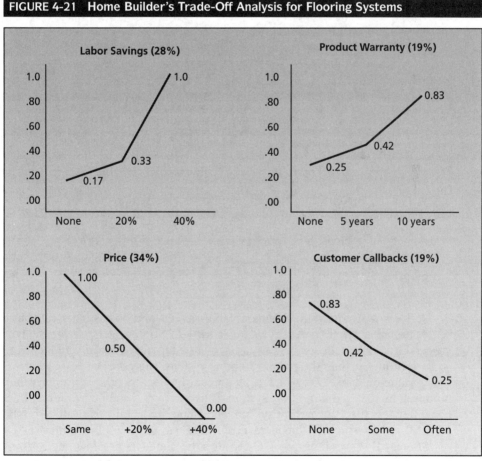

Note: To estimate the importance of each preference curve the low to high score is summed for each of the preference curves (2.99) and then each low to high range divided by this sum. When each is expressed as a percent it represents the importance that performance feature had on the ranking of alternatives.

FIGURE 4-22 Customer Value: Conventional and Value-Added Flooring Systems

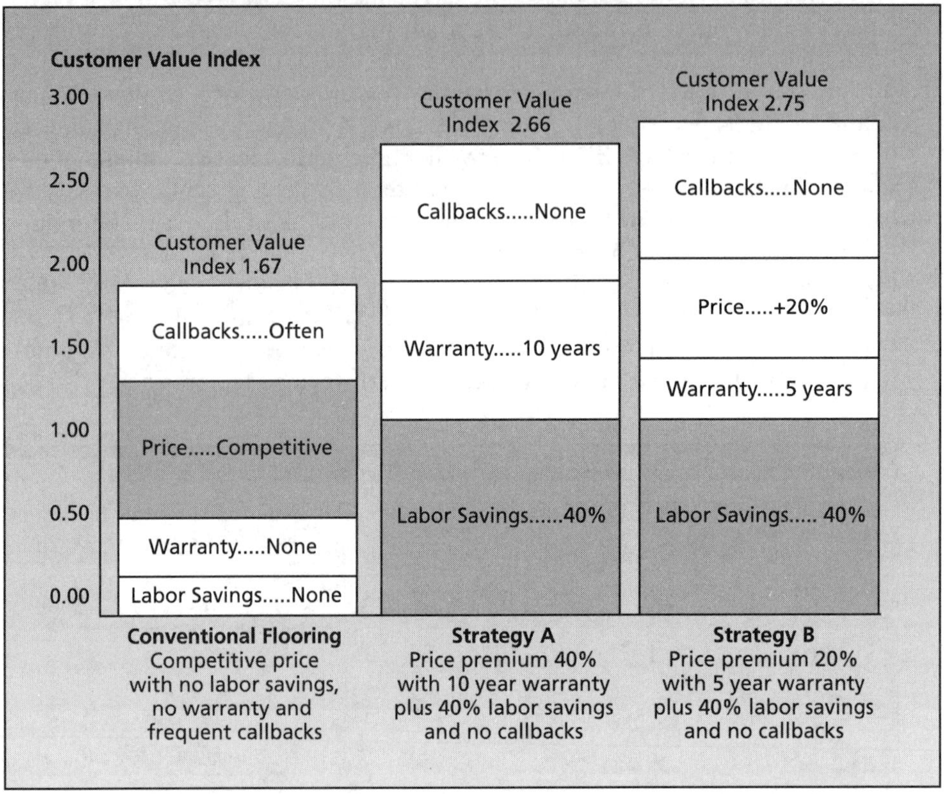

Customer Value Index

3.00		Customer Value Index 2.75
	Customer Value Index 2.66	
2.50	Callbacks.....None	Callbacks.....None
	Customer Value Index 1.67	
2.00		
	Callbacks.....Often	Price.....+20%
1.50		Warranty.....10 years
	Price.....Competitive	Warranty.....5 years
1.00		
0.50	Warranty.....None	Labor Savings......40%	Labor Savings..... 40%
0.00	Labor Savings.....None		

Conventional Flooring	**Strategy A**	**Strategy B**
Competitive price with no labor savings, no warranty and frequent callbacks	Price premium 40% with 10 year warranty plus 40% labor savings and no callbacks	Price premium 20% with 5 year warranty plus 40% labor savings and no callbacks

below. For the current flooring system, price is clearly the value driver (1.0 of 1.67) since it makes up 60 percent of the total CVI.

Customer Value Index = Labor Savings + Warranty + Price + Callbacks

CVI of Current Flooring System = None (.17) + None (.25) + $\dfrac{\text{Commodity}}{(1.0)}$ + $\dfrac{\text{Often}}{(.25)}$

= 1.67

A flooring system with 40 percent labor savings and no customer callbacks could be positioned in two ways. As shown in Figure 4-22, Strategy A offers the full labor savings and customer callback benefits along with a ten-year warranty and a price that is 40 percent higher than the current flooring system. This combination produces a customer value index of 2.66, which is 59 percent higher than the customer value index produced by the current flooring system. Thus Strategy A should be more attractive to home builders than the current system. The value driver for this strategy is labor savings (1.0 of 2.66) since it is the largest contributor to the overall customer value index.

Strategy B shown in Figure 4-22 provides the same labor savings and customer callback performance as Strategy A but is priced only 20 percent higher than the current flooring system and offers only a five year warranty. The customer value index for this combination of performance and price is 2.75, which is 65 percent higher in value than the current flooring system. The value driver for Strategy B is also labor savings. Strategies A and B are both superior to the current flooring system in terms of customer value. Strategy A, however, is likely to be more profitable, given a much higher price premium.

Summary

At the core of any market-based strategy are a strong customer focus and an ongoing commitment to understanding customers' needs and the problems customers encounter. Too often, businesses oversimplify the analysis of customer needs by narrowly focusing on specific product features and price. Although this assessment is important, it is also important for a business to look beyond current product features and price to more broadly see and understand the complete process or cycle the customer goes through in acquiring and using a product. Spending a day in the life of a customer or lead user provides a practical way for managers to more fully understand customers' needs and discover new opportunities to improve customer value and satisfaction.

While end-user customers are interested in product benefits, service benefits, brand image (emotional benefits) and the cost of purchase, channel intermediaries who sell manufacturers' products to these customers have a different way of assessing customer value. Intermediaries are attracted, satisfied and retained with a superior transaction value. Transaction value is the economic value derived from marketing a product based on the margin it produces per square foot of space, required inventory (square feet of space), inventory turnover (the number of times per year the inventory sells), and marketing expenses associated with promoting the product. Any one of these components can be modified to improve an intermediary's transaction value. When we look across the entire supply chain we may find different members of the supply chain have different ways of inferring customer value. This presents an additional challenge to manufacturers who rely on others to reach and serve end-user customers.

We examined three areas of customer analysis that influence customer benefits (economic benefits, perceived benefits, and emotional benefits) and the way customers derive value from these customer benefits. Economic benefits are a measurable difference in savings that enables a business to create an economic value that is greater than that of competing products. Although a lower price is an obvious source of economic value, there are nonprice areas from which economic benefit can be created. Savings derived from lower acquisition, usage, ownership, maintenance and repair, and disposal costs offer ways to lower the total cost of purchase for a target customer. However, not all benefits can be quantified into an economic value expressed in dollar savings.

Customer benefits derived from a product's appearance, exceptional service, or reputation are more difficult to put a dollar value on. Likewise, customer perceptions of performance have a strong influence on product preference and purchase behavior. By measuring customer perceptions of product benefits, service benefits, and brand benefits relative to competition, we are able to develop an overall index of total benefits derived from a particular business's product. By also measuring perception of price and nonprice costs of purchase relative to competition, we can develop an overall index of the total cost of purchase. The difference between total perceived benefits and cost provides a measure of perceived customer value. The larger the customer value, the greater the potential to attract, satisfy, and retain customers.

A third area of customer benefit and value creation is emotional benefits. Products that serve an underlying psychological need, type of personality, or personal values are creating emotional benefits that add value for the customer. Understanding these aspects of a target market are important in positioning a product and enhancing its perceived value. Products, like people, have personalities, and the closer we are able to position the product with respect to the target customer's emotional needs, the greater potential value we will be able to create with a given product.

Finally, trade-off analysis was introduced to help us better quantify the value created by different combinations of price and product positioning. The customer trade-off process enables us to uncover the degree to which different aspects of a product are driving customer preferences. This analysis in turn enables a business to index the value it creates relative to key competitors and to evaluate the impact alternative positioning strategies would have on customer preference and relative value. Overall, customer analysis and value creation are important inputs in developing marketing strategies designed to yield high levels of customer satisfaction.

Market-Based Logic and Strategic Thinking

1. What is the danger in asking customers what is important to them in a particular product purchase?
2. How do product features differ from customer benefits?
3. What is meant by "Staple Yourself to an Order"? How would this process increase opportunities to improve customer value?
4. How does Empathic Design help a business to discover customer problems and new opportunities for value creation?
5. What is the purpose of spending a day in the life of a customer?
6. Why should the scenes in each videotape of a day in the life of a customer go beyond the use of our product or service?
7. What is economic value to the customer?
8. What are the ways in which a business can create a more attractive economic value?
9. Why is it important to measure perceived benefits and perceived costs?
10. What are the ways in which a business can improve the perceived value of its product?
11. How should customer preference and purchase behavior change as a function of different levels of perceived customer value?
12. Why are emotional benefits important?
13. How do psychological motives help shape emotional benefits and customer perceptions of value?
14. How does the personality of a spokesperson help shape the emotional benefits of the product being endorsed?
15. Using Figure 4-16, discuss the brand personalities of Kodak film, Mountain Dew, and Prudential Insurance, and how these brand personalities were created?
16. What is transactional value?
17. Explain how a convenience store selling Coca-Cola products could estimate its transaction value in selling Coca-Cola products?
18. How could Coca-Cola improve the convenience store owner's transaction value?
19. What is trade-off analysis? How does it help us understand customer preferences?
20. How could a business determine if customers would prefer a new service?

APPLICATION PROBLEM: ADVAN-TECH SOFTWARE

Advan-Tech Software (ATS) is a start-up company that designs and markets software-engineering products. Industry surveys report that a software engineer costs $100,000 per year (including all benefits). The industry data also show that software engineers are productive (actually producing computer code) only 40 percent of the time. Advan-Tech Software can improve software-engineering productivity to 60 percent.

Competing products are well known and well supported by their manufacturers. Advan-Tech Software was not well known and had a limited staff to support customers technical problems and inquiries. These types of products are licensed with an annual fee. Competing products cost about $1,000 per year per software engineer. Advan-Tech Software's licensing fee is $1,500 per year per software engineer.

The product has been on the market one year, and management felt it was a good time to evaluate customer perceptions of their product relative to competing products. The results of the customer survey are summarized below.

Software Engineer Product Benefits (60%)	Relative Importance	ATS Rating	Competitor 1	Competitor 2	Competitor 3
Compatibility	**60**	**8**	8	5	6
Ease of Use	**40**	**9**	7	5	5

Software Engineer Service Benefits (30%)	Relative Importance	ATS Rating	Competitor 1	Competitor 2	Competitor 3
Quality of Support	**70**	**5**	8	6	7
Support Availability	**30**	**5**	7	6	7

Software Engineer Company Benefits (10%)	Relative Importance	ATS Rating	Competitor 1	Competitor 2	Competitor 3
Known/Reliable	**60**	**5**	9	7	6
Cutting Edge	**40**	**8**	8	6	5

Overall Cost of Purchase	Relative Importance	ATS Position
Labor Cost	**80**	–20%
Price of Software	**20**	100%

For access to interactive software to answer the questions below go to www.RogerJBest.com or www.prenhall.com/best.

1. Compute Advan-Tech Software's relative product, service, and company benefits and its overall relative benefits.
2. Compute Advan-Tech Software's relative cost of purchase.
3. Create a value map and interpret the value Advan-Tech Software provides relative to the competition.
4. Based on these results, assume Advan-Tech Software dedicates resources to improving its service ratings from 5 to 7 and improving its image of being known/reliable from 5 to 6 by adding resources to a marketing communications program. With these improvements, how would Advan-Tech Software's overall customer value change?

Notes

1. Readings in *Positive Impact:* William Henry Jr., "Walking in the Customer's Shoes" (November 1994):6–7; Paul Tulenko, "It's Important to Know What Customers Want" (August 1994):9–10; American Marketplace, "Author Says Success Lies in Customer Value Management" (August 1994):11–12.
2. Dorothy Leonard and Jeffrey Rayport, "Spark Innovation through Empathic Design," *Harvard Business Review* (November–December 1997).
3. Michael Lanning, *Delivering Profitable Value* (Reading, MA: Perseus Books, 1998):228–253.
4. Eric von Hippel, "Lead Users: An Important Source of Novel Product Concepts," *Management Science* 32, no. 7 (July 1986): 791–805.
5. Craig Henderson, "Finding, Examining Lead Users Push 3M to Leading Edge of Innovation," In Practice Case Study Series, *American Productivity & Quality Center,* 2000.
6. Gary Lillien, Pamela Morrison, Mary Sonnack, and Eric von Hippel, "Performance Assessment of the Lead User Idea Generation Process for New Product Development," working paper ISBM No. 4-2001, (The Pennsylvania State University).
7. Benson Shapiro, V. Kasturi Rnagan, and John Sviokla, "Staple Yourself to an Order," *Harvard Business Review,* (July–August 1992): 113–22
8. Robert Yeager, "Customers Don't Buy Technologies; They Buy Solutions: Here's How Five Advanced Technology Marketers Saw the Light and Avoided Becoming High-Tech Commodities," *Business Marketing* (November 1985):61–76.
9. Michael Hammer, *The Agenda,* Crown Business (2001).
10. John Forbis and Nitin Mehta, "Value-Based Strategies for Industrial Products," *Business Horizons* (May 1981):32–42.
11. "Ratings and Recommendation: Toasters and Toaster-Oven/Broilers," *Consumer Reports* (August 1998):42–43.
12. "Perceptions of Quality," *Journal of Marketing* (October 1993):18–34.
13. Bradley Gale, *Managing Customer Value* (New York: Free Press, 1994).
14. Morris Holbrook, "The Nature of Customer Value: An Axiology of Services in the Consumption Experience," in *Service Quality: New Directions in Theory and Practice,* ed. Roland Rust and Richard Oliver (London: Sage Publications, 1991):21–71.
15. Delbert Hawkins, Roger Best, and Kenneth Coney, "The Changing American Society: Values and Demographics," in *Consumer Behavior: Implications for Marketing Strategy,* 6th ed. (New York: Irwin, 1995):66–88.
16. Jennifer Aaker, "Dimensions of Brand Personality," *Journal of Marketing Research* (August 1997):347–56.
17. Donald Tull and Delbert Hawkins, *Marketing Research: Measurement and Method,* 6th ed. (New York: Macmillan, 1993):406–18; and M. Agarwal and P. Green, "Adaptive Conjoint Analysis versus Self-Explicated Models," *International Journal of Research* (June 1991):141–46.
18. John Morton and Hugh Devine, "How to Diagnose What Buyers Really Want," *Business Marketing* (October 1985):70–83.
19. J. Axelrod and N. Frendberg, "Conjoint Analysis," *Marketing Research* (June 1990):28–35; P. Green and V. Srinivasan, "Conjoint Analysis in Marketing Research," *Journal of Marketing* (October 1990):3–19; D. Wittink and P. Cattin, "Commercial Use of Conjoint Analysis," *Journal of Marketing* (July 1989):19–96; and A. Page and H. Rosenbaum, "Redesigning Product Lines with Conjoint Analysis," Journal of Product Management (1987):120–37.

Appendix 4.1

TRADE-OFF ANALYSIS COMPUTATIONS

Step 1. Determine individual scores for each attribute (factor/level) by summing the scores for that attribute.

Labor Savings	Price		
	Same	+20%	+40%
None	Some 5 years (A) [5]	Often 10 years (B) [6]	None None (C) [8] = 19
20%	None 10 years (D) [1]	Some None (E) [7]	Often 5 years (F) [9] = 17
40%	Often None (G) [3]	None 5 years (H) [2]	Some 10 years (I) [4] = 9
	= 9	= 15	= 21

Product Warranty

None	= 8 + 7 + 3	= 18
5 years	= 5 + 9 + 2	= 16
10 years	= 6 + 1 + 4	= 11

Customer Callbacks

None	= 8 + 1 + 2	= 11
Some	= 5 + 7 + 4	= 16
Often	= 6 + 9 + 3	= 18

Step 2. Rank attributes and summed attribute scores from lowest to highest. (X's below)

	X	Y
+40% Labor Savings	9	1.00
Same Price	9	1.00
10 Years Product Warranty	11	0.83
No Call	11	0.83
Price +20%	15	0.50
5 Years Product Warranty	16	0.42
Some Call Backs	16	0.42
+20% Labor Savings	17	0.33
No Product Warranty	18	0.25
Often Call Backs	18	0.25
None Speed	19	0.17
Price + 40%	21	0.00

Step 3. Determine the maximum score, minimum score, and difference between the maximum and minimum scores.

Step 4. Rescale the raw scores, (X's) using the following Normalization Formula:

Normalization Formula:

$$Y = \frac{X_{max} - X}{X_{max} - X_{min}}$$

$$Y = \frac{21 - X}{21 - 9}$$

$$Y = \frac{21 - X}{12}$$

Now, all scores will vary between zero and one, depending on their overall attractiveness to this customer segment.

CHAPTER 5

MARKET SEGMENTATION AND SEGMENTATION STRATEGIES

Market segmentation is the cornerstone of a market-based strategy. A market segment is a specific group of customers with unique customer needs, purchase behaviors, and identifying characteristics. Market segmentation opens the door to multiple market-based strategies and greater marketing efficiency. It creates the opportunity for sales and profit growth.

The Gap is well known for its product positioning as expressed by its products, merchandising, pricing, locations, and advertising. With a successful marketing strategy the Gap grew sales and profits through store expansion until it reached a point of diminishing returns. At this point the Gap extended its market segmentation strategy to cover the price-quality needs of adjacent segments of the casual clothing market.

The Banana Republic enabled the Gap to reach the *fashion segment* with higher quality and higher prices for the merchandise listed in Figure 5-1. Old Navy was geared to a more price-sensitive segment. At Old Navy, target customers can buy the same set of products at less than half the purchase price of Banana Republic. The product quality of Old Navy is lower, store layout is basic, and service is limited. While the Gap is posi-

FIGURE 5-1 Gap Market Segmentation and Product Positioning

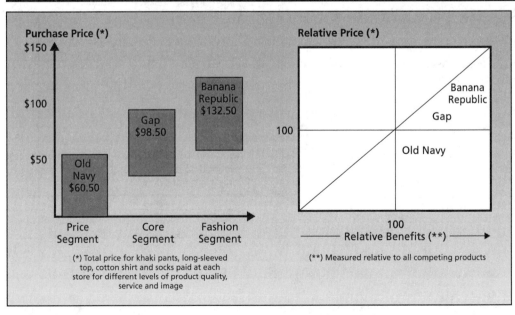

(*) Total price for khaki pants, long-sleeved top, cotton shirt and socks paid at each store for different levels of product quality, service and image

(**) Measured relative to all competing products

FIGURE 5-2   Fundamental Forces That Shape Differences in Consumer Needs

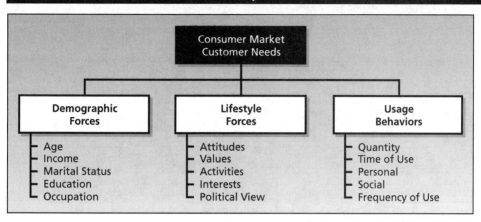

tioned with average prices and average product quality, this multisegment marketing strategy allowed the Gap to reach different segments of the clothing market with different product positions, each creating value for uniquely different customer needs.

Customer Needs

Understanding customer needs is the first step in successful market segmentation. A business with a strong market orientation will seek to understand customer needs and develop strategies to attract, satisfy, and retain target customers. Because potential customers will rarely all have the same needs, a business with a strong market orientation will divide its served market into segments as described below.

> A market segment is a specific group of customers with similar needs, purchasing behaviors, and identifying characteristics.[1]

Both consumers and businesses have market needs, but the factors influencing their needs differ in important ways. Understanding why customers have different needs is helpful in determining how to divide up a market into useful needs-based market segments.

Forces That Shape Consumer Market Needs

Consumers differ in a great many ways. Obviously people have different preferences for automobiles, toothpaste, and entertainment. Not so obvious are the factors that influence their preferences. Although there are many factors that contribute to these differences,[2] there are three primary forces that shape the needs of consumers, as summarized in Figure 5-2.

Demographic Influences

Consider how customer needs and preferences for an automobile change as one moves *demographically* from college student to management trainee. Changes in income, occupation, and educational status each contribute to a changing set of customer needs for a variety of products such as an automobile. A few years later, the same person may get married and start a family; changes in marital status and household will once again shift needs and automobile preferences. Because there are a large number of demographic

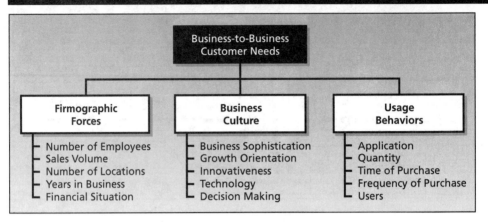

FIGURE 5-3   Fundamental Forces That Drive Differences in Business-to-Business Customer Needs

differences between both individuals and households, we should expect a large array of differences in what these consumers need, can afford, and buy.

Lifestyle Influences

Demographics are not alone in shaping customer needs and market demand. *Lifestyle forces* created by differences in values, attitudes, and interests also contribute to differences in customer needs. Two consumers who are demographically the same may differ significantly in their attitudes and value orientations. A consumer with strong environmental values is likely to prefer a different type of car than a demographically identical person whose values are more focused on fun, enjoyment, and personal gratification. These differences, as well as differences in preferred activities and interests, contribute to lifestyle forces that shape customer needs and product preferences.

Usage Behaviors

A third major force in shaping customer needs is *usage behavior*. How the product is used, when it is used, and how much it is used are likely to shape customer needs for certain products. A family with two or three children under ten will have a different set of usage behaviors for an automobile than a family with two children over the age of sixteen. In addition, if parents are buying a first car for their child as a graduation gift, their needs are likely to be different from those of people who are buying a car for the family or for business.

Forces That Shape Business Market Needs

Quite often, discussions of market segmentation are limited to consumer markets and, as a result, managers in business-to-business, industrial, high-tech, and commercial markets are left to extrapolate how segmentation might apply to their markets. Actually, there is very little difference in how fundamental forces shape customer needs, but there are fairly large differences in the types of factors that contribute to these fundamental forces, as shown in Figure 5-3.

Firmographics

In consumer markets, one of the key forces is *demographics*. A more appropriate term in business-to-business markets would be *firmographics*. Differences in the size of a

FIGURE 5-4   Market Segmentation of the Small Business Market

Growth-Oriented Entrepreneurs

Core Business Need
Ways to invest and grow

Firmographics
Medium size
More sophisticated
Higher in education
Ongoing financial plan

Purchase Behavior
Products that enhance productivity
High revenue per customer
Willing to buy value-added solutions

Value Proposition
*Solutions that help you grow
your business*

Cost-Focused Sustainers

Core Business Need
Ways to continue and save

Firmographics
Small in sales/employees
Less sophisticated
Lower in education
Limited or no financial plan

Purchase Behavior
Products that lower cost
Low revenue per customer
Confused by value-added solutions

Value Proposition
*Solutions that save your
business money*

commercial or industrial business in both employees and sales are likely to contribute to differences in customer needs. Industries can also be identified by the Standard Industrial Classification (SIC) code.

These industry differences often correspond to different product applications and different needs for products. Likewise, the newness of a business, number of locations, and financial stability are also important firmographics that may play a role in shaping customer needs in nonconsumer, business-to-business markets.

Business Culture

Just as consumer markets have lifestyles, businesses have *cultures* (styles) that can have a profound impact on their needs. Two firms that are very similar in firmographics may have very different needs due to major differences in their corporate style, or culture. A firm with a strong technological base and growth orientation is going to have a different set of needs from a commodity business with no aspirations for growth. Other differences in attitudes with respect to innovation and risk and centralized versus decentralized decision making are also likely to shape the customer needs and requirements in a purchase decision.

Usage Behaviors

Finally, as in consumer markets, usage behavior can play a role in shaping business customer needs. How much a business buys, how often it purchases, who uses the product, and how it is used all influence the specific needs a business-to-business customer will have in selecting one vendor or product over another. Quite often, it is not simply the product a customer is buying but the support, service, and integrity of the company from which it is buying. For example, though there are several million small businesses in the United States, they can be divided into two core segments: *growth-oriented entrepreneurs* and *cost-focused sustainers*. As shown in Figure 5-4, each segment is different in business need, firmographics, and purchase behavior. Growth-oriented entrepreneurs are better educated, more sophisticated, and better organized, and they have a passion to grow their business. By contrast, cost-focused sustainers are more centered on maintaining the status quo at the lowest cost. These small businesses also tend to be less sophisticated in their operations, have a lower level of formal education, and are less likely to have a working financial plan. To sell successfully in either segment requires a strategy that recognizes the unique needs and behaviors of each segment.

NEEDS-BASED MARKET SEGMENTATION

Understanding customer needs is a basic tenet of market-based management. Although demographics, lifestyle, and usage behaviors help to shape customer needs, they are not always the best way to identify groups of similar customers. There are simply too many variables and too many meaningless combinations. Instead, the market segmentation process should start with customer needs as described below:

> *First*, group customers with like needs and then discover which demographics, lifestyle forces, and usage behaviors make them distinct from customers with different needs.

In this way, we are able to let customer needs drive the market segmentation process and let the unique combination of external forces that shaped them follow. This approach reduces the chance of an artificial segmentation of the market based on a combination of demographics and usage behaviors that are *not* the key forces that shape customer needs. However, before we proceed with the process of needs-based segmentation, let's first examine the *demographic trap*.

The Demographic Trap

Marketers new to market segmentation will often fall into the *demographic trap*. Given the strong role demographics, lifestyle, and usage play in shaping customer needs, it would seem logical to segment a market on the basis of these differences. For example, in the consumer financial services market we could segment the market on the basis of differences in income, education, and age, as well as differences in amount invested, frequency of transactions, and type of investments purchased. If we created three meaningful categories for each of these six variables, we would have over 700 possible market segments!

$$\text{Number of Segments} = (3 \text{ categories per variable})^6 = 729$$

This is too many segments to consider if we are to develop a meaningful marketing strategy for each customer group. Perhaps even more important, it is possible that none of the over 700 segments have anything to do with customer needs. It may be convenient to group customers into demographic, lifestyle, or usage categories, but the demographics selected may or may not be relevant in shaping customer needs. Although markets are heterogeneous, and people differ from one another by demographics, personal attitudes, and life circumstances, *demographic segmentation seldom provides much guidance for product development or message strategies.*[3] Thus, it makes more sense to start the market segmentation process with customer needs and group customers on the basis of similar needs.

FIGURE 5-5 Key Steps in a Needs-Based Market Segmentation Process

Steps in Segmentation Process	Description
1. Needs-Based Segmentation	Group customers into segments based on similar needs and benefits sought by customer in solving a particular consumption problem.
2. Segment Identification	For each needs-based segment, determine which demographics, lifestyles, and usage behaviors make the segment distinct and identifiable (actionable).
3. Segment Attractiveness	Using predetermined segment attractiveness criteria, determine the overall attractiveness of each segment.
4. Segment Profitability	Determine segment profitability (net marketing contribution).
5. Segment Positioning	For each segment, create a "value proposition" and product-price positioning strategy based on that segment's unique customer needs and characteristics.
6. Segment "Acid Test"	Create "segment storyboards" to test the attractiveness of each segment's positioning strategy.
7. Marketing Mix Strategy	Expand segment positioning strategy to include all aspects of the marketing mix: product, price, promotion, and place.

Needs-Based Market Segments

To illustrate the importance of needs-based segmentation, consider how we might segment the market for investment services. Relevant demographics that might be considered to cause differences in needs could include income, assets, age, occupation, marital status, education, and, perhaps, others. Relevant use behaviors might include experience with investments, size of investment portfolio, portfolio diversification, and amount of average transaction. Each of these influences could be legitimately argued to be an important force in shaping customer needs. However, consider the hopeless task that would emerge if one were to attempt to segment the market on the basis of all of these differences.

Instead, the first step in the market segmentation process outlined in Figure 5-5 is to determine customers' investment needs and the benefits they hope to derive from their investment decisions. A study of female investors' needs produced three *needs-based segments*:[4]

- **Segment A:** Investors who sought investments that outperform inflation with minimum tax consequences.
- **Segment B:** Investors who sought investments that provide appreciation with limited risk.
- **Segment C:** Investors who sought investments that produced high levels of current income with minimal risk.

It would not take much of a financial adviser to figure out which type of investments would best suit each segment of investors. However, on the basis of needs alone, we do not know who these customers are. The primary *benefit* of needs-based market segmentation is that segments are created around specific customer needs. The primary *disadvantage* is that we do not know who these customers are. We need to determine what observable demographics and behaviors differentiate one segment from another in order to make a needs-based segmentation actionable.

FIGURE 5-6   Segment Identification: Female Investor Market Segments

Segment Profile	Segment: Segment Need		
	A: Growth without Taxes	B: Appreciation with Minimal Risk	C: Income with Minimal Risk
Demographics			
Age	35–45	35–55	55–75
Income > $50,000	86%	3%	63%
Working	100%	43%	17%
Professional	83%	9%	13%
Married	56%	13%	35%
Youngest Child < 5	24%	83%	5%
College Educated	78%	23%	17%
Lifestyle			
Investment Attitude	Confident	Concerned	Conservative
Interests	Sports/Reading	Family	Leisure
Entertainment	Concerts	Movies	Television
Key Value	Individualistic	Cooperative	Traditional
Usage Behaviors			
Experience	Some/Extensive	None/Limited	Limited/Moderate
Risk Preference	Moderate/High	Low	Low/Moderate
Net Worth	Growing	Fixed	Fixed

Segment Identification

After grouping customers into needs-based segments, step 2 in the segmentation process is segment identification.

> For a segmentation scheme to be actionable, it must characterize segments by demographic variables for purposes of targeting and positioning.[5]

For each needs-based segment, we need to determine the demographics, lifestyles, and usage behaviors that make one segment meaningfully different from another. The key descriptive factors that make segment A distinct from the other segments are career orientation, occupation, college education, and above-average income, as shown in Figure 5-6. Women in this segment are also more likely to be self-confident and competitive and to have interests outside the home. On the basis of these characteristics, this segment is labeled the *career woman*. With accurate delineation of segment needs and identification, one can begin to visualize a self-confident career woman who has discretionary income to invest but wants her investments to grow at a rate greater than inflation without the burden of additional taxes.

Although segment B is in the same general age category as segment A, customers in segment B have lower incomes, are more likely to have young children, and are less likely to be married. They have less experience with investments and are more likely to be fearful of investment decisions. This segment is labeled the *single parent*, given both the unique family situation and lifestyle orientation.

FIGURE 5-7   Forces that Shape Segment Attractiveness

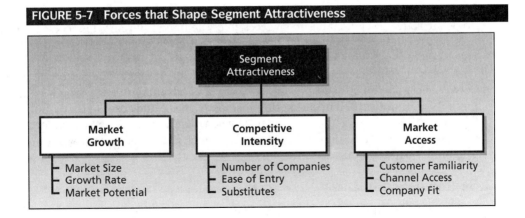

Segment C is called the *mature woman*, because of age, conservative outlook, and wealth position. These investors want investments that deliver high levels of current income with limited risk. Thus, all three segments have unique needs and identities that enable us to successfully accomplish the first two steps in the needs-based segmentation process outlined in Figure 5-5.

Segment Attractiveness

What makes one segment attractive and another not attractive? Although every business might answer this question somewhat differently according to its industry perspective, when we step back and look more broadly at the factors that make a market attractive, we find few differences. Common to most assessments of segment attractiveness would be measurements of *market growth*, *competitive intensity*, and *market access*.

Market Growth

As shown in Figure 5-7, forces that shape market growth include the size of the segment, rate of growth, and market potential. Large, growing segments with potential for future growth are more attractive than combinations of small segments without potential for growth. Each of these forces directly affects the opportunity for profitable growth. A first step in assessing segment attractiveness is to identify the key market forces that contribute to an attractive market opportunity for growth.

Competitive Intensity

The number of competitors, the number of substitutes, and the competitive rivalry among competitors affect the attractiveness of a segment. Even if the market growth for a segment is attractive, the competitive intensity could more than offset its attractiveness and opportunity for profitable growth. If there are many competitors and market entry is relatively easy, market attractiveness diminishes because it becomes more difficult to achieve market share and margin objectives. In addition, if there are many substitute products and very limited product differentiation, margins will be further compressed. An attractive segment is one with relatively few competitors, little price competition, very few substitutes, and high barriers to competitor entry.

Market Access

To be attractive, a segment has to be accessible. The first requirement is access to channels that reach target segment customers. Without customer familiarity and channel access, there is little opportunity for success. Market access also requires a good fit between a business's core capabilities and target segment needs. The better the match between customer needs and a business's sources of advantage, the easier it is to access markets. Without sufficient marketing resources, market access is greatly impeded. Segment attractiveness is greatly enhanced when a business has good customer access, sufficient marketing resources to access customers, and a good fit between business capabilities and customer needs.

Segment Profitability

Although the market attractiveness of a segment may be acceptable, a business may elect not to pursue that segment if it does not offer a desired level of profit potential. To estimate segment profitability, we can use the net marketing contribution expected with a certain level of segment market penetration.

For any segment there is a certain level of market demand. For example, the segment demand among *growth-oriented entrepreneurs* in the small-business market may be 100,000 in a particular geographic region. Assume that a business believes it can achieve a 10 percent penetration of this market segment with an average revenue per customer of $1,000 per year and variable cost per customer of $600. Marketing expenses are estimated to be $1 million. Based upon these estimates, the net marketing contribution, or segment profitability, would be $3 million, as the following shows.

$$\text{Net Marketing Contribution} = \left[\text{Segment Demand} \times \text{Segment Share} \times \left(\text{Revenue per Customer} - \text{Variable Cost per Customer}\right)\right] - \text{Marketing Expense}$$

$$= [100{,}000 \times 0.10 \times (\$1{,}000 - \$600)] - \$1 \text{ million}$$
$$= 10{,}000 \times \$400 - \$1 \text{ million}$$
$$= \$4 \text{ million} - \$1 \text{ million}$$
$$= \$3 \text{ million}$$

The importance of market segmentation and segment profitability is highlighted in Figure 5-8. Without a segmentation of customers, this health insurance business attempted to sell to all willing buyers. However, customer segmentation based on insurance needs revealed that their greatest market penetration was in the smallest and least profitable segment, segment I. Given the relative attractiveness of the other two segments because of their revenue per customer and claims problems, the health insurance provider revised its marketing efforts around segments II and III.

A key benefit of market segmentation is identifying segments that should *not* be pursued. As Chuck Lillis, the CEO of MediaOne Group, put it, "I will know when our businesses are doing a good job of market segmentation when they can articulate who we should *not* sell to." Businesses that do not segment their markets generally sell to everyone, and in doing so may hurt profits without even knowing it.

FIGURE 5-8   Market Segmentation of the Business Insurance Market

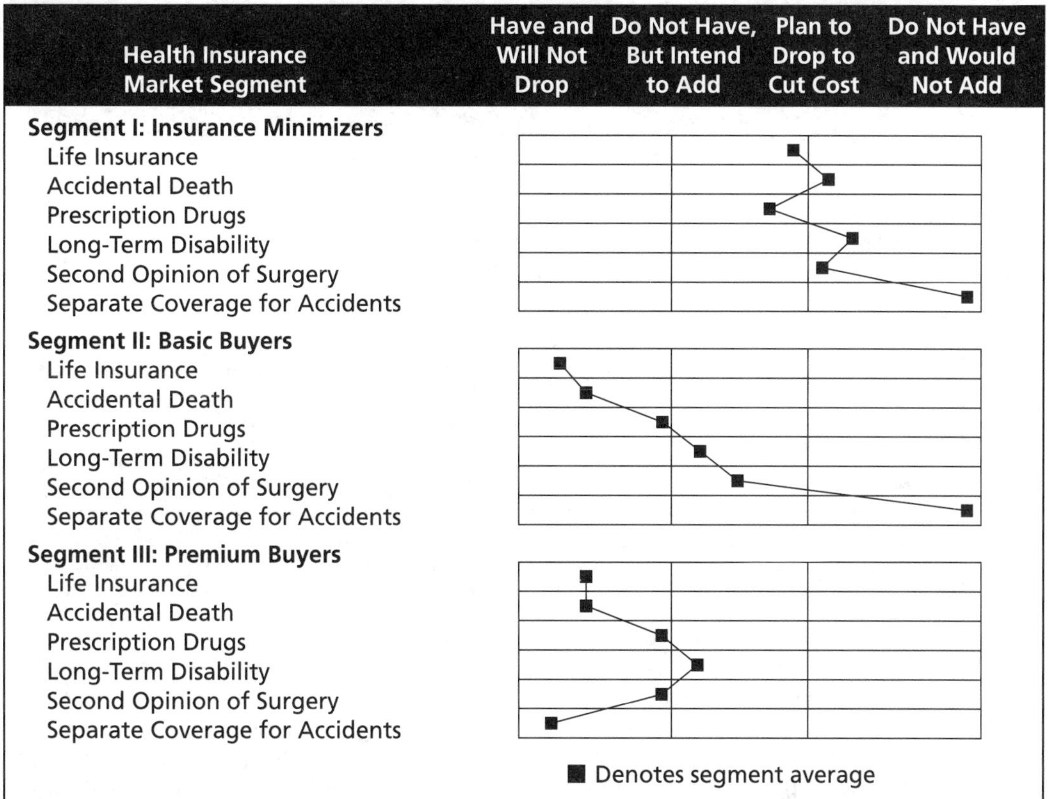

Health Insurance Market Segment	Have and Will Not Drop	Do Not Have, But Intend to Add	Plan to Drop to Cut Cost	Do Not Have and Would Not Add
Segment I: Insurance Minimizers				
Life Insurance				
Accidental Death				
Prescription Drugs				
Long-Term Disability				
Second Opinion of Surgery				
Separate Coverage for Accidents				
Segment II: Basic Buyers				
Life Insurance				
Accidental Death				
Prescription Drugs				
Long-Term Disability				
Second Opinion of Surgery				
Separate Coverage for Accidents				
Segment III: Premium Buyers				
Life Insurance				
Accidental Death				
Prescription Drugs				
Long-Term Disability				
Second Opinion of Surgery				
Separate Coverage for Accidents				

■ Denotes segment average

Segment	Size	Revenue per Customer*	Claims Problems*	Company Share
Insurance Minimizers	30%	100	100	40%
Basic Buyers	34%	163	71	27%
Premium Buyers	36%	181	66	19%

*Indexes set equal to 100 for Insurance Minimizers.

Segment Positioning

For each target segment, a new set of marketing challenges needs to be addressed. A business needs to develop a customized *value proposition* and *positioning strategy* that deliver value to target customers in each segment.[6] A value proposition includes all the key elements of the situation and the benefits the target customer is looking for in this purchase. For the female investor market described in Figure 5-6, segment A included middle-aged professional women who were seeking investments that would have above-average growth with minimal tax consequences. The value proposition developed for this segment was: "How to beat inflation and taxes with thoughtful investment planning."

Ideally, the value proposition for a segment should be built around the key benefits sought by the target customer. As a result, the value proposition for segments B

FIGURE 5-9 Segment Storyboards for Acid Test of Segment Strategies

Investment Program A	Investment Program B	Investment Program C
How to Beat Inflation and Higher Taxes	*Special Help for Women with Special Money Problems*	*Safe Investment Solutions That Pay Good Income*
Key Benefits	**Key Benefits**	**Key Benefits**
• Capital Appreciation • Minimal Taxation	• Growth/Appreciation • Safety	• Safety • Income
Products	**Products**	**Products**
• Growth Stocks • Municipal Bonds • Growth Funds	• Growth Mutual Funds • Blue-Chip Stocks • High-Grade Bonds	• Utility Stocks • High-Grade Bonds • High-Dividend Stocks

Potential customers are instructed to examine each "segment storyboard" and select the one that best fits their investment needs. The degree to which target segment customers select the storyboard designed for them determines the degree to which the segment positioning strategy would be judged to be working.

and C would be radically different because the needs, benefits, and purchase behaviors of these segments are radically different.

To develop a *segment positioning strategy* for each of the three segments, we need to return to Figure 5-6 as a guide. Because the three segments differ in primary needs, demographics, lifestyle, and purchase behaviors, it is important to use all this information in developing a customized positioning strategy for each segment.

Although there could be many possible strategies for each segment, Figure 5-9 outlines a *value proposition* and *positioning strategy* designed to meet the unique needs of each of these three segments. Product differences based on segment needs are relatively easy to determine. This is the first sign of a good segmentation program. If a business can readily link customer needs to specific product features and benefits, then it is on the right track in developing a successful segment strategy. If this linkage is difficult or arbitrary, target customers will be less likely to recognize a segment strategy as being unique.

Because pricing is less important in the investment market than in, for example, the retail market, it is not a key part of the segment positioning strategy for any of the three segments. Had a segment emerged as price-sensitive, then pricing may have become a critical issue in both the value proposition and the segment positioning strategy.

Promotion is critical in delivering the value proposition and communicating the identity of the customer it is intended for. Thus, both the ad copy and the media selected for advertising communications are crucial. For segment A, the ad copy would portray a career woman in a business setting; potential media could include *Business Week*. Segment B requires a different approach because the family plays a larger role, as does limited experience in financial planning. Likewise, the promotion strategy for segment C has to be carefully customized to the needs, lifestyles, and usage behaviors of mature female investors.

To reach customers in each of these segments, a business has to again be sensitive to the needs and lifestyle of the target customer. For the career woman, lunchtime seminars at or near her place of work are used to more effectively deliver the value proposition and product portfolio that would best serve her needs and desired benefits. Morning or evening seminars at local schools are more likely to meet the place needs of the single parent segment. A convenient location would be a key consideration in drawing mature women to a seminar customized to their needs. Interestingly, seminars targeted at the mature segment are given on cruise ships, where participants are able to write off a portion of their trip by attending a short seminar each day.

Segment Strategy Acid Test

To test our understanding of segment needs and our ability to translate that understanding into a value proposition, the next step in the segmentation process is an *acid test* of our strategy.[7] To conduct an acid test, we need to create at least three distinct *segment storyboards*, each of which delineates a different value proposition and segment positioning strategy. We would then ask potential customers to examine the segment storyboards and to select the one that best meets their needs. Figure 5-9 illustrates a sample storyboard for each of the female investor segments. A sample of female investors would be asked to evaluate each value proposition and each segment storyboard and to select the one that most appealed to them and their situation.

If the strategy is successful, the majority of the potential customers from any given target segment will select the segment storyboard created for them. The higher the percentage of correct classification, the better the chance the business has of delivering a meaningful segment strategy. Of course, if target segment customers indicate that none of the segment storyboards fits their needs, then the business has failed to translate segment needs into a meaningful value proposition and segment positioning strategy.

A telecommunications business found in an acid test that five segments found the storyboard created for them attractive, though they had suggestions on how to improve them, while one segment failed to find any of the segment storyboards attractive. The business had to do more research, probing deeper into the overall needs of customers in the segment that failed to find an attractive segment storyboard. After additional customer research, and a second time through the acid test, the business was able to attract enough target segment customers to a revised storyboard to warrant moving forward in the segmentation process.

In another acid test, a segment of bank customers rejected a segment storyboard designed for them because it did not include the cost of a new service. A revised value proposition included both the benefits and the cost of this new service. In all cases, an important part of the acid test is to ask customers for ways in which the value proposition can be modified to better fit their needs, usage behavior, and lifestyle.

Segment Marketing Mix Strategy

Although this last step may seem a bit trivial given the preceding steps, a major cause of failure is ineffectively *executing* the segment strategy. To be successful, the segment strategy next needs to be expanded to include all elements of the marketing mix. The segment positioning strategy may include both product and price, but a complete marketing mix strategy needs also to include promotion (communications) and place

FIGURE 5-10   DuPont Segment Value Propositions and Positioning Strategies

Commercial Fishing

Value Proposition: *This boat hull of Kevlar saves fuel, gets there faster, and can carry more fish.*

Aircraft Design

Value Proposition: *Our L-1011 is 807 pounds lighter because of Kevlar 49.*

(sales and distribution) strategies.[8] If target segment customers are not adequately aware of the segment value proposition or cannot acquire the product at preferred points of purchase, the segment strategy will fail.

For example, in Figure 5-10 we can see how DuPont developed different advertisements to execute a multisegment strategy for Kevlar. Note the attention to distinct segment value propositions and product positioning differences that are unique to each target segment.[9] A generic ad highlighting product features would not have the impact that each segment-specific ad was designed to have.

SEGMENTATION STRATEGIES

On the basis of segment attractiveness, profit potential, and available resources, there are several segment strategies a business could pursue. As shown in Figure 5-11, segment strategies can range from a *mass market* strategy with no segment focus to a *mass customization* strategy with numerous niche segments within segments. This section discusses these various segment strategies and the circumstances under which they are used.

Mass Market Strategy

When differences in customer needs are small or demographics are not distinctive, a business may elect to use a mass market strategy. This strategy presents a generic value proposition built around the core customer need and the business's generic positioning strategy.

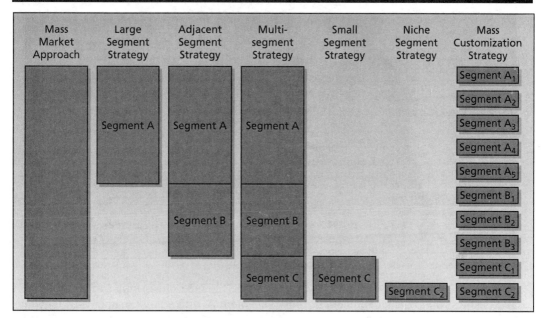

FIGURE 5-11   Segmentation Hierarchy: Mass Market to Mass Customization Strategies

Wal-Mart, for example, pursues a mass market strategy built around a low-cost value proposition that has worked very effectively for thirty years. Coca-Cola, Caterpillar, Sony, Marlboro, Phillips, Toyota, Volvo, and Kodak are some of many well-recognized global brands that use a global marketing strategy, while sometimes modifying their products and market communications to meet specific customer needs in specific international markets.

Large Segment Strategy

When a market is segmented and marketing resources are limited, a business could elect to pursue a *large segment* strategy. As illustrated in Figure 5-11, a mass market strategy could be segmented into three core segments. A large segment strategy would focus on segment A, because it is the largest, representing 50 percent of the market. Unlike a mass market strategy, a large segment strategy addresses one set of core customer needs. Thus, a large segment strategy engages the benefits of market segmentation while also providing a relatively large market demand. Chevy's truck strategy is a large segment strategy. Because market demand is somewhat limited and a large segment exists, this large segment strategy provides a cost-effective way to reach a large number of target customers.

Adjacent Segment Strategies

Quite often, businesses find themselves in a situation in which they have pursued a single segment focus but have reached the point of full market penetration. When this is the case, an *adjacent segment* strategy offers an attractive opportunity for market growth. Because resources are limited, a closely related attractive segment is tackled next. With profits derived from the primary target segment, the next most attractive adjacent segment is addressed.

FIGURE 5-12 Toyota's Adjacent Segmentation Strategy

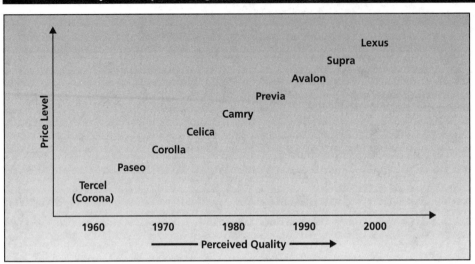

In Figure 5-11, segment B is profiled to be the next most similar to segment A. A business that reaches full penetration of segment A with a large segment strategy may pursue new growth by entering segment B, an adjacent segment with respect to product and price needs.

An example of this segmentation strategy is Toyota's adjacent segment strategy in the U.S. car market. Toyota entered the U.S. market with the Corona at the low-price end of the market (today the Tercel serves this segment). As Toyota penetrated this segment, it moved to an adjacent segment in terms of price and quality by adding the Corolla, as shown in Figure 5-12. By the late 1980s, additional products were developed for higher price-quality segments. Next came entry into the luxury car segment with Lexus and an adjacent segment for the Supra and Avalon. Over a thirty-year period, Toyota effectively used an adjacent segment strategy, and today it has a strong market position in each segment.

Multisegment Strategies

Market segmentation opens the door to multiple market-based strategies and greater marketing efficiency. For example, many retail gasoline companies operated for more than twenty years on the fundamental belief that gas purchases were made primarily on the basis of price. This marketing belief guided their marketing strategy. However, a study of gas station customer needs uncovered five distinct segments, only one of which would be described as price shoppers.[10] The top three segments illustrated in Figure 5-13 are more concerned with quality, service, and the availability of other products such as coffee, soft drinks, sandwiches, and snack foods. In addition, each of the top three segments in the figure (Road Warriors, Generation F3, and True Blues) produced more revenue per customer than Home Bodies (convenience buyers) and Price Shoppers.

These three target segments, which make up 59 percent of the gas customers, produce higher revenue per customer because they buy more gas, premium products, and food products. In addition, the average margin per customer in each of these segments

FIGURE 5-13   Mobil Corporation's Segment Selection and Multisegment Strategy

Segment	Size	Core Customer Needs	Use Behavior	Key Demographics
Road Warriors	16%	Premium Products and Quality Service	Drive 25,000 to 50,000 miles a year; buy premium gas, drinks, and sandwiches.	Higher income, middle-aged men.
Generation F3	27%	Fast Fuel, Fast Service, and Fast Food	Constantly on the go; drive a lot, snack heavily, and want fuel and food fast.	Upwardly mobile men and women, half under 25.
True Blues	16%	Branded Products and Reliable Service	Brand- and station-loyal; buy premium gas, pay cash.	Men and women with moderate to high income.
Home Bodies	21%	Convenience	Use whatever gasoline is conveniently located.	Usually housewives who shuttle children during day.
Price Shoppers	20%	Low Price	Neither brand- nor station loyal.	Usually on tight budget.

is also higher than in the other two groups because the products they buy often have higher margins. By focusing on these three segments, a gas retailer could implement a series of marketing strategies to better serve the needs of these target segments and, if successful, grow its revenues and profits.

Perhaps an even more challenging multisegment marketing strategy was one developed by an electric equipment manufacturer. The power generation and distribution market in the United States includes 7,000 entities. A segmentation study of this market produced twelve distinct needs-based segments that differed in customer needs, firmographics, and usage behavior, [11] as shown in Figure 5-14. At one extreme was a segment that included large, publicly owned utilities that had large engineering and maintenance staffs, and at the other extreme were small rural co-ops that produced electricity for small farm communities. Another segment actually included businesses that produce electricity for their own consumption and sell excess power to the local utilities. The Los Angeles Performing Arts Center is a customer in this segment.

The electric equipment manufacturer found each of the segments attractive and already had sales to customers in each of the segments. The only difference was that before the segmentation study the business used a mass market strategy and treated all customers roughly the same. On the basis of the unique needs of each segment, twelve separate marketing programs were designed. Designing them required twelve different segment product-positioning and marketing approaches in order to build a strong value proposition for each segment.

The year the multisegment strategy was implemented, the entire market experienced a decline of 15 percent in sales. In addition, one regional vice president had elected not to participate in the implementation of the multisegment marketing strategy. Despite the market's decline, there were significant increases in sales in regions A and B and a smaller increase in region C, the control group, as shown in Figure 5-14. Overall, the business achieved a sales growth of more than 10 percent in a year that the

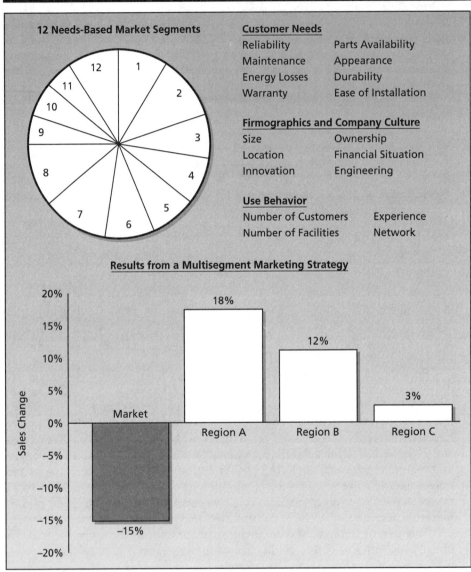

FIGURE 5-14 Multisegment Power Generation Market Strategy

12 Needs-Based Market Segments

Customer Needs

Reliability	Parts Availability
Maintenance	Appearance
Energy Losses	Durability
Warranty	Ease of Installation

Firmographics and Company Culture

Size	Ownership
Location	Financial Situation
Innovation	Engineering

Use Behavior

Number of Customers	Experience
Number of Facilities	Network

Results from a Multisegment Marketing Strategy

market declined by 15 percent in sales volume. It is also important to note that this increase was achieved with essentially no change in marketing budget—simply better market focus and reallocation of marketing resources.

Small Segment Strategy

Although a market may provide three segment opportunities, a business with limited resources and certain capabilities may elect to compete in the smallest segment. The smallest segment, as represented by segment C in Figure 5-11, is often ignored by large competitors, who may use mass market or large segment strategies. Even businesses with a multisegment strategy may not be able to compete effectively with a business that has a singular-focus small segment strategy.

For example, Mercedes for many years used a small segment strategy to stay focused on the luxury car market. Having built a certain prestige in this market, Mercedes was reluctant to move down into lower price-quality adjacent segments. However, because of the increased attractiveness of adjacent segments, Mercedes is now pursuing a dual-segment strategy.

Niche Segment Strategies

Market segmentation is a process of grouping customers with like needs into homogeneous segments, but the process is never perfect. That is, even when customers in a given segment share common needs, there are still differences in demographics or usage behaviors that cannot be fully addressed with a single segment strategy. As a result, there is the opportunity for a business to carve out a niche within a segment and further customize its marketing effort to that group of target customers.

Consider the case of Sub-Zero refrigerators.[12] This business, with less than a 2 percent share of the U.S. refrigerator market, competes with industry giants who have large economies of scale and marketing resources. However, Sub-Zero holds 70 percent of the "Super Premium" segment, a niche market segment in the refrigerator market. Sub-Zero specializes in very expensive built-in refrigerators that start at $3,500. Target customers claim, "to own a Sub-Zero refrigerator is to have something special."

It is hard to outperform niche competitors such as Sub-Zero because they have all their marketing resources focused on the specific needs of a certain type of customer. Within that segment, Sub-Zero can focus on a *niche market* that includes only high-end customers who are seeking a super premium refrigerator. For Sub-Zero, a needs-based market strategy is customized to the specific needs, lifestyle, and usage behavior of their niche customer.

Mass Customization

The complete opposite of a mass market strategy is a *mass customization* strategy. A mass customization strategy treats every unique group of customer needs as a niche market. As shown in Figure 5-11, a mass customization strategy recognizes all ten unique groups of customer needs. The objective is to customize a segment strategy for each customer segment. *Mass customization* is a term used in conjunction with database marketing. With the use of customer databases,[13] a segment can be further divided into customized subsegments, as shown in Figure 5-11.

Figure 5-15 illustrates how mass customization would work for a printer purchase. Shown to the left in Figure 5-15 are five aspects of performance and price, each with three levels of performance. This creates 243 possible product-price configurations. The most expensive printer with next-day delivery would cost $750 and the least expensive with one-week delivery would cost $110. These price points may serve as reference prices from which customers can gauge their cost savings or price premium based on their preferred level of performance, delivery, and price.

In this example the customer was willing to pay $310 for a business-quality printer with greater than four pages per minute, a ninety-day warranty, 800 Hotline technical service and next-week delivery. When subtracted from the highest reference price

FIGURE 5-15   Mass Customization for On-Line Printer Purchase

Product Performance – Menu	
Print Quality	**Prices**
Home Use	$50
Business	$100
Professional	$250

Print Quality	**Prices**
2 pages per minute	$50
4 pages per minute	$100
>4 pages per minute	$150

Warranty	**Prices**
90 days	Free
1 year	$50
2 years	$100

Technical Service	**Prices**
Online	Free
800 Hotline	$50
On-Site Service	$200

Delivery	**Prices**
1 Week	$10
3 – 4 Days	$25
Next Day	$50

Purchasing Instructions

Purchasing Your Printer

Build your own printer based on preferred features and your spending budget.

1. For each five performance features select your preferred level of performance and enter it in the Printer Purchase Table below.

2. The total cost is computed based on the price of the preferred features selected.

3. If you want to modify your purchase, just make the needed changes under Preferred Features and a new total cost will be computed.

4. When satisfied with your printer purchase click on send.

SEND	Submit printer purchase as specified

Performance Feature	Preferred Features	Price
Print Quality	Business	$100
Print Speed	>4 pages	$150
Warranty	90 days	$0
Technical Service	800 Hotline	$50
Delivery	1 Week	$10
Total Cost		**$310**

($750) this is a $440 savings. When compared to the lowest possible price ($110), the $310 printer is $200 more than the price of the most basic printer with limited warranty and delivery and the lowest price.

The use of mass customization allows customers to create their own segments. This is good for the customer as well as the business, because even the same customer may shift buying needs based on a changing situation. Assume in the example above that the customer was replacing a printer that just broke down and needed to use the printer the next day. In this situation the customer would probably pay $350 for the same printer.

Or assume a small business customer just took on some new clients with higher quality expectations. That could result in shifting to a professional-quality printer and two-year warranty with the same print speed (greater than four pages per minute) and same technical support (800 Hotline). This would result in a price of $560 with a one-week delivery. The whole point of mass customization is to let the customer "*build their product*" according to their individual needs and price sensitivity. Mass customization combines the advantages of a niche segment strategy with the breadth of opportunity available with multisegment marketing strategies.

CUSTOMER RELATIONSHIP MANAGEMENT

A logical extension of market segmentation and mass customization is **Customer Relationship Management (CRM)**. A business using market segmentation strives to build programs around a group of target customers in an effort to satisfy and retain them. The ultimate goal of a customer-relationship focus is to build individual relationships between a business and individual customers. Customer Relationship Management is also referred to as *One-On-One Marketing*.[14]

While many businesses work hard to get new customers, this is where the customer relationship often stops. By contrast, CRM is more focused on what happens after the transaction where real profits are made through customer loyalty and repeat purchases as described below.[15]

> "Much of the time, the opening of a new customer account is simply an opportunity to lose money. Most single-account households are unprofitable. We have to build a relationship to make a profit. If we can build a relationship, then we can keep customers through relationship building—not pushing products. They will reward us by buying more, buying profitably, and keeping more of their money with us"
>
> —TERRI DIAL, CEO, WELLS FARGO

While advances in telecommunications and the Internet have enhanced our ability to connect with customers, in today's world the customer experience is often made worse with electronic messaging, online service, and self-help menus built into products. Just when customers really need to connect with the company they buy from, they are passed off to an endless stream of voice messages or directed to an online service program that is even more confusing.

The rapid growth of CRM technologies designed to support customer relationship management has lured many businesses down the wrong road to where technology is seen as the solution instead of a tool. Without a solid grounding in the function and process of building customer relationships, these businesses fall into a *technology trap*. Many millions of dollars have been wasted implementing technological solutions without first building a customer relationship program.

Building a Customer Relationship Management Program

The first step in building an effective customer relationship management program is market segmentation and a complete understanding of customer needs. Without an adequate understanding of customer needs, usage behaviors, and customer profitability, a business is likely to fail in building customer relationships and delivering solutions that meet customer needs and that are profitable.[16] While technology can help facilitate the process, a successful CRM program starts with market segmentation (Step I) as outlined in the following:

STEP I   **Market Segmentation**—Understanding customer needs, behaviors, and profitability

STEP II   **Customer Identification**—Individual customer identification

STEP III **Customized Solution**—Deliver a value based on individual needs

STEP IV **Customer Interaction**—Build cost-efficient and effective ongoing customer interaction

STEP V   **Customer Loyalty**—Track customer satisfaction, commitment, and profitability

Step II requires customer identification. This is similar to step 2 (segment identification) in needs-based segmentation, but even more demanding. Each customer needs to be identified individually and must be accessible so that a One-On-One Marketing program for that customer may be built. Step II requires that a business identify individual customer needs that require individual solutions that add value to the customer. Customer interaction without adding value will ultimately fail as customers are vulnerable to competitors' efforts to win them away from the business.

For example, Marriott International treats the business traveler as a separate needs-based segment (Step I). To build Customer Identification and link it to individual needs (Step II) Marriott maintains an individual customer profile based on customer requests and stored preferences from past visits when a business customer calls to make a reservation at Marriott. Based on individual customer needs, tee times are scheduled, dinner reservations arranged, and recreation itineraries are created based on individual preferences (Step III).

With an individualized solution in place, Step IV requires a cost-efficient and effective way to maintain ongoing interaction with customers. This step is critical, because the ongoing interaction is the key source of information feeding a continuous process of refining the customized solution. From the beginning, every interaction with target customers is a *Customer Touch Point*—an opportunity to build customer relationships one by one. Customer Touch Points also include voice mail systems, direct mail advertising, storefronts, websites, mass E-mail messages, order desks, return counters, and service calls. At every point of contact—before, during, and after a sale—the way a business communicates shapes its relationships with customers and potential customers. The way a business manages its customer relationships determines the potential profitability of those customers in the long run.

Marriott maintains individual contact with customers to measure all aspects of the customer experience. This level of customer interaction (Step IV) facilitates the process of building customer loyalty (Step V). Step V in the CRM program involves tracking customer satisfaction, loyalty, and profitability for each individual customer identified for customer relationship management. For Marriott, high customer-satisfaction scores have translated into higher levels of repeat business and customer loyalty. Marriott has learned that customers who participate in their Personal Planning Service (a one-on-one marketing program) produce significantly higher customer-satisfaction scores and spend an average of $100 per day *more* on services beyond the room rate. This higher revenue per customer and higher levels of loyalty has translated into a hotel occupancy rate ten percentage points higher than the industry average.

Summary

At the heart of market-based management is a skillful execution of market segmentation. It is the core of a market-based strategy because it is built around customer needs, unique lifestyles, and usage behaviors. To the degree to which a business understands differences in customer needs, it can translate them into actionable segment strategies.

A specific segmentation process was presented with special emphasis on creating needs-based segments. Although it may be easy to create segments on the basis of differences in demographics or behavior, doing so may lead to a marketing strategy that does not deliver a needs-based customer solution. However, needs-based segments need to be demographically identified so that actionable strategies can be created for each segment. These first two steps are crucial.

The next steps in the segmentation process require that we index overall segment attractiveness and estimate segment profit potential to select target segments. A value proposition and marketing mix strategy must be developed for each target segment selected. To ensure that we have accurately translated target customer needs and identity characteristics into our positioning strategy (value proposition and marketing mix), a segment acid test is carried out. This enables a business to determine if customers are adequately attracted to the combination of a target segment value proposition and segment strategy designed for them. On the basis of customer feedback, a revised strategy can be finalized and implemented.

In some instances, resources may be limited and only a single segment or niche (subsegment) within a segment may be pursued. In other instances, a multisegment strategy may fit the resources and capabilities of a business. Of course, the more segment strategies a business has, the more difficulty it encounters in maintaining a distinct marketing strategy for each segment. With the use of database marketing, a business can actually take either a segment strategy or a multisegment strategy one step further with mass customization. With mass customization, a business is able to further customize its value proposition and segment positioning through customized product positioning and communications. Mass customization enables a large business to obtain the advantages of a niche marketer while also serving many segments and niches within segments.

A logical extension of mass customization is Customer Relationship Management. The ultimate goal of customer relationship management is an individual relationship between a business and individual customers. Because not all customers can be served by Customer Relationship Management, a critical first step is market segmentation. Once target customers are profiled, customized solutions can be built through individual Customer Touch Points in an effort to satisfy and retain target customers.

Market-Based Logic and Strategic Thinking

1. How did market segmentation help The Gap in its marketing strategy?
2. Why should customer needs be the driving force in segmenting a market?
3. What kind of problems can occur if a business segments a market on the basis of demographics or usage?
4. How are customer needs shaped, and what role do these forces play in the segmentation process?
5. What happens when a business is able to segment a market on the basis of needs but unable to demographically or behaviorally identify the segments?

6. How does firmographics help shape business-to-business customer needs?
7. What forces shape market attractiveness, and how should they be measured in order to develop an overall index of market attractiveness?
8. What criteria should be used in determining which segments a business should pursue?
9. What is a segment value proposition? Why is it a crucial part of the segmentation process?
10. How would you develop a value proposition for a retail gasoline business's target customers?
11. What is a segment marketing mix strategy? How did the marketing mix strategy differ for each of the three segments of the female investor services market?
12. What is an "acid test"? What are the advantages of performing an acid test?
13. How did DuPont create an effective multisegment strategy for Kevlar?
14. What is an adjacent segment strategy? Why would a business pursue an adjacent segment strategy when more than one segment of the market is attractive and offers good profit potential?
15. When would a business pursue a single segment market strategy?
16. Why is a niche strategy often difficult for competitors to outperform?
17. What is mass customization? How could a business using a mass customization strategy match the effectiveness of smaller niche competitors?
18. What is Customer Relationship Management? Why should it improve customer satisfaction and retention?
19. Why is market segmentation a critical first step in building a Customer Relationship Program?
20. What are "Customer Touch Points" and what role do they play in Customer Relationship Management?

APPLICATION PROBLEM: US FIBER SIDING

US Fiber Siding manufactures a fiber cement product that is used in siding houses and commercial buildings. Fiber cement is a composite of fiber and cement that is resistant to fire, rot, and termites. It is durable and will last over 50 years. It is aesthetically attractive and is a growing segment of the siding market. At 13 percent it is second to vinyl siding (40 percent) and well ahead of hardboard (9 percent) and brick (8 percent).

COMPANY PERFORMANCE

US Fiber Siding is the market leader in the fiber cement market with a 70 percent market share. Their sales in 2002 were over $1 billion with profits before taxes of $129 million as shown below.

Performance (millions)	2002	2001	2000
Volume	1.96	1.7	1.45
Average Price	$550	$525	$500
Sales Revenues	$1,078	$893	$725
Cost per Unit	$385	$368	$350
Cost of Goods Sold	$755	$625	$508
Gross Profit	$323	$268	$218
Marketing & Sales Expense	$129	$107	$87
Other Operating Expense	$65	$54	$44
Operating Income (before taxes)	$129	$107	$87

These results evolved with a mass market penetration pricing strategy. This marketing strategy has worked well and has allowed US Fiber Siding to penetrate the market and achieve a dominate share position. However, market research shows that many customers would have payed more for the benefits provided by fiber cement siding.

MARKET RESEARCH SEGMENTATION

A market research study commissioned by US Fiber Siding uncovered three distinct needs-based segments as shown and described below:

- **"Total Quality" Segment:** This segment (10 percent of current customers) wants total quality and is not price sensitive. These customers want all the benefits of fiber cement but are sensitive to appearance and will pay more to get a high quality appearance. These customers have higher income and buy expensive homes. They are heavily influenced by

Segment Profiles

US Fiber Siding Customer Profile	Total Quality	No Problems	Price Buyer
Core Need	Quality	Safety	Cost
Benefits	Long Life	Long Life	Long Life
	Appearance	No Problems	Installation Cost
Demographics	High Income	Average Income	Low Income
	Expensive Homes	Track Homes	Multifamily
	Custom Homes	Remodels	Commercial
Price Point (*)	$2.50/sq ft	$1.00/sq ft	$.50/sq ft
Channel Influencer	Architect	Contractor	Wholesaler
Media—Print	Architecture	Sunset	Contractor
	Digest	Magazine	Magazines
Media—Television	Important	Important	Not Needed

(*) Maximum price at which segment volume can be obtained

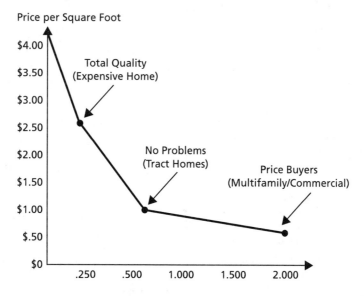

Continued

architects and read upscale home building magazines. They would buy a total quality fiber cement product at $2.50 per square foot.

- **"No Problems" Segment:** These customers (30 percent of annual customer demand) want no problems and a long life. Customers in this segment have average incomes and buy average price homes. They are influenced by articles and ads in magazines such as *Sunset*. A "no problems solution" comes before price in this segment which will pay up to $1.00 per square foot.

- **"Price Buyer" Segment:** These customers are contractors building multi-family apartment and commercial buildings. They are sensitive to cost of materials and the cost of installation. While they are attracted to the core benefits of fiber cement siding, the total cost of installation is a driving need. These customers will buy at wholesale prices and pay up to $.50 per square foot. This segment is price sensitive, makes up roughly 60 percent of current customers, and is attracted to fiber cement siding at $2.50 per square foot.

Segment Strategy

- **"Total Quality" Segment**—A pre-painted, pre-drilled product with a fifty year warranty addresses the total quality needs of this segment. Higher marketing and sales expenses are needed to contact architects and develop ad copy for this segment. The product will be called Cape Cod Siding. The price, volume, unit cost, and marketing expenses (as percent of sales) are shown below.

- **"No Problems" Segment**—The current product will be repositioned for this segment stressing no problems (fire, rot, and termites) as well as long life. This will be supported with a forty year warranty and sold at $1.00 per square foot. Advertising and point of purchase retail displays raise the marketing and sales expenses to 15 percent of sales.

- **"Price Buyer" Segment**—A new product, Fast-Track Siding, will be easier to use and install. At a price of $.50 per square foot this fiber cement product is more expensive than vinyl but a lower installation cost makes it more cost competitive. Marketing and sales expenses are planned at 8 percent of sales.

US Fiber Siding Performance (millions)	Total Quality	Security Seekers	Cost Conscious
Volume	210	640	1100
Average Price (*)	$2.50	$1.00	$0.50
Unit Cost	$1.50	$0.70	$0.40
Marketing & Sales (% sales)	20%	15%	8%

(*) Price at which segment volume can be obtained

Questions

For access to interactive software to answer the questions below go to ww.RogerJBest.com or www.prenhall.com/best.

1. Using the interactive software estimate the sales impact of the proposed segment strategy and contrast it with the current mass-market strategy.

2. Compute the gross profit for each segment and compare the overall gross profit of the segment strategy to the mass-market strategy.

3. Estimate the net marketing contribution for each segment and the overall net marketing contribution for the segment strategy and mass-market strategy.

4. Estimate operating income (assuming operating expense remains at 6% of sales) for each segment and compare the overall operating income of the segment strategy to the mass-market strategy.

Notes

1. Wendell Smith, "Product Differentiation and Market Segmentation As Alternative Marketing Strategies," *Marketing Management* (Winter 1995):63–65.
2. Delbert Hawkins, Roger Best, and Kenneth Coney, *Consumer Behavior: Implications for Marketing Strategy*, 6th ed. (New York: Irwin, 1995):4–25.
3. Marshall Greenberg and Susan McDonald Schwartz, "Successful Needs/Benefits Segmentation: A User's Guide," *Journal of Consumer Marketing* (Summer 1989):29–36.
4. "Merrill Lynch Campaign Targeted at Women Stresses Investment Options," *Marketing News* (November 30, 1979):11.
5. Sachin Gupta and Pradeep Chintagunta, "On Using Demographic Variables to Determine Segment Membership in Logit Mixture Models," *Journal of Marketing Research* (February 1994):128.
6. Michael Lanning, *Delivering Profitable Value* (Reading, MA: Perseus Books, 1998):39–88.
7. William Band, "Customer-Accelerated Change," *Marketing Management* (Winter 1995):19–33.
8. P. Dickson and J. Ginter, "Market Segmentation, Product Differentiation, and Marketing Strategy," *Journal of Marketing* (April 1987):1–10.
9. G. Coles and J. Culley, "Not All Prospects Are Created Equal," *Business Marketing* (May 1986):52–59.
10. Allanna Sullivan, "Mobil Bets Drivers Pick Cappuccino Over Parties," *Wall Street Journal* (January 30, 1995).
11. Dennis Gensch, "Targeting the Switchable Industrial Customer," *Marketing Science* (Winter 1984):41–54.
12. J. Levine, "Cool!" *Forbes* (April 1996):98.
13. Stan Rapp and Tom Collins, *MaxiMarketing* (New York: McGraw-Hill, 1987); Jonathan Berry, "Database Marketing—A Potent New Tool for Selling," *Business Week* (September 5, 1995):56; Robert Buzzell and Rajendra Sisoda, "Information Technology and Marketing," in *Companion Encyclopedia of Marketing*, ed. Michael Baker (Los Angeles: Rutledge, 1995).
14. Don Peppers and Martha Rogers, *The One-On-One Future: Building Relationships One Customer at a Time* (Doubleday, 1997).
15. Melinda Nykamp, *The Customer Differential* (New York, Amacom, 2001):11.
16. Don Peppers and Martha Rogers, *One to One B2B: Customer Development Strategies for the Business to Business World* (Doubleday, 2001).

CHAPTER

6 | COMPETITOR ANALYSIS AND SOURCES OF ADVANTAGE

Google has quickly become the preferred search engine for the Internet. By 2002 Google.com became the market leader in Internet web search with a search share more than twice that of its closest competitor as illustrated in Figure 6-1. While this has resulted in sales growth, even more impressive is Google's profitability. Google's $70 million in sales produced an estimated $15 million in profits. This is three times the profits of eBay for its first three years as an online business. To better understand Google's market and financial performance, we need to understand its sources of competitive advantage as summarized below:

- **Differentiation**—A product differentiation is built around superior technology that provided customers with greater speed, accuracy and ease of use. As important is the sustainability of this advantage that is based on a knowledge advantage. More than 50 of Google's 400 employees have Ph.Ds and are encouraged to come up with new innovative solutions.
- **Marketing**—High awareness, high customer loyalty and superior market reach (10,000 servers do 1800 searches a second in 72 languages in 32 countries) along with innovative advertising programs provide important marketing benefits to advertisers.
- **Cost**—To maintain a lower cost Google builds its own computers with commodity hardware and builds them in a way that eighty servers can be used in the same space that normally accommodates ten servers. Google servers also run the free Linux operating system instead of expensive systems offered by Microsoft and Sun.

COMPETITION AND COMPETITIVE POSITION

While Google's success is impressive, it is often difficult to hold a competitive advantage due to changing competition. When one thinks about General Motors, NBC, or IBM, one does not have to go back too far in time to see how the competitive position of each of these market leaders has changed. For General Motors, it was foreign competition that eroded its competitive position, first with lower prices, and then with higher levels of product quality. For NBC, CBS, and ABC, it was first ESPN, CNN, and Fox and then a multitude of cable networks and the Internet. And for IBM, DEC, and others, it was Compaq, Dell, Toshiba, and a flood of new competitors. These competitors could buy the basic hardware and software for a computer and assemble and market it at lower prices.

138

FIGURE 6-1 Sources of Competitive Advantage for Google

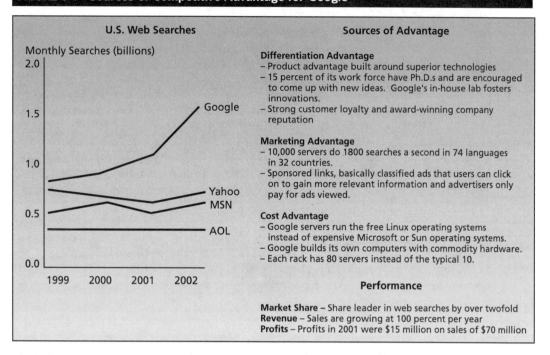

U.S. Web Searches

Monthly Searches (billions)

- Google
- Yahoo
- MSN
- AOL

1999   2000   2001   2002

Sources of Advantage

Differentiation Advantage
– Product advantage built around superior technologies
– 15 percent of its work force have Ph.D.s and are encouraged to come up with new ideas. Google's in-house lab fosters innovations.
– Strong customer loyalty and award-winning company reputation

Marketing Advantage
– 10,000 servers do 1800 searches a second in 74 languages in 32 countries.
– Sponsored links, basically classified ads that users can click on to gain more relevant information and advertisers only pay for ads viewed.

Cost Advantage
– Google servers run the free Linux operating systems instead of expensive Microsoft or Sun operating systems.
– Google builds its own computers with commodity hardware.
– Each rack has 80 servers instead of the typical 10.

Performance

Market Share – Share leader in web searches by over twofold
Revenue – Sales are growing at 100 percent per year
Profits – Profits in 2001 were $15 million on sales of $70 million

In each case, the market leader once held a strong, almost impenetrable competitive position. And, in each case, new competitive forces emerged and the competitive position of the market leader was seriously eroded. It is important to recognize that in each example, the market leader had not lowered quality, raised prices, or cut back on marketing efforts. On the contrary, each had made serious efforts to improve products, reduce prices, and expand marketing efforts to retain customers. However, in each case, the competitive forces brought to bear on its market first challenged, and then eroded, the market leader's competitive position.

There are three important aspects of competition that affect a business's competitive position and profitability, as outlined in Figure 6-2. The first, *industry forces,* has to do with the competitive forces within an industry. These competitive forces shape a market's attractiveness and profit potential. An important step in market analysis is an industry analysis of markets in order to select those markets that offer the best profit potential.

Second, within an industry or market, it is important for a business to benchmark its *competitive position.* External market measures of *relative* product quality, service quality, customer satisfaction, brand awareness, and market share are crucial market metrics that benchmark the strength of a business's competitive position. Internal metrics such as unit cost, order cycle time, delivery costs, accounts receivable, and sales per employee are equally important in benchmarking and managing competitiveness. However, to improve on an important competitive weakness, a business needs to benchmark world-class performance outside its industry in order to gain a competitive advantage.

Finally, to achieve a superior level of profitability, a business needs to attain a source of sustainable *competitive advantage.* This could be a cost advantage that yields

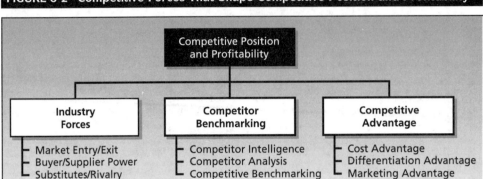

FIGURE 6-2   Competitive Forces That Shape Competitive Position and Profitability

more attractive prices, a quality advantage that enhances product preference or price premiums, or a marketing advantage that achieves greater customer awareness and availability. The purpose of this chapter is to examine each of these areas of competition and how they are used in the development of market-based strategies.

INDUSTRY ANALYSIS

A first step in industry analysis is to determine the attractiveness of the competitive environment. Developing a strong competitive position in an unattractive market has the potential to lessen profitability even when a business's competitive position in that industry is relatively strong.[1] Picking the right markets (industries) in which to compete is a crucial step in market analysis and strategy development.

Shown in Figure 6-3 are industry forces that shape the attractiveness of a competitive environment. Each of these industry forces can be evaluated along a continuum from unfavorable to favorable. As the sum of these forces favors a more attractive competitive environment, there is greater profit potential. A business in a market with low entry barriers, high exit barriers, high levels of customer and supplier power, many substitutes, and intense rivalry among competitors will have a lower profit potential than a business with a more favorable set of competitive forces.

Barriers to Entry

Market entry can be blocked in many ways. Many international markets are blocked by political barriers. These barriers reduce competition and enhance profit potential for protected competitors. Technology or low-cost manufacturing can also create entry barriers. Businesses with a superior cost or technological advantage create a market entry barrier that discourages competitors from entering a market. In addition, the resources needed to compete in a given market could be so great that entry is limited. High advertising expenditures, R&D spending, and sales force expenditures can each require resource levels that can block market entry for businesses with limited resources. For example, barriers to entry in the pharmaceutical industry are relatively high. Patents on prescription drugs, high R&D investments, and large sales forces

FIGURE 6-3   Industry Analysis: Industry Forces and Profit Potential

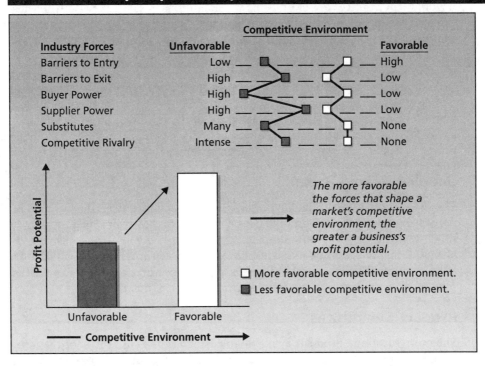

needed to contact physicians deter competitor entry and contribute to the attractiveness of this competitive environment.

Barriers to Exit

The competitive environment is also enhanced when weak competitors can easily exit a market. Legal barriers, specialized assets, or the strategic importance of a business often prevent businesses from exiting markets when they should. A pharmaceutical company that is losing money on a particular prescription drug may want to exit, but legal, political, or social forces could create an environment in which market exit would be very difficult. The struggle to survive can lead to competitive practices that adversely affect industry profits.

Likewise, a business that has invested in specialized assets (capital or people or both) may find it difficult to exit a market because these assets are not easily sold or transferred to another business application. Businesses that have specialized in nuclear fuel reprocessing may find market exit difficult because of their specialized assets. Finally, a business that is dependent on products that are strategically important to its image or ability to market other products may not exit a market even though it is producing less-than-desired levels of profitability.

Customer Buying Power

When relatively few customers buy in large quantities, and can easily switch suppliers, there is considerable customer buying power, which lowers market attractiveness.

Large, concentrated groups of customers possess a buying power that enables them to negotiate lower prices or better terms and conditions of sale. Likewise, when customers can easily switch from one supplier to another, they force increased competition, which can lower prices as well as raise the cost of serving customers. In addition, when the purchased product or service is of limited importance to the customer, supplier dependence is much lower.

For the pharmaceutical industry, customer buying power is relatively low. Many well-known prescription drugs, such as Prozac, have many individual customers to whom the product is extremely important and who have limited opportunities to switch. As a result, the pharmaceutical industry has relatively low customer buying power, which enhances the competitive environment and profit potential.[2]

Supplier Selling Power

The flip side of customer buying power is supplier selling power. If a business is a large purchaser of a commodity product (less important to the buyer) and is in an industry in which switching costs are low, supplier power is generally low. For a business, this is an attractive market situation that contributes to industry attractiveness and profit potential. For many pharmaceutical businesses, supplier power is relatively low for these reasons, which contributes to the overall attractiveness of the industry.

Product Substitutes

The more substitute products available to customers, the easier it is for them to switch. Ease of switching intensifies competition and lowers profit potential and industry attractiveness. For example, in the soft drink industry, there are many product substitutes, so premium pricing is impossible. However, if the market definition is broadened to include non–soft drink substitutes, such as mineral water, fruit drinks, fruit juices, and sports drinks, one can begin to understand the enormous pressure this level of choice brings to bear on competitors serving these markets. It is important to have a broad market definition as presented in Chapter 3 in order to understand the full impact of substitutes in evaluating industry attractiveness. For example, in the pharmaceutical industry, there are fewer substitutes than in the beverage or automobile industry.

Competitive Rivalry

The more competitors in an industry, the lower the differentiation between competitors, and the larger the excess industry capacity, the more likely the industry will engage in intense competitive rivalry. More intense competitor rivalry tends to lower prices and margins and raise marketing expenses in the battle to attract and retain customers. The net effect is a less attractive competitive environment in which the profit potential is lower.

The personal computer industry is an industry that is becoming increasingly more competitive due to price rivalry. The market has attracted many competitors with considerable capacity. In addition, product differentiation among personal computer products has become minimal. These factors, along with slower market growth, have intensified competition. By contrast, the pharmaceutical industry has fewer competitors for specific drugs, and product differentiation is much greater. As a result, the pharmaceutical industry is less likely to engage in intense competitive rivalry.

| Business's Marketing | Competitor's Marketing Strategy | |
Strategy	Hold Price	Cut Price 5%
Hold Price	Market Share = 10% Volume = 1 million units Price = $100 per unit Margin = $40 per unit Total Contribution = $40 million	Market Share = 8% Volume = 800,000 units Price = $100 per unit Margin = $40 per unit Total Contribution = $32 million
Cut Price 5%	Market Share = 12% Volume = 1.2 million units Price = $95 per unit Margin = $35 per unit Total Contribution = $42 million	Market Share = 10% Volume = 1 million units Price = $95 per unit Margin = $35 per unit Total Contribution = $35 million

FIGURE 6-4 Performance Impact of Price Rivalry and Prisoner's Dilemma

Prisoner's Dilemma

Intense competitive rivalry can evolve into what is known as a *prisoner's dilemma*.[3] In such situations, downward price moves by one competitor force "follower moves" by other competitors in order to minimize lost profits. Actually, all competitors would be better off if none cut prices to begin with.

Consider the example presented in Figure 6-4. The current scenario with both the business and its competitor holding price yields a total contribution (margin per unit multiplied by unit volume) of $40 million. If the competitor cuts price by 5 percent and the business holds price, the business will lose two share points and $8 million in total contribution. Of course, if the business were to lead with a price cut against a competitor who did not follow, the business could gain two share points and $2 million in total contribution. The worst effect of the prisoner's dilemma occurs when one competitor cuts price and the other matches that price in order to minimize losses. As shown in Figure 6-4, this combination results in no share gain or loss and a total contribution $5 million lower than when the two competitors both held at the higher price.

COMPETITIVE POSITION

Although selecting competitive environments that favor profit potential is an important aspect of competitive analysis, it has been shown that it is equally important for businesses to develop a strong competitive position in the markets in which they compete.[4] To understand the degree to which a business has a position of competitive advantage, we need to engage in a detailed analysis of competitors. An important question is "Which competitors should a business analyze?" We want to maintain a very broad market definition to include all meaningful competing substitutes, but, at the same time, a business cannot engage in a detailed analysis of every competitor.[5] Thus, we need a mechanism to help us identify a relevant competitor set that will help us prioritize which competitors to analyze and benchmark.

Benchmark Competitors

There is a variety of ways to identify a business's competitors. Perhaps the best is to have customers evaluate the degree to which they consider competitors as interchangeable substitutes. The closer customers perceive two competitors to be, the more likely they are to switch from one to the other. Likewise, the more dissimilar customers perceive any pair of competitors to be, the less likely they are to switch from one to the other. In addition, customers can rate each competitor on the basis of how far that competitor is from their ideal product or supplier. From these customer perceptions we can create a *perceptual map,* which is very useful in gaining a better understanding of both competitive position and key competitors to benchmark.

Perceptual mapping is a technique used to capture customer perceptions of competing products or services.[6] Without specifying criteria for evaluating differences between competing products, customers are simply asked to rate the degree to which they perceive each pair of competitors to be *different* from one another. For example, in the luxury car market, the Volvo 700, Mercedes 420, BMW 525, Lincoln Towncar, Buick Regal, and Honda Prelude are competing substitutes. As shown in Figure 6-5, the Volvo 700 and BMW 525 were rated very close in *perceived similarity,* whereas the Lincoln Towncar and Honda Prelude were rated as very dissimilar.

By asking customers to also rate each car shown with respect to how close it is to their *ideal* car, we can gain a better understanding of competitive position and key competitors. In the example presented in Figure 6-5, the customer ratings of the cars shown relative to the ideal car produced two different segments. There were two different sets of customer needs and product preferences operating in this sample market. The ideal car for segment A is almost equidistant from the Honda Prelude, Buick Regal, BMW 525, and Volvo 700. Thus, these four competitors would be the most likely choices for customers in segment A. If you were on the marketing team for Buick Regal, you should view Honda, Volvo, and BMW as your key competitors in serving segment A, even though Mercedes and the Lincoln Towncar are equally close to the Buick Regal. However, if Buick Regal were more interested in serving segment B, then Lincoln Towncar and Mercedes would be their competitors to benchmark.

A variety of multidimensional scaling programs can be used to create a perceptual map,[7] such as the one shown in Figure 6-5. In this example, a graphical representation of interbrand differentiation was created in two dimensions.[8] In most applications, over 90 percent of competitor differentiation can be captured in two dimensions. With a perceptual map of competition, a business can easily discern two things: (1) which competitors it will compete against in a particular market segment and (2) its competitive position relative to these competitors in attracting and satisfying customers in this segment. However, to improve or maintain a position relative to competitors and the customer's ideal car, a business must also know on what basis target customers are differentiating competing products.

Competitor Analysis

Once a business has identified which competitors it should benchmark, the business now has to engage in a more detailed analysis of these competitors. A competitor analysis such as this is difficult to conduct and something a business may do only periodically.

FIGURE 6-5 Customer Perceptions of Interbrand Differentiation

Competing Alternatives	←				Degree of Perceived Differentiation					→
	Very Similar								Very Different		
Mercedes–Volvo	0	1	2	3	4	5	(6)	7	8	9	10
Mercedes–Towncar	0	1	(2)	3	4	5	6	7	8	9	10
Mercedes–Prelude	0	1	2	3	4	5	6	7	8	(9)	10
Mercedes–Buick	0	1	2	3	4	5	(6)	7	8	9	10
Mercedes–BMW	0	1	2	(3)	4	5	6	7	8	9	10
Mercedes–Ideal A	0	1	2	3	4	5	(6)	7	8	9	10
Mercedes–Ideal B	0	1	(2)	3	4	5	6	7	8	9	10
Volvo–Towncar	0	1	2	3	4	5	6	(7)	8	9	10
Volvo–BMW	0	1	2	(3)	4	5	6	7	8	9	10
Volvo–Buick	0	1	2	3	(4)	5	6	7	8	9	10
Volvo–Prelude	0	1	2	3	4	(5)	6	7	8	9	10
Volvo–Ideal A	0	1	(2)	3	4	5	6	7	8	9	10
Volvo–Ideal B	0	1	2	3	4	(5)	6	7	8	9	10
Towncar–Prelude	0	1	2	3	4	5	6	7	8	9	(10)
Towncar–BMW	0	1	2	3	(4)	5	6	7	8	9	10
Towncar–Buick	0	1	2	3	4	5	(6)	7	8	9	10
Towncar–Ideal A	0	1	2	3	4	5	6	7	(8)	9	10
Towncar–Ideal B	0	1	(2)	3	4	5	6	7	8	9	10
BMW–Prelude	0	1	2	3	4	5	6	7	(8)	9	10
BMW–Buick	0	1	2	3	4	(5)	6	7	8	9	10
BMW–Ideal A	0	1	2	3	4	(5)	6	7	8	9	10
BMW–Ideal B	0	1	2	(3)	4	5	6	7	8	9	10
Buick–Prelude	0	1	2	3	4	(5)	6	7	8	9	10
Buick–Ideal A	0	1	(2)	3	4	5	6	7	8	9	10
Buick–Ideal B	0	1	2	3	(4)	5	6	7	8	9	10
Prelude–Ideal A	0	1	2	3	(4)	5	6	7	8	9	10
Prelude–Ideal B	0	1	2	3	4	5	6	7	8	(9)	10

Perceptual Map

Dimension II

+10

• Volvo 700

• Honda Prelude

• BMW 525

Ideal Car Segment A

−10   • Buick Regal   0   • Mercedes   +10   Dimension I

Ideal Car Segment B

• Lincoln Towncar

−10

145

FIGURE 6-6   A Competitor Information Search

Outlined below are the questions posed and the sources of information from which competitive intelligence was gathered in one hour by a research expert.

1. How big is the circuit board market served by Merix, and what is its current market share?

The *Market Share Reporter* gives market size and share of hundreds of sectors in the economy, but Merix did not appear. *Predicast* provides market sizes and reference to *SMT Trends* (a trade journal) that reports the market share statistics of the top 10 circuit board producers, but not Merix. However, the *CorpTech Dictionary of Technology Companies* turned out to be the mother lode. It gives Merix's SIC (standard industrial classification) and lists other companies in that sector. From this information, an estimate of market size and share was computed.

2. Merix has been dependent on a few large customers. Is it adding to its customer base?

A search of a local newspaper uncovers an article "Merix Wants More Customers." It quotes the company as saying 70 percent of revenues come from its top five customers. Merix's most recent annual report also states that 69.3 percent of revenues come from four customers. In addition, the *SEC Edgar* Web site reports Merix's 10K and states that not much progress has been made in adding new customers to its customer base.

3. Develop a biographical profile of Merix's CEO and her approach to business.

Standard and Poor's *Register of Directors and Executives* provides a short bio on the CEO, Debi Coleman, and her e-mail address. The *Biography and Genealogy Master Index, Dun & Bradstreet Reference Book of Corporate Management, Who's Who,* and *Who's Who of American Women* provide no details. However, *Who's Who* in Finance and Industry provides a detailed resume.

4. Will Merix have a booth at any upcoming trade shows? If so, where and when?

Trade Shows Worldwide and the current editions of *Trade Show and Exhibits Schedule* and *Trade Show Week Data Book* provide the answers needed.

5. Merix hired a new chief operating officer. What biographical information is available?

Predicast reported that a chief operating officer was hired, and *Business Wire* press releases provided a bio on the new COO.

Other sources considered but not used included *Business News Bank* (a CD-ROM database), *Business Index* (another CD-ROM database), *Value Line*, and *Red Chip Review*. Had time permitted, the *Manufacturers Register* (every state has one) and trade magazines would have been used.

However, a market-based business with a strong market orientation is *gathering competitor intelligence all the time* and, as a result, has continuously evolving competitor profiles from which to evaluate its own competitiveness and competitive advantages.[9]

Competitor Intelligence

A great deal of competitive intelligence is public and readily available from dealers, trade press, business press, industry consultants, trade shows, financial reports, industry reports, general press, government documents, and customers.[10] However, unless a business has created a market-based culture in which everyone in the organization is an *information gatherer,* the more valuable and difficult to find sources of competitive intelligence will slip by unnoticed.

In today's growing information age, information on markets and competitors is becoming rapidly more available. For example, the reference librarian at Multnomah County Library in Portland, Oregon, was challenged to see how much competitor intelligence he could gather in one hour. Five questions were posed with respect to the Merix Corporation, a small circuit board manufacturer. Outlined in Figure 6-6 is a summary of

FIGURE 6-7 Competitor Analysis (2001): Dell vs. Benchmark Competitors				
Market-Based Performance	**Dell**	**Compaq**	**Gateway**	**Advantage**
Market Share	14.2%	11.2%	2.0%	Dell
Percent Gross Margin	20.2%	20.6%	13.8%	Compaq
Marketing Budget (% sales)	10.0%	15.9%	33.2%	Dell
New Marketing Contribution (millions)	$3,250	$1,776	($1,184)	Dell
Marketing Productivity	1.02	0.33	–0.59	Dell
Operating Performance				
Return on Sales	6.8%	–2.3%	–17.0%	Dell
Return on Assets	16.1%	–2.6%	–34.0%	Dell
Sales-to-Asset Ratio	2.4	1.4	2.04	Dell
Days of Inventory	4	24	12	Dell
Days Accounts Receivable	32	58	17	Gateway

the competitive information and sources used to answer the questions posed. As shown, all five questions were adequately answered in one hour by a skilled person.[11]

A Sample Competitor Analysis

Dell Computer is the market leader in the personal computer market. Although there are over 100 competitors in this market, it is important that Dell understand its strengths and weaknesses relative to its two largest competitors, Compaq and Gateway. Using publicly available information, Dell can create a competitor analysis that benchmarks its performance against these two competitors.

Shown in Figure 6-7 are five market-based performance metrics and five operating performance metrics for Dell, Compaq and Gateway for 2001. With regard to market-based performance, Dell has a higher market share, higher net marketing contribution, higher marketing productivity with a smaller marketing budget based on percentage of sales. Compaq is only slightly ahead of Dell in percent gross margin. Dell also leads competitors in four of five operating performance metrics and in 2001 was the only one of the three with a positive net income. Dell produces $2.40 per $1 of assets while Gateway has an asset turnover (sales-to-asset ratio) of 2.04 and Compaq 1.4. Compaq's poorer sales-to-asset ratio is in part due to higher levels of inventory and much larger accounts receivable. This difference in operating performance is largely due to a difference in marketing strategies; Dell and Gateway are direct marketers, whereas Compaq relies more heavily on PC resellers to reach target customers.

The level of detail included in a competitor analysis can vary considerably from what is shown in Figure 6-7. In the example shown in Figure 6-8, the competitor analysis is broken down into two categories: *market-based performance* and *operating performance.* And, as shown, each area is further broken down into more specific performance metrics and then measured for the business and a benchmark competitor. In this example, the business has almost one-third of the market share of the benchmark competitor. This competitive gap corresponds closely with similar competitive gaps in number of distributors, number of distributor locations, and sales force coverage. To close its share gap, the business undoubtedly needs to address adverse competitive gaps in distribution and sales coverage.

FIGURE 6-8   Competitor Analysis for an Industrial Business

Dimension of Competitiveness	Business Performance	Competitor Performance	Performance Gap*
Market-Based Performance			
Market Share	6%	17%	11 behind
Relative Price	115	100	15 higher
Relative Product Quality	115	105	10 better
Relative Service Quality	93	113	20 worse
Number of Distributors	87	261	174 fewer
Sales Force (number)	36	60	24 fewer
Advertising & Promotion (% of sales)	0.5%	0.5%	0 equal
Marketing Budget (% of sales)	16.0%	17.0%	1.0 lower
Operating Performance			
Unit Manufacturing (% of sales)	48.0%	50.8%	2.8 lower
Direct Materials (% of sales)	26.0%	17.6%	8.4 higher
Overhead (% of sales)	38.0%	31.0%	7.0 higher
Return on Assets (%)	17.1%	19.5%	2.4 lower
Return on Sales (%)	7.4%	11.1%	3.7 lower
Asset Turnover	2.3	1.6	0.7 higher
Accounts Receivable (days)	46	38	8 higher
Sales per Employee	$1.5 mil	$2.1 mil	0.6 lower

* Performance Gap = Business Performance − Competitor Performance

Overall, the business is behind its benchmark competitor in most aspects of market-based performance. The competitive gaps shown help create performance targets and management incentives to close these gaps. This, of course, is a key input into the development of a successful market-based strategy. From an internal perspective, this business is also poorly positioned in almost all areas of operating performance. Higher overhead costs and accounts receivable and lower return on sales per employee lower profitability and productivity. Each of these gaps may be difficult to close, and competitors are not likely to help. Thus, to successfully close important competitive gaps, a business may have to go outside its industry to find better competitive practices.

Competitive Benchmarking

Sometimes a business needs to go outside its industry to benchmark a business known to be superior in a particular business process. General Mills, for example, uses the same production lines to make a variety of related food products. For example, the same production line used for scalloped potatoes is used for au gratin potatoes. To change over from the production run to another requires as much as twelve hours. While there were on going efforts to reduce downtime during the production changeover, only small incremental improvements could be achieved. Recognizing that NASCAR pit teams have to change equipment during a race with minimum loss of time, General Mills decided to benchmark NASCAR pit teams' process of changing equipment when a race car can off the track for servicing. What they learned allowed them to implement a new process that reduced production change time to as little as twenty minutes.

FIGURE 6-9 Competitive Benchmarking: Xerox Billing Errors	
Competitive Benchmarking	*Xerox: Billing Errors*
1. Identify a key area of competitive weakness	1. Xerox found billing errors were more frequent than those of competitors.
2. Identify a benchmark company.	2. Xerox looked at Citicorp, AT&T, and American Express.
3. Track the benchmark company's process advantage.	3. With the cooperation of American Express, Xerox developed new systems to reduce billing errors.

Competitive benchmarking is a process developed initially at Xerox to improve its competitive position relative to key competitors. The idea is for a business to identify a key area of competitive weakness, such as billing errors in Figure 6-9, and then benchmark a company, *outside* its industry, that is recognized as a *world-class performer* in this area.[12] In this way, a business can hope to gain access to the underlying processes that produce this *best practice* and develop a system that, when successfully implemented, has the potential of being better than that of its key competitors.

The first step in competitive benchmarking is to identify a key area of competitive weakness that affects customer satisfaction or profitability or both. For Xerox, a large number of billing errors was an annoying competitive weakness, as outlined in Figure 6-9. This was a source of considerable customer frustration and hurt overall perceptions of performance and customer satisfaction. The second step was to identify several companies that would be recognized as among the very best in the world in this area of performance. Xerox identified Citicorp, American Express, and AT&T. After talking with these companies, Xerox selected American Express and gained the cooperation of American Express in order to study its billing systems, which had a significantly lower error rate and many more transactions.

Once inside American Express, Xerox could observe the systems and processes that led to a more error-free billing system. This knowledge was transferred into several programs to begin the process of becoming more competitive in this key area of competitive weakness. Performance benchmarks were set in an effort to work toward decreasing billing errors. These efforts took time, but Xerox reached its goal and turned a competitive weakness into a competitive strength. Xerox had a similar success story in competitive benchmarking of order cycle time (the time it takes to deliver the product after the customer places the order), using L.L. Bean as a benchmark company.

SOURCES OF COMPETITIVE ADVANTAGE

As a business begins to more fully grasp its position relative to key competitors, it gains better insight into potential sources of competitive advantage. For a source of relative advantage to be a competitive advantage requires (1) that the area of relative advantage be meaningful to target customers and (2) that the relative advantage be sustainable (not easily copied by competitors).

Wal-Mart, for example, has developed a low-cost advantage that has enabled it to attract and satisfy target customers by offering lower prices. Hewlett-Packard, by contrast, has built a differentiation advantage with product innovation and quality, and Nordstrom has built a differential advantage with service quality. Each attracts and

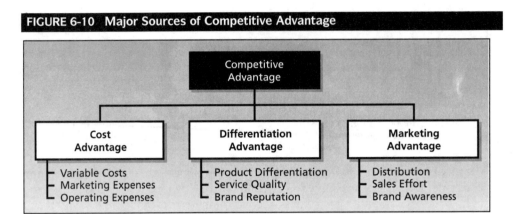

FIGURE 6-10   Major Sources of Competitive Advantage

satisfies customers with differentially superior products or services. Nike, on the other hand, has developed a marketing advantage with creative and aggressive marketing efforts and with retailing that attracts and satisfies target customers.

In each case, the business developed a source of competitive advantage that is meaningful to target customers. It becomes an area they work on each day in order to sustain their level of competitive advantage. While there are potentially many areas of competitive advantage, the three primary areas are described next and in Figure 6-10.

- **Cost Advantage:** A significantly lower cost position from which to create lower prices while still achieving desirable profit margins.
- **Differentiation Advantage:** A meaningful differentiation that creates desired customer benefits at a level superior to competition.
- **Marketing Advantage:** A marketing effort that dominates the competition in sales coverage, distribution, or brand recognition, or some combination of the three.

COST ADVANTAGE

A business can achieve three different types of cost advantage, as outlined in Figure 6-10. It can achieve a lower variable cost per unit sold, a lower level of marketing expenses, or a lower level of operating and overhead expense. Each of these cost advantages is achieved in different ways.

Variable Cost Advantage

Businesses with a lower unit cost are able to achieve the same (or better) unit margin at lower prices than competing businesses. Unit or variable costs include manufacturing costs and variable costs associated with distribution, such as discounts, sales commissions, transportation, and other variable transaction costs. As demonstrated in Figure 6-11, a unit cost advantage relative to competition contributes to higher levels of profitability.

But how does a business achieve a low variable cost advantage? Volume is a key factor. Businesses with a substantial market share (volume) advantage can generally achieve a lower unit cost.[13] As volume increases, the cost per unit generally decreases.

FIGURE 6-11   Profit Impact of a Variable Cost Advantage

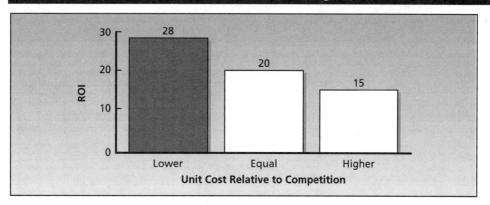

For example, as demonstrated in Figure 6-12, the cost of cellular phone service decreases at the rate of 18 percent every time the volume of customers in a geographic market doubles. Thus, when a cellular business in a given market doubles its customer base from 400,000 to 800,000, the unit cost decreases by 18 percent. In this case, the business that attains the largest customer penetration (volume) achieves a lower unit cost.

FIGURE 6-12   Unit Cost Advantage Due to Volume Advantage

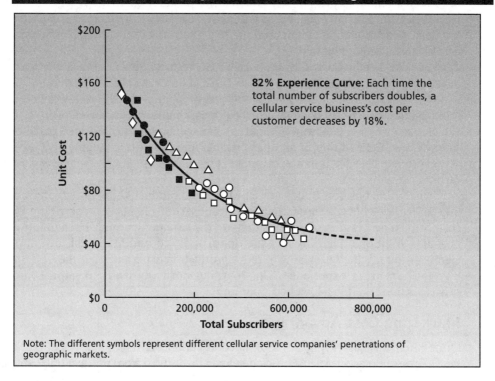

82% Experience Curve: Each time the total number of subscribers doubles, a cellular service business's cost per customer decreases by 18%.

Note: The different symbols represent different cellular service companies' penetrations of geographic markets.

FIGURE 6-13   Ignition Switch Cost Advantage Due to Scale and Scope Effects

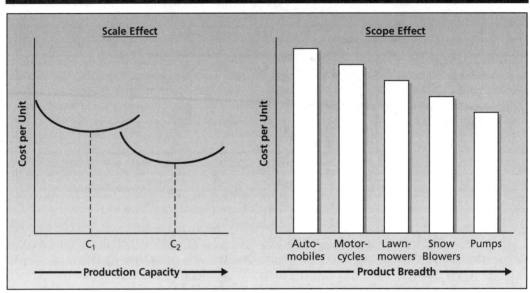

A larger production volume allows for production and purchasing economies that lower the unit cost of a product, thereby creating a *scale effect*. With volume purchases, Wal-Mart has been able to negotiate a lower cost of goods. The same scale effect would occur for a manufacturer who had twice the production capacity. For example, as Honda has moved from one level of production capacity to an increased capacity, there has been some reduction in unit cost due to a scale effect for certain component products, as illustrated in Figure 6-13.

Likewise, as a business adds products to its product line that have similar purchased materials and manufacturing processes, it is able to lower the average unit cost of all products. This is a *scope effect*. For Honda, the cost of ignition switches is lower because the same ignition switch components are used in cars, motorcycles, lawnmowers, all-terrain vehicles, snow blowers, snowmobiles, jet skis, and generators, as illustrated in Figure 6-13. In each case, the addition of another product line provides a volume-cost advantage across product lines for common component parts such as ignition switches, spark plugs, carburetors, and so on.

Finally, as a business builds more of the same product, there is a greater opportunity for *learning effects*. These are nonscale, nonscope effects that contribute to lower cost through process improvements that are the result of learning. Each unit produced provides additional learning and the opportunity to build the next unit more efficiently. Naturally, the business with more production experience has the best opportunity to learn from experience. This learning normally leads to improvements in processes that result in a lower cost per unit.

Marketing Cost Advantage

Quite often, businesses may not look beyond variable costs for sources of cost advantage. However, marketing cost efficiencies can be derived from product line extensions.

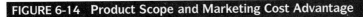

FIGURE 6-14 Product Scope and Marketing Cost Advantage

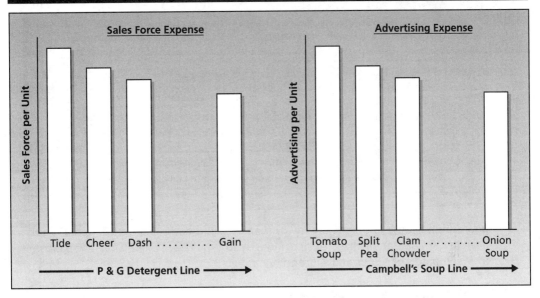

For example, it takes a certain number of salespeople to adequately cover a target market. As the sales force is given more products to sell to the same customers, a *marketing cost scope effect* is created. As illustrated in Figure 6-14, Procter & Gamble sales force expense per pound of soap detergent sold should decrease as more brands of soap detergent are added to its product line. A competitor with far fewer brands would have to have the same sales call frequency to adequately serve retailers and, therefore, would experience a higher cost per pound sold because it had fewer brands to sell.

Another area of marketing cost advantage is derived from the advertising cost efficiency of a brand extension strategy. For example, Campbell's Soup is the banner brand from which a whole line of soup brands has been created. Each time an individual soup is advertised, it is reinforcing top-of-the-mind awareness of Campbell's Soup and each soup in the product line. In this way, the scope effect created by additional soups should lower the advertising dollars spent per ounce of soup sold.

Operating Cost Advantage

Although an operating cost advantage is generally outside the control or influence of the marketing function, lower operating expenses relative to competitors contribute to a low-cost advantage. For example, Wal-Mart achieves an operating expense to sales ratio under 20 percent of sales; many of its competitors' operating expenses are well over 20 percent. This difference gives Wal-Mart another source of cost advantage from which to create greater customer value with lower prices and greater shareholder value with lower operating expenses.

Likewise, McDonald's has been able to cut the cost of construction of new McDonald's restaurants by 50 percent since 1990 by sticking to standardized building designs. Because the building is an asset that needs to be depreciated, this source of

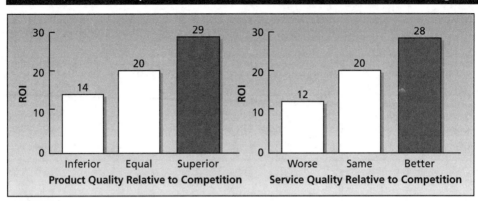

FIGURE 6-15   Profit Impact of a Differentiation Product and Service Advantage

operating expense is drastically lower than it would be if each building had a unique design. Using a standardized design, along with rapid store expansion, has contributed to McDonald's earnings and shareholder value.

DIFFERENTIATION ADVANTAGE

Every business must manage its costs, but not every business can have a cost advantage. To achieve above-average profits, a business needs some source of competitive advantage. A differentiation advantage with respect to product, service, or brand reputation is a potential source of competitive advantage as outlined earlier. However, as do all sources of competitive advantage, a differentiation advantage has to be meaningful to target customers and sustainable (not easily duplicated by competitors).

Product Advantage

There are many aspects of a product around which a business can build a differentiation advantage. A product's durability, reliability, performance, features, appearance, and conformance to a specific application each has the potential of being a differential advantage.[14] For example, the ESCO Corporation is a manufacturer of earth-moving equipment parts that are used in very demanding mining and construction applications. The company has developed a differential advantage in the wearlife of its products due to proprietary steel chemistry and product design. The end result is that its products last longer and are less likely to break than are the products of its competitors. Both of these customer benefits save the customer money even when its products are sold at a higher price. Overall, businesses with a relative advantage in product quality produce higher levels of profitability, as illustrated in Figure 6-15.

Service Advantage

A business can achieve a differentiation service advantage in the same way it can achieve a differential product advantage.[15]The same baseline conditions are required: First, the service advantage has to be meaningful and important to target customers, and second, it has to be sustainable. FedEx tracks its performance each

FIGURE 6-16   Price Impact of Relative Quality and Reputation

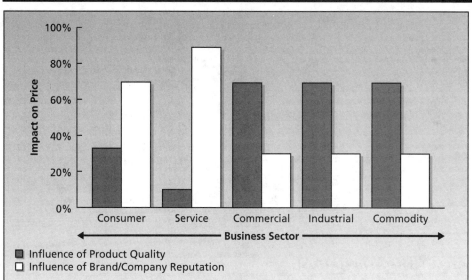

day on ten service quality indicators (each weighed by the customer pain a failure creates). This service quality index is carefully monitored each day to help FedEx maintain a service quality advantage. As its service quality index improves, customer satisfaction improves and the overall cost per package decreases. Thus, on the days that its service quality is at its highest level, FedEx is able to create greater overall customer satisfaction with fewer errors, lower costs, and greater profits for share-holders. As shown in Figure 6-16, businesses with a service quality advantage pro-duce higher levels of profitability.

Reputation Advantage

Another source of differential competitive advantage is brand reputation. Although competing watchmakers may match the quality of a Rolex watch, they cannot easily match Rolex's brand reputation advantage. Products such as Chanel, Nikon, and Perrier have built successful brand reputations that provide a source of competitive advantage in their ability to attract target customers. Their reputation or status adds a dimension of appeal that is an important customer benefit to many less price-sensitive, more image-conscious consumers.

A brand reputation advantage can be measured in the same way as a product or service differential advantage. We find that businesses with an advantage in brand reputation are able to both attract customers and obtain a price premium. As shown in Figure 6-16, the reputation of a consumer product or service can have a bigger impact on price premiums than a product advantage. Even in business-to-business markets, an advantage in brand or company reputation helps to support price and, hence, margins.

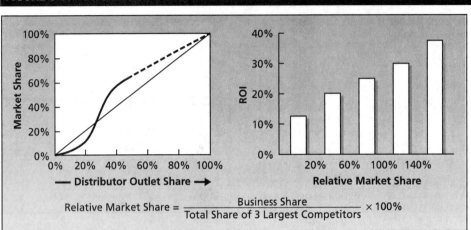

FIGURE 6-17   Distribution Outlet Share vs. Market Share

$$\text{Relative Market Share} = \frac{\text{Business Share}}{\text{Total Share of 3 Largest Competitors}} \times 100\%$$

MARKETING ADVANTAGE

A business that dominates markets with a relative advantage in distribution, sales coverage, or marketing communications can control (and often block) market access. This is also a source of competitive advantage. Whether through sales and distribution or marketing communications, Eastman Kodak, Procter & Gamble, Campbell's Soup, and many others have developed a source of competitive advantage around their marketing expertise.

Channel Advantage

In all markets in which distribution is required for market access, there are a finite number of distributors, whether retailers in consumer markets or dealers in business-to-business markets. Furthermore, there are even fewer top-notch distributors. Therefore, a business that is able to dominate these distributors can control channels in a given market and, to some degree, control market access. This is a source of competitive advantage independent of cost or differential advantage.

Shown in Figure 6-17 is the relationship between distributor share and market share, along with the impact of market share advantage on profitability. What this suggests is that as a business is able to dominate the channels to market, it is able to achieve a higher relative market share. As shown, larger relative shares tend to correspond with greater levels of profitability.[16]

Sales Force Advantage

In both consumer and business-to-business markets, certain levels of sales call frequency and after-sale service are required. Because there is a limit to how many sales calls a salesperson can make in a given time period, a business with more salespeople will simply be able to reach and serve more customers. For example, on the basis of a certain call frequency and purchase behavior in a given industry, assume that the sales per salesperson is $2 million per year. If one business has 100 salespeople, it is able to achieve sales of $200 million. A business with twenty salespeople would achieve an estimated sales level of $40 million, assuming equal sales force capabilities and competitive products in terms of price and quality. Thus, the business with a sales force that is five times larger has a marketing advantage. For the competing business to neutralize this advantage, it would have to increase its sales coverage, assuming no change in price or differentiation advantage.

Brand Awareness

Nike has very good products with attractive prices. But what makes Nike a tough competitor is the level of market awareness and identity it has been able to develop with creative ad copy, pervasive promotion of the Nike swoosh, careful selection of product spokespersons, and heavy advertising. This level of competitive advantage makes it difficult for competitors who may in fact have a better product or lower price with comparable quality. Nike's name, logo recognition, and top-of-the-mind awareness make it easier for Nike to attract customers for existing products and to launch line extensions or entirely new product lines under the Nike name and logo.

This type of competitive advantage, like all others, is relevant only when the communications created are meaningful and important to target customers. To obtain and sustain a marketing communications advantage takes more than advertising dollars. It goes right to the core of market-based management. Who are our customers? What do they want? And how do we communicate our product in a way that best serves their needs?

Summary

Competitive analysis is an important aspect of marketing strategy and market orientation. There are three primary dimensions to competitor analysis: industry forces, competitor benchmarking, and competitive advantage. The first aspect of competitive analysis is an analysis of industry forces. Industry forces such as competitor entry and exit, number of substitutes, buyer and supplier power, and competitive rivalry each affect profit potential. When the collective sum of these forces is favorable, the profit potential is greater. Thus, to obtain the best profit potential, a business needs to assess its industry forces.

Competitor analysis is a way of bringing all these sources of competitiveness together to help understand a business's competitive position in a given market. A complete competitor profile enables a business to better understand its key strengths and weaknesses. Quite often, a business may be overlooking several fundamental weaknesses in its competitive makeup. A competitor gap analysis is intended to expose these major weaknesses.

Often, a competitor analysis will lead to an area of weakness that needs to be further examined and better understood. Competitive benchmarking is a process in which a business identifies a business outside its industry that is known for excellence in a given area. By studying a world-class business, a business can hope to not only improve in its area of weakness but to also improve to the extent it could gain a competitive advantage over its competitors.

There are three primary sources of competitive advantage: cost advantage, differentiation advantage, and marketing advantage. A cost advantage in either variable costs, marketing expenses, or overhead expenses enables a business to price more aggressively in building customer value. Share leaders often have a cost advantage due to economies of scale, economies of scope, and experience curve effects. Niche businesses can also achieve a cost advantage with lower overhead and lower marketing expenses.

Differentiation is a second major source of advantage. An advantage in product quality, service quality, or reputation (image) provides a unique source of differential advantage. In each case, a business with a differential advantage that is meaningful to target customers is in a position to charge more for its products and enhance profitability through higher margins. For markets in which service quality is more important than product quality, profitability is even greater. In some industries, particularly service industries, a business's reputation for quality has a very large impact on its price positioning.

A third major source of advantage is a marketing advantage. A business with a strong distribution system can control market access and limit competitors' ability to reach target customers. Likewise, a business with a large, well-trained, and well-supported sales force is able to better serve customers and respond more quickly to their problems or changing needs. This again is a considerable source of market-driven advantage. Finally, businesses that have a core competency in marketing communications are able to build and sustain market awareness and customer preference effectively and cost efficiently. Again, this is a tremendous source of advantage because these businesses will be able to more easily attract new customers and maintain a presence with existing customers.

APPLICATION PROBLEM: NEW VECTOR

NewVector is a strategy consulting firm that helps businesses assess their sources of competitive advantage. **NewVector** specializes in industrial markets and has built a database of over 1,000 industrial businesses. Each business in the database is profiled on several measures of financial performance, market performance and sources of competitive advantage. From these data **NewVector** has built the performance model on the next page.

In the **NewVector** competitive advantage model there are both *direct* and *indirect* effects on financial performance. The direct effects are indicated with solid arrows and indirect effects with dashed arrows. The numbers along each path reflect the relative impact of that variable. As shown, a business's cost advantage and its differentiation advantage have both direct and indirect effects on financial performance. A marketing advantage, however, only impacts financial performance indirectly through market performance. To estimate the financial impact of a client's competitive position, NewVector determines the business's relative competitive position with respect to cost, differentiation, and marketing, and then estimates an index of relative financial performance using the model on the next page.

$$\text{Market Performance Index (MPI)} = \left[-.40 \times \frac{\text{Cost}}{\text{Adv.}}\right] + \left[.75 \times \frac{\text{Differentiation}}{\text{Adv.}}\right] + \left[.90 \times \frac{\text{Marketing}}{\text{Adv.}}\right]$$

$$\text{Financial Performance Index (FPI)} = 100 + \left[-.60 \times \frac{\text{Cost}}{\text{Adv.}}\right] + \left[.20 \times \frac{\text{Differentiation}}{\text{Adv.}}\right] + \left[1.50 \times \text{MPI}\right]$$

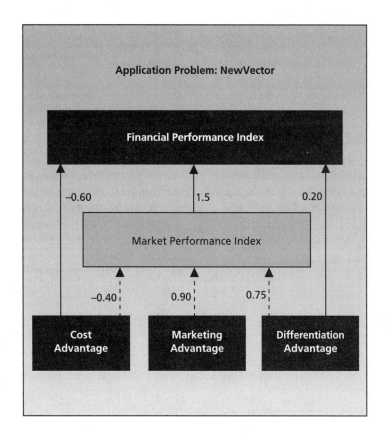

Application Problem: NewVector

Financial Performance Index

−0.60   1.5   0.20

Market Performance Index

−0.40   0.90   0.75

Cost Advantage   Marketing Advantage   Differentiation Advantage

Consider the business profiles below. This business has a relative cost position of 70 which translates into a 30 percent lower cost advantage. A relative position of 100 with respect to differentiation is equivalent to a zero competitive advantage. A relative marketing position of 90 means the business is 10 percent behind the competition in marketing presence and effectiveness.

Source of Advantage	Relative Position	Competitive Advantage	Interpretation
Cost Advantage	70	−30	30% lower cost
Differential Advantage	100	0	no difference
Marketing Advantage	90	−10	10% behind competition

Using this information and the Competitive Advantage Model shown above, we can first compute the effects on market performance.

Continued

Market Performance Index

$$\begin{matrix} \text{Market} \\ \text{Performance} \\ \text{Index (MPI)} \end{matrix} = \left[-.40 \times \frac{\text{Cost}}{\text{Adv.}}\right] + \left[.75 \times \frac{\text{Differentiation}}{\text{Adv.}}\right] + \left[.90 \times \frac{\text{Marketing}}{\text{Adv.}}\right]$$

$$= -.40 \times -30 \quad + \quad .75 \times 0 \qquad\qquad + \quad .90 \times -10$$
$$= \qquad \mathbf{12} \qquad + \qquad \mathbf{0} \qquad\qquad\qquad + \qquad \mathbf{-9}$$
$$= \qquad \mathbf{3}$$

This business's primary sources of advantage are in cost advantages. With no measurable differentiation advantage and a below-par market position, this business has a relatively low market performance index of 3.0.

The next step is to incorporate these results into financial performance as shown below. What we can learn is that the financial performance of this business is driven by its cost advantage. The strength of its cost advantage creates a financial index of 122.5. This is interpreted to mean that this business should have profitability metrics that run 22.5 percent higher than competitors.

Financial Performance Index

$$\begin{matrix} \text{Financial} \\ \text{Performance} \\ \text{Index (FPI)} \end{matrix} = 100 + \left[-.60 \times \frac{\text{Cost}}{\text{Adv.}}\right] + \left[.20 \times \frac{\text{Differentiation}}{\text{Adv.}}\right] + \left[1.50 \times \text{MPI}\right]$$

$$= 100 + \mathbf{-.60} \times -30 \;+\; .20 \times \mathbf{0} \qquad\qquad + \; 1.50 \times \mathbf{3.0}$$
$$= 100 + \qquad\quad \mathbf{18} \qquad + \qquad \mathbf{0} \qquad\qquad\qquad + \qquad \mathbf{4.5}$$
$$= \mathbf{122.5}$$

To better understand the dynamics of competitive advantage and financial performance, let's address the questions below.

For access to interactive software to answer the questions below go to www.RogerJBest.com or www.prenhall.com/best.

1. What would be the profit impact if a business matched competitors with respect to marketing position while maintaining its 30 percent cost advantage? What would be the impact of a 20 percent advantage in marketing position?

2. Evaluate the contribution of a cost advantage and market performance to the financial performance index for the current strategy, matching competition in marketing position, and building a 20 percent market advantage.

3. Using NewVector's Industry Performance Model, what level of differentiation advantage would a competitor with 10 percent marketing advantage and a 30 percent cost disadvantaged need to equal NewVector's client financial performance index of 122.5?

Market-Based Logic and Strategic Thinking

1. Why is competitor orientation an important element of a business's market orientation?
2. How could the industry forces for a regional phone company be different from the industry forces for a regional bank?
3. How will the industry change as competitors enter the regional phone market? How will profit potential be affected?
4. What impact would Procter & Gamble's everyday low price strategy have on competitive rivalry and the prisoner's dilemma?
5. How will the Internet affect competitor intelligence gathering? What traditional sources of competitor intelligence will most likely be available on the Internet?
6. What is the benefit of a competitor gap analysis? How would the results be used in strategy development?
7. When should a business do a competitive benchmarking study?
8. What are the benefits of competitive benchmarking?
9. Cost and differentiation are well-known sources of competitive advantage, but why is a marketing advantage also a potential source of competitive advantage?
10. What are the various ways a business can achieve a cost advantage?
11. Why do share leaders often have a cost advantage?
12. What areas of relative advantage does Wal-Mart use to drive its competitive position? How should Kmart and Sears drive their competitive positions?
13. Why are businesses with a relative advantage in either market share, unit cost, or product quality more profitable than businesses that have no advantage in any of those areas?
14. Identify for each area of differential advantage a business that uses this as a source of competitive advantage. Explain how each source of differential advantage helps the business attract and satisfy target customers.
15. Identify businesses that have developed different types of marketing advantage, and explain for each how this advantage affects profitability.
16. How could a business with a niche market strategy develop a marketing advantage as a source of competitive advantage?

Notes

1. Michael Porter, *Competitive Strategy* (New York: Free Press, 1980): chapter 1.
2. Anita McGahan, "Industry Structure and Competitive Advantage," *Harvard Business Review* (November–December 1994):115–24.
3. Sharon Oster, "Understanding Rivalry: Game Theory," in *Modern Competitive Analysis*, 2nd ed. (Kinderhook, NY: Oxford 1994), 237–51.
4. George Day and Prakash Nedungadi, "Managerial Representations of Competitive Advantage," *Journal of Marketing* (April 1994):31–44; Richard Rumelt, "How Much Does Industry Matter?" *Strategic Management Journal* (March 1991):67–86; and Ralf Boscheck, "Competitive Advantage: Superior Offer or Unfair Dominance," *California Management Review* (Fall 1994):132–51.
5. Joseph Porac and Howard Thomas, "Taxonomic Mental Models of Competitor Definition," *Academy of Management Review* 15 (1990):224–40.
6. Hugh Devine Jr. and John Morton, "How Does the Market Really See Your Product?" *Business Marketing* (July 1984):70–79.
7. Donald Tull and Delbert Hawkins, *Marketing Research: Measurement and Method*, 6th ed. (New York: Macmillan, 1993):431.

8. Glen Urban and Steven Star, *Advanced Marketing Strategy* (Upper Saddle River, NJ: Prentice Hall, 1991):144.

9. Stanley Slater and John Narver, "Does Competitive Environment Moderate the Market Orientation–Performance Relationship?" *Journal of Marketing* (January 1994):46–55; and John Narver and Stanley Slater, "The Effect of Market Orientation on Business Profitability," *Journal of Marketing* (October 1990):20–35.

10. Leonard Fuld, *The New Competitive Intelligence—The Complete Resource for Finding, Analyzing, and Using Information about Your Competitors* (New York: John Wiley & Sons, 1995).

11. "Intelligence," *Oregon Business* (May 1988):28–32.

12. Robert Camp, *Benchmarking—The Search for Industry Best Practices That Lead to Superior Performance* (Milwaukee, WI: Quality Press, 1989); Kathleen Leibfried and C. McNair, *Benchmarking: A Tool for Continuous Improvement* (New York: Free Press, 1992); Jeremy Main, "How to Steal the Best Ideas Around," *Fortune* (October 9, 1992):102–6; Gregory Watson, *Strategic Benchmarking* (New York: Wiley, 1993); and Gregory Watson, *Benchmarking for Competitive Advantage* (Portland, OR: Productivity Press, 1993).

13. William Boulding and Richard Staelin, "A Look on the Cost Side: Market Share and the Competitive Environment," *Marketing Science* (Spring 1993):144–66.

14. David Garvin, "Competing on the Eight Dimensions of Quality," *Harvard Business Review* (November–December 1987):101–9.

15. Bradley Gale, *Managing Customer Value* (New York: Free Press, 1994):309.

16. Robert Buzzell and Bradley Gale, *The PIMS Principles: Linking Strategy to Performance* (New York: Free Press, 1987).

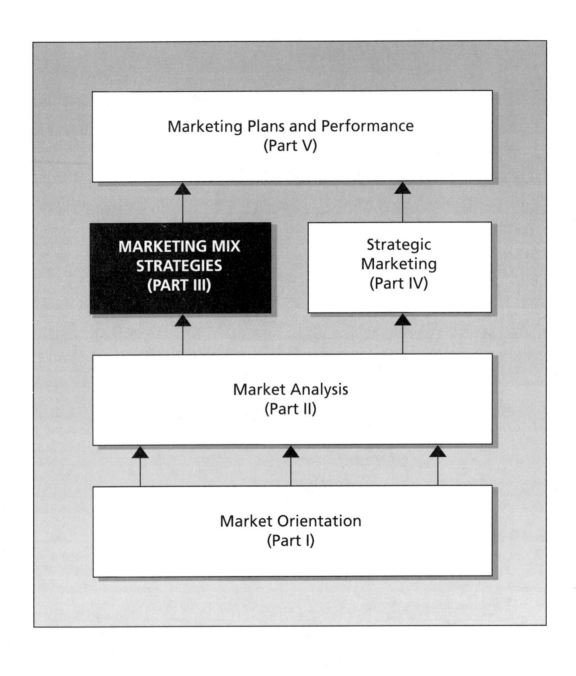

PART

III

MARKETING MIX STRATEGIES

*"Price is only relevant in the context of the value
of what it is you're offering. If you've got a really good product,
people will afford it. Whereas if you've got a product nobody wants,
it doesn't matter how cheap you make it."*
—JOEL HOESKTRA
CEO, General Mills

Businesses that lack a market orientation are more likely to price their products by simply checking the competition or marking up their costs to achieve a desired profit margin. There are good odds that these businesses will hurt their customer value, market share, and profit margins. A market-based business will set prices based on customer needs and the strength of its product position relative to competitors.

Part 3 focuses on short-run tactical marketing strategies designed around the marketing mix for a particular target market. The market analysis presented in Part 2 is a prerequisite for the development of a tactical marketing strategy because these strategies are built around market demand, the needs of a target segment, and within the context of a competitive environment.

Chapter 7 is devoted to product positioning and differentiation, branding and brand management, and product-line strategies. Chapter 8 presents alternative market-based pricing strategies. The combination of product and price creates a certain level of customer attractiveness for a business's product position. Without a strong marketing effort in terms of sales effort, distribution, advertising, and promotion, however, the share potential of a business cannot be fully realized. Chapter 9 examines the various marketing systems (channels and sales) that can be used to effectively reach target customers, and chapter 10 focuses on the role marketing communications play in delivering a successful tactical marketing strategy.

7 | PRODUCT POSITIONING AND BRAND STRATEGIES

When the Loctite Corporation launched a product branded RC-601, management was confident that it had the potential to be a great success. RC-601 could be applied, shaped, and cured to repair worn or broken metal machine parts. In one customer test, one tube of RC-601 saved 800 hours of machine downtime.

Because production engineers were suspicious of using a gel-like substance to repair critical machine parts, Loctite's marketing strategy was to confront the production engineers' skepticism head on. Sales literature and advertising copy were created with great technical detail in order to convincingly document the strength and engineering characteristics of RC-601.

The pricing was also designed to be attractive and to not present a barrier to trial usage. Pricing RC-601 under $10.00 per tube, the new product team felt there should be little opposition to trying the new Loctite product. What more could the target customer want than an *inexpensive solution to machine downtime when a part breaks or needs repair?*[1]

Unfortunately, the RC-601 marketing strategy failed. After an extensive marketing effort, Loctite distributors were requesting refunds on RC-601 inventory that was not selling. Though the product was proven to work reliably, the market failed to accept it, even at an inconsequential price. RC-601 was removed from the market less than one year after its market launch.

After several months of internal speculation, a customer research project was designed to determine why customers rejected RC-601. This research uncovered the fact that production engineers were risk-averse and wanted proven solutions. The low price may have created even greater suspicions with regard to reliability and quality. Moreover, the customer research also revealed that the real target customer was the maintenance worker, not the production engineer or supervisor. Maintenance workers were more open to new ideas, preferred pictures of how things worked, and could purchase supplies such as RC-601 when they cost under $25.00. With this customer intelligence, a revised target market strategy was formulated around maintenance workers' *product* needs as well as their *personal* needs. Recognizing these needs, the company included the following changes in its revised product positioning strategy:

- RC-601 was renamed Quick Metal to better communicate the primary benefits of the product (speed and strength). Also, the advertising copy focused on "how to use" the product rather than on technical data.

FIGURE 7-1   Loctite's Product Positioning for Quick Metal

- A new logo and new packaging were created that featured a metallic-colored tube and a box with bold lettering, as shown in Figure 7-1.
- The price was modified to capture more of the economic value created by the product while keeping the purchase decision within the discretion of the maintenance worker.

The revised product positioning strategy was a huge market success. This success was based upon finding the right target customer and then building a product positioning strategy around the needs of that target customer. Thus, the first step in successful product positioning is to determine the appropriate target customers and to understand their needs, both product and personal.

PRODUCT POSITIONING

The cordless drill market is partitioned into five needs-based product segments, as illustrated in Figure 7-2.[2] At the low end are light-duty cordless drills, which are relatively low in power, torque, and endurance (time to a battery change). At the other extreme are heavy-duty power cordless drills, which are high in power, torque, and endurance. Sears has elected to position products in each of the price-performance segments. Black & Decker, on the other hand, has positioned itself in four of the five

FIGURE 7-2   Cordless Drill Product Line Positioning

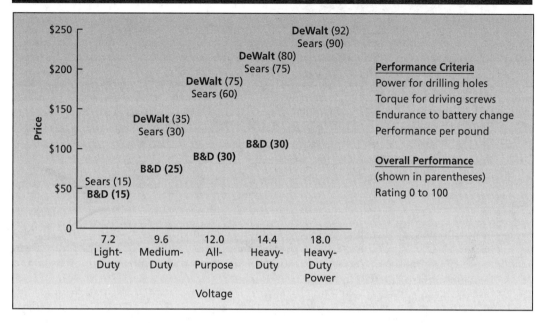

segments at much lower prices. DeWalt (a Black & Decker brand) is positioned higher than Sears in four of the five segments.

Although the Sears' product positioning strategy covers all five price-performance segments, its relative position is not the same in all five segments. At the low-price end of the market (light duty), Sears is higher-priced than Black & Decker for roughly the same performance. At the high-price end of the market (heavy duty power), Sears is priced just below DeWalt. In the midprice segments (medium duty, all-purpose, and heavy duty), Sears faces both brands. In these segments, Sears is rated and priced slightly lower than DeWalt. Black & Decker is rated and priced significantly lower in the all-purpose and heavy-duty segments.

Product Positioning and Market Share

The goal of a positioning strategy is to create a product-price position that is attractive to target customers and creates a good source of cash flow for the business. Achieving a certain level of market share is a key factor in the success of a marketing strategy and directly dependent on the strength of a business's *product positioning* and *marketing effort.*

As shown in Figure 7-3, market share is represented as the business's product position multiplied by its marketing effort. Thus, a weak product position with a strong marketing effort will fail to deliver a desired level of market share. Likewise, an attractive product position that is supported with a weak marketing effort will also fail to achieve a desired level of market share. To be successful, a business needs both.

Also shown in Figure 7-3 are the various factors that contribute to a business's product position and marketing effort. Product differentiation, price, product breadth,

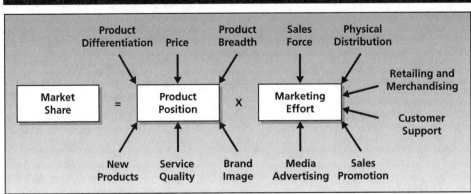

FIGURE 7-3   Product-Price Position, Marketing Effort, and Market Share

new products, service quality, and brand image each contribute to the strength of a business's overall product position. As these inputs to product positioning outperform those of competitors, the strength of a business's product position increases and becomes more attractive to target customers.

In this chapter, we will cover each of the inputs to product positioning shown in Figure 7-3. In Chapter 8, we will focus on pricing strategies used to enhance a business's product position. Inputs to marketing effort include the sales force, customer support, distribution, retailing, advertising, and sales promotions. The importance of each input to marketing effort varies from business to business, but the combination in any specific marketing situation is critical. Marketing effort and the inputs shown in Figure 7-3 will be addressed in Chapters 9 and 10.

Product Positioning Strategies

To create an attractive product position and achieve a desired level of market share and profitability requires several ongoing product management efforts. The first is very basic. Who is our target customer? What is our positioning strategy? Will the positioning strategy create a superior value for target customers? For a particular target price, a business needs to develop a position based on either a low price or some source of *differentiation and product positioning* that is meaningful to target customers. As shown in Figure 7-4, a differential advantage could be built around some combination of price, product, service, and brand.

A second important area of product management is *branding and brand management strategies.* How broad should the product line be? How should brands be created to communicate a consistent image and desired target market identity? How can a brand's assets and potential liabilities be managed to create higher levels of brand equity? And finally, a third area of product management is *brand and product line strategies.* To what degree should flanker brands be added as extensions of a strong umbrella brand? And when should a business bundle or unbundle products in order to attract and satisfy target customers? From a core product positioning strategy, these types of product line strategies need to be developed in order to fully leverage a business's capabilities and profit potential. The remainder of this chapter is devoted to the three areas and specific topics identified in Figure 7-4.

FIGURE 7-4   Product Positioning Strategies

PRODUCT POSITIONING AND DIFFERENTIATION

On the basis of target customer needs, a business must develop a product position that is in some way differentially superior to competitors' product positions. In a price-sensitive market, product positioning generally requires a lower price, because other sources of differentiation are not valued by target customers. For markets in which differentiation is possible and valued by target customers, a variety of strategies are possible. Product, service, and brand image differences that are meaningful to target customers and differentially superior to those of competitors offer the potential to create a more attractive product position. Regardless of the product positioning strategy pursued, our goal is to create a customer value superior to that offered by competitors, as illustrated in Figure 7-5. The remainder of this section will be devoted to these product positioning and differentiation strategies.

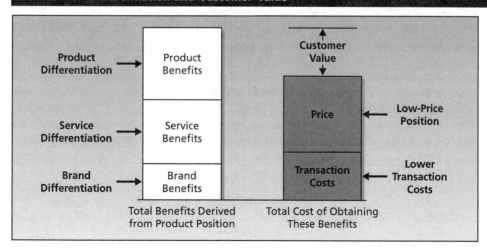

FIGURE 7-5   Differentiation and Customer Value

FIGURE 7-6 Dimensions of Product Quality

Quality Killers

Reliability: Time to failure or malfunction for a given product
Conformance: Incidence of defects that should not have occurred

Quality Drivers

Performance: Operational characteristics that distinguish product performance
Durability: Product life and ability to endure demanding use conditions

Quality Enhancers

Features: Number and type of options that can be added
Serviceability: Ease, speed, and cost of maintenance and repair

Quality Aesthetics

Appearance: The fit, finish, and appearance of a product
Reputation: The image created by the brand name or company

Product Differentiation

Many customers are not seeking the lowest price, and many are willing to pay a higher price for products that deliver important customer benefits. Differences in product quality, reliability, and performance can attract customers who are seeking products that perform better than average products. There are eight dimensions of product quality that can serve as bases for product differentiation.[3] These dimensions can be arranged into four hierarchical categories of product quality, as shown in Figure 7-6. If a business fails to deliver acceptable or expected levels of reliability and conformance, an advantage in other dimensions of product quality will not matter. At the other extreme, quality aesthetics as a source of differentiation is of value only when all other aspects of quality are met with respect to customer quality expectations.

Quality Killers

Customers expect reliability and conformance to specifications. Whether they are buying a computer, an automobile, or a Boeing jet, customers expect the product to conform to the specifications that are basic elements of the product. For example, Nescafé creates different blends of coffee to match customers' taste preferences in different international markets. This is conformance to expectations (i.e., specifications).

Customers also expect products to operate reliably. Companies such as General Electric, Motorola, and Allied Signal have engaged in *six sigma* programs. At two sigma, a business with one million products would experience 40,000 failures. At six sigma, the failure rate drops to as close to failure-free as one could expect to get. GE has spent $1 billion to convert all its divisions to six sigma principles. Higher conformance to specifications and fewer failures enhance customer retention and are also raising GE profit margins.

Quality Drivers

Performance and durability are the workhorses of product quality. Improvements in steering, braking, and fuel economy have been key aspects of improved automobile performance. For example, BMW adds an extra coat of paint to its vehicles sold in Japan in order to meet the quality expectations of the Japanese luxury car buyer.

Manufacturers who cannot keep pace with performance improvements will simply lose market share over time. Those who can lead with improved product performance will have created a position on a basis of product differentiation and competitive advantage. Intel, for example, seeks to stay ahead of competitors by continuously improving its products. For over three decades, Intel has followed *Moore's Law: Every eighteen months the operating performance per unit of space should double.* This pursuit of performance has enabled Intel to dominate the market it serves, with an 85 percent market share.

Durability is also a key component of product quality. Customers have expectations with respect to how long the product should last and how well it should stand up in normal usage. A business that fails to meet customer expectations with respect to durability will face difficulty in both attracting new customers and retaining existing customers. Durability is a common source of advantage in demanding industrial product use situations. For example, ESCO corporation is a specialty steel manufacturer that makes wear parts for front-end loaders and buckets for mining and construction applications. With proprietary steel chemistry and product designs, ESCO is able to offer customers greater product durability that extends the life of its products and reduces the incidence of breakage in extreme earthmoving applications.

Quality Enhancers

A product that meets customer expectations with respect to conformance, reliability, performance, and durability can be differentiated with enhanced quality features. Additional options that can improve the use, safety, or enjoyment of a product can be important sources of product differentiation. Air bags, automotive entertainment systems, cruise control, and navigation maps are examples of features that have been added to automobiles to enhance their quality. Features, as a source of differentiation, become more important as a business serves more affluent segments of the market. These customers often want more than the basic elements of product quality. They are seeking enhanced quality in the products they purchase.

Serviceability is another quality enhancer. Products that are easier to maintain and repair save time and money. The Saturn was engineered to make automotive repair easier and less time-consuming. The net result is lower repair costs. This design has also produced lower insurance costs due to lower-than-normal cost of repair in the event of an accident. Both lower the total cost of ownership for Saturn owners.

Quality Aesthetics

The appearance of a product and its reputation can also serve as sources of product differentiation. In Japan, the appearance of a product, or even of the package around the product, can have an enormous impact on the success of that product. For example, a British stereo manufacturer introduced its very high quality system into the Japanese market but failed because the box it was packaged in did not match the quality of the product it contained.

Likewise, the image a brand projects or reputation a company has established can be important in some markets. The quality of products such as Porsche, Rolex, and Chanel is judged not only on their functional characteristics but also on their aesthetic characteristics, which are derived from the image they project. A watch comparable on all seven other aspects of quality listed in Figure 7-6, but not made by Rolex, will fail to attract customers who value the Rolex name and the image it projects.

FIGURE 7-7 Key Dimensions of Service Quality	
Reliability:	Ability to perform the promised service dependably and accurately
Responsiveness:	Willingness to help customers and provide prompt service, and readiness to provide prompt service
Assurance:	Employee knowledge, courtesy, and ability to convey trust and confidence
Empathy:	Caring, individualized attention the business offers its customers
Tangibles:	Facilities that enhance service quality

Service Differentiation

Nordstrom, FedEx, and Caterpillar are well-recognized businesses that have sought to attain a superior position in the area of service differentiation. Many competitors carry the same brand name products and can match the atmospheres found in Nordstrom stores. However, Nordstrom's positioning strategy has always been an unparalleled service advantage. This position of superior service differentiates it from competitors by creating a customer benefit that target customers find attractive. In this way, Nordstrom delivers a greater customer value to target customers.

For FedEx, the promise of "when it absolutely, positively has to get there" communicates its service position around reliability. And, as shown in Figure 7-7, reliability is one of the key dimensions of service quality.[4] The other service dimensions shown in Figure 7-7 are also important and may provide a good opportunity to build a service advantage in other business situations. For example, Caterpillar has sought to strengthen its competitive position and customer benefits with a differential advantage in responsive service. A twenty-four-hour parts and repair service anywhere in the world has helped Caterpillar differentiate itself from competitors and create a valued service benefit for Caterpillar customers.

Brand Differentiation

In many consumer and business-to-business purchases, customers are influenced by the status of a brand name or by the assurance of a well-known company. Brands such as Lexus and Mercedes have strong associations with prestige or status. The importance of these brand benefits to many target customers enhances their positioning and differential advantage.[5]

Brand differentiation provides another way to position a business's products relative to competitors and to create incremental customer benefits and value, as illustrated in Figure 7-8. For example, Marriott estimated that adding its name to Fairfield Inn increased Fairfield Inn's occupancy by 15 percent. Kellogg found that in matched product tests, customer choice of corn flakes cereal increased from 47 percent, when the brand was not known, to 59 percent, when the Kellogg name was identified. And when Hitachi and a competitor jointly manufactured TVs in England, Hitachi sold its TVs at a $75 price premium and achieved a higher market share.[6] Each of these examples illustrates the importance of brand benefits to target customers and the brand equity these brand reputations create for the business.[7]

A strong brand enhances positive evaluations of a product's quality, maintains a high level of product awareness, and provides a consistent image or brand personality. A strong brand, such as Coca-Cola, extends each of these positive customer evaluations to brand extensions that include Coke Classic, Diet Coke, Caffeine Free Coke, and Cherry

FIGURE 7-8 Differentiation and Customer Value

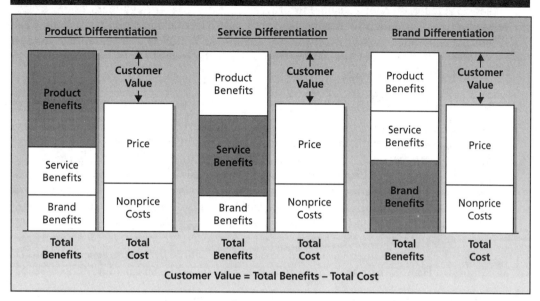

Customer Value = Total Benefits – Total Cost

Coke. Brand differentiation can be an important source of differentiation and extend the positioning benefits of a core brand to many closely related flanker brands. However, there are limits to brand extensions.[8] At some point, it may be necessary to create new brand names and build another area of brand equity as Coca-Cola did when entering the sports drink market with Powerade and the fruit juice market with Fruitopia.

Low Cost of Purchase

Thus far, we have focused on the benefit side of differentiation. A business can also create a source of advantage with low price and, hence, lower the cost of purchase. Businesses with a low-cost advantage in markets in which price is an important determinant of customer value can utilize a low price as a basis for product positioning. However, in these market situations, a business cannot ignore product, service, or brand issues. A business must still meet customer expectations in these areas, even though the strength of its product position is built around a more attractive price.

Low-Price Position

For example, Wal-Mart utilizes low prices to create an attractive position relative to competing retail stores. With a low-price positioning strategy, Wal-Mart must achieve a lower cost of buying, inventorying, and retailing the products it sells. This positioning strategy requires Wal-Mart to continuously find ways to contain or lower costs in order to maintain low prices as a source of competitive advantage while still meeting target customer needs for product, service, and brand. With this positioning strategy, Wal-Mart creates customer value and a competitive advantage by offering lower prices.

Gateway Computer and Dell Computer have positioned themselves with a lower cost of purchase by eliminating the retailer markup. Target customers who are price-sensitive can achieve greater customer value with lower prices by purchasing directly from these businesses but must give up the convenience and confidence of buying from a local retailer. Of course, using low price as a positioning strategy requires these businesses to pay attention to all aspects of achieving a low-cost position because they are not the only ones pursuing a low-price advantage. Gateway, for example, is able to achieve its low-price positioning strategy with a lower cost of operations by locating in South Dakota, where wage rates and taxes are low.

Lower Transaction Costs

The total cost of purchase also includes transaction costs, as shown in Figure 7-5. These are costs associated with the acquisition of a product. A business can build a low-cost advantage and customer value by lowering these nonprice costs of purchase. For example, American Hospital Supply found that $0.50 of every $1 a hospital spent to buy hospital equipment was spent on acquiring and inventorying the equipment. In response, American Hospital Supply devised a computerized ordering and inventory management system that would lower a hospital's cost of acquiring and inventorying equipment by 50 percent. In lowering these transaction costs, American Hospital Supply created a greater customer value and developed a source of advantage that enabled American Hospital Supply to grow to become the market share leader in this market.

BRANDING AND BRAND MANAGEMENT STRATEGIES

To fully capture the total value of a product's positioning it is important to brand a product in a way that communicates its intended positioning. A brand name gives an identity to a product or service, providing a way to quickly comprehend the brand's primary benefits whether rational or emotional.

Brand Identity

The successful management of brands is built around sound marketing practices. A business with a strong market orientation that has segmented its target markets and tracks customer behavior by segment is in the best position to build a successful brand.[9] An internally focused business simply does not have the market intelligence needed to build a brand identity that is meaningful to target customers. The first step in developing a brand identity is to define the desired product positioning and value proposition for a specific target market. Without these specifications the branding identification process would quickly deteriorate into an internal process built around product features rather than customer benefits.

Brand Encoding

A great deal of strategy goes into the branding process and the creation of specific brand names.[10] Because there are a great number of options, we have created a brand encoding system to help us understand how to encode a product's positioning into a brand name for a specific market and desired image. The encoding system is presented as a hierarchy of possible naming components that starts with the company name, followed by a brand name and further enhanced or modified by sub-brand names, numbers, letters, product names, and benefits. A brand can be as broad as a company name like Dell, as narrow as a specific version of a product like Microsoft Windows ME, or a brand name can be as abstract as Altoids.

Company brand names such as Nike and General Electric create an image and umbrella brand under which a wide range of products can be communicated to diverse product–markets. The Nike name carries an image of competitiveness and winning across product–markets that include track, golf, soccer, football, basketball and many others. General Electric's image for reliability and good value reaches across light bulbs, appliances, plastics, medical systems, power generation systems, electric motors, transportation equipment, electrical distribution equipment, jet engines, credit and other financial services.

Companies such as Sony, Intel and Ford have created specific brand names to supplement their company names and enhance the identity and position of their products. Ford, for example, brands its cars as Ford Explorer, Ford Taurus, and Ford Mustang. Intel adds to its company name and brand name a product name to further distinguish its product positioning with Intel Pentium Processors, Intel Celeron Processors, and Intel Xeon Processors. Other companies such as Procter & Gamble use only a brand name like Tide, Cheer, Bold, Bounce, Gain, and Ivory Soap in their line of laundry soaps.

In each case, some combination of elements from the brand encoding system allowed these companies to achieve their desired product positioning for each brand while building a portfolio of brands that has both meaning and synergy.[11] A brand name may or may not use each of the elements in the code. Choosing which specific elements to include in a brand is a matter of determining which combination is most likely to exert the full power of a product position as presented in the following brand encoding strategies..

Company and Brand Name

This is the branding strategy used by many automobile companies such as Ford. Shown below is Ford's branding strategy for its line of SUV's. While the first brand was Ford Explorer, Ford was able to expand this very popular brand to include a variety of related brands under the banner of Ford Explorer.

Company	Brand	Sub-Brand	Numbers/Letters	Product	Benefits
Ford	Escape				
Ford	Explorer Sport				
Ford	Explorer				
Ford	Eddie Bauer Explorer				
Ford	Expedition				
Ford	Excursion				

Brand and Sub-Brand Name

Some businesses, like Eastman Kodak, use a brand and sub-brand to further clarify and enhance a brand's identity and intended differentiation. Shown below are the major color film brands that Eastman Kodak has developed to position its different film products.

Company	Brand	Sub-Brand	Numbers/Letters	Product	Benefits
	Kodak	Gold			
	Kodak	Gold 400			
	Kodak	Royal Gold			
	Kodak	Advantix			
	Kodak	Elite			
	Kodak	Gold Max			
	Kodak	Insight			

Company and Product Name

General Electric serves a diverse set of product markets that range from consumer goods to medical and industrial and financial services. The GE name and logo are key factors in communicating the company's long tradition of providing quality products and services at prices that deliver customer value. Within each of these major GE product lines, branding is enhanced with numbers and letters to further identify levels of performance and specification. However, General Electric has elected not to include the brands NBC and CNBC under the GE flagship brand. For strategic reasons GE has preferred to minimize the association between GE and NBC and CNBC.

Company	Brand	Sub-Brand	Numbers/Letters	Product	Benefits
GE				Aircraft Engines	
GE				Appliances	
GE				Capital	
GE				Industrial Systems	
GE				Lighting	
GE				Medical Systems	
GE				Plastics	
GE				Power Systems	
GE				Specialty Materials	
GE				Transportation Systems	
	NBC				
	CNBC				

Company, Brand and Product Name

Intel encodes its brand names to include the company name, a unique brand name, and the product name. As the following shows, this helps Intel communicate the positioning of four microprocessor families (Celeron, Pentium, Xeon, and Itanium) while also branding a Micro-Architecture with NetBurst and a memory chip with StrateFlash. For its more complex products, Intel uses letters or letters and numbers to abbreviate the product name using names such as the Intel IXP 1200 Network Processor, Intel PCA (Personal Client Architecture) and Intel IEA (Internet Exchange Architecture).

Company	Brand	Sub-Brand	Numbers/Letters	Product	Benefits
Intel	Pentium		4	Processor	
Intel	Xeon			Processor	
Intel	Celeron			Processor	
Intel	Itanium			Processor	
Intel	StrateFlash			Memory	
Intel	NetBurst			Micro-Architecture	
Intel				Network Processor	
Intel			IXP 1200		
Intel			PCA		
Intel			IEA		

The Intel company name provides an umbrella brand name that communicates Intel's reputation for quality and innovation. The individual brand names enable Intel to position multiple products in the same markets. The addition of product names allows Intel to sell multiple products to the same customer without confusing the product application.

Company Name, Brand Name and Number

Microsoft uses a variation of the Intel strategy of leveraging its company name and branding individual products. However, rather than a use product name, Microsoft uses numbers and letters to communicate versions of its software brands. For example, Microsoft Outlook Express 6 allows buyers and users to quickly identify the Microsoft product and its newness relative to older versions of the same brand. This strategy allows the brand to date itself, as in the case of Microsoft Windows 95, 98, and 2000.

Company	Brand	Sub-Brand	Numbers/Letters	Product	Benefits
Microsoft	Windows		2000		
Microsoft	Outlook Express		6		
Microsoft	Excel		97		
Microsoft	Word		98		
Microsoft	Office		2000		
Microsoft	Windows		XT		

Brand Name and Benefit

Braun has successfully branded the Oral-B toothbrush. Taking advantage of the well-known name and image for quality in the Oral-B brand, Braun extended the Oral-B brand name by including primary benefits that differentiate the brands. The Oral-B Ultra Plaque Remover is clearly targeted at customers seeking the benefit of plaque removal, which customers can quickly tell is different from the intended benefit of the regular Oral-B toothbrush.

Company	Brand	Sub-Brand	Product	Benefits
	ORAL-B			Cross Action
	ORAL-B			Ultra Plaque Remover
	ORAL-B			Excel Pulsating Toothbrush

Brand Name Only

Procter & Gamble has long been known for its "brand-name-only" strategy. In markets served by multiple P&G brands, P&G Brand Teams work hard to maintain their unique product positions. For example, the following are the P&G brands positioned for the laundry soap market. Each brand has a unique focus and product-positioning strategy. Including the P&G name as a prominent component of the brand names

Company	Brand	Sub-Brand	Product	Benefits
	Tide			
	Downy			
	Gain			
	Cheer			
	Bounce			
	ERA			
	Febreze			
	Dreft			
	Dryel			
	Ivory Snow			
	Bold			

FIGURE 7-9 Top Ten Global Brands in 2002			
Rank	*Brand*	*Value**	*Business Week Comment*
1	Coca-Cola	$70	Still the best brand by far. Growth in the developing world offset so-so new products . . .
2	Microsoft	$64	Still dragging through the courtroom, its biggest challenge is stagnant PC purchases.
3	IBM	$51	Good thing Big Blue was rebuilt on services—still the most promising segment.
4	GE	$41	Jack Welch's retirement took a toll on the GE name.
5	Intel	$31	"Intel Inside" put it on the map, but it faces tough competition and sluggish PC sales.
6	Nokia	$30	Still the cell phone of choice, but overall sales of mobile handsets are weak.
7	Disney	$30	Even monster hit Monsters Inc. couldn't offset a post-9/11 falloff at theme parks.
8	McDonald's	$26	Who remembers Mad Cow disease? Global expansion continues; negative PR fades.
9	Marlboro	$24	Line extensions and merchandising clout overcome court challenges and rising prices.
10	Mercedes	$21	The leading luxury-car brand, but its low-end models suffered from poor reviews.

* $ billions

could dilute the positioning of the individual product brands. Also, because the products are well understood and sold in specific retail locations, there would be little value in adding a product name, letters or sub-brand name. In the brand-name-only encoding strategy, the primary benefit is often embedded in the name to further communicate the desired product position of the brand.

Brand Assets and Liabilities

Brand names like Coca-Cola, Microsoft and GE are worth billions of dollars, as shown in Figure 7-9. These top ten global brands are ranked on the basis of their estimated value.[12] However, how did they achieve this level of value? What are their brand assets? Do they have any brand liabilities? The comments suggest that some brands have well protected assets while others clearly have brand liabilities to deal with.

Brand Assets

A brand, like any business with financial assets, has varying brand assets.[13] A brand such as Coca-Cola creates brand assets based on its market leadership and high level of awareness. Brand assets that impact brand value are also derived from an exceptional reputation for quality, brand relevance, and high levels of customer loyalty. While a variety of other influences could create brand assets,[14] these five brand assets can be found to some degree in the top ten global brands listed in Figure 7-9.

- **Brand Awareness:** Brands with high awareness can more easily introduce new products and enter new markets, such as Nike with the Nike name and logo.
- **Market Leadership:** Market-share leaders such as Intel dominate the markets they compete in.

FIGURE 7-10 Brand Asset Score Card						
Brand Assets	*Below Average (0)*	*Somewhat Below (50)*	*About Average (100)*	*Somewhat Above (150)*	*Top Performer (200)*	*Brand Asset Score*
Brand Awareness						
Market Leadership						
Reputation for Quality						
Brand Relevance						
Brand Loyalty						
Total Brand Assets						

- **Reputation for Quality:** A superior reputation for quality is a brand asset for companies such as Lexus.
- **Brand Relevance:** A brand must be relevant to consumers within a product–market to be a brand asset. Over the past fifteen years Lexus has gained brand relevance among luxury car buyers while Cadillac has lost brand relevance as the lifestyle and demographics of this market changed.
- **Brand Loyalty:** For brands such as E-Trade, a high level of customer retention is a profitable brand asset that lowers marketing expenses and increases customer profitability.

While there are several ways to measure these brand assets, one is with the Brand Asset Score Card shown in Figure 7-10. In this case, a brand is rated relative to the average brand in its competing market. Individual brand-asset scores can range from zero to 200. With five assets, the overall brand-asset score ranges from zero to 1000. An average brand would attain an overall brand-asset score of 500. Thus, top-ten global brands such as Coca-Cola, Microsoft, and GE should produce brand asset scores much greater than 500.

To understand how the Brand Asset Score Card would work consider how you might have assessed each of the brand assets presented in Figure 7-10 for Cadillac and Lexus in 1990. Lexus was a relatively new brand, while Cadillac was the market leader with a 30 percent market share. Most luxury car buyers in 1990 would have rated Cadillac's brand assets higher than Lexus. If this analysis were performed again between 2000 and 2005, we would most likely see Lexus climb in brand assets and Cadillac slide in brand assets as its market share eroded to below 20 percent.[15]

Brand Liabilities

Brands can also incur brand liabilities due to a product failure, a lawsuit, or questionable business practices. Prior to the Enron collapse, Arthur Andersen would have had relatively low levels of brand liabilities. Their involvement and questionable accounting practices led to considerable customer dissatisfaction and lawsuits, which in turn created brand liabilities that lowered Arthur Andersen's brand equity. At the same time, Arthur Andersen's brand assets were drastically reduced by declining market share, an eroding reputation for quality, and declining brand loyalty. The net result was a significant increase in brand liabilities and a corresponding reduction in brand assets. While other brand liabilities could be considered, the following are five potentially harmful brand liabilities.

FIGURE 7-11 Brand Liability Score Card						
Brand Liabilities	*Below Average (0)*	*Somewhat Below (50)*	*About Average (100)*	*Somewhat Above (150)*	*Major Problem (200)*	*Brand Liability Score*
Customer Dissatisfaction						
Environmental Problems						
Product Failures/Recalls						
Lawsuits/Boycotts						
Questionable Bus. Practices						
Total Brand Liabilities						

- **Customer Dissatisfaction:** Brands with high levels of customer complaint and customer dissatisfaction incur a brand liability that detracts from brand equity. Customer complaints in the telecommunication industry have created brand liabilities for some telecom companies.
- **Environmental Problems:** Brands associated with poor environmental practices may create a certain level of brand liability. The brand equity of many oil companies is lower when associated with oil spills or poor environmental drilling practices.
- **Product or Service Failures:** Product failures, like those experienced by Firestone Tires, result in brand liabilities that can potentially destroy a powerful brand.
- **Lawsuits and Boycotts:** Lawsuits and consumer boycotts create brand liabilities. Class-action lawsuits against Cadet Manufacturing Company for defective heaters became a brand liability that the company is still working hard to overcome.
- **Questionable Business Practices:** Questionable or unethical business practices that surface as negative news create brand liabilities. Nike, for example, lost some of its brand equity due to questionable working conditions at its foreign production sites.

As with brand assets, brand liabilities can be assessed using the Brand Liabilities Score Card presented in Figure 7-11. For most strong brands, brand assets should exceed brand liabilities. Using the Brand Liabilities Score Card one could make an assessment of Arthur Andersen before and after the Enron debacle. Again, while opinions will vary, most would find that their estimate of Arthur Andersen's brand liabilities increased after the Enron scandal. Thus, for Arthur Andersen the Enron scandal resulted in a likely decrease in brand assets and a likely increase in brand liabilities, both contributing to a significant drop in brand equity.

Brand Equity

In a business, the owner's equity is the value of the owner's holdings in the company. It is determined by the difference between what a company owns in assets and what a company owes in liabilities. The larger the ratio of assets to liabilities the greater the owner's equity. As Figure 7-12 shows, brand equity can be assessed in the same way. To calculate brand equity, simply subtract the total brand-liability score from the total brand-asset score. Tracking changes in brand equity over time is an important part of the brand-management process since brand equity is not static.

FIGURE 7-12   Brand Balance Sheet and Brand Equity

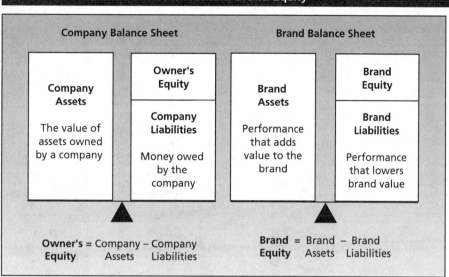

For businesses such as Firestone, Cadet, and WorldCom, one can easily envision how brand equity quickly eroded as brand assets declined and brand liabilities grew. Likewise, it should be easy to comprehend how the brand equity of companies such as Dell Computer, Lexus and Target has grown over the last fifteen years as their brand assets grew without burdensome brand liabilities. In either situation, the brand-equity model can be a useful way to understand and manage brands.

BRAND AND PRODUCT LINE STRATEGIES

The more products a business has to sell, the more ways it has to attract and satisfy potential customers. A broad line of products creates more selling opportunities for the sales force and channel partners. A business with a narrow line of products has to be more focused in order to be cost-effective in its marketing efforts.

Because a broad product line provides a business with more potential customers and the potential to sell more to each customer, this type of marketing efficiency translates into more sales and higher levels of profitability. For example, in Figure 7-13, we can see that businesses with broad product lines are more profitable during the emerging and growing stages of a product life cycle than are businesses with a narrow product line. Thus, it is particularly important to expand a business's product line during these stages of the product life cycle. This is exactly what Microsoft did in the 1980s and 1990s in growing the computer market.

Product-Line Development

Quite often, a company will want to expand from one market segment into an adjacent segment in order to grow sales and profits. Product line expansion requires considerable

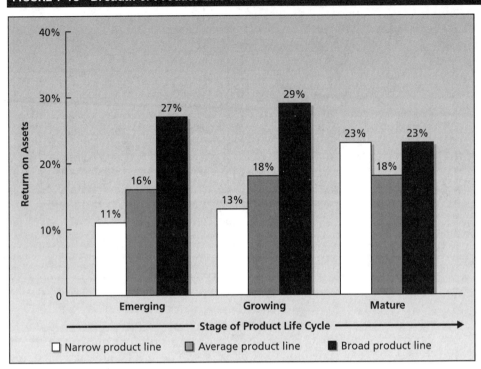

FIGURE 7-13   Breadth of Product Line and Return on Invested Assets

product differentiation and careful positioning because the same company is now going to ask for a different price for a different combination of product, service, and brand benefits. Toyota sequentially expanded its product line from a very low product-price segment in the 1960s to the point where, today, Toyota offers a full line of automobiles, each with a different product-price position and unique brand name identity, as illustrated in Figure 7-14.

In the beer market, Anheuser-Busch's product line strategy utilizes separate brand names for each of the five beer marketing positioning strategies it has pursued, as outlined in Figure 7-14. Each brand has a distinct product-price position that is attractive to different types of customers or different use situations. In recent years, Anheuser-Busch expanded its product line to the micro beer segment with the introduction of Michelob HefeWeizen, and it added Kirin to create an import brand position.

Umbrella and Flanker Brands

An *umbrella brand* is the core product of a business such as Ivory (soap), American Express (credit cards), Betty Crocker (cake mix), Gerber (baby food), Kodak (film), and Johnson & Johnson (baby shampoo). From a consumer's point of view, the core product is the most visible embodiment of the brand name. Accumulated exposure and experience with the core product solidifies a certain image and quality expectation. Umbrella branding involves the transfer of quality perceptions derived from a core product or brand to product line extensions that use the same brand name. The intent of umbrella branding is to enhance the effectiveness of marketing programs and to

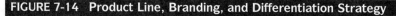

FIGURE 7-14   Product Line, Branding, and Differentiation Strategy

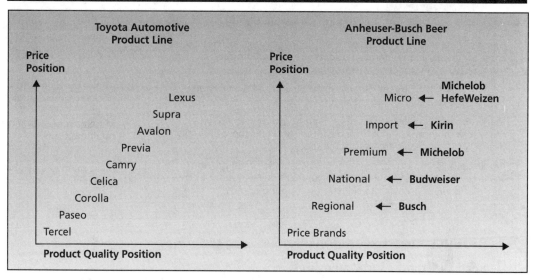

increase demand for product extensions by transferring brand awareness and perceptions of quality from the umbrella brand.[16]

For example, the Frito-Lay core brands capture 59 percent of the U.S. snack chip market. In 2001, sales growth of the Frito-Lay brands was largely due to the introduction of new flanker brands under the core brands of Fritos, Lay's Potato Chips, Cheetos, and Doritos as illustrated in Figure 7-15. These umbrella brands create a base from which to introduce flanker brands which enhance market penetration at a lower cost.[17] Summarized in Figure 7-16 are four ways a flanker brand benefits from a strong umbrella brand and how each of these benefits contributes to the profitability of the flanker brand.

FIGURE 7-15   Frito Lay Umbrella and Flanker Brands

Frito's Corn Chips	Lay's Potato Chips	Ruffles Potato Chips	Cheeto's Cheese Snacks	Tostitos Tortilla Chips	Doritos Tortilla Chips	Rold Gold Pretzels	Granola Bars	Cracker Jack
Frito's Twist	Lay's Bistro Gourmet Chips		Cheeto's Mystery Colorz Snacks		Dorito's Extremes Tortilla Chips			

The purpose of brand and line extensions is to leverage the awareness and image of the flagship brand while, at the same time, not diluting its image or perceived quality. However, line extensions may not grow market demand and can cannibalize the core brand or other extensions while raising the total cost of marketing. Thus, careful product line accounting is needed to ensure that product line extensions are profitable and, overall, that they incrementally improve the profitability of the entire product line.[18]

FIGURE 7-16   How Umbrella Brands Impact the Performance of Flanker Brands

Benefits an Umbrella Provides Flanker Brands	Performance Impact
Brand Awareness: The high level of market awareness attained by the core brand creates an umbrella under which related products can be introduced at a much lower cost of advertising.	Lowers a flanker brand's advertising expenses
Known Quality: The quality image of the core brand is conferred to brand-line extensions under the umbrella brand.	Allows for premium pricing (higher margins)
Market Reach: Retailers are more inclined to give precious shelf space to well-known brands. Brand extensions under these umbrella brands also gain easier access to retail space.	More volume with more retail shelf space
Product Mix: Brand extensions under the umbrella brand provide customers more variety and the opportunity to buy variations of the core brand without having to switch to competing brands.	More sales volume and higher customer retention

Product-Line Extensions

Vertical Brand-Line Extensions

A successful brand can often be "franchised," meaning it can be extended to other versions of the product. This can be accomplished most easily with *"vertical brand extensions"* of the core brand. Gardenburger is a company that manufactures meatless products. Its core brand is shown in Figure 7-17 as the *original*. Vertical brand names subsequently added to the basic Gardenburger brand name include *Gardenburger Flame Grilled* and *Gardenburger Santa Fe*. These vertical brand extensions provide variety for Gardenburger customers who may tire of the same taste of one product, and may attract new customers from other meatless products or even customers trying meatless products for the first time.

Horizontal Brand-Line Extensions

Horizontal brand extensions within a product class are possible by adding complementary products. For Gardenburger this meant adding horizontal product lines that included meatless chicken, sausage, ribs, diners and veggie entrees. Furthermore, a horizontal brand extension in Veggie brands opened the door to additional vertical brand extensions. Each of these combinations leveraged the core *Gardenburger* brand while growing sales and profits.

FIGURE 7-17   Gardenburger Vertical and Horizontal Brand Extensions

Vertical Brand	*Horizontal Brand Extensions*					
	1	*2*	*3*	*4*	*5*	*6*
Extensions	**Hamburgers**	**Chicken**	**Sausage**	**Veggie**	**Ribs**	**Diners**
1	Original	Chick'n Grill	Breakfast Sausage	Savory Portabella	Meatless Riblets	Diner Deluxe
2	Flame Grilled			Veggie Medley		
3	Santa Fe			Fire Roasted Vegetable		

FIGURE 7-18 Honda Product Line for Multiple Product-Markets									
Auto-mobiles	*Motor-cycles*	*Scooters*	*Jet Skis*	*ATVs*	*Lawn and Garden*	*Snow Blowers*	*Pumps*	*Generators*	*Engines*
Accord	Touring	Silver Wing	Aqua Trax F-12	Utility	Lawn Mowers	Wheel Drive	Construction	Handheld	GX Series
Civic Sedan	Sport Touring	Reflex	Aqua Trax F-12X	Sport	Tillers	Track Drive	De-Watering	Economy	GC Series
Civic Coupe	Sport	Elite-80			Trimmers	Light Weight	Multi-Purpose	Industrial	Mini 4 Stroke
Civic Hybrid	Cruiser	Metro-politan					Submersible	Super Quiet	
Insight	Standard	Metro-politan II						Deluxe	
Odyssey	Moto-cross								
Pilot	Off-Road								
S-2000									

New Product–Market Brand Extensions

Vertical and horizontal brand extensions provide excellent opportunities for growth within a given product–market. However, eventually a business will hit a point of diminishing returns and will need to examine the potential of its proven brand name in other product–market applications. Honda built a reputation in the automotive and motorcycle markets for reliable, high quality products. This brand reputation allowed easy entry to each of the other product–markets listed in the following, often at a price premium. The Honda brand name was so strong that it was easily transferred to related product–markets such as lawn mowers, snow blowers, pumps, generators, skimobiles, and jet skis, as illustrated in Figure 7-18. Each product–market had a "related relevance" to what the Honda brand name stood for in terms of quality and reliability, and the benefits of Honda's core brand carried over to these new products.

Co-Branding

A successful brand can also be leveraged by entering another product–market with co-branding rather than creating a brand extension. For example, Yoplait yogurt co-branded with Trix, a children's cereal, to create Trix Yoplait yogurt produced for children.[19] High awareness and brand preference for Trix among children quickly led to sales of Trix Yoplait yogurt with no advertising.

Co-branding takes advantage of the potential synergy of two brands that share a common market space. Healthy Choice had many brand extensions in the frozen-food category. To enter the cereal market, co-branding with Kellogg's cereals saved considerable advertising money and provided easier access to cereal shelf space in retail stores. The composite product—"Healthy Choice from Kellogg's"—uses the Healthy Choice logo, colors, and packaging. Co-branding provided Healthy Choice with easy access to the already crowded cereal market, while it gave Kellogg's a credible product-line extension that included a dimension of weight loss and health—a product concept that had failed without the Healthy Choice name and credibility.

Trix Yoplait yogurt and Healthy Choice from Kellogg's are composite co-brands that merge two brands together. Co-branding can also include ingredient co-branding strategies. "Intel Inside" is a classic example of *ingredient co-branding*. The Intel micro-processor chip is an ingredient—a key component—of a personal computer. Intel's reputation for quality in personal computers adds perceived quality to the personal computer. Dell Computer with "Intel Inside" is a co-branding strategy that has helped Dell grow its sales of personal computers and helped Intel grow its sales of micro-processors. Using the "Intel Inside" logo on all personal computers using Intel micro-processors was a low-cost way to keep the Intel company name in front of personal computer customers.

Bundling and Unbundling Strategies

Products are often enhanced with additional features and services to provide customers with more complete solutions. Most personal computers are purchased with a variety of software packages to enable easier and faster usage of common programs such as word processing, spreadsheets and Internet access. In other instances, customers may have designed their own specialty software and would seek to purchase a personal computer without this software (i.e. unbundled) in order to lower their total cost of purchase. Each of these product strategies can be used to further enhance a product's benefits or lower cost by removing product features and services.

Product Bundling

Bundling products serves to create a complete customer solution that has the potential to create a superior customer value and attract customers. Products such as living room sets, entertainment packages, and software offered with the purchase of computers are product bundles that have the potential to create a superior value (economic and perceived) for target customers. There are two approaches to product bundling.

A *pure product bundling* strategy involves the sale of two or more products at an overall price lower than the total price that would be paid if the products were purchased separately. Even when the products are offered individually at a discounted price that makes the total cost equal to the bundled purchase price, customers rate the bundled offering higher in perceived value.

A *mixed bundling* strategy offers the customer the opportunity to purchase each of the items separately at a sale price or bundled with an additional level of savings. There is evidence that when both options are available, customer perceptions of value exceed those produced with a pure bundling strategy.[20] In addition, a mixed bundling strategy has been shown to be more profitable than pure bundling strategies.[21]

Product Unbundling

Unbundling a set of products that is normally sold as an integrated bundle or system can also be desirable in attracting and satisfying customers. For many complex industrial and commercial purchases, customers may want to purchase individual products or components and integrate them into a certain configuration that best serves their needs.[22] In some instances, value-added resellers (VARs) fulfill this role. For specialized applications in architecture, agriculture, or chemical processing, VARs will purchase

FIGURE 7-19   Umbrella Brand and Flanker Brand Product Line Profitability

Performance ($ millions)	Core Brand	Flanker Brand A	Flanker Brand B	All Brands
Volume (millions pounds)	120	60	20	200
Price per pound	$ 1.00	$ 0.90	$ 0.80	$ 0.95
Sales	$120.00	$54.00	$16.00	$190.00
Variable Cost	$ 0.40	$ 0.45	$ 0.55	$ 0.43
Margin per pound	$ 0.60	$ 0.45	$ 0.25	$ 0.52
Total Contribution	$ 72.00	$27.00	$ 5.00	$104.00
Manufacturing Expenses	$ 36.00	$18.00	$ 6.00	$ 60.00
Gross Profit	$ 36.00	$ 9.00	($ 1.00)	$ 44.00
Marketing Expenses	$ 10.00	$ 3.00	$ 1.00	$ 14.00
Net Marketing Contribution	$ 26.00	$ 6.00	($ 2.00)	$ 30.00
Operating Expenses	$ 13.00	$ 5.00	$ 2.00	$ 20.00
Operating Income	$ 13.00	$ 1.00	($ 4.00)	$ 10.00

unbundled products and integrate them in a customized bundle that best suits the target customers' application. Hewlett-Packard may have a very attractive product bundle, but it cannot meet the specific needs of all customers. By unbundling and selling individual products or component products to VARs and systems integrators, HP has been able to create value for its customers and sales growth opportunities for the business.

In the early evolution of a market, customer needs are generally less fragmented than in the later stages, and bundled product solutions are often very attractive. However, as markets grow and new customers enter, segments of the market emerge, and more customized product solutions are needed to satisfy different customers.[23] As a market matures, unbundling often becomes more important in attracting and satisfying customers.[24]

Product Elimination

Product elimination decisions need to be done with care. Often the cost accounting used to produce product-line profitability statements includes allocations of fixed manufacturing expenses to a line of products, which can distort the stated profitability of any single brand or product.

For example, consider a line of corn chips with a well-known core brand and two flanker brands. Each variation of the core brand is different but all are made in the same manufacturing facility that is operating at 60 percent of capacity. As shown in Figure 7-19, the core brand produces an operating income of $13 million while Flanker Brand A is barely profitable at $1 million and Flanker Brand B is operating at a loss of $4 million. Many managers would be tempted to eliminate Flanker Brand B in an effort to improve profits. However, eliminating Flanker Brand B would actually lower profits by $4 million. Flanker Brand B produces a total contribution of $5 million while costing $1 million in marketing expenses. If Flanker Brand B were eliminated, the $6 million in manufacturing expense would have to be reallocated to the two other brands. While the $1 million in marketing expenses associated with Flanker Brand B would be eliminated, so would the $5 million in total contribution. Hence, there is a loss of $4 million in operating profit.

Summary

For any specific target segment, a business needs to develop a tactical marketing strategy that involves positioning its product with respect to products and price and marketing its product with respect to promotion and place. This chapter focused on product position and product strategies, but a successful marketing strategy requires a highly integrated mix of product, price, promotion, and place.

Product positioning and differentiation are key parts of a successful marketing strategy. How should a business position its products relative to customer needs and competitors? And what source of differentiation is needed to make this product position differentially superior to competitors' products? Low-price differentiation is an important position to develop for businesses serving price-sensitive markets. However, lowering the customer's transactions costs can also be a valuable way to achieve a low-cost advantage. For markets in which differentiation is possible, a business could build its differentiation around a product or package advantage, service advantage, or an advantage in brand reputation. To be successful, the differentiation underlying the positioning strategy must be meaningful to target customers and sustainable (not easily duplicated by competitors).

A positioning strategy is further enhanced by the brand name used to identify a product. Because a company may have many products and serve many diverse markets, special care has to be given to how brand names are encoded to ensure both meaning and consistency across the product line. Commonly used brand encoding systems include (1) company and brand name, (2) company, brand and sub-brand name, (3) company and product name, (4) company, brand and sub-brand name, (5) company, brand name and number or letter, (6) brand name and benefit and (7) brand name only. Each of these brand-encoding systems has advantages and disadvantages with respect to distinctiveness, consistency, and communicating the product's positioning.

To grow, a business needs to leverage its product knowledge, production capabilities, marketing systems, and brand equity. Product line strategies provide an excellent opportunity to grow and leverage current assets and expenses. Related product line extensions that are built off an existing brand or a new brand are important ways to achieve profitable growth. Brands that are well known for above-average quality create a basis from which to create flanker brands. One has to be mindful of sales cannibalization, damaging the image of the core brand, and the diminishing returns of adding a number of brands. Product bundling and unbundling are also product strategies that can enhance customer attractiveness in certain customer markets.

Finally, new product development is an essential part of market-based product management. Without new product success, a business's long-run survival is in question, as is its short-run ability to grow the business. The higher a business's percentage of new product sales, the higher its level of real sales growth will be. And when new product sales are also a source of relative competitive advantage, even higher rates of sales growth are achievable. A market-based business should manage the new product development process on the basis of three important areas of input: customer, competitor, and technology. The goal is to develop a new product that is responsive to an unfulfilled customer need in a manner that is superior to what the competition is offering.

APPLICATION PROBLEM—SILICONE SEALANTS

Silicone Sealants manufactures and markets a wide range of silicone sealants used in the electronics, electro-mechanical, and construction markets. The silicone is the same in each market application but is branded and marketed differently in each market.

As shown in the diagram below, the EL-9100 is sold direct to end-users at $9.00 per pound along with applications engineering, technical support, and applicator designed for electronics applica-

tions. The EM-3100 is sold at $6.00 per pound with a direct sales force but is distributed by industrial distributors with a special applicator at a customer price of $8.00 per pound. The direct sales force provides limited applications for engineering but can resolve problems quickly. The C-3100 is sold at $4.00 per pound to construction retailers who resell the silicone sealant for $6.00 per pound with no applicator or technical support.

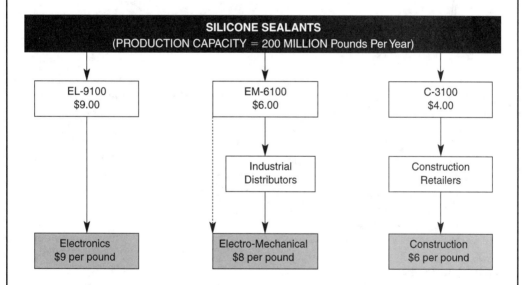

The combined sales of the Silicone Sealants are $880 million per year. Each product–market has different costs associated with packaging, sales, and marketing. The manufacturing expense of $175 million is shared based on vol-

ume produced, and the operating expenses of $80 million are shared on the basis of sales. As shown below, the electronics product–market is clearly the most profitable, and the construction market is losing money.

Continued

Silicone Sealant's Product-Line Income Statement

Performance (millions)	EL-9100 Electronics	EM-6100 Electro-Mech.	C-3100 Construction	Sealants Total
Volume	40	60	40	140
Price per lb.	$ 9.00	$6.00	$ 4.00	$ 6.29
Sales	$360.00	$360.00	$160.00	$880.00
Variable Cost	$ 4.50	$3.50	$ 2.25	$ 3.43
Margin per lb.	$ 4.50	$2.50	$ 1.75	$ 2.86
Total Contribution	$180.00	$150.00	$ 70.00	$400.00
Manufacturing Expenses	$ 50.00	$ 75.00	$ 50.00	$175.00
Gross Profit	$130.00	$ 75.00	$ 20.00	$225.00
Marketing Expenses	$ 36.00	$ 28.80	$ 9.60	$ 74.40
Net Marketing Contribution	$ 94.00	$ 46.20	$ 10.40	$150.60
Operating Expenses	$ 32.73	$ 32.73	$ 14.55	$ 80.00
Operating Income	$ 61.27	$ 13.47	($ 4.15)	$ 70.60

The finance manager has called a meeting to discuss C-3100 profits in the Construction market. He recommends that they exit the construction market since they are losing over $4 million per year.

The construction-marketing manager responds with the following proposal.

"Construction retailers are split into two segments, 75 percent "**price buyers**" and 25 percent "**security seekers**," (those who want a supply guarantee). I propose we offer an e-marketing sales program in construction with variations to accommodate both customer needs:

- **Price Buyers:** A construction silicone product sold online at market prices of $4.00 per pound with no guaranteed availability.
- **Security Seekers:** Guaranteed supply and first to be shipped whenever you call at $4.50 per pound.

The marketing expense for the *price buyer* program would be 2 percent of sales, and marketing expenses for the *security seekers* program would be 4 percent of sales.

Questions

For access to interactive software to answer the questions below go to www.RogerJBest.com or www.prenhall. com/best.

1. What would be the profit impact (change in net marketing contribution) of exiting the construction market as proposed by the finance manager?

2. How would the net marketing contribution change in the other markets if the business exited the construction market?

3. What is the profit impact of the proposed market multi-segment strategy? Assume the same total volume in the construction market would be retained.

4. Would it be the profit impact in the "Security" segment if the marketing budget was doubled in order to double the volume sold in this segment?

Market-Based Logic And Strategic Thinking

1. Why did Loctite's initial Quick Metal marketing effort fail?
2. How would you evaluate the product line positioning of Black & Decker relative to Sears in terms of customer choice and customer value? See Figure 7-2.
3. How does Compaq's product positioning strategy differ from IBM's?
4. How could a business with a very attractive product position achieve a lower market share?
5. What is Dell's source of customer attractiveness and differentiation? How does Compaq approach the same market?
6. How would a business use the eight dimensions of quality differentiation in developing a product and package differentiation strategy?
7. How does a business such as McDonald's develop a positioning strategy around some aspect of service differentiation?
8. Why would a brand name such as Kodak, Disney, or Coca-Cola create customer value and provide a basis for product positioning and differentiation?
9. Why would the occupancy of a Fairfield Inn increase by 15 percent when the Marriott name is added to the building?
10. Why would a mere extension of a line of related products contribute to higher levels of profitability?
11. What is the marketing logic that underlies Anheuser-Busch's product line and bundling strategy for the beer market?
12. What are the advantages of a product strategy involving a strong core brand with flanker brands? Under what conditions would this product line strategy fail?
13. Why are vertical brand-line extensions less expensive than horizontal brand-line extensions?
14. How does a well-known brand help in the marketing and profitability of a flanker brand?
15. Why would a company like Ford co-brand with Eddie Bauer to create a unique brand of Ford Explorer within the Ford SUV product line?
16. Under what conditions would the elimination of a flanker brand with a negative operating income result in lower overall operating income if eliminated?

Notes

1. Bill Abrams, "Consumer-Product Techniques Help Loctite Sell to Industry," *Wall Street Journal* (April 2, 1981).
2. "Drills for All Reasons," *Consumer Reports* (November, 1997):24–28.
3. David Garvin, "Competing on Eight Dimensions of Quality," *Harvard Business Review* (November–December 1987):101–5.
4. Valarie Zeithaml, A. Parasuramon, and Leonard Berry, *Delivering Quality Service* (New York: Free Press, 1990): chapter 1.
5. Bradley Gale, "Creating Power Brands," in *Managing Customer Value* (New York: Free Press, 1994), 153–74.
6. Peter Farquhar, "Managing Brand Equity," *Marketing Research* (September 1989):24–33.
7. David Aaker, *Managing Brand Equity: Capitalizing on the Value of a Brand Name* (New York: Free Press, 1991).
8. Daniel Sheinin and Bernd Schmitt, "Extending Brands with New Product Concepts: The Role of Category Attribute Congruity, Brand Affect, and Brand Breadth," *Journal of Business Research* 31 (1994):1–10.
9. D. Aaker, *Building Strong Brands* (The Free Press, 19996), 356–357.
10. D. D'Alessandro, *Brand Warfare* (McGraw-Hill, 2001).
11. S. Hill and C. Lederer, C. Lederer, and K. Keller, *The Infinite Asset: Managing Brands to Build New Value* (Harvard Business School Press, 2001).

12. "The Top 100 Brands," *Business Week,* (August 5, 2002), 95–99.

13. S. M. Davis, *Brand Asset Management* (Jossey-Bass, Inc., 2000).

14. K. Keller, "The Brand Report Card," *Harvard Business Review* (January-February, 2000),147–157.

15. C. Lederer and S. Hill, "See Your Brands Through Your Customers' Eyes," *Harvard Business Review* (June, 2001), 125–133.

16. T. Erdem, "An Empirical Analysis of Umbrella Branding," *Journal of Marketing Research* (August 1998): 339–51; David Aaker, *Building Strong Brands* (New York: Free Press, 1995); P. Dacin and D. Smith, "The Effect of Brand Portfolio Characteristics on Consumer Evaluations of Brand Extensions," *Journal of Marketing Research* (May 1994): 229–42; A. Rangaswamy, R. Burke, and T. Oliver, "Brand Equity and Extendibility of Brand Names," *International Journal of Research in Marketing* (March 1993):61–75.

17. M. J. Hatch and M. Schultz, "Are the Strategic Stars Aligned for Your Corporate Brand?" *Harvard Business Review* (February, 2001), 129–134.

18. Bruce Hardle, "The Logic of Product-Line Extensions," *Harvard Business Review* (November– December 1994):53–62.

19. D. Aaker, *Building Strong Brands* (The Free Press, 19996), 298–300.

20. Manjit Yadav and Kent Monroe, "How Buyers Perceive Savings in a Bundle Price: An Examination of a Bundle's Transaction Value," *Journal of Marketing Research* (August 1993): 350–58.

21. William Adams and Janet Yellen, "Commodity Bundling and the Burden of Monopoly," *Quarterly Journal of Economics* (August 1976):475–98; and Richard Schmalensee, "Gaussian Demand and Commodity Bundling," *Journal of Business* 57(1984):211–30.

22. Lynn Wilson, Allen Weiss, and George John, "Unbundling of Industrial Systems," *Journal of Marketing Research* (May 1990):123–38.

23. Roger Best and Reinhard Angelmar, "Strategies for Leveraging Technology Advantage," in *Handbook on Business Strategy* (Boston: Warren, Gorham, and Lamont, 1989):2–1-2-10.

24. Barbara Jackson, *Winning and Keeping Industrial Customers* (Lexington, MA: Lexington Books, 1985); and Michael Porter, *Competitive Advantage* (New York: Free Press, 1985).

8

MARKET-BASED PRICING AND PRICING STRATEGIES

In the early 1990s, Compaq Computer used cost-based pricing to price its personal computers.[1] This pricing process started with the cost of making a personal computer (purchased parts, labor, and equipment) and adds on a profit margin to achieve a desired price as illustrated in Figure 8-1. In this example the cost to make a low-priced computer for the under-$1000 segment of the PC market was $600. A desired profit margin of 25 percent was added to the cost to produce a price to retailers of $840. Retailers also used cost-based pricing and marked their cost of $840 up to a price of $940 to achieve a 15 percent profit margin. In this case, everybody should be happy: the target end-user customer got a personal computer for under $1000, retailers obtained a desired margin of 15 percent, and the computer manufacturer achieved a desired margin of 25 percent.

But something is missing from this approach to pricing. First, cost-based pricing ignores what the customer would be willing to pay for a certain level of product performance. Second, this approach to pricing overlooks what the competition is offering relative to the customer's needs and price affordability. Recognizing these flaws in its pricing logic, Compaq shifted from cost-based pricing to market-based pricing in the mid-1990s. As shown in Figure 8-1, market-based pricing starts with the customer, the

FIGURE 8-1 Cost-Based Pricing versus Market-Based Pricing

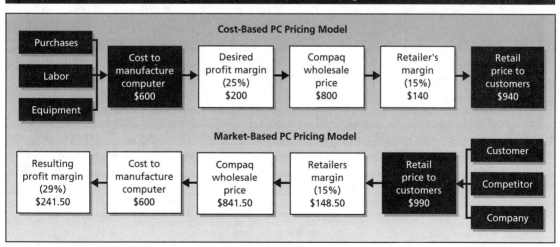

FIGURE 8-2 Pricing Strategy Process Template

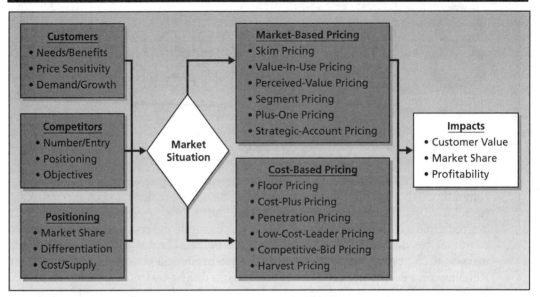

competition, and company positioning. Based on customer needs price sensitivity, and competing products a price is developed around a product's relative strengths to provide a better value than competing products. In this example, the customer would have paid $990 for the same computer based on its benefits and price relative to competing computers. Retailers would still want their traditional 15 percent margin, resulting in a market-based price of $841.50 from the PC manufacturer. At a cost of $600 per unit, the margin would be $241.50 per unit. This would be $41.50 higher than the margin obtained with cost-based pricing. In this instance, market-based pricing achieved a higher profit while delivering an attractive customer value. It may appear that market-based pricing is the preferred approach to pricing, but there are situations in which cost-based pricing may be a better approach depending on the market situation, as illustrated in Figure 8-2.

Cost-based pricing is the most commonly used approach to pricing in business.[2] This is largely because customer and competitor intelligence are hard to obtain and because cost-based pricing is relatively easy to do. One study found that over 60 percent of the businesses surveyed used cost-based pricing as their primary basis for setting price.[3] This is consistent with an ongoing worldwide study of over 15,000 managers from over 60 countries where 64 percent of those surveyed used cost-based pricing to set price. As shown below those in general management are more likely to use market-based pricing while many in marketing management and other related job functions are more likely to use cost-based pricing. In this study managers who use market-based pricing had much higher levels of marketing knowledge and stronger market-oriented attitudes.[4]

Pricing Strategy	Senior Management	Marketing Management	Product Management	Sales/Sales Management	Marketing Communications
Market-Based	55%	37%	34%	31%	17%
Cost-Based	45%	63%	66%	69%	83%

FIGURE 8-3   Customer and Competitor Intelligence and Pricing Orientation

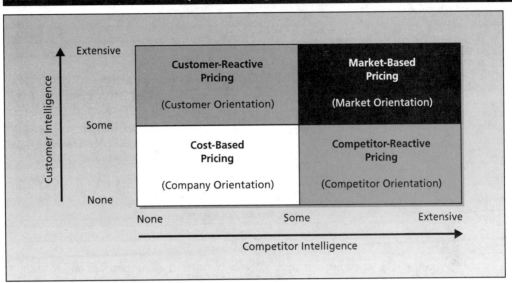

MARKET-BASED PRICING

At the heart of market-based pricing is extensive customer and competitor intelligence.[5] Without high levels of both, market-based pricing is simply not possible. This is why most businesses fall back into cost-based pricing as illustrated in Figure 8-3. A business with a strong customer orientation may believe it is using market-based pricing but without competitor intelligence the business cannot fully gauge its price position. Likewise, a business focused on competitor's pricing and positioning but ignoring customer needs will evolve into reactive competitive pricing. Thus, only businesses with a strong market orientation that focus on both customers and competitors have the possibility to engage in market-based pricing.

Market-based pricing starts with a good understanding of customer needs and the benefits a product creates relative to competitors' products.[6] On the basis of customer benefits, price is set relative to competition to create a superior value. In this way, price is set in the market, not at the factory or in the financial department. This section reviews the various market-based pricing strategies while the following section reviews commonly used cost-based pricing strategies

Skim Pricing

Skim pricing is most likely to occur at the early stages of the product life cycle as illustrated in Figure 8-4. In some situations, a business holds a proprietary product advantage relative to competition because it holds a patent or the product has a unique capability. In such a case, a business will pursue a premium price strategy while still delivering superior customer value until competition can match its source of competitive advantage. For example, many prescription drugs are patented. Under the protection of a patent, the holder may charge higher-than-normal prices. During this period,

FIGURE 8-4   Skim Pricing

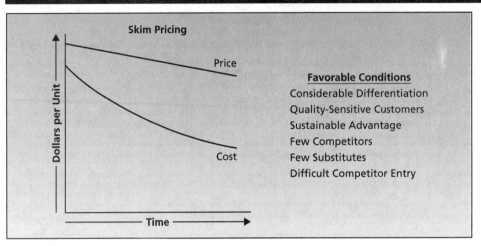

Skim Pricing

Favorable Conditions
Considerable Differentiation
Quality-Sensitive Customers
Sustainable Advantage
Few Competitors
Few Substitutes
Difficult Competitor Entry

the business is able to create a *price umbrella* because the competition cannot match the business's relative advantage, as shown in Figure 8-4.

But under what conditions is a skim pricing strategy likely to work? As summarized in Figure 8-4, when a business has a considerable, and sustainable, differentiation advantage in a quality-sensitive market that has few competitors and is difficult for competitors to enter, a *skim pricing* strategy is a viable market-based pricing strategy. When feasible, a skim pricing strategy allows a business to systematically penetrate markets as it adds production capacity. As the demand for a high-priced segment is sat-

FIGURE 8-5   Market-Based Value Pricing

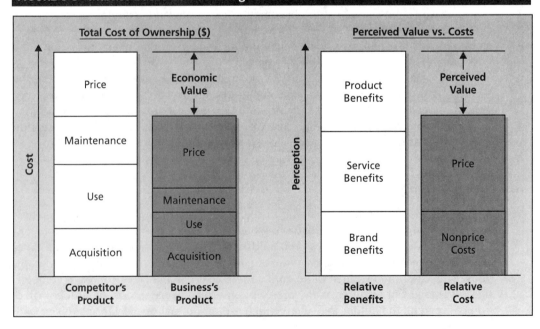

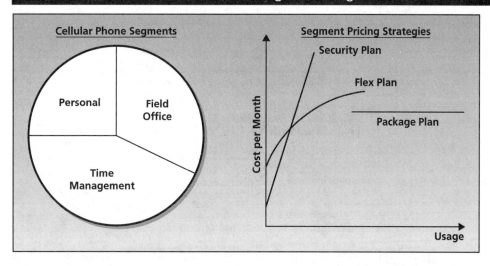

FIGURE 8-6 Cellular Phone Market-Based Segment Pricing

urated, price can be lowered to systematically attract more customers until prices reach a level affordable to most potential customers.

Value-In-Use Pricing

As a business moves into the growth stage of the product life cycle it will have to find a way to lower the cost to potential customers in order to attract their purchase volume. However, this does not have to mean lower prices. By considering the total cost of ownership incurred by target customers, a business can utilize market-based pricing to produce an attractive savings (economic value) while maintaining a premium price. For example, in Figure 8-5, the price of a business's product is higher than the price of the competitor's product, but the customer's total cost of ownership is lower. The business saves the customer money on the basis of lower acquisition, use, and maintenance costs over the life of the product.

The level of economic value and price are set relative to what is an attractive savings to customers, not on the cost of manufacturing and marketing the product. In market-based pricing costs and margins are the business's problem, not the customer's. Customers are interested in savings or economic value, and the higher the savings, the more attractive the business's product. Chapter 4 discusses the various ways a business can lower the cost of ownership and, hence, achieve higher price levels while still creating a superior value for target customers.

Perceived Value Pricing

Some customer benefits are more difficult to quantify in terms of economic value, yet they have an important perceived value. Another approach to market-based pricing is *perceived value pricing*. As illustrated in Figure 8-5, the perceived benefits derived from the product, service, and brand (image or reputation) yield a certain level of total perceived benefits. The overall perceived cost of purchase is made up of the price paid, the terms of purchase, and any transaction costs that contribute to the total perceived

FIGURE 8-7 Product Life Cycle Pricing Strategies

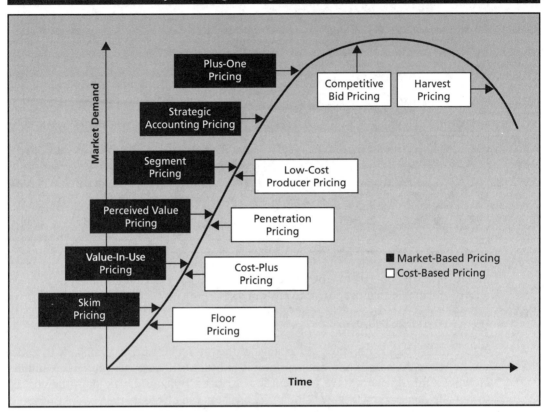

cost of purchase. The net difference between perceived overall benefits and cost is perceived customer value. In this example, the strength of the business's overall benefits enables it to charge a price higher than the competition's (price premium) and still create a larger overall perceived value for customers. Chapter 4 provides a detailed discussion of how to measure perceived customer value and the various ways a business can improve its perceived benefits in order to obtain higher prices and still create a superior value when compared with competitors. One should keep in mind that market-based value pricing is only possible with a good understanding of customer needs and competitor's positions as presented earlier in Figure 8-3.

Segment Pricing

At the heart of market segmentation is market-based pricing strategies. Customers in different segments generally have different product needs and different price sensitivities. A price-sensitive segment would be attracted to low price regardless of additional product or service benefits. A quality-sensitive segment may pay more for the extra benefits (product, service, or brand) they desire. Thus, the market-based price could be different for different segments within a market.

Let's consider the cellular phone market. There are many potential segments, but the three outlined in Figure 8-6 are typical of many cellular phone markets. Customers in the *field office* segment are heavy users who work away from the office. The *package plan,* which provides a fixed monthly cost for a wide range of usage, provides considerable economic value and cost certainty to businesses in the field office segment. Customers in the *time management* segment work at and away from their offices but use the cellular phone to manage their time, both business and personal. Their usage varies from month to month. A *flex plan* best fits their needs because it provides for usage discounts during periods of heavy use. Finally, the *personal* user is a nonbusiness customer with low usage. This user is sensitive to the cost of cellular phone service but likes the security and convenience a cellular phone offers. For this segment, a *security plan* offers a very low minimum monthly access fee but a higher usage fee. Because all three market-based price programs are available to any customer, we would expect customers in the various segments to prefer the market-based pricing alternative that best fits their usage patterns and price sensitivity. As shown in Figure 8-7, Segment Pricing is most likely to be used during the growth stage of the Product Life Cycle.

Strategic-Account Pricing

Customers that are large and very important to a business's sales and profits become strategic accounts. Pricing for strategic accounts is market-based and customized to the unique needs of a strategic customer and competitive market conditions. The market-based pricing perspective is also longer range and may include a pricing mechanism to adjust prices over a period of several years. A primary goal of strategic-account pricing is to maintain a strong business-to-business relationship even when market conditions in an industry change. For example, sellers may be required to take a slightly lower price in a "seller's market" when average prices are generally high. Likewise, buyers may be asked to pay a slightly higher price in "buyer's markets" where average prices are generally very low. This market-based price-sharing helps reduce large swings in margins while maintaining large volumes of the customer's business. Strategic account pricing will not work without a strong commitment to serving customer needs and a price that creates a superior value when compared to competitor's offerings.

Plus-One Pricing

As products mature in most competitive markets, businesses are able to emulate the best features of competitors' products. As a result, it is difficult to stand out as unique. To succeed in these markets, a business needs some source of differentiation in order to build a unique product position. It needs to establish a plus-one product position[7] in order to justify a market-based price with a slight premium relative to competing products.

A plus-one market-based pricing strategy product position is one in which a business can equal competitors on all areas of product and service quality but can find one area of meaningful performance in which it is clearly superior. For example, Volvo, in the luxury car market, must meet customer expectations in all aspects of performance but uses safety as its plus-one product differentiation strategy in achieving a market-based price relative to competing luxury cars. This is what makes Volvo uniquely different, and it is a central part of its product-price positioning and value proposition. On the other hand, Lexus uses performance as its plus-one pricing strategy while Mercedes uses its reputation. As illustrated in Figure 8-7, a plus-one pricing strategy is a market-based pricing strategy that is most likely to be used in late stages of the product life cycle.

COST-BASED PRICING STRATEGIES

While it may appear that market-based pricing is the preferred approach to pricing in a market-focused business, there are situations in which cost-based pricing may be an appropriate pricing approach. Market-based pricing starts with the customer, competition, and a business's competitive position, as illustrated in Figure 8-1. In this manner, price is set in the market to create a desired level of customer attractiveness and delivered customer value. In contrast, cost-based pricing starts with the cost of the product and a desired margin. On the basis of these requirements, a price is set and the product is sold to channel intermediaries who mark up the price to a level that allows them to achieve a desired margin. This, of course, is the price the customer sees in the marketplace, as illustrated in Figure 8-1. In markets where product differentiation is minimal, cost-based pricing is often a reasonable alternative to market-based pricing.

Floor Pricing

Floor pricing is an internal, cost-based price computation based on a desired level of profitability. The floor price could be based on a desired margin or return on investment. As a result, floor pricing is often used in the early stages of the product life cycle (see Figure 8-4) when target customers are less price sensitive.

For example, a new product has an available production capacity of two million units per year. At that capacity the cost per unit is $5.00 and the fixed manufacturing expense is $5 million per year. The business is not interested in launching new products with less than a 30 percent gross profit. Given these financial parameters, a price of $10.70 per unit will yield annual sales of $21.4 million and a gross profit $6.4 million— a 30 percent gross profit margin.

$$\textbf{\% Gross Profit} = \frac{\text{Volume} \times \textbf{Price} - \text{Volume} \times \begin{matrix}\text{Unit} \\ \text{Cost}\end{matrix} - \begin{matrix}\text{Manufacturing} \\ \text{Exp.}\end{matrix}}{\text{Volume} \times \textbf{Price}}$$

$$\textbf{.30} = \frac{2{,}000{,}000 \times \textbf{Price} - 2{,}000{,}000 \times \$5.00 - \$5 \text{ million}}{2{,}000{,}000 \times \textbf{Price}}$$

$$\textbf{Price} = \textbf{\$10.70} \text{ per unit}$$

A cost-based floor price of $10.70 has nothing to do with what customers would pay for the product or what competitors are charging for a comparable product. However, the floor price of $10.70 does serve the purpose of establishing the lowest price the business could charge and still make its financial objective of a 30 percent gross-profit margin.

Another common floor-pricing approach is based on return on investment or return on invested capital. Assume the same business wanted a minimum of a 30 percent pretax return on investment on the same project and required $20 million in investment. In this case we need to include the operating expenses, which are estimated at $2 million per year. Based on these financial parameters, a price of $11.50 would be needed to achieve a desired pretax return on investment.

$$\text{Return on Investment} = \frac{\text{Volume} \times \textbf{Price} - \text{Volume} \times \frac{\text{Unit}}{\text{Cost}} - \frac{\text{Manufacturing}}{\text{Exp.}} - \frac{\text{Operating}}{\text{Exp.}}}{\text{Investment}}$$

$$.30 = \frac{2{,}000{,}000 \times \textbf{Price} - 2{,}000{,}000 \times \$5.00 - \$5\text{ million} - \$2\text{ million}}{20{,}000{,}000}$$

Price = **$11.50** per unit

Again, this price has nothing to do with market reality. It is an internally generated price that benchmarks what is needed to achieve a desired return on investment. If this price or a higher price cannot be obtained, the product will fail to earn the desired return on the $20 million investment. Again, the floor price should not be used to set price; it should only be used to calibrate the lowest price at which a product can be sold and still meet the financial benchmarks set by the company.

Cost-Plus Pricing

Cost-plus pricing is also often referred to as markup pricing since the price is determined by using a standard markup on cost. For an internally focused business, cost-plus pricing is likely to be used in the early stages of the product life cycle as a business's costs come down as volume grows. The exact markup on cost will depend on the company and industry. However, channel intermediaries, who typically use cost-plus pricing, utilize standard markups that vary by industry

For example, Figure 8-8 illustrates the cost-plus channel markups typically used in five different product–markets.[8] An average furniture manufacturer that sells to a wholesaler at a price index of 100 will see its furniture marked up by 38.9 percent to a price index of 138.9. At a wholesale index price of 138.9, the furniture is sold to furniture retailers who mark up the price by 63.6 percent. This results in a buyer's price index of 227, a price 2.27 times the manufacturer's selling price based on industry markup pricing in the furniture industry. Again, we should emphasize that this approach to pricing has little to do with customer needs, price sensitivity and competitor's product and price positioning.

Penetration Pricing

Businesses focused on building volume may use a cost-based penetration-pricing strategy. As illustrated in Figure 8-4, this cost-based pricing strategy is most likely to be employed in the growth stage of the product where volumes are likely to grow fastest

FIGURE 8-8 Cost-Plus Pricing and Channel Markups					
Business Sector	*Manufacturer's Price Index*	*Wholesaler's Markup*	*Wholesale Price*	*Retailer's Markup*	*Buyers Price Index*
Furniture	100	38.9%	138.90	63.6%	227
Gasoline	100	19.8%	119.80	22.8%	147
Groceries	100	23.5%	123.50	28.5%	159
Sporting Goods	100	34.8%	134.80	57.8%	213
Liquor	100	21.6%	121.60	37.1%	167
Average	**100**	**27.7%**	**127.70**	**38.8%**	**177**

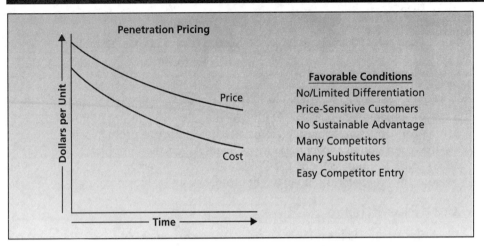

FIGURE 8-9   Penetration Pricing

Penetration Pricing

Favorable Conditions
No/Limited Differentiation
Price-Sensitive Customers
No Sustainable Advantage
Many Competitors
Many Substitutes
Easy Competitor Entry

in response to lower prices. Thus, the primary objective of penetration pricing is to build volume that drives down cost as illustrated in Figure 8-9.

Cost-based penetration pricing is a mass market strategy that is used most often when product differentiation is minimal, customers are price-sensitive, there are many competitors or substitutes, and competitor entry is easy. The volume leader can often gain a cost advantage and continue to lower prices, discouraging competitor entry as well as encouraging competitor exit. The price of DRAMs (Dynamic Random Access Memory) is a good example of volume-sensitive pricing as illustrated in Figure 8-10. In this product–market prices decrease by 30 percent every time cumulative volume doubles.[9]

A volume leadership position can enable a business to use penetration pricing to build market share and discourage competition from either entering the market or staying in the market. In this situation, the share leader is simply further down the cost curve and is able to price at a lower level and still maintain a desirable contribution margin. Thus, when cost reduction is volume-sensitive and product differentiation is minimal, a penetration pricing strategy may be a viable path to market leadership and profitable growth.

Low-Cost Leader Pricing

The producers of Bic pens and lighters have always sought to have the lowest cost and a price that no competitor could get below. Likewise, from its beginnings Wal-Mart sought to be the low-cost leader in retail, and this was accomplished with a variety of management systems that lowered the cost of goods sold as well as lower operating expenses. A low-cost leader does not always have to be the volume leader, however. While many companies may achieve a cost advantage based on volume and economies of scale, this is not required. There are even low-share businesses that have moved into the low-cost producer position.

Chi Mei, for example, is a low-cost producer of plastics and other chemicals. The company operates with a minimal sales force, minimal management staff, and no technical service. All aspects of its business are designed to maintain a low-cost leadership position. While not the share or volume leader, Chi Mei is the lowest-cost producer and offers the lowest prices based on their low cost position. Even in situations where cus-

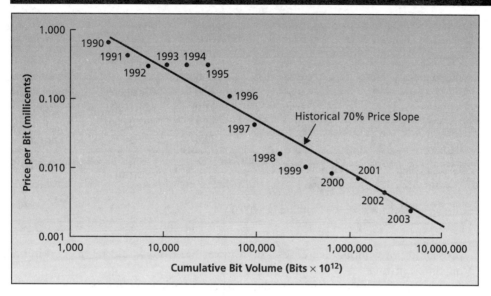

FIGURE 8-10   DRAM Price Curve

tomers may pay more due to short supply, low-cost leaders base their prices on costs and slim margins. As illustrated in Figure 8-4 low-cost producer cost-based pricing is most likely to occur in the late stages of their product life cycle when product differentiation is minimal and prices very competitive.

Competitive Bid Pricing

Competitive bid pricing is a cost-based pricing approach that is used in markets where there is little or no product differentiation. In such markets, bidders are prequalified and bids must meet product specifications and delivery dates in order to be considered. Of those meeting the required specifications, suppliers are selected on the basis of the lowest price. For example, in the corporate purchase of personal computers, product features are specified, bidders qualified, and price bids submitted. For example, Dell Computer has been successful in winning 50 percent of its bids in customer purchases with specific product performance and service requirements. Competitive bid pricing is a cost-based pricing strategy designed for this type of pricing.

Shown in Figure 8-11 is a ratio of price to cost called the *bid ratio*.[10] Alongside the bid ratio is a history of winning bids that the company obtained at different bid ratios. For example, a bid ratio of 1.2 (price is 20 percent over cost) resulted in winning bids 63 percent of the time. The probability of actually winning is also a function of the number of bidders. In this example, there are two bidders, and the probability of winning a bid with a 1.2 bid ratio is 0.40. The profit at this price level is $1 million, and the expected value, based on the probability of a winning bid, is $400,000. In this case, a bid ratio of 1.2 (with two bidders) is also the best cost-based price because it provides the highest expected value. Thus, in a given year, if the business bid 100 contracts in competition against one other bidder, and used a 1.2 bid ratio, it would achieve the best level of overall profitability for the year. Of course, as the number of bidders increases, the

FIGURE 8-11   Cost-Based Competitive Bid Price Strategy

Bid Ratio	Percentage of Winning Bids	Probability* of Winning	Profit of Winning Bid (millions)	Expected Value	Cost-Based Pricing Logic
0.90	100	1.00	−$.05	−$500,000	A price
1.00	92	0.85	0	0	20 percent
1.10	80	0.64	+$.50	+$320,000	higher than cost
1.20	63	0.40	+$1.0	+$400,000 ◄──	offers the best
1.30	21	0.04	+$1.5	+$60,000	long-run
1.40	3	0.00	+$2.0	+$0	profitability.

$$*\text{Probability of Winning} = \left(\frac{\% \text{ Winning Bids}}{100\%}\right)^{\text{No. of Bidders}} = \left(\frac{63\%}{100\%}\right)^{2} = 0.40$$

Expected value $= 0.40 \times \$1 \text{ million} = \$400,000$

probability of winning decreases, and a lower bid ratio would be needed in order to maximize profits.

On the basis of this logic, we might expect a business to always use a certain cost-based price bid ratio, but this is not the case. For example, consider an aerospace contractor that is using a 1.2 bid ratio but has won more bids than expected and is now approaching full manufacturing production capacity. For the next bid, this contractor might purposely bid higher, knowing the chances of winning are lower. However, if the bid was won, it would be at a higher profit level and it would be worth the extra cost needed to complete another job while at full capacity. The opposite might also be true. If that contractor's capacity utilization is very low, it may bid below the optimal bid price to improve its odds of winning. In these instances, volume is needed, and the business may forgo higher profits in exchange for a better chance of obtaining a certain volume of work.

Harvest Pricing

At the late stages of a product's life cycle, margins are often very low and volumes flat or declining The net result is poor profits with little prospect for improvement. In these situations, many businesses will use a cost-based harvest pricing strategy as illustrated in Figure 8-7. Based on cost and the need for higher margins, the business will raise prices in anticipation of a reduction in volume. Subsequent cost-based price increases will follow to improve margins as volume continues to fall. This sequence of cost-based price increases and volume reductions is normally continued until the business exits the market at a price customers simply will not pay.

However, there is an interesting twist to harvest pricing. In many instances a business will raise price to improve margins and expect to lose volume. This was true for a manufacturer of automotive components that raised prices 15 percent and lost 30 percent of its business volume. A subsequent price increase of 10 percent, however, resulted in a modest decrease of 1 million in volume while another 10-percent price increase a year later resulted in no decrease in volume. At this combination of price and volume the business had uncovered a profitable niche market and managed price and volume to produce an attractive total contribution as illustrated in Figure 8-12.

FIGURE 8-12 Harvest Pricing and Profitability

Market Situation	Price	Volume	Sales	Unit Cost	Margin per Unit	Total Contribution
Late in life cycle	$10.00	10 million	$100 million	$10.00	$ 0	$0
15% Price Increase	$11.50	7 million	$80.50	$10.00	$1.50	$10.5 million
10% Price Increase	$12.65	6 million	$75.90	$10.00	$2.65	$15.9 million
10% Price Increase	$13.92	6 million	$83.49	$10.00	$3.92	$23.5 million

PRICING AND PROFITABILITY

Sales growth is an obsession in most businesses. Marketing and sales managers as well as general managers and CEOs generally believe that more is better: If those in marketing can deliver more volume, more market share and more sales revenues, we can grow profits. This may be true in many instances, but managers need to be especially careful when using price to achieve this objective. Let's examine a fairly common business situation.

The marketing and sales team of a business is challenged to grow sales revenues at a rate greater than 10 percent. Their product–markets are price-sensitive and they judge a 10 percent price decrease would yield a 25 percent gain in volume. If this were achieved, sales revenues would go up 12.5 percent as shown in the following. Furthermore, market share based on sales dollars would increase by 10 percent.

The problem with this sales-oriented scenario is that the strategy would lose money! As the analysis illustrates in Figure 8-13, this lower-price strategy would grow sales revenues but lower profits. This is because the increase in volume (25 percent) was not sufficient to offset the reduction in margin (30 percent). The goal of a pricing strategy should be to make more profits—not more volume or more sales dollars. In this example a price strategy to grow sales 12.5 percent would lower total contribution by almost 12.5 percent. Since all other fixed manufacturing, marketing, and operating

FIGURE 8-13 Sales Obsession versus Profit Orientation

Sales Obsession Performance Metrics	Original Situation	Growth Strategy	Percent Change
Market Demand (millions)	200	200	0%
Price (per unit)	$6.00	$5.40	−10%
Volume (millions)	40	50	25%
Market Share (units)	20%	25%	25%
Market Share (dollars)	20%	22%	10%
Sales Revenues (millions)	**$240**	**$270**	**12.5%**

Profit Orientation Performance Metrics	Original Situation	Growth Strategy	Percent Change
Price (per unit)	$6.00	$5.40	−10%
Unit Cost	$4.00	$4.00	0%
Margin per Unit	$2.00	$1.40	−30%
Volume (millions)	40	50	25%
Sales Revenues (millions)	$240	$270	12.5%
Total Contribution (millions)	**$80**	**$70**	**−12.5%**

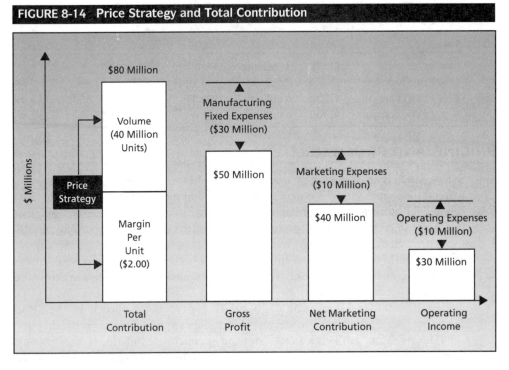

FIGURE 8-14   Price Strategy and Total Contribution

expenses are not likely to change, this price strategy to grow sales would lower overall profits. Marketing strategies like this that deliver superior sales growth but fail to contribute to profits will eventually bankrupt a company.

Total Contribution

The objective of a pricing strategy should be to improve profits. While growth in volume, market share, and sales sounds great, more is not always better. Any price change impacts *volume* and *margin.* As shown in Figure 8-14, the goal of pricing should be to determine what price produces a combination of volume and margin that increases the business's total contribution. When the total contribution produced by a price strategy is lower, overall profits will also be lower because fixed costs are deducted from the total contribution.

The total contribution of a pricing strategy is the product of the unit volume sold and the margin per unit. For example, in the case study presented in Figure 8-13 the total contribution before the price change was $80 million. This was the result of a volume of 40 million units and a $2.00 margin per unit. The strategy to grow sales would produce a volume of 50 million units but a lower margin ($1.49 per unit). The net result would be a gross profit of **$70** million, **$10** million lower than the original level of business profits.

$$\textbf{Total Contribution} = \text{Volume (units)} \times \text{Margin (per unit)}$$
$$\text{(original situation)} = \quad 40 \text{ million} \quad \times \quad \$2.00$$
$$= \quad \textbf{\$80 million}$$

$$\textbf{Total Contribution} = \text{Volume (units)} \times \text{Margin (per unit)}$$
$$\text{(price strategy)} = \quad 50 \text{ million} \quad \times \quad \$1.40$$
$$= \quad \textbf{\$70 million}$$

Price-Volume Break-even Analysis

Break-even analysis is generally viewed as an accounting concept, but it is extremely useful in evaluating the profit potential and risk associated with a pricing strategy, or any marketing strategy. The purpose of this section is to examine, from a marketing viewpoint, the usefulness of break-even volume and break-even market share.

$$\text{Operating Income} = \text{Volume} \times \text{Margin per Unit} - \text{Fixed Expenses}$$
$$0 = \text{Volume} \times \$2.00 - \$50 \text{ million}$$

$$(\text{Break-even Volume}) = \frac{\$50 \text{ million}}{\$2.00 \text{ per unit}} = 25 \text{ million units}$$

Price and Break-even Volume

For a given price strategy and marketing effort it is useful to determine the number of units that need to be sold in order to break even (produce a net profit equal to zero). For example, in the business situation presented in Figure 8-14 the margin per unit was $2.00 and the total fixed expenses (manufacturing, marketing, and operating expenses) were $50 million. Sales of 25 million units would be required to break even.

Break-even volume is the volume needed to cover fixed expenses on the basis of a particular margin per unit. Although break-even volume can be estimated graphically, as illustrated in Figure 8-15, it can be computed more directly with the following formula:

$$\text{Break-Even Volume} = \frac{\text{Fixed Expenses}}{\text{Margin per Unit}}$$

The lower the break-even volume is relative to manufacturing capacity or expected sales volume, the greater the profit potential.

Price and Break-Even Market Share

Because break-even volume is an unconstrained number, the reasonableness of the break-even volume requires additional considerations. Because market share is constrained between zero and 100 percent, break-even market share provides a better framework from which to judge profit potential and risk. To compute break-even market share requires only that we divide the break-even volume by the size of the target market, as shown next.

$$\text{Break-Even Market Share} = \frac{\text{Break-Even Volume} \times 100}{\text{Market Demand}}$$

If the market demand for the product were 200 million units per year, then the breakeven market share would be 12.5 percent when the break-even volume is 25 million units. In this case the business has a 20 percent market share which is 8.5 share points above break-even. If the business's target share was 15 percent, then the risk of a loss is greater because the breakeven share is close to the target market share.

PRICE ELASTICITY AND PERFORMANCE

Market demand and market growth are often dependent on price level. At high prices, many customers simply cannot enter the market, as described in Chapter 3. As the price of cellular phone services, CD players, and computers decreased, more customers entered these markets. In one sense, price regulates both the size of a market and how fast it will grow.

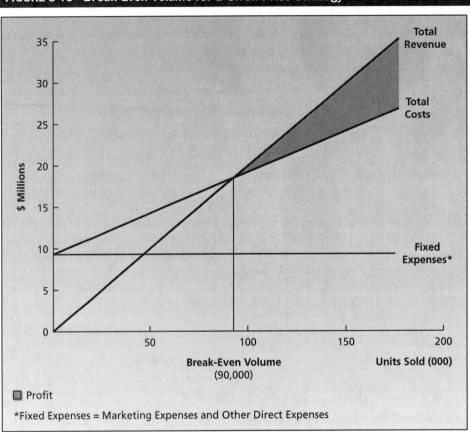

FIGURE 8-15 Break-Even Volume for a Given Price Strategy

Profit

*Fixed Expenses = Marketing Expenses and Other Direct Expenses

For example, Figure 8-16 shows how market demand for voice messaging (a telecommunications service) varies as a function of price. A business that wants to limit initial demand because of a lack of capacity to add the service may price the service at $5 per minute. This price produces an estimated demand of 9,000 customers in a particular geographic market. In addition, at this price, the price elasticity is −2.20, which means that for each 1 percent reduction in price, demand would grow by approximately 2.2 percent. Therefore, a 10 percent price reduction from $5 to $4.50 should yield a 22 percent increase in customer demand (from 9,000 to 10,980).

A business might continue to lower price to grow demand, but when the price elasticity reaches −1.0, the sales revenue will have reached its maximum. At this point, up or down price moves will result in lower overall sales revenue. This is the price point at which a nonprofit organization doing fundraising events would be able to maximize the revenues received, if that is their objective. However, a business wanting to grow profits may price above or below this price point, at which *revenues,* not necessarily *profits,* are maximized.[11]

FIGURE 8-16   Voice Messaging Price Elasticity of Demand

At each price along the diagonal curve, there is a different level of price elasticity.

Price (P)	Elasticity (e)
$6.00	−4.80
$5.00	−2.20
$4.00	−1.15
$3.00	−0.70
$2.00	−0.38
$1.00	−0.16

$$e = \frac{\Delta Q/Q}{\Delta P/P}$$

Elasticity = −2.2

Elasticity = −0.38

(Chart: Price Cost per Minute (P) vs. Market Demand (Q) (millions))

Inelastic Price Performance

As shown in Figure 8-17, when a price is inelastic, all aspects of performance are improved when prices are increased. Lowering price when it is inelastic will hurt sales, margins, and total contribution and increase unit volume, as presented in Figure 8-17.

For example, Yellow Pages advertising is known to be price inelastic, with an elasticity of approximately −0.7. What would be the consequence of a Yellow Pages business lowering prices on its $100 ads by 10 percent? Assume that the business normally sells one million of these ads and that its variable cost is $50 per ad. The results are a

FIGURE 8-17   Price Elasticity and Performance

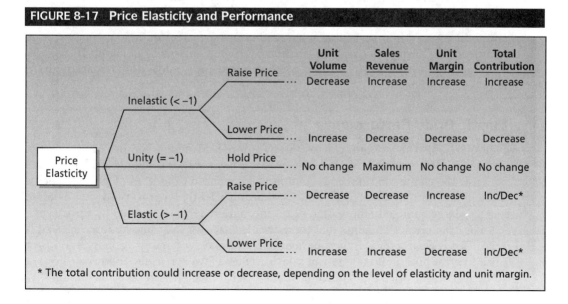

		Unit Volume	Sales Revenue	Unit Margin	Total Contribution
Inelastic (< −1)	Raise Price	Decrease	Increase	Increase	Increase
	Lower Price	Increase	Decrease	Decrease	Decrease
Unity (= −1)	Hold Price	No change	Maximum	No change	No change
Elastic (> −1)	Raise Price	Decrease	Decrease	Increase	Inc/Dec*
	Lower Price	Increase	Increase	Decrease	Inc/Dec*

* The total contribution could increase or decrease, depending on the level of elasticity and unit margin.

unit margin of $50, sales revenues of $100 million, and a total contribution of $50 million, as shown in the following.

Current Price Situation

Price per Ad	= $100	Variable Cost per Ad	= $50
Ad Volume	= 1 million ads	Margin per Ad	= $50
Sales Revenue	= $100 million	Total Contribution	= $50 million

A decision to lower prices by 10 percent when the price elasticity is equal to -0.70 would produce the following performance:

Lower Price Strategy

Price per Ad	= $90	Variable Cost per Ad	= $50
Ad Volume	= 1.07 million ads	Margin per Ad	= $40
Sales Revenue	= $96.3 million	Total Contribution	= $42.8 million

As shown above, a decision to lower price by 10 percent when prices were inelastic lowered margins by $10 per ad, lowered sales by $3.7 million, and lowered total contribution by $7.2 million, even though volume increased. This would have been a disastrous pricing decision. A business that did not know that its price was inelastic could easily follow a strategy of lowering prices in response to competitors or customer concerns about price.

The correct strategy in this case would be to raise price, because the price is inelastic. A strategy to raise price by 10 percent when the price elasticity is -0.70 would produce the following estimate of performance:

Raise Price Strategy

Price per Ad	= $110	Variable Cost per Ad	= $50
Ad Volume	= 0.93 million ads	Margin per Ad	= $60
Sales Revenue	= $102.3 million	Total Contribution	= $55.8 million

As shown, this strategy would increase margins by $10 per ad, sales by $2.3 million, and total contribution by $5.8 million. Knowing the correct direction to move price improved this business's total contribution by 10 percent, while giving up 70,000 ads. Although there was a loss of unit market share (ads sold), dollar market share improved significantly.

Elastic Price Performance

Figure 8-17 also shows that price strategy is more difficult when prices are elastic. Although sales revenues will increase with a price cut and decrease with a price increase, the change in total contribution will depend on the level of price elasticity. Though a price may be elastic, it may not be sufficiently large to produce a volume increase large enough to more than offset the margin decrease created by a price cut.

For example, let's assume that the price elasticity for the same Yellow Pages ad is -1.5. This is clearly an elastic price, and one that may lead many businesses to lower price to grow both unit volume and sales revenue. However, as the following shows, a strategy to lower price by 10 percent would lower total contribution by $4 million.

FIGURE 8-18 Forces that Shape Price Elasticity				
Ease of Customer Switching	*0*	*0.5*	*1*	*Score*
Product Differentiation	Extensive	Some	None	
Cost of Switching Suppliers	High	Modest	Low	
Customer Loyalty	High	Modest	Low	
Ease of Switching Index				**0**
Supply/Demand Conditions	*0*	*0.5*	*1*	*Score*
Supply Conditions	Short	Adequate	Excess	
Demand Conditions	Strong	Modest	Weak	
Substitutes	None	Few	Many	
Supply/Demand Index				**0**

Lower Price Strategy

Price per Ad	= $90	Variable Cost per Ad	= $50
Ad Volume	= 1.15 million ads	Margin per Ad	= $40
Sales Revenue	= $103.5 million	Total Contribution	= $46 million

A strategy to raise prices by 10 percent when the price elasticity is equal to -1.5 would yield less ad volume and less sales revenue but would produce higher margins and a larger total contribution.

Raise Price Strategy

Price per Ad	= $110	Variable Cost per Ad	= $50
Ad Volume	= 0.85 million ads	Margin per Ad	= $60
Sales Revenues	= $93.5 million	Total Contribution	= $51 million

The biggest challenge in using price elasticities is not the calculations—it is estimating a value for price elasticity. However, every time a business changes its price it has the opportunity to compute the actual price elasticity. But, because market conditions can change, the same price move can have different price elasticities. For example, if the ease of switching suppliers is average in a "buyer's market" where supply exceeds demand, price elasticities could be very high as illustrated in Figure 8-18. However, if the market shifted to a "seller's market" during a period of short supply, the price elasticities could drop to much lower levels for the same product.

Ease of Switching

One dimension of price elasticity is the ease of switching. The easier it is for customers to switch suppliers of a product or to substitute products, the higher the price elasticity since customers can easily move to obtain lower prices. The level of product differentiation, cost of switching, and customer loyalty each impact the ease of switching as described in the following:

- **Product Differentiation**—The more unique a product is in its product and service benefits, the harder it is to replace with other products or substitutes. In markets where product differentiation is strong, price sensitivity is often lower.

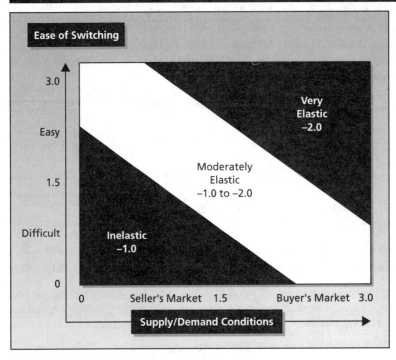

FIGURE 8-19   Guidelines for Estimating Price Elasticity

- **Cost of Switching**—The more expensive it is to switch suppliers, the harder it is for customers to switch suppliers when prices increase. Thus, higher switching costs generally result in lower price elasticities.
- **Customer Loyalty**—The more loyal a customer is to a brand or company the less likely they will switch suppliers when prices go up. When customer loyalty is low, however, the ease of switching is much greater and prices are more elastic.

A manager can assess the ease of switching for a specific product–market by estimating levels of product differentiation, switching costs, and customer loyalty, and then calculating an Ease-of-Switching Index as shown in Figure 8-18. This would provide a rough estimate of one dimension of price elasticity using the guidelines presented in Figure 8-19.

Supply/Demand Conditions

In many markets supply generally outpaces demand. In the automobile market, for example, price elasticity is going to be higher since customers can easily get a comparable product from several sources. In markets where demand outpaces supply, as was the case for Chrysler's PT Cruiser, the price elasticity was much lower. The supply conditions, demand conditions, and substitutes each have an impact on price elasticity, as described in the following guidelines:

- **Supply Conditions**–In markets with excess supply, prices are generally more elastic. In short-supply situations—even in commodity markets—price increases can be inelastic.

FIGURE 8-20 Forces That Help Shape Competitor Price Response			
	Competitor Response Elasticity		
	None	*Partial*	*Full*
Supply Forces			
Variable Cost Structure	High		Low
Capacity Utilization	Full		Low
Product Perishability	None		High
Product Differentiation	High		None
Competitor Financial Position	Poor		Strong
Strategic Importance	Low		High
Demand Forces			
Price Elasticity	Inelastic		Elastic
Efficiency in Price Shopping	Low		High
Customer Loyalty	High		Low
Market Growth Rate	High		Low
Complementary Products	None		Important
Substitute Products	None		Many

- **Demand Conditions**–When demand is strong and growing, prices tend to be less elastic. On the other hand, in markets with weak or flat demand, prices tend to be more price-sensitive.
- **Substitutes**–In markets with many substitutes, like beverages, price-sensitivity is high since there are many substitute products to choose from. In many prescription-drug markets there are very few substitutes, which lowers price elasticity.

Using these guidelines and the scale presented in Figure 8-18, a manager can make a rough estimate of market conditions and how they will potentially impact price elasticity. Using this **Supply/Demand Index** along with the **Ease of Switching Index,** a manager can then apply the guidelines in Figure 8-19 to gain a better understanding of the price elasticity for a given situation. Of course, noting these conditions and calculating the actual price elasticity after a price change would provide a basis for revising Figure 8-17 to be more representative of a specific product–market.

Competitor Price Response

The question that keeps many managers awake at night is, "What will my competitors do in response to my price change?" If a business lowers price to gain share, and competitors follow, there is likely to be very little real share gain. And at reduced margins, with a limited increase in volume, total contribution is likely to go down. On the other hand, if a business raises prices to improve margins and competitors do not follow, the business could lose share and lower total contribution, even with higher margins.

In any given market, competitor response to price change is going to depend on a variety of supply and demand forces,[12] as outlined in Figure 8-18. As the supply and demand forces in Figure 8-20 align to the left, competitors are less likely to respond to a price cut. As these forces shift to the right, they will contribute to the likelihood of a full and fast competitor response to a price cut. Overall, there is generally a high degree of price interdependence among competing firms. One study showed that the average competitor price response elasticity was 0.71.[13] This means that if a business lowered its prices by 10 percent, it could expect competitors to follow with a 7.1 percent price decrease.

PRODUCT LINE PRICING

As a business adds more products to its product line, it enhances sales growth but also increases the chances of cannibalization of existing product sales. It is necessary to know both a product's price elasticity and the degree to which there is a cross-elasticity with other products. Products that have a *positive* cross-elasticity are *substitutes*; lowering the price of one product will decrease the demand for the other product. Products that have a *negative* cross-elasticity are *complementary* products; lowering the price for one product will increase the demand for both products. Because the margins may be different for alternative products in a product line, one has to give careful consideration to any price change to ensure that the total profits are increased for the entire product line.

Pricing Substitute Products

In extending the product line of a business, one has to recognize that there will be some cannibalization when one product in the line may be substituted for another. For example, a business that offers both Yellow Pages advertising and direct-mail advertising would find that there is a cross-elasticity of demand between the two of approximately +0.80. This means that if the business were to raise the price of Yellow Pages advertising by 10 percent, the demand for direct mail would go up an estimated 8 percent, assuming no change in direct-mail prices. The cross-elasticity between these products and other media, such as newspaper, television, and radio advertisement, is less than +0.3. Thus, the rate of product substitution based on price change is much less.

Figure 8-21 shows the price elasticities and market shares for nine competing laundry detergents as well as their cross-elasticities.[14] The results of this empirical

FIGURE 8-21 Price and Cross Price Elasticity of Competing Laundry Detergent Brands

Brand	Share (%)	Wisk	Tide	Surf	Era	Solo	Cheer	Bold-3	All	Fab
Wisk	22.7	−1.37	0.31	0.37	0.23	0.11	0.12	0.09	0.08	0.07
Tide	21.5	0.33	−1.39	0.37	0.23	0.11	0.13	0.09	0.08	0.07
Surf	19.5	0.48	0.46	−1.91	0.33	0.16	0.16	0.12	0.11	0.09
Era	13.5	0.36	0.33	0.39	−1.57	0.11	0.12	0.10	0.08	0.07
Solo	5.9	0.36	0.34	0.41	0.25	−1.78	0.13	0.11	0.10	0.07
Cheer	4.9	0.46	0.47	0.47	0.31	0.15	−2.20	0.12	0.13	0.09
Bold-3	4.4	0.49	0.44	0.49	0.34	0.18	0.16	−2.32	0.11	0.10
All	3.6	0.48	0.46	0.50	0.32	0.17	0.20	0.12	−2.36	0.10
Fab	3.6	0.50	0.50	0.49	0.33	0.16	0.17	0.14	0.12	−2.41

Elasticities: A 1 percent price change in the brand column creates the percent change in market share for each row of brands.

study illustrate the price elasticity of each brand of detergent as well as the cross-elasticity of competing substitutes. As shown, cross-elasticities are much higher for higher-share brands.

Pricing Complementary Products

Of course, products that are complements will also be affected by price change. Software and printers are products that complement personal computers. Therefore, the demand for these products varies with the price of personal computers. If the cross-elasticity between PCs and spreadsheet programs were −0.6, then for each 1 percent change in the price of PCs, there would be a 0.6 percent change in the demand for spreadsheet programs. Thus, if computer industry prices decreased by 10 percent, the demand for spreadsheet programs should go up by 6 percent. Conversely, if the price of personal computers were to increase by 10 percent, the demand for spreadsheet programs would decrease by 6 percent.

PROMOTION PRICING

The average price elasticity for consumer products has been estimated to be −1.76.[15] Promotional price elasticities are much greater for the four product categories shown in Figure 8-22.[16] The overall average promotional price elasticity for these products is −8.3, approximately three times their average price elasticity.

A promotional price elasticity of −8.3 means that a price promotion of a 10 percent discount should produce an increase in demand of over 80 percent, on average. These product categories are very price-sensitive, and promotional pricing is common. However, promotional price elasticity varies substantially among brands and product categories, depending on differences in market share and promotional activity.[17]

Price Promotion Bundling Strategies

Price promotion bundling involves combining two or more complementary products and selling that bundle at promotion prices.[18] Consider a telecommunications company that offers a basic phone service along with the options of having voice mail and a hot line. Voice mail is priced at $5.50 per month and the hot line service at $5.00. The table on the next page shows the maximum price each of four different customers would pay for each of these services and for both.

FIGURE 8-22 Price and Promotional Price Elasticities

Product Category	Promotional Elasticity	Price Elasticity	Ratio of Deal to Price
Flour	−8.9	−2.1	4.2
Bathroom Tissue	−10.3	−3.2	3.2
Tuna	−8.7	−2.9	3.0
Margarine	−5.1	−2.8	1.9
Average	**−8.3**	**−2.8**	**3.0**

Customer	Maximum Price Customers Will Pay (per month)		
	Voice Mail	Hot Line	Both
A	$5.00	$3.50	$8.50
B	$5.50	$4.00	$9.50
C	$4.00	$5.00	$9.00
D	$3.50	$4.50	$8.00

Note that the current pricing strategy, with no bundling, attracts only one customer (B) to voice mail and only one customer (C) to hot line. The combined result is revenue of $10.50, as shown in Figure 8-23. Since each service costs the company $3.00 to provide, the total cost for both services is $6.00, and the gross profit is $4.50, as also shown in Figure 8-23.

Discount Price Strategy

A *discount price* strategy designed to attract all customers to at least one service would require a price of $5.00 per month for voice mail and a price of $4.50 per month for the hot line service. This strategy would attract both customer A and customer B to voice mail and customers C and D to the hot line service. This would result in total revenue of $19.00, a variable cost of $12.00, and a gross profit of $7.00, as shown in Figure 8-23.

Pure Bundling Strategy

A *pure bundling* price strategy would use the lowest total price a customer would pay for both services in an attempt to get all customers to buy both these services. Thus, the pure bundling price would be $8.00 (the price customer D would pay for the combination of services). A price of $8.00 per month should attract all four customers to buy both services. This would result in total revenue of $32.00, a variable cost of $24.00, and a gross profit of $8.00, as also shown in Figure 8-23.

Mixed Bundling Strategy

A *mixed bundling* price strategy is designed to offer both discount prices and a bundled price at levels that will attract customers from each segment. Offering a discount price of $5.00 for voice messaging and $4.50 for hot line as well as a bundled price for both services of $9.00 accomplishes this objective. Customers B and C are attracted to the bundled price for both services since they are available at or below what these customers would pay for both. Customer A will find the bundled price of $9.00 is too high, but will purchase voice mail at the discounted price of $5.00. Customer D will also find

FIGURE 8-23 Performance Impact of Price Bundling

Price Strategy	Price (per month)			Services Purchased	Sales Revenue	Variable Cost	Gross Profit
	Voice Mail	Hot Line	Both				
No Bundling	$5.50	$5.00	—	2	$10.50	$ 6.00	$4.50
Discount Only	$5.00	$4.50	—	4	$19.00	$12.00	$7.00
Pure Bundling	—	—	$8.00	8	$32.00	$24.00	$8.00
Mixed Bundling	$5.00	$4.50	$9.00	6	$27.50	$18.00	$9.50

the bundled price of $9.00 too high but will purchase the hot line service at the discounted price of $4.50. As Figure 8-21 illustrates, this mixed bundling price strategy will result in total revenue of $27.50 (less than pure bundling), but a gross profit of $9.50, highest of these alternative pricing strategies.

Summary

Pricing is a critical part of customer value and business profitability. If prices are high, it is great for margins but could result in a low customer volume if perceived benefits are less than perceived price. In competitive markets where product differentiation is feasible, market-based pricing presents a pricing logic designed to deliver high levels of customer value and business profitability.

Market-based pricing starts with customer needs, competitors' positions, and the business's product positioning, and works backward to margin. By contrast, a cost-based pricing approach starts with the cost of the product and a desired margin and works forward to a market price. Cost-based pricing can lead to under- and overpricing in markets in which differentiation is possible. However, in markets in which differentiation is minimal and customers are price-sensitive, cost-based pricing can be a viable approach to pricing.

Changes in price affect both volume and margin. A price decrease that grows volume and sales revenues but results in a decrease in total contribution adversely impacts a business's profits. The goal of any pricing strategy should be to grow or maintain profits. Therefore, it is critical to evaluate how total contribution will change with a price increase or decrease. Since the total contribution is the product of volume times margin, a change in price will affect both volume and margin and total contribution.

Because price affects margin and a certain level of fixed expenses is needed to achieve a certain level of market penetration, a break-even analysis is useful in assessing profit potential and risk. However, break-even volume, although a useful target, is not as useful in risk assessment as break-even market share. Because market share is constricted between zero and one (100 percent), it provides a relative index by which risk can be judged. Break-even market share enables a business to gauge profit potential and risk by the difference between target share and the break-even market share.

Price-volume relationships are made more complex by varying degrees of price elasticity. Price elasticity is a measure of price sensitivity. When prices are inelastic price increases result in a decrease in volume but increase in sales and profits. A price decrease when prices are inelastic would result in higher volume but lower sales and lower profits. When prices are elastic a price decrease will result in higher volumes and higher sales revenues. However, profits may go down if margins are low or up when margins are large. Price elasticities are not easy to estimate and vary based on a customer's ease of switching and a market's supply/demand conditions. Understand these forces and tracking price elasticities that result when prices are changed allows a business to build a set of guidelines for estimating price elasticity.

Product line price decisions are also complicated by cross-elasticity. The price elasticity of demand for a given product may signal a particular price strategy. When cross-elasticity exists between products, a business needs a more careful analysis of profit impact. The demand for products that are substitutes will change in the direction of the price change of the substitute. The demand for complementary products will change inversely to a price change in a complementary product.

Promotional price elasticities are much higher than nonpromotion price elasticities. The full profit impact of a price promotion requires a business to evaluate profit impact over a time span that includes periods before and after the price promotion. Forward consumer buying during a promotion, inventory depletion before a promotion by retailers, and forward buying by retailers lower demand in adjacent nonpromotional periods. This effect lowers the overall contribution of the promotional strategy.

APPLICATION PROBLEM: MICROSOFT WINDOWS 95

In the late nineties, the U.S. government brought an antitrust lawsuit against Microsoft. Professor Richard Schmalansee, an economics professor at the Massachusetts Institute of Technology, defended Microsoft Windows' 90 percent market share. In his testimony, Professor Schmalansee provided the following insights.

Schmalansee disclosed that "the company had sold 125 million copies of Windows 95 for more than $7 billion—an average price of $56." Schmalansee also estimated "that if Microsoft could increase the price of Windows by 5 percent, it could raise its pretax revenues by $173 million. A 10 percent increase would earn the company an additional $345 million." Schmalansee asked, "Why would a profit-driven firm, not known for leaving money on the table, pass up such easy money?" "No one," he suggested, "could possibly conclude that Microsoft enjoys the quiet life of a monopolist."[15]

Questions
For access to interactive software to answer the questions below, go to www.RogerJBest.com or www.prenhall.com/best.

1. How many copies of Windows would Schmalansee estimate to be sold if Microsoft increased its price by 5 percent? How many copies would have been sold if Microsoft had raised the price 10 percent?

2. What is the price elasticity at a 5 percent higher price? At a 10 percent higher price?

3. On the basis of the estimated price elasticities, what would a monopolist do with respect to price?

Market-Based Logic and Strategic Thinking

1. Why would Compaq Computer shift from cost-based pricing to market-based pricing?
2. Why might GE Aerospace use cost-based pricing instead of market-based pricing in developing a bid for a U.S. Air Force contract?
3. How would an earthmoving equipment manufacturer with superior productivity price its product using economic value?
4. How would you approach pricing the Lexus sport-utility vehicle? What elements of perceived value would be important in developing a market-based price?
5. Is Compaq pursuing a cost-based pricing strategy in the personal computer market? Why? What is the underlying pricing logic that supports Compaq's pricing strategy?
6. How does the three-segment–based price strategy for cellular phones described in the text contribute to the customer value in each segment?

7. When would a business use cost-based pricing?
8. How can a price decrease that increases volume and sales result in a profit decrease?
9. Explain how ease of switching and supply/demand conditions operate for an inelastic service such as a dentist and a very elastic service such as a plumber.
10. In 2000, the market demand for personal computers was 129 million and the average price was $1922. The average margin was 20 percent of sales. By 2003, prices dropped to an average price of $1708 and grew to 161 million while average margins slipped to 17 percent of sales. What is the price elasticity over this time period and how did sales revenues and total contribution (volume x margin) change?
11. If coffee and doughnuts were both price elastic and also cross-elastic complements, with the margin on doughnuts being much higher, how would you vary prices to increase overall profitability?
12. What factors would you want to consider in evaluating profitability if you were a beverage manufacturer and going to engage in a price promotion?
13. How would Dell Computer use competitive bid pricing in responding to an insurance company's request for a quote on 1,000 PCs of a certain type?
14. Which pricing strategy would you have recommended for Gillette's Mach3 razor: skimming, competitive, or penetration? What factors and assumptions influence your choice of new product-price strategies?
15. Why is break-even market share potentially more valuable to a marketing manager than break-even volume?

Notes

1. A. Cleland and A. Bruno, *The Market Value Process* (San Francisco: Jossey-Bass, 1996): 106; D. Kirkpatrick, "The Revolution at Compaq Computer," *Fortune* (December 14, 1992):80–88.
2. P. Noble and T. Gruca, "Industrial Pricing: Theory and Managerial Practice," *Marketing Science,* Vol. 18, No. 3, 1999, 435–454.
3. G. Cressman, Jr., "Commentary on Industrial Pricing: Theory and Managerial Practice," *Marketing Science* Vol. 18, No. 3, 1999, 455–457.
4. R. Best, Marketing Excellence Survey, *www.MESurvey.com*
5. Michael Morris and Gene Morris, *Market-Oriented Pricing* (Lincolnwood, IL: NTC Business Books, 1990):93–100.
6. R. Dolan and H. Simon, *Power Pricing* (New York: Free Press, 1966) 82–83.
7. California Technology Stock Letter (February 4, 1999):4.
8. Annual Statement Statistics, (Robert Morris Agency), 1996.
9. Thomas Nagle and Reed Holder, *The Strategy and Tactics of Pricing* (Upper Saddle River, NJ: Prentice Hall, 1995):199–206.
10. Gerald Smith and Thomas Nagle, "Financial Analysis for Profit-Driven Pricing," *Sloan Management Review* (Spring 1994):71–84.
11. R. Dolan and H. Simon, *Power Pricing* (New York: Free Press, 1996):222–41.
12. J. Lambin, *Advertising, Competition and Market Conduct in Oligopoly Over Time* (Amsterdam: North Holland-Elsevier, 1976).
13. R. Bucklin, G. Russell, and V. Srinivasan, "A Relationship between Market Share Elasticities and Brand Switching Probabilities," *Journal of Marketing Research* (February 1998):99–113.
14. Gerard Tellis, "The Price Elasticity of Selective Demand: A Meta-Analysis of Econometric Models of Sales," *Journal of Marketing Research* (November 1988):331–41.
15. Robert Blattberg and Scott Neslin, *Sales Promotion Concepts, Methods, and Strategies* (Upper Saddle River, NJ: Prentice Hall, 1990):356.
16. Ruth Bolton, "The Relationship between Market Characteristics and Promotional Price Elasticities," *Marketing Science* (Spring 1989):153–69.
17. R. Dolan and H. Simon, *Power Pricing*: 222–45.
18. Ted Bridis, "Witness Says Price for Windows Cheap," *The Oregonian* (January 22, 1999):B2.

9 | MARKETING CHANNELS AND E-MARKETING

The worldwide business-to-business (B2B) market demand for epoxy is approximately $5 billion. This market includes 2,000 customers, with 20 percent of them accounting for 80 percent of the purchases. For these 400 customers the average revenue per customer is $10 million per year and Dow Chemical serves this group of customers with a direct-marketing channel as shown in Figure 9-1. While this marketing channel is cost-effective and profitable, it could not be used to reach the 1,600 smaller epoxy customers who buy considerably less and are often geographically hard to reach.

In 2000 Dow Chemical launched e-epoxy.com, investing $2 million in an e-marketing channel in an effort to reach these 1,600 smaller customers in a cost-effective way. In the first seven weeks e-epoxy.com attracted 200 new visitors per week and 100 repeat visitors per week. Two-thirds of the sales produced through this e-marketing channel were from customers who had never done business with Dow Chemical.[1] The end results were gains in market share, sales, and new customers.

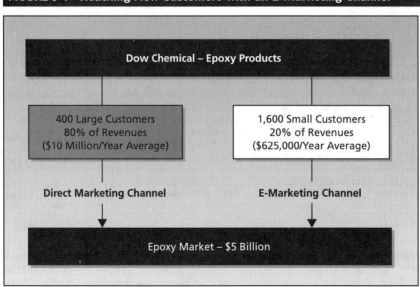

FIGURE 9-1 Reaching New Customers with an E-Marketing Channel

The choice and management of marketing channels directly impacts three important areas of performance.

- **Customer Value:** Marketing channels can enhance or reduce customer value based on the service quality and the efficiency with which end-user customers are served.
- **Sales Revenues:** Marketing channels determine customer reach which impacts sales to existing customers as well as sales to potential customers.
- **Profitability:** Marketing channels have a direct impact on margins and marketing expenses and play a critical role in the profits that can be obtained in any given marketing channel.

For dot.com businesses such as Amazon.com, E*Trade Group, and eBay, e-marketing is their primary marketing channel and a core component of their business model. The customer value these businesses create and the sales and profits they obtain are directly related to their successful management of an e-marketing channel. These businesses have chosen e-marketing as their means of building a brand, interfacing with customers, and delivering products. The e-marketing channel is vital to the existence and survival of these companies.

For established businesses like Dow Chemical, General Electric, and Charles Schwab, an e-marketing channel provides another marketing channel for them to reach new customers and serve existing customers more efficiently. For these businesses, e-marketing channels leverage existing brand equity, supply-chain capabilities, and operating expenses already in place.

In the personal-computer market, a variety of marketing channels have emerged in an effort to reach and serve many different types of customers. As shown in Figure 9-2,

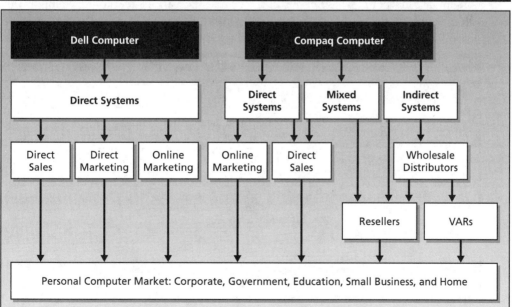

FIGURE 9-2   Personal Computer Marketing Channels: Dell vs. Compaq

Compaq Computer has built its business using a complex marketing channel system, relying heavily on a combination of direct and indirect marketing channels. In contrast, market leader Dell Computer has grown to the number one position by honing its direct marketing channel approach with direct marketing, e-marketing and direct sales as also depicted in Figure 9-2.

MARKETING CHANNELS AND CHANNEL MANAGEMENT

Marketing channels are a key component of a supply chain that links manufacturers with end-user customers as illustrated in Figure 9-3. As shown, *Supply Chain Management* involves the management of materials, information, and money that flow from suppliers to a business to marketing channel partners who provide the business's products to target customers. Companies such as SAP, which has established itself as a market leader in supply chain management, has developed systems to help businesses more efficiently manage supply chain functions such as order entry, inventory, and shipping between a business and its suppliers and channel partners.

Because many businesses sell through channel partners, they do not directly interface with the end-user customer. *Customer Relationship Management* (CRM) is a channel management activity that helps businesses establish one-on-one marketing relationships with customers, even when channel partners are needed to reach target customers. With the advent of Internet technologies and e-marketing channels, CRM allows a business to gain a much better focus on its customers' individual needs and preferences. In a rapidly growing market for CRM solutions, Siebel Systems has emerged as a market leader in helping businesses better manage this process and improve customer satisfaction and retention.

There are many different marketing channels that can be used to connect businesses with customers. The purpose of this chapter is to understand how channel partners impact marketing channel performance and the various marketing channels that can be configured to reach customers with different needs. We will also examine how marketing channels can serve as a source of competitive advantage.

FIGURE 9-3 Marketing Channels and Channel Activities

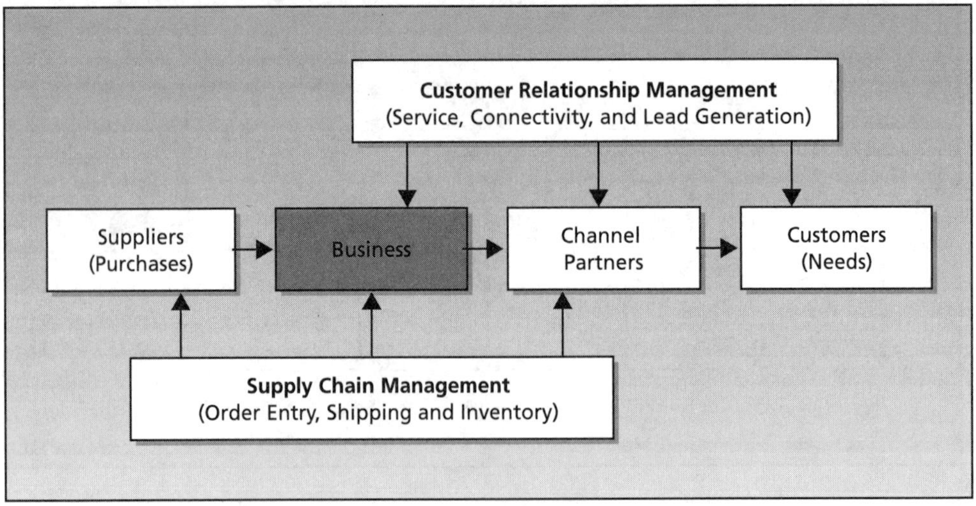

MARKETING CHANNEL PERFORMANCE

Marketing channel performance is based on three things: customer reach, operating efficiency, and service quality. All three are needed for a customer-effective and cost-efficient marketing channel. If a business cannot reach potential customers, sales will not happen. If operations are not efficient, the cost to serve customers will be too high to be profitable. Without service quality, customer retention will suffer, even if customers can be reached effectively and served cost-efficiently. All three components of marketing channel performance outlined in Figure 9-4 must be operating at satisfactory levels for a marketing channel to achieve desired sales, profits, and customer satisfaction.[2]

Customer Reach

One of the primary objectives of a marketing channel is to reach target customers. Of course, this has to be done in a way that is cost-effective and provides the level of service quality sought by target customers. Every marketing channel differs in its structure and its ability to reach customers. With direct marketing channels, a company engages in direct contact with its customers. This can be accomplished with direct sales, direct marketing, telemarketing, and e-marketing. Indirect marketing channels include channel intermediaries such as wholesalers, distributors, retailers, Original Equipment Manufacturers, and value-added resellers.

To illustrate the impact of marketing channels on customer reach and sales let's examine how Hewlett-Packard's marketing channels have expanded. Prior to the mid-1980s HP had built its business around direct sales and what was called "The HP Way." This business model relied upon one-on-one relationships between HP engineers and customer engineers. This direct sales channel (shown in bold in Figure 9-5) worked well for many years. While successful, this business model limited HP's growth since many potential customers could not be economically served with a direct sales approach. To reach more potential customers and grow sales, HP expanded its business model and added new marketing channels as shown in Figure 9-5. These new channels, along with new products to serve the needs of new customers, allowed HP to grow from $5 billion in the early 1980s to over $50 billion twenty years later.

The marketing channel with perhaps the most potential to expand customer reach is the e-marketing channel. The ability to reach a world of potential new customers at an insignificant marginal marketing cost has led most businesses to invest to some

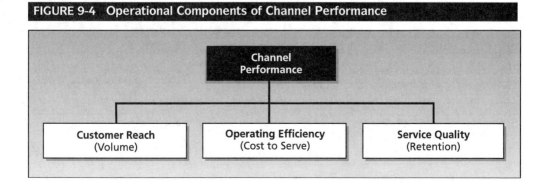

FIGURE 9-4   Operational Components of Channel Performance

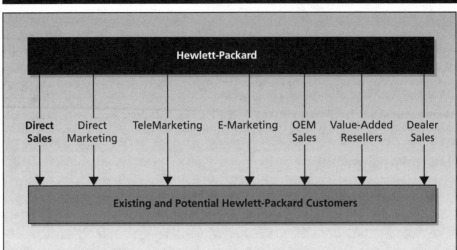

FIGURE 9-5 Hewlett-Packard Marketing Channels

degree of e-marketing. General Electric, for example, added an e-marketing channel to supplement its traditional marketing channels, much like Dow Chemical did with e-epoxy.com. GE saw immediate results as its e-marketing channel sales grew from $7 billion in 2000 to $14 billion in 2001. Much of this growth in e-marketing channel sales was attributed to new customers.[3]

Operating Efficiency

Marketing channels also vary in their cost structure. A direct marketing channel offers higher margins but the company must bear the full cost channel management and of marketing expenses. An indirect marketing channel has lower margins but lower channel management and marketing expenses. In this case the channel intermediary receives a portion of the margin in exchange for distribution and carrying out some of the marketing channel functions.

In the following example, the net marketing contribution of each marketing channel is the same but the revenue and cost structures differ. Each channel produced unit sales of 100,000 units. The direct marketing channel had a higher margin per unit ($5.00) but higher marketing expenses ($250,000). The indirect marketing channel had a lower margin per unit ($3.00) and lower marketing expenses ($50,000). In this example, both channels produced the same marketing profitability.

$$\text{Net Marketing Contribution} = \text{Volume} \times (\text{Price} - \text{Unit Cost}) - \text{Marketing Expenses}$$

$$\text{(Direct Marketing Channel)} = 100,000 \times (\$10.00 - \$5.00) - \$250,000$$

$$= \$500,000 - \$250,000$$

$$= \$250,000$$

$$\text{Net Marketing Contribution} = [\text{Volume}] \times [(\text{Price} - \text{Unit Cost})] - \text{Marketing Expenses}$$

$$\begin{aligned}\text{(Indirect Marketing Channel)} &= 100,000 \times (\$8.00 - \$5.00) - \$50,000 \\ &= \$300,000 - \$50,000 \\ &= \$250,000\end{aligned}$$

E-marketing channels have improved the operating efficiency of many businesses. A well-designed and implemented e-marketing channel can lower variable costs and marketing expenses as well as reduce other operating expenses in many cases. For example, in 2001 GE's cost to serve customers was reduced by $1 billion with the implementation of e-marketing channels. For many businesses e-marketing channels have provided a low cost way to reach smaller, hard to reach customers.

Online buying also saved GE $14 billion on the purchase of goods and services in 2001. In 2002 Hewlett-Packard introduced e-sourcing with b2eMarkets.com for conducting electronic Request(s) for Information and Request for Proposals/Quotes. This has allowed HP to reduce costs and time in their procurement of products and services.

Service Quality

Every channel also has different levels of service quality. With direct marketing channels, companies have the opportunity to control service quality since they have the advantage of a direct customer interface. This allows for service enhancements, mass customization, and quick response to customer problems.

Indirect marketing channels remove the business from the end-user customer. As a result they are dependent on channel partners to adequately deliver desired levels of customer service. Because indirect channel intermediaries often represent many different lines of products, their product knowledge and commitment to specific customer needs may not be as complete.

E-marketing channels that improve order fulfillment and track deliveries without multiple phone calls have the potential to lower cost and improve customer satisfaction. To further enhance e-marketing channels, Customer Relationship Management (CRM) systems are designed to facilitate a one-on-one customer relationship with target customers. One of the primary goals of CRM is to identify problems, resolve them, and maintain a dialogue with customers as to how the company can improve its service quality.

ALTERNATIVE CHANNEL SYSTEMS

The first decision a business must make is whether to use a *direct, indirect,* or *mixed* channel system.[4] All things being equal, a business would generally prefer to sell and distribute directly to target customers, because this combination of channel and sales responsibility offers the most control and greatest potential for value-added sales and services. On the other hand, a business may not have the expertise or resources needed to fund and support a direct channel system and therefore might elect to reach target customers through an indirect channel system. A business may also need to use a combination of direct, indirect, and mixed channel systems in order to reach different target

FIGURE 9-6   Alternative Channel Systems

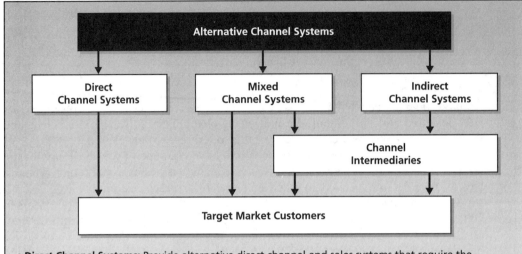

- **Direct Channel Systems:** Provide alternative direct channel and sales systems that require the business to retain ownership (title) of products sold and responsibility for delivery to customers and value-added functions desired by customers.
- **Indirect Channel Systems:** Provide varying degrees of sales and value-added functions while taking ownership and responsibility for delivery to target customers or other intermediaries.
- **Mixed Channel Systems:** Provide direct sales contact and technical support while the actual purchase is made at a channel intermediary who has taken title (ownership) of the products being sold.

markets cost-effectively and to deliver the service level expected by target customers. These three channel systems are shown in Figure 9-6.

Direct Channel Systems

As illustrated in Figure 9-7, a direct approach can include a direct sales force, direct marketing, telemarketing, online marketing, manufacturer's representatives, sales agents, or brokers. In each case, the business retains *ownership* of the products and *responsibility* for sales, distribution, service, and collection of payment for products sold.

Although a direct sales force offers the best opportunity for sales communication and customer interaction, it is often too expensive to reach target customers with a direct sales approach. The cost of direct customer sales contact is both high and increasing. For example, the fully loaded cost (salary, benefits, and expenses) of a direct salesperson in many business-to-business markets can range from $100,000 to over $300,000 per year. Direct marketing, which includes direct mail and catalog sales, offers a less expensive alternative, but the opportunity for sales communications is more limited. Telemarketing provides a greater opportunity for a sales communication but is more labor-intensive and often more expensive than direct marketing. Emerging electronic marketing channels in home shopping and Internet computer-based purchasing are offering greater opportunities for customer interaction.[5] Finally, manufacturers' representatives, sales agents, and brokers can assume the selling responsibility for the business and are paid a sales commission only when a sale occurs. E-marketing channels

FIGURE 9-7   Alternative B2C Marketing Channels

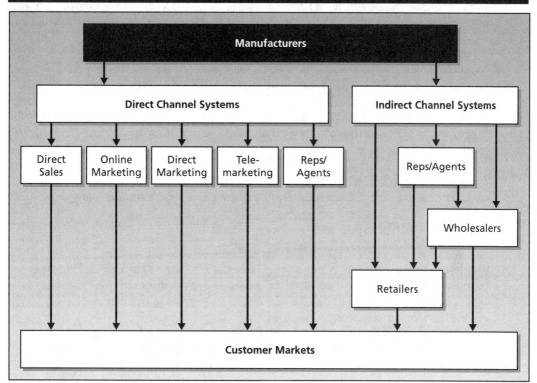

have greatly enhanced customer reach, customer interactivity, online information searches, purchasing, and after-sale customer service.

Indirect Channel Systems

Because using a direct channel system is often expensive, it limits the number of customers a business can profitably reach. As a result, many potential customers who buy in smaller purchase amounts cannot be profitably served with a direct channel system. In these situations, a business has to at least consider using indirect channel systems.

Indirect channel systems are inherently more complex, because they involve at least one intermediary who takes over both ownership of the product and the majority, if not all, of the control in both sales and distribution. As shown in Figure 9-7, an indirect channel system could include retailers, commercial distributors (also called dealers), full-function wholesalers, and specialty wholesalers.

Retailers take over the sales and point of purchase distribution in consumer markets, and distributors or dealers assume this responsibility in business-to-business markets. Compensation for their services is usually in the form of a discount off the customer selling price. This discount can range from 10 percent to over 50 percent.

Wholesalers offer an intermediate point of sales and physical distribution between a business and retailers or dealers. There are full-function wholesalers, who offer a full range of products and services (inventory, delivery, credit, and stocking), and limited-function wholesalers, who offer a limited range of products and services. For example, a cash-and-carry wholesaler does not deliver the product or offer credit. In most cases, the discount offered to wholesalers is less than that offered to retailers or dealers, because the range of services is considerably less.

VARs and OEMs are unique indirect channel system alternatives in that they buy products, directly or indirectly, add value to them, and resell them. These alternatives will be discussed at greater length in the discussion of business-to-business alternative channels.

While e-marketing channels can be a distinct indirect channel, it can also enhance or supplement existing channel systems. It can improve many interactions along the supply chain. Also, customers often go online to gather information and then buy the product at a wholesaler or retailer. Others may place orders online but take actual delivery at a retail outlet. E-marketing channels can also be used to help track orders, especially in complex industrial purchases where lead times can be long and deliveries complicated, as in the case of a Caterpillar grader or avionics for a Boeing jet.

Mixed Channel Systems

In some instances, a combination of direct and indirect channel systems provides the best way to reach and serve target customers.[6] For example, many industrial and business- to-business firms use a direct sales force or manufacturers' representatives to perform the sales contact while localized dealers and distributors provide product availability, delivery, and service, as well as terms of payment.

Mixed channel systems are particularly important when products are fairly technical and localized availability and service are important. For example, Microsoft, Compaq Computer, and others have direct sales forces that call on large corporate accounts, often referred to as enterprise businesses. While the technical sales team works with the customer to create a desired customer solution, the local reseller of their products will handle the actual sales, delivery, and service.

B2C Channels

In consumer markets, businesses are likely to use indirect channel systems to effectively and cost-efficiently reach target customers. Innovations in direct marketing, online marketing, and wholesale shopping have opened new channel systems that may be equally attractive. Outlined in Figure 9-7 are the various channel systems typically used in consumer markets. As shown, there are both direct and indirect channel systems. In consumer markets, a direct channel system is less likely to be used. Direct marketing through consumer catalogs, direct-mail marketing, telemarketing, and electronic marketing have grown significantly in recent years and offer future growth opportunities with innovations in telecommunications. Catalog companies, such as Esprit, Eddie Bauer, and L.L. Bean, have had noteworthy success in recent years, whereas Mary Kay Cosmetics, Electrolux, and Amway have used a direct sales approach to reach target consumers. In each case, a different direct channel system is required to effectively meet customer needs and to produce acceptable levels of profitability. And, if there were a more efficient way to accomplish these objectives, it would be marketing's responsibility to find that alternative.

Online marketing is an emerging direct consumer channel system that involves Internet computer-based purchasing and includes new businesses such as Amazon.com,

Peapod, and Auto-By-Tel. These channel intermediaries buy their products from manufacturers and wholesalers and resell them through the Internet:

- Amazon.com is an online book retailer that purchases books from large book wholesalers and resells them online with next-day UPS delivery, if desired. Amazon.com also purchases and resells CDs.
- Peapod shoppers pay a monthly fee of $4.95 and 5 percent of the purchase price for groceries purchased online and delivered to the shoppers' homes.
- Auto-By-Tel helps customers in their car purchases. They are an online broker that shops for the car and price the customer wants. In this case, Internet shoppers do not directly pay Auto-By-Tel for this service. Rather, the dealers pay monthly fees for referrals of consumers who visit the Auto-By-Tel Web site.

B2B Channels

Software manufacturers, such as Adobe, serve both consumer and business customers. As illustrated in Figure 9-8, these companies use a direct marketing channel to reach and serve large enterprises such as Fortune 500 companies. To reach medium-sized to smaller businesses and individual consumers, these manufacturers use online marketing as part of their direct channel, but, to a greater degree, they use an indirect channel to reach these customers. As shown in Figure 9-8, software producers will sell direct to large national chains, but they use independent, commissioned representatives to reach smaller independent retailers. Each of the channels has different levels of cost, control, sales contact, and ownership.

FIGURE 9-8 Marketing Channels and Sales Systems Used to Reach Software Buyers

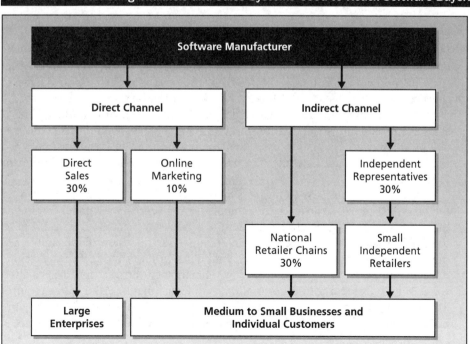

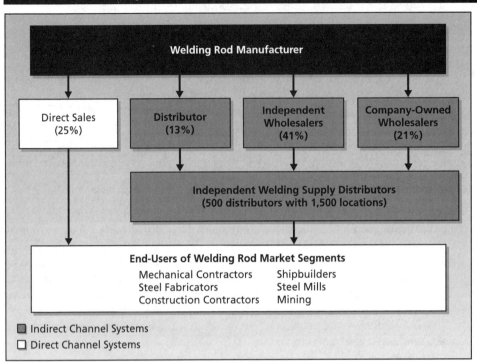

FIGURE 9-9   Channel Systems for a Manufacturer of Welding Rods

As stated earlier, most businesses would prefer to sell and distribute with a direct channel system. This provides a greater degree of control and specialized knowledge that can be customized for the end customer. Yet, for industrial products, such as the one illustrated in Figure 9-9, only 25 percent of sales are via direct channel systems.[7]

This percentage is partly the result of the cost of a business-to-business direct sales call, which ranges from $100 to over $300. In industrial markets, approximately 50 percent of all sales are derived from the combination of manufacturers' reps or sales agents and industrial distributors. For many inexpensive industrial and commercial products, wholesalers are used. In some instances, as in hospital supply products, the large hospital supply wholesaler may sell directly to hospitals and other medical institutions.

Unique to the business-to-business market, as outlined in Figure 9-10, are VARs and OEMs. VARs purchase a variety of equipment from several manufacturers and package them as a system. A VAR often provides the total system, as well as specialized services, to help the customer learn, use, maintain, and upgrade the system. For example, a VAR in the agricultural market may purchase computers, printers, modems, fax machines, and telecommunications equipment from several manufacturers, along with specialized software, to help farmers with crop rotation, fertilizing, planting, and water requirements. The agricultural customers could buy all these products separately, but they prefer to purchase a complete (bundled) system that is customized to their specific needs.

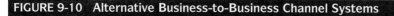

FIGURE 9-10   Alternative Business-to-Business Channel Systems

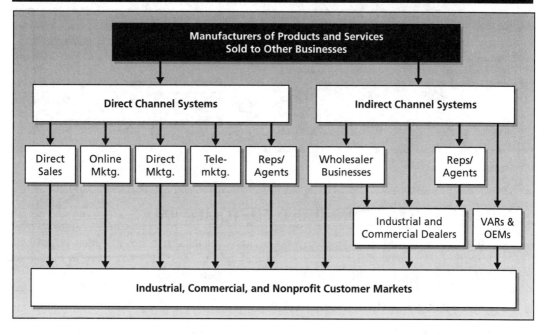

An OEM is very similar but actually creates a new manufactured product. OEMs, such as Ford, IBM, or Caterpillar, buy component products from other manufacturers to incorporate into their products. For example, Ford does not manufacture tires; it purchases them from a tire manufacturer such as Firestone. Although Firestone operates primarily through company-owned retail tire stores, it also sells tires to automobile manufacturers, who provide another important, indirect channel sales opportunity. Likewise, IBM may buy disk drives from Seagate and computer chips from Intel, as well as make its own.

Virtually all B2B businesses now have some e-marketing capability. Many components of e-marketing are informational while others involve order placement. An excellent example of total commitment to an e-marketing channel is Dow Corning—a technology leader and major manufacturer of silicone products.

Dow Corning found that many of its products were overpriced and overloaded with features and services that some customers did not want to pay for. In response the company created a new B2B e-marketing channel to reach price-sensitive customers as illustrated in Figure 9-11. Products were rebranded under the name Xiameter and sold without after-sales service at price breaks of up to 10 percent to 15 percent through an e-marketing channel (www.xiameter.com). This allowed Dow Corning to maintain both a direct and an indirect marketing channel for value-added products while remaining price competitive with standardized products branded as Xiameter in the price-buyer segment as shown below. When 80 percent of Xiameter orders are processed free of human intervention, Dow Corning plans to reduce costs by $100 million by selling through this new e-marketing channel as well as grow sales revenues in this segment of the silicone market.[8]

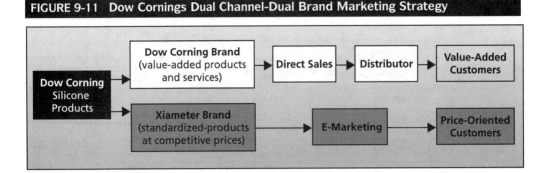

FIGURE 9-11   Dow Cornings Dual Channel-Dual Brand Marketing Strategy

CHANNEL SYSTEMS THAT BUILD CUSTOMER VALUE

There are many alternative channel systems a business can use to reach target customers. To be successful, however, a channel system must enhance *customer value* by either increasing customer benefits or lowering customer cost of purchase, or both.

Delivering Product Benefits

Because many products are perishable or easily damaged, it is important to select a channel that will be able to deliver a business's product to target customers in the form that meets or exceeds customer expectations. In selecting a particular channel system, a business needs to consider how that channel system either enhances or detracts from the following product benefits:

- **Product Quality:** Can the channel system deliver the product or service with the quality level required and expected by target customers?
- **Product Assortment:** Can the channel system provide the range of products required in order to achieve a desired level of customer appeal?
- **Product Form:** Can the channel system provide the product, as it is needed, to both intermediaries and final customers?

In each case, a channel system is not a viable alternative if it cannot meet the product benefits sought by target customers.[9] Customers simply will not buy products that do not meet their buying needs. There are almost always competing alternatives, so customers will satisfy their buying needs by purchasing a competing product.

Delivering Service Benefits

Every channel has advantages and limitations with respect to service. The need for delivery, installation, training, technical support, repair, terms of payment, credit, and easy return are all service benefits that a business has to consider in selecting a particular channel system. To determine if a channel system is viable, a business has to consider the following questions with respect to a customer's service needs and expectations.

- **After-Sale Services:** What are the after-sale services that are critical to achieving total customer satisfaction with the product or service?

- **Availability/Delivery:** To what degree do customers benefit from quick access to goods or services and immediate delivery?
- **Transaction Services:** Can the channel system provide for the customer's credit needs, terms of payment, warranty, FOB pricing, and return of faulty products?

Each of these service benefits can be critical. A business with a better product may not achieve market success if it fails to provide the service benefits required by target customers. To be successful in meeting customer expectations, a business has to make the product available at the target customer's desired point of purchase. In addition, it must meet or exceed each of its customer's product and service requirements, whether the final customer or a channel intermediary.

Building Brand Image

It is important to carefully consider how a channel system will affect the image of a product or manufacturer. Hartman Luggage, for example, manufactures a high-quality line of luggage and has a certain image for quality. Hartman is very selective in choosing retailers who will support or enhance this brand image, as pointed out in Figure 9-12.

Likewise, Perfume de Paris manufactures and markets perfume at approximately one-third the price of Chanel and other higher-priced perfume products. It is important for Perfume de Paris to have its product sold through mass merchandisers who emphasize price, because mass merchandising is consistent with its target customer and product and price-positioning strategy.

Building Company Benefits

Overall benefits can be enhanced and contribute to building customer value with *relationship marketing*.[10] Direct channel systems offer the greatest opportunity for presenting product information, controlling the selling effort, and offering specialized selling skills. This opportunity to enhance the total benefits through personal relationships

---

FIGURE 9-12   How Channel Systems Contribute to Customer Value

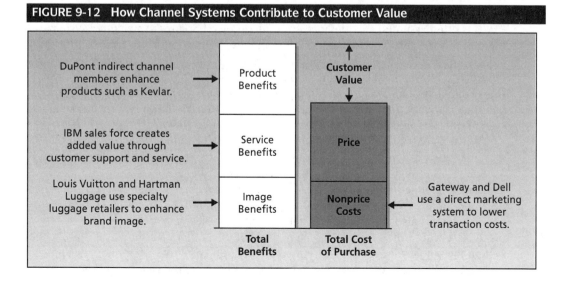

developed with customers or channel intermediaries can be very important. Strong customer-firm relationships produce high degrees of commitment by both parties, and high commitment has the potential to enhance customer value.

When a business cannot directly interact with target customers, it must take care in selecting a channel system that will be capable of fulfilling these customer relationships effectively.[11] For a given product and customer, this selection may require a certain level of product knowledge, sales and negotiation skill, call frequency, and follow-up after-sales service. The bottom line is that any channel system is of little value if the sales interaction with the target customer is ineffective.

With an e-marketing channel, a business with 10,000 customers should look at customers not as a segment of 10,000 customers but as 10,000 segments, each with one customer. Today e-marketing channels can be extended with Customer Relationship Management and the development of one-on-one marketing relationships. Whether a consumer business with thousands of customers or an industrial business with hundreds, the use of Customer Relationship Management and e-marketing enables businesses to interact with customers, make customized offerings, and build customer loyalty.

Improving Cost Efficiency

By making a product readily available, a business can lower a customer's transaction costs. Customers have preferred points of purchase. If a business does not make products readily available at these points of purchase, it inherently raises the cost of the transaction. For undifferentiated products, this type of transaction cost is high. Customers will not make the effort to purchase the product if it is not conveniently available. On the other hand, the more differentiated a product, and the greater its perceived value, the more willing the customer may be to incur this type of transaction cost.

Another way to affect customer value (total benefits less total costs) is to lower the cost of reaching customers. The more cost-efficient a channel system, the greater the opportunity to lower customer costs or to increase business profitability. An important marketing responsibility is to find and develop channel systems that are cost-efficient while still delivering the benefits sought by customers.

It is often assumed that the more intermediaries there are in a channel system, the higher the total cost of purchase. In general, that assumption is not true, or that channel system would not exist. Consider, for example, the channel system presented in Figure 9-13, in which 100 manufacturers each contact 20,000 retailers once a month. In this channel system, there is a monthly transaction cost of $50 for order placement, handling, delivery, and billing. The net result is an industry that has an overall channel system transaction cost of approximately $1.2 billion, as shown.

When an extra layer (wholesalers) is added to the channel system, each of the 100 manufacturers can now sell each month to wholesalers at a cost of $25,000 per month, as illustrated in Figure 9-14. This cost is much higher because a great deal more merchandise is handled and delivered each month. In this channel system, the wholesalers need to then distribute to the 20,000 retailers each month. Their cost is $750 per transaction, which is also considerably higher because wholesalers are shipping a variety of products, because they represent a large number of retailers. As shown, in this channel system the wholesaler lowers the annual transaction costs to $210 million, or approximately $1 billion less than the channel system without a wholesaler function.

FIGURE 9-13   Transaction Costs in a Channel without Wholesalers

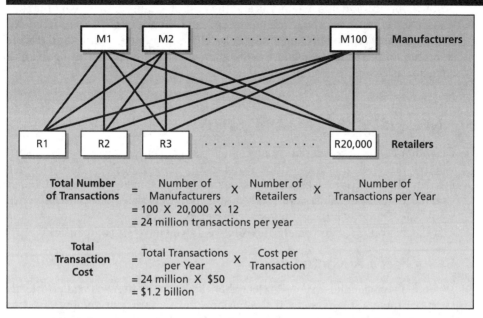

FIGURE 9-14   Transaction Costs in a Channel with Wholesalers

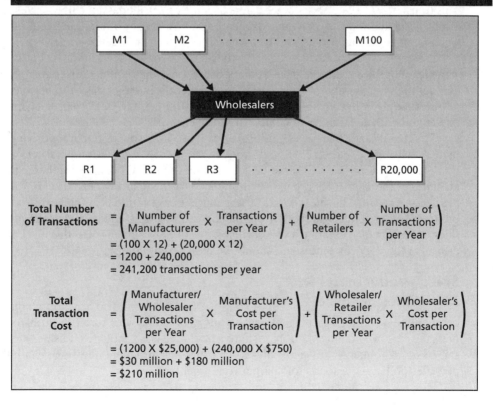

Although a business generally builds customer value through a combination of product, service, and image benefits and the cost of acquiring these benefits (price and transaction costs), any given channel system can enhance or detract from the delivered customer value. Thus, selecting a particular channel system requires both careful consideration of the benefits sought by customers and the cost of delivering them through a particular channel system.

CHANNEL SYSTEMS AND COMPETITIVE ADVANTAGE

Customer contact is essential for any sale to occur. This contact can take many forms, whether direct or indirect. For direct channel systems, a business must have a certain number of salespeople to establish and maintain a certain level of contact. For indirect channel systems, a business must have a sufficient number of outlets, whether retail or wholesale. Either can be a source of competitive advantage when done in a manner that creates value for customers and relative advantage over competitors.

Sales Force Advantage

When a direct channel system is selected as the best way to reach and effectively serve target customers, it is essential that a business have a sufficient number of salespeople. Assume that a business has 1,000 target customers and the required rate of customer contact for sales effectiveness and customer satisfaction is two customer visits per month. This translates into 24,000 customer contacts per year. Further assume that a salesperson in this particular industry can make three customer visits per day and has four days per week to make customer calls. This translates into a need for 38 salespeople.

If competitors have an average of only 20 salespeople, they cannot accomplish the same level of sales coverage. These competitors will either contact fewer customers or contact the same number of customers less frequently. In either case, the business with 38 salespeople is better able to reach more customers and better serve customers' needs, and both are sources of competitive advantage.

The quality of a business's sales force can also be a source of competitive advantage. A sales force with exceptional product knowledge and a strong market orientation is in a good position to serve target customer needs. Of course, the behavior and attitudes of the sales force are in part influenced by the market orientation of the business.[12] As a result, a business with a strong market orientation is in the best position to build customer relationships that enhance customer satisfaction and retention. The sales force is, in fact, creating a source of competitive advantage when this level of sales effort is valued by customers and cannot be matched by competitors.[13]

Sales Productivity

Businesses that have a high level of sales productivity can also develop a source of competitive advantage. A business with a more efficient sales force, in terms of sales per salesperson, will have a lower cost per sale than a less productive business with the same sales revenue. An efficient sales force translates into higher levels of profitability per sales dollar and a source of competitive advantage.

But how does a business develop high levels of sales productivity? Businesses with high-quality products, broad lines of related products, and efficient sales administrative systems produce high levels of sales per salesperson. High-quality products are easier to sell than are low-quality products, and they often have premium prices. A broad product line provides more sales opportunities per sales call. And the use of computers and other telecommunications systems has been shown to improve sales administrative efficiency and to allow for more time with customers.

Distribution Advantage

For markets in which indirect channel systems are the dominant channel system used to reach target customers, share of distributor outlets can be directly linked to market share. As shown in Figure 9-15, generally the higher a drug store's outlet share, the higher its market share. Empirical studies have shown that the relationship between outlet share and market share is nonlinear and generally S-shaped, as shown in Figure 9-16. A small distributor share produces proportionately smaller market shares. However, as outlet share grows, market share grows at a faster rate until it exceeds outlet share. Then, as outlet share continues to increase, the rate of market share growth decreases.

There are only a few cases in which very high outlet and market shares have been observed. The lower part of the curve, below a 50 percent outlet share, is well documented.[14] But, because market share must equal 100 percent when outlet share equals 100 percent, the upper half of the curve in Figure 9-16 can be extrapolated with some confidence. Recognizing this relationship, for markets in which indirect retail or dealer channel systems are required to reach and serve target customers, businesses with dominant distribution shares have a source of competitive advantage. Why? Because in any given market, there is a finite number of distributors, and fewer good ones. The business that dominates this channel system can control market access by blocking market entry because the number of available distributors or retailers is limited.

FIGURE 9-15 Drug Store Chain Market Share vs. Outlet Location Share					
North American Drug Store Chains	*Sales ($ billions)*	*Market Share (%)*	*Number of Stores*	*Outlet Share (%)*	*Sales per Store ($ millions)*
Walgreens	$13.4	23	2,363	14	$ 5.67
Rite Aid	11.8	20	3,963	23	2.97
CVS	11.1	20	3,909	23	2.84
Eckerd	8.8	15	2,786	17	3.16
American Drug Stores	5.2	9	882	5	5.93
Longs Drug Stores	2.8	5	337	2	8.40
Shoppers Drug Mart	2.8	5	801	5	3.52
Jean Coutu	1.2	2	483	3	2.38
Phar-Mor	1.1	2	104	1	10.38
Medical Shoppe Int'l.	1.0	2	1,236	7	0.84
Total/Average	**$59.2**	**100%**	**16,864**	**100%**	**$ 3.51**

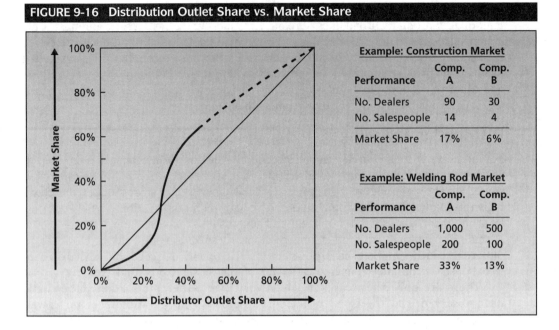

FIGURE 9-16 Distribution Outlet Share vs. Market Share

Example: Construction Market

Performance	Comp. A	Comp. B
No. Dealers	90	30
No. Salespeople	14	4
Market Share	17%	6%

Example: Welding Rod Market

Performance	Comp. A	Comp. B
No. Dealers	1,000	500
No. Salespeople	200	100
Market Share	33%	13%

PROFIT IMPACT OF ALTERNATIVE CHANNEL SYSTEMS

Several aspects of profitability come into play in determining the profitability of any channel system. Consider for example a manufacturer who sells ten million units per year of industrial lubricant in a market in which it has a 5 percent market share. The business currently sells its lubricants to independent wholesalers for $1.50 per unit, as shown in Figure 9-17. The wholesalers mark up the price of these lubricants 50 percent to $2.25 to achieve a 33.3 percent margin. Supply house distributors, in turn, mark up the price to $3 to achieve a 25 percent margin. The manufacturer's variable cost per unit is $0.90. In addition, the producer spends $3.5 million on fixed marketing expenses for advertising, selling, and administrative expenses. With this channel system and marketing expense, the business is able to achieve a 5 percent market share and $2.5 million in net marketing contribution:

$$\begin{matrix} \textbf{Net} \\ \textbf{Marketing} \\ \textbf{Contribution} \end{matrix} = \left[\begin{matrix} \text{Market} \\ \text{Demand} \end{matrix} \times \begin{matrix} \text{Market} \\ \text{Share} \end{matrix} \times \left(\begin{matrix} \text{Revenue} \\ \text{per} \\ \text{Customer} \end{matrix} - \begin{matrix} \text{Variable} \\ \text{Cost per} \\ \text{Customer} \end{matrix} \right) \right] - \begin{matrix} \text{Marketing} \\ \text{Expenses} \end{matrix}$$

$$= [200 \text{ million} \times 0.05 \times (\$1.50 - \$0.90)] - \$3.5 \text{ million}$$
$$= [10 \text{ million} \times \$0.60)] - \$3.5 \text{ million}$$
$$= \$2.5 \text{ million}$$

At this point, management might ask, "What is an alternative channel system worth?" To answer this question, we need to compute the net marketing contribution of an alternative channel system and compare it with the business's current net marketing contribution.

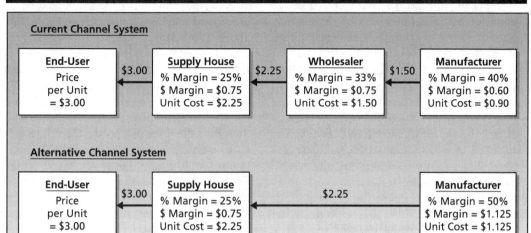

FIGURE 9-17   Alternative Channel Systems for Industrial Lubricants

Assume that the lubricant manufacturer feels that it could capture more margin and maintain the same market share by selling and distributing direct to the supply houses, as illustrated in Figure 9-17. The business estimates that this channel system would raise its variable cost per unit to $1.125 and would require twice the marketing budget ($7 million). These numbers translate into a net marketing contribution of $4.25 million, as shown in the following, $1.75 million greater than the current net marketing contribution.

$$\begin{aligned} \text{Net Marketing Contribution} &= [200\ \text{million} \times 0.05 \times (\$2.25 - \$1.125)] - \$7\ \text{million} \\ &= [10\ \text{million} \times \$1.125] - \$7\ \text{million} \\ &= \$4.25\ \text{million} \end{aligned}$$

Thus, the value of this alternative channel system would be $1.75 million, the increase in net marketing contribution that it would provide.

Summary

Regardless of how attractive a business's products or services may be, if the business cannot reach target customers with a desired level of services, it has little chance of marketing success. Customers have product and service requirements along with preferences of where to buy. Likewise, a business has image requirements and the need for sales effectiveness and cost-efficiency. To be successful, a channel system must meet both customer and business requirements.

The biggest decision is whether to use a direct or an indirect channel system. In a direct system, the business retains ownership of its products and is responsible for many of the selling, delivery, warehousing, and transaction activities. Direct channel systems include direct selling, direct marketing, telemarketing, and the use of manufacturers' reps and sales agents. An indirect system takes ownership of the product and varying degrees of responsibility for selling, warehousing, delivery, and transaction activities. Indirect systems include different combinations of wholesalers and retailers in the consumer market. In the business-to-business market, indirect systems can also include different combinations of wholesalers and dealers, value-added resellers (VARs) and original equipment manufacturers (OEMs).

The biggest change in marketing channels is the use of e-marketing channels. For businesses like General Electric, it leveraged their ability to reach customers and capitalize on existing brand awareness, order entry systems, and operating expenses. For dot.com businesses like e-Bay, e-marketing is the primary marketing channel and a core element of their approach to serving customers. Without an effective e-marketing channel strategy many dot.com businesses

did not survive. Managed successfully e-marketing channels have proved to be an important marketing channel in both B2C and B2B markets.

In many instances, multi-tiered channel systems are more customer-effective and cost-efficient than direct systems. Thus, the belief that having more intermediaries in a channel system pushes up the cost, and, therefore, the price of a product, is not true. If a more efficient system were available, marketers would find it. However, rarely is one channel and sales system sufficient to reach all target customers. And, the greater a business's market coverage, with either a direct or an indirect system, the greater its market share. Thus, an important part of a profitable marketing strategy is a well-thought-out and well-managed channel system strategy.

APPLICATION PROBLEM: WWW.MESURVEY.COM

Companies		
3M	IBM	Portland General
ANZ Bank	ICI	PPG Industries
Arrow Electronics	Indium	Praxair
BASF	Ingersoll-Rand	Reilly Inc.
Ceridian	Itron	Reiter Auto.
Dow Automobile	James Hardie	Roche
Dow Chemical	Kennametal	Shell
Dow Corning	Lucas Industries	Southern Co.
DuPont	MediaOne	Sprint
Eastman Kodak	Moore Corporation	Tektronix
ECMRA	Motorola	Telstra
Ericsson	Northwest Natural	Unisys
Exxon-Mobil	Natl. Australian Bank	US West
Ferro Corp.	Pharmacia	WestPac Bank
Hewlett-Packard	Pitney Bowes	Xerox

Geographic Area	Countries	Percent
North America	3	62%
Europe	10	19%
Asia Pacific	8	14%
Latin America	4	2%
All Others	5	3%

Job Function Presentation			
Marketing Mgrs.	21%	Gen./Snr. Mgmt	9%
Product Mgrs.	11%	Bus. Planning	4%
Sales Mgmt.	11%	Bus. Support	8%
Marketing Supp.	8%	R&D/Engineering	5%
MARCOM	2%	Mfg./Distribution	3%
Svc./Tech. Supp.	2%	Other	16%

The **Marketing Excellence Survey** (MES) is a program developed to assess a manager's marketing knowledge and marketing attitudes. Each manager completing

the survey receives a *confidential* Personal Feedback Report that benchmarks their performance relative to peers in their business and MES database of over 15,000 managers from over 60 countries. Businesses receive a Benchmark Summary Report that summarizes overall results.

"PAPER AND MAIL" BUSINESS MODEL: 1992–1997

The Marketing Excellence Survey operated for five years with a traditional business model in which customer contact and sales were accomplished over the telephone and printed Marketing Excellence Surveys were mailed to managers participating in the survey. As shown below, the entire process relied on phone, fax, copies and FedEx.

The average revenue per customer during this period was $7,500. The variable cost of administering the Marketing Excellence Survey and producing reports was approximately 40 percent of sales. Marketing expenses were 20 percent of sales. The Net Marketing Contribution for the average customer was **$3,000 (40 percent of sales).** Non-marketing fixed expenses included rent, utilities, telephone, equipment and supplies which were deducted from the overall net marketing contribution at the end of the year to determine the MESurvey.com operating income.

Promotion Materials **Copy & FedEx**	Pre-Survey Materials **Copy & FedEx**	Survey **Copy & FedEx**	Survey Completed **& Mailed**	Data Entry **Manual**	Report Production & Editing **Manual**	Report **Copy & FedEx**

——————————— **MES Paper and Mail Process** ——————————————⟶

"E-MARKETING" BUSINESS MODEL: 1998–PRESENT

In 1998 MESurvey.com shifted from a *"paper and mail"* business to an *"e-marketing"* business in which virtually every aspect of the business was digitized. As

shown below, e-mail, online survey completion, and online editing of reports replaced phone, fax, paper, and FedEx although a certain amount of phone contact was still necessary.

Promotion Materials **E-mailed**	PreSurvey Materials **E-mailed**	Survey Setup **Online**	Survey Completed **Online**	Survey Data **Uploaded**	Report Production & Editing **Online**	Report **E-mailed &** hard copy mailed

——————————— **MES E-Marketing Process** ——————————————⟶

The switch to an "e-marketing" business model had a dramatic impact on revenue per customer, variable costs, error rate, marketing expenses, and productivity as summarized below:

- **Revenue per Customer:** Increased by 33 percent from $7,500 to $10,000. This was due to a higher response rate and

easier survey assess for managers located outside the USA.

- **Customer Reach:** MESurvey.com could now simultaneously serve 5 to 10 different clients across 60 countries at the same time.

- **Error Rate:** With no data input required the error rate due to typing errors or misreading handwriting disappeared.

continued

Also, online editing reduced report production errors and time.

- **Variable Cost:** Costs associated with presurvey copying and mailing and data input were eliminated. The cost of report production dropped also as all editing was done online. The cost of delivered reports decreased with a combination of electronic reports and hard copy. Other variable costs that now included related Internet charges increased. The net result was a reduction in variable cost from 40 percent of sales to 30 percent.

- **Marketing Expenses:** Promotional and advertising expenses and sample reports were now sent electronically. This cut marketing and sales expenses from 20 percent of sales to 10 percent of sales.

- **Productivity:** The e-marketing business model allowed the business to double its number of customers served with the same staff and fixed expenses, because less time was needed for promotional mailing, presurvey setup, data entry, report production and editing.

Questions

For access to interactive software to answer the questions on the next page go to www.RogerJBest.com or www.prenhall.com/best.

1. Ignoring the cost reductions achieved by e-marketing, estimate how the net marketing contribution would have changed with only a 33 percent increase in revenue per customer.

2. What impact did e-marketing have on the variable costs, and how did this change alone affect the net marketing contribution per customer?

3. What impact did e-marketing have on the marketing expenses, and how did this change alone affect the net marketing contribution per customer?

4. Taking into account all the cost reductions and revenue increases from switching to an e-marketing business model, how did the overall net marketing contribution per customer change?

Market-Based and Strategic Thinking

1. Why is it advantageous to view a combination of sales and channels of distribution as a channel system?
2. How has the use of a direct channel system helped Dell Computer grow over the last 10 years?
3. How has Compaq Computer's channel system contributed to its growth over the last 10 years?
4. What is the difference between a direct and an indirect channel system? Why might a business use both?
5. What is a mixed channel system? Why would Microsoft's Office suite be marketed with a mixed channel system to large business customers?
6. What are the various direct sales and channel systems that could be used in the consumer market? How do they differ from the business-to-business market?
7. What role do online channel systems play in the way we buy airline tickets and stocks?
8. How does e-marketing help businesses reach customers, lower cost, and improve customer service?
9. What role do VARs play in business-to-business markets? How do they enhance customer value?
10. How does the use of multiple channel systems affect the growth of a business?
11. How does the use of a channel system either enhance or detract from customer value? What specific factors need to be considered in selecting one channel system over another?
12. Why can a channel system be a source of competitive advantage?

13. What are some of the ways a channel system can be a source of advantage and contribute to a higher market share?
14. How can increased sales force quality and sales force productivity be developed into a source of competitive advantage?
15. How would you go about determining the profit impact of an alternative channel system?

Notes

1. K. Schnepf, "Customers of Epoxy Resin and Related Products Find e-epoxy.com a Powerful Procurement Channel," (www.dow.com-new/prodbus/2001).
2. M. Understrom and T. Anderson, *Brand Building On the Internet*
3. J. Welch, *Jack: Straight from the Gut* (Warner Business Books, 2001), 341–351.
4. Kasturi Rangan, Melvyn Menezes, and E.P. Maier, "Channel Selection for New Industrial Products: A Framework, Method and Application," *Journal of Marketing* (July 1992):69–82.
5. R. Oliva, "Painting with Business Marketers' Web Palette," *Marketing Management* (Summer 1998):50–53.
6. F. Cespedes and R. Corey, "Managing Multiple Channels," *Business Horizons* (July–August 1990):72.
7. Robert Haas, *Industrial Marketing Management: Text and Cases,* 4th ed. (Northridge, CA: Kent, 1989); 239; and Michael Morris, *Industrial and Organizational Marketing* (Old Tappan, NJ: Macmillan, 1988):489–523.
8. *SPECIAL REPORT: THE CORPORATE NET The Cultural Key to Net Gains,* http://www.businessweek.com/technology/content/apr2002/tc20020415_9527.htm, April 15, 2002.
9. Niraj Dawar and Philip Parker, "Marketing Universals: Consumers' Use of Brand Name, Price, Physical Appearance, and Retailer Reputation As Signals of Product Quality," *Journal of Marketing* (April 1994):81–95.
10. James Anderson and James Narus, "A Model of Distributor Firm and Manufacturer Firm Working Partnerships," *Journal of Marketing* (January 1990):42–58.
11. David Morris, "What's Old Is New in Relationship Marketing," *Marketing News* (February 1994):4, 8; and Robert Robicheaux and James Coleman, "The Structure of Marketing Channel Relationships," *Academy of Marketing Science* (Winter 1994):38–51.
12. Judy Siguaw, G. Brown, and Robert E. Widing, "The Influence of Market Orientation of the Firm on Sales Force Behavior and Attitudes," *Journal of Marketing Research* (February 1994):106–16.
13. Robert Ping, "Does Satisfaction Moderate the Association between Alternative Attractiveness and Exit Intention in a Marketing Channel?" *Academy of Marketing Science* (Fall 1994):364–71.
14. Gary Lilien, Philip Kotler, and K. Moorthy. *Marketing Models* (Upper Saddle River, NJ: Prentice Hall, 1992):434–38; P. Hartung and J. Fisher, "Brand Switching and Mathematical Programming in Market Expansion," *Management Science* (August 1965):231–43; and Gary Lilien and Ambar Rao, "A Model for Allocating Retail Outlet Building Resources across Market Areas," *Operations Research* (January–February):1–14.

CHAPTER 10

MARKETING COMMUNICATIONS AND CUSTOMER RESPONSE

At an Intel conference Paul Otellini, President and Chief Operating Officer, began with a story about Wayne Gretzky and his famous quote: "*I skate to where the puck is going, not to where it is.*" Building on this theme, Mr. Otellini handed out a hockey puck to each of the Intel managers in attendance. On one side of the puck was written "*Follow Me*" and on the other side was the now legendary logo "*intel inside™*" as shown in Figure 10-1.

Mr. Otellini's point was that market leaders skate to where the puck is going, and the "*intel inside*" advertising program has led the way. This logo catapulted Intel from technological obscurity to the fifth most valuable brand in 2002, valued at an estimated $31 billion.[1]

Firms like Nike, Ford, and Procter & Gamble spend millions more than Intel does on advertising but have achieved far less brand value than Intel—a brand not endorsed by any athlete, Hollywood star, cartoon figure, or noted public figure. "*intel inside*" with its logo and sound has cleverly become a highly recognized brand. The cost of this advertising effort was also low relative to major brand promotions because Intel co-branded its advertising with personal-computer manufacturers wanting to associate their brand with the latest technology and the Intel brand.

FIGURE 10-1   Intel Inside

MARKETING COMMUNICATIONS

The first job of a marketing communication is to build awareness: to inform customers of a business's products. Second, marketing communications need to continually reinforce messages in order to maintain awareness. Third, it is often the job of a marketing communication to motivate a target customer to take action. Thus, there are three fundamental marketing communications objectives, any one of which can be the focus of a particular marketing communication.

- **Build Awareness:** Build a level of awareness with respect to important information about the organization and its products and/or services.
- **Reinforce the Message:** Sustain a desired level of retention with respect to image, key benefits, and name recognition over time.
- **Stimulate Action:** Motivate target customers to take a specific action in a relatively short time.

Because message reinforcement and action can come only after a reasonable level of awareness, businesses need to first build awareness and comprehension before moving on to other marketing communications objectives.

Building awareness, comprehension, and interest in a business's products are major steps in the hierarchy of customer response. As illustrated in Figure 10-2, there is a hierarchical set of customer response effects. If a marketing communication fails to create target customer awareness, the first stage in the hierarchy, none of the customer response effects that follow are possible. In this example, 37 percent of the target market will not be reached with the marketing communication and will therefore not have a chance to comprehend, develop interest, form intentions, or take action.

Of the 63 percent of the customers who are aware of the business's marketing communication, 54 percent can accurately recall the important content (comprehension). This means that 29 percent (the 46 percent who don't comprehend, out of the 63 percent who are aware) are removed from further customer response because they do

FIGURE 10-2 Marketing Communications and Customer Response Index

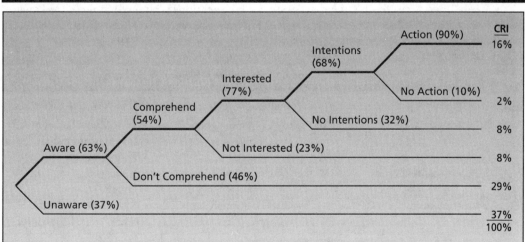

The overall customer response index for any combination of effects in the customer response hierarchy is the product of the proportions of individual effects that make up that combination. For example, the customer response index for customers who are aware of the communication (63%), comprehend its content (54%), but are *not* interested in the product or service (23%) is as follows:

CRI = % that are aware X % that comprehend X % that are not interested
    = 0.63 X 0.54 X 0.23
    = 0.08, or 8%

not fully comprehend the marketing communication content. Thus, the combination of target customers lost due to lack of awareness (37 percent) and insufficient message comprehension (29 percent) is 66 percent.

Of those target customers who are aware of and adequately comprehend the marketing communication, 77 percent express an interest in the product and its benefits, leaving 23 percent who are uninterested and creating a lost customer response of approximately 8 percent. Of those who are interested, 68 percent intend to take a desired action. However, those who are interested, but not sufficiently motivated to take action, create another loss in customer response of 8 percent.

Finally, target customers who are aware, comprehend, are interested, intend to take action, and take the desired action produce a customer response of 16 percent. Target customers who intend to take action, but do not, create an additional loss of potential customer response of 2 percent. In order to achieve a higher overall level of customer response, a business would need to improve its performance at specific stages in the customer response hierarchy in which the business has not performed well.

STRATEGIES TO INCREASE CUSTOMER RESPONSE

The potential causes of low levels of customer response in the customer response hierarchy are outlined in Figure 10-3. Marketing communications play a major role in low levels of awareness and comprehension. Low levels of awareness can be caused by poor media selection, insufficient message frequency (repetition), or poor ad copy. Low levels of comprehension can also be the result of insufficient frequency or poor ad copy. Correcting these problems is essential to improving overall customer response.

For example, assume that for the situation presented in Figure 10-1, the business developed a more effective marketing communications strategy that increased awareness from 63 percent to 75 percent. This increase would translate into a potential increase in customer response index (CRI), from 16 percent to 19 percent.

FIGURE 10-3 Marketing Causes of Low Levels of Customer Response		
Poor Response	*Marketing Problem*	*Underlying Cause*
Low Awareness	Marketing Communications	• Poor Media Selection • Insufficient Frequency • Poor Ad Copy
Poor Comprehension	Marketing Communications	• Insufficient Frequency • Poor Ad Copy
Low Interest	Product Positioning	• Insufficient Benefits • Weak Value Proposition • Poor Ad Copy
Low Intentions	Price and Transaction Cost	• High Price • Need for Low-Cost Trial • High Switching Cost
Low Purchase Level	Distribution and In-Store	• Not Readily Available • Hard to Find In-Store • Insufficient Sales/Service

$$\text{CRI (current)} = 0.63 \times 0.54 \times 0.77 \times 0.68 \times 0.90 = 0.16$$
$$\text{CRI (improved)} = 0.75 \times 0.54 \times 0.77 \times 0.68 \times 0.90 = 0.19$$

Assume, also, that the comprehension of its marketing communication was increased because of improved ad copy from 54 percent to 67 percent. The combined effects of increased awareness and comprehension increase the overall CRI from 16 percent to 24 percent, as illustrated.

$$\text{CRI (improved)} = 0.75 \times 0.67 \times 0.77 \times 0.68 \times 0.90 = 0.24$$

A well-positioned product with an attractive customer value (perceived benefits that are greater than perceived costs) and a strong marketing (channel) system will still not achieve full marketing success without a good marketing communications program. If target customers are unaware of a product's benefits, cost, and value, there is little opportunity for purchase.

For example, Johnson Controls is a Fortune 500 business that serves a variety of markets, one of which is the commercial building services market. Johnson Controls has achieved an excellent reputation among customers. However, a market research study revealed a low level of awareness in the commercial building services market; customers mentioned Johnson Controls with disappointing frequency when asked to identify suppliers of this service.[2]

In response to this information, Johnson Controls developed the "Classic Buildings" marketing communication illustrated in Figure 10-4. These print ads were

FIGURE 10-4   Johnson Controls' "Classic Buildings" Print Ad

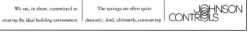

run in *Forbes, Fortune, Business Week,* and the *Wall Street Journal,* each of which reaches building and facilities managers (the target customers) in Fortune 1000 businesses. Nine months after the campaign, measurements were made. Unaided recall of Johnson Controls had increased by 30 percent. The marketing communication effort increased company awareness and helped presell the company. Both effects contributed to an increase in sales.

BUILDING CUSTOMER AWARENESS AND COMPREHENSION

Creating awareness among a large number of people is not the objective of most marketing communications. The objective is to create awareness among and communicate effectively to *target customers.* A memorable advertisement that is well known among the general population will fail if it does not achieve a high level of awareness and comprehension among target market customers.

Media Selection and Customer Awareness

As outlined in Figure 10-3, target customer awareness and comprehension are affected by media selection, message frequency, and ad copy. To effectively reach target customers, a business has to have a good understanding of their media habits. Do they watch television, and, if they do, which programs? Do they listen to the radio, and, if they do, which stations and at what time? Which newspapers and which sections of the newspaper do they read? Which magazines do they subscribe to? How do they go to work, with respect to exposure to outdoor signage? Do they use the Yellow Pages; are they Internet users or cable TV shoppers, or do they respond to direct-mail advertising? All of these questions must be answered in order to purchase the combination of media that will effectively reach as many target customers as economically possible.

A key measure of effective media selection is *target market reach.* Target market reach *is the percentage of target customers who will be exposed to the business's message given a certain combination of media.* For example, a golf ball manufacturer wants to reach golfers. To do so, the manufacturer might advertise in print media such as *Golf Digest, Golf Magazine,* the *Wall Street Journal,* and *Business Week* and on television during golf tournaments. Through this combination of media, the manufacturer might, for example, be able to reach 63 percent of the golfers it considers target customers for its golf balls.

To get a target market reach greater than 63 percent would require the manufacturer to add media that reach target customers not reached with the current combination of media. If the incremental reach were more expensive than the incremental economic benefit derived from reaching these target customers, then the business would not seek to go beyond its current level of target customer reach.[3]

Message Frequency and Customer Awareness

Once a business has found the right combination of media to effectively reach target customers, the next question becomes how often the business needs to expose target customers to its message in order to achieve a certain level of awareness. Using too few messages may prevent information from getting through to target customers and will probably result in low levels of awareness and comprehension. On the other hand, too

FIGURE 10-5   Advertising Frequency and Awareness in a Business-to-Business Market

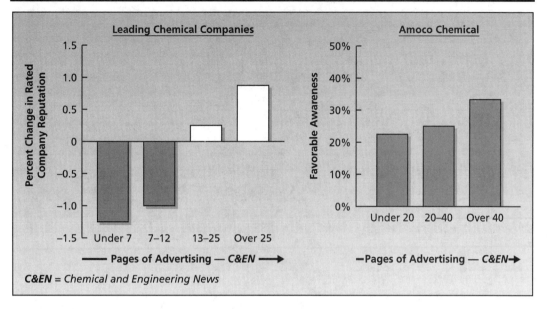

many exposures could irritate target customers and potentially have an adverse effect on retained information and perceptions of the ad, product, or company.

For example, the frequency of print advertising by leading chemical companies affects the year-to-year change in ratings of company reputation, as shown in Figure 10-5. Leading chemical companies that advertise fewer than seven to twelve times per year in *Chemical and EngineeringNews (C&EN)* adversely affect their reputation, whereas those at higher levels of frequency positively affect their reputations.[4] For Amoco Chemical, the level of favorable awareness steadily increased with the level of message frequency in *C&EN*.

If Amoco Chemical were to stop its marketing communications, over a relatively short time its level of awareness would diminish. Shown in Figure 10-5 are the results of a classic study on message frequency and awareness.[5] In a "concentrated frequency" strategy, thirteen consecutive messages were exposed to target customers over thirteen weeks. As shown, the message awareness steadily increased each week until it reached its highest level in week thirteen. However, after week thirteen, no more messages were exposed to target customers for the remainder of the year and, as shown, the message awareness decayed back down almost to zero. This marketing communications strategy would be appropriate for building awareness and comprehension for seasonal products, political candidates, and special events.

The same message was also sent to a different group of target customers once every four weeks throughout the year in a "distributed frequency" strategy. These target customers also received thirteen message exposures, but they were spread out over the entire year. In the four-week period following each exposure, recall of the message decreased, but it did not go below the level prior to the last exposure. Hence, each additional exposure built from a higher base position. And, as shown, although this pattern of exposure frequency produced a longer-lasting effect, it never reached the highest

FIGURE 10-6   Message Frequency and Message Awareness

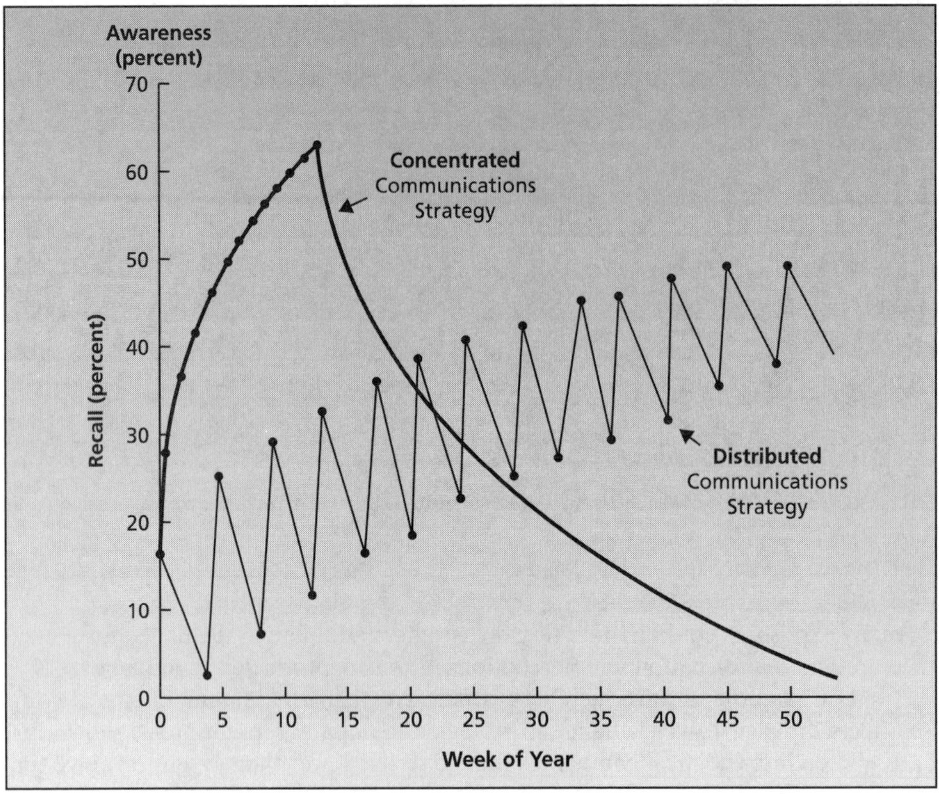

level of awareness produced by the concentrated frequency effort. This approach to marketing communications would be appropriate in building and maintaining target customer awareness and comprehension.

In Figure 10-6, target customers were exposed to each of the thirteen messages sent. A more typical situation is one in which target customers are exposed to only a fraction of the messages sent. So, for most marketing communications, there are more messages sent than received, as illustrated in the following:

Number Recalled	Proportion Recalling	Weighted Average
0	0.10	0.00
1	0.10	0.10
2	0.10	0.20
3	0.10	0.30
4	0.15	0.60
5	0.20	1.00
6	0.15	0.90
7	0.05	0.35
8	0.05	0.40
Total	**1.00**	**3.85**

In this example, eight marketing communications were directed to target customers. Ten percent did not recall seeing any of these ads, while 5 percent recalled seeing all eight. A weighted average of this recall yields an average message frequency of approximately four. This means the average target customer was exposed to the business's marketing communication approximately four times during the exposure period even though eight communications were directed at the target market. In television advertising, the combined impact of message frequency and reach produces an index called *gross rating points* (GRPs). A business with a 60 percent reach and a frequency of four produces an impact of 240 GRPs. This is a far better measure of advertising effectiveness than the dollars spent on advertising, because GRPs better measure how well the ad reached a target market and how often it was seen.

$$\text{Gross Rating Points} = \text{Reach} \times \text{Frequency} = 60 \times 4 = 240$$

Ad Copy and Customer Response

A highly memorable marketing communication that does not communicate the product and its benefits will fail to enhance interest in the product and will lower the overall level of customer response. Ad copy is best able to attract customers when it is based on customer needs and situations familiar to customers. It needs to integrate customer needs and situations with the product's benefits and business name.[6] If an ad is attractive but fails to create product interest, the ad copy is of limited value to the customer or to the business.

MESSAGE REINFORCEMENT

Although building awareness, comprehension, and interest are critical to achieving a high level of target customer response, these levels will diminish, as shown in Figure 10-5, if the message is not continually reinforced. Johnson Controls' marketing communications program improved ad awareness, but to hold or continue to grow a high level of awareness, a company would have had to continually keep the message in front of target customers.

Message Reinforcement and Pulsing

Maintaining a high level of awareness is expensive and requires new ad copy as the old copy begins to wear out. One approach to message reinforcement that maintains awareness, reduces copy wearout, and is cost-efficient is *pulsing*.[7] Pulsing involves the use of alternating exposure periods. An example of pulsing is a television advertisement that achieves 150 gross rating points over a four-week exposure period and is run in alternating four-week periods. As shown in Figure 10-6, a certain level of awareness is built up during a four-week exposure period; it then diminishes to some degree over the following four-week period in which there is no message exposure, and then awareness is built up again in a subsequent four-week exposure period.

If a business can maintain a desired level of awareness with pulsing, it can reduce the cost of advertising because there is no advertising expenditure in alternating non-exposure four-week periods. A secondary benefit of pulsing is that it reduces the potential for copy wearout due to overexposure to the same message. Because the

FIGURE 10-7   Message Reinforcement Strategies

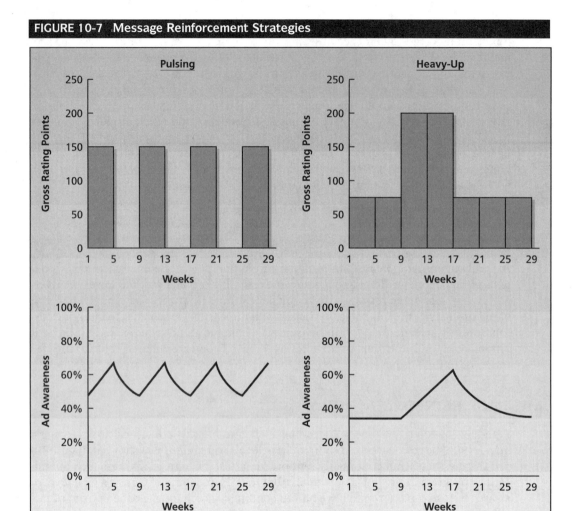

marketing message is not seen on a continual basis, the ad copy's novelty and appeal wear out at a slower rate. Also, pulsing reduces the potential for overexposure, which can cause customer irritation and reduce ad effectiveness.

Heavy-Up Message Frequency

Because certain products can be purchased more readily at some times of the year than at others, a business may use a heavy-up exposure pattern to build higher levels of awareness, comprehension, and, it is hoped, interest in the advertised product or service. Figure 10-7 illustrates a heavy-up marketing communications program for a well-known brand that is consumed most heavily in the summer. Many other exposure patterns are possible, but in this example, the business elects to maintain a certain level of base awareness throughout most of the year and to heavy-up its message frequency just before and during the prime buying period for this product. The business could also combine a heavy-up strategy for its primary promotion period and a pulsing strategy throughout the rest of the year.

STIMULATING CUSTOMER ACTION

Quite often, simply informing target customers and maintaining awareness are not enough to stimulate customer action. More is needed, particularly for new products whose benefits cannot be fully realized until they have been tried. For example, advertising copy that attempted to explain the benefits of the Post-it Note was simply not taken seriously by target customers.[8] And after eighteen months in four test markets, 3M's efforts to communicate the benefits of Post-it Notes led nowhere. A further complication was that 3M had a policy against giving away free goods on a new product introduction. The marketing director opened a fifth test market to specifically get around the corporate policy and to generate trial purchase through a free sample program. This move enabled customers to discover the benefits of Post-it Notes by using them, and the product went on to be a great commercial success.

PUSH VS. PULL COMMUNICATIONS STRATEGIES

One almost always thinks of marketing communications as being directed toward customers, but an important aspect of marketing communications is communications directed toward channel intermediaries. Approximately one-third of marketing communications dollars is spent on customer advertising, and two-thirds on sales promotions. The largest portion of the sales promotion expense (37 percent of total spending) is spent on intermediary promotions, and the remaining portion (29 percent of total spending) on customer promotions. In total, approximately 63 percent of the marketing communications budget is spent on customers and 37 percent on intermediaries.

Customer-targeted marketing communications are *pull* type communications. The objectives of a pull-through marketing communication are to build awareness, attraction, and loyalty and to reduce search costs, as shown in Figure 10-8. When pull marketing communications are successful, customers will seek out certain products or services and, in essence, by the interest they create, pull the product through the channel. A pull strategy requires channel intermediaries to carry certain products or brands in order to attract and satisfy target customers.

Push communications are directed at channel intermediaries. The objective in this case is to motivate channel intermediaries to carry a particular product or brand and, in this way, make it more available to customers. When successful, push communications result in a wider range of availability, fewer stockouts, greater merchandising (shelf space), and a greater marketing effort than would have been achieved with little or no push communications.

It is important, however, to understand that it is the combination of both push and pull marketing communications that creates the greatest impact on customer response and, therefore, market share gains.[9]

FIGURE 10-8 Push–Pull Communications and Customer Response

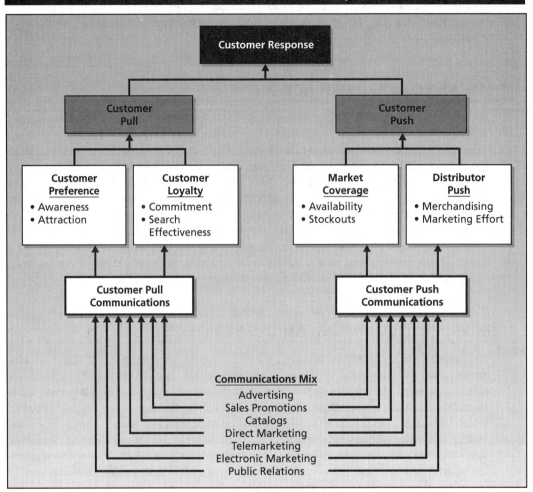

PULL COMMUNICATIONS AND CUSTOMER RESPONSE

As also shown in Figure 10-7, a wide range of alternative marketing communications can be used to create a communications mix designed to create customer pull.[10] To illustrate the power of media advertising, consider the fate of L&M cigarettes. Before cigarette advertising on television was banned, L&M had a 17 percent market share. After the ban, the decision was made to not advertise, because L&M management believed that other forms of advertising were ineffective. They were wrong, and today L&M is no longer on the market. The brand had good brand recognition and good customer pull. But, without continued reinforcement of the brand name and its positioning, it faded from customers' minds and, eventually, from the marketplace.

There are many forms of customer-directed sales promotions, such as coupons, rebates, sweepstakes, gifts, and rewards. When United Airlines initiated its Mileage Plus program, it changed how customers selected airlines and flights. Catalogs such as

L.L. Bean, Eddie Bauer, Spiegel, and many others stimulate customer pull every month with mailings to targeted customers. Direct marketing and, more recently, electronic marketing on the Internet, take a similar, but even more customized, approach to creating customer pull in the marketplace.

Advertising Elasticity

The percent change in sales volume per one percent change in advertising effort is a measure of advertising elasticity. Although there are considerable variations among products and market situations, short-run advertising elasticities are relatively small when compared with price elasticities. A study of 128 advertising elasticities produced an average advertising elasticity of 0.22, with very few advertising elasticities greater than 0.5. This means that for every 1 percent change in advertising expenditures, there will be an estimated 0.22 percent change in volume sold.[11]

For instance, a business with a sales volume of 200,000 units and a 0.22 advertising elasticity could estimate its sales to increase to a volume of 208,800 units with a 20 percent increase in advertising, as shown below:

$$\frac{\text{Sales}}{\text{Volume}} = \frac{\text{Current}}{\text{Volume}}\left[1 + \left(\text{Ad Elasticity} \times \frac{\text{Percent Change}}{\text{in Advertising}}\right)\right]$$
$$= 200{,}000 \times [1 + (0.22 \times 0.20)]$$
$$= 200{,}000 \times 1.044$$
$$= 208{,}800 \text{ units}$$

It is important to keep in mind that there are certain limits to what advertising can accomplish with respect to sales response at different stages of a product's life cycle. During the introductory stage, a business builds awareness, comprehension, and interest, but the market demand is small, and even when advertisements are very effective, only a limited volume and sales response are achievable.

The growth stage of a product's life cycle offers the greatest opportunity for sales gains using advertising. A business that does not invest in advertising during this phase is missing its best opportunity to grow sales, because advertising elasticities will be greatest during this period. However, as a market matures, there is less new volume coming into the market, and the effects of advertising on sales response begin to diminish. Finally, in declining markets, a business needs to cut back on advertising because dollars spent on advertising produce little, if any, sales response.

Advertising Carryover Effects

In addition to a short-run advertising impact on sales response, advertising also has been shown to have a long-run carryover effect. That is, the advertising effort made in a given period will produce some additional sales response in subsequent sales periods. Advertising carryover coefficients range from zero to less than one, with the average carryover coefficient equal to approximately 0.5.[12] This means that in the period immediately following the ad effort, a 0.50 sales effect from the previous period will carry over. In the second period, the carryover effect of 0.50 is squared, and 0.25 of the sales response produced two periods earlier occurs, and so on, as shown in Figure 10-9.

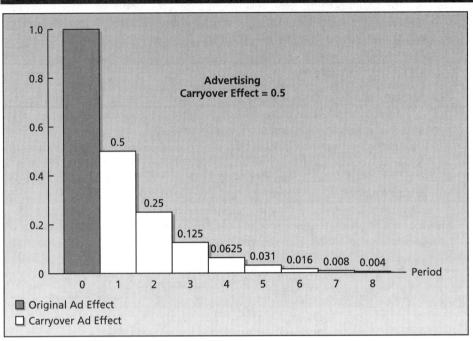

FIGURE 10-9   Media Advertising and Sales Carryover

Recall the business with a short-run advertising elasticity of 0.22 that could expect a short-run increase of 80,000 units in sales revenue from a 20 percent increase in advertising expenditures. The total impact of this ad expenditure, using a 0.50 carry-over effect, is approximately 160,000 units, as shown next. Thus, the overall sales response to the advertising effort would have been double the short-run effect as shown in Figure 10-10 and calculated below:

$$\frac{\text{Total Sales}}{\text{Effect}} = \frac{\text{Original Sales Effect}}{(1 - \text{Carryover Effect})} = \frac{80,000 \text{ units}}{(1 - 0.5)} = 160,000 \text{ units}$$

Direct Marketing Promotions

Database marketing makes customized direct-mail programs a viable opportunity to efficiently reach target customers and provide them with an incentive to take action. For example, consider a new sparkling wine, for which the producer direct mailed 100,000 known champagne consumers a $5 coupon good on the purchase of its sparkling wine. As shown in Figure 10-9, only 5 percent of the target customers responded by using the coupon. Of these 5,000 customers, 2,000 tried the new sparkling wine but did not repurchase; 1,000 used the coupon and became occasional buyers at the rate of one bottle per year; and 2,000 used the coupon and became regular purchasers at the rate of four bottles per year. Among the 95 percent who did not respond, 30 percent never opened the mailer and 65 percent opened it and were favorably impressed. Of these 65,000 customers, 5,000 purchased the product without the coupon at a later date. In total, 16,000

FIGURE 10-10   Customer Response to a Direct Marketing Promotion

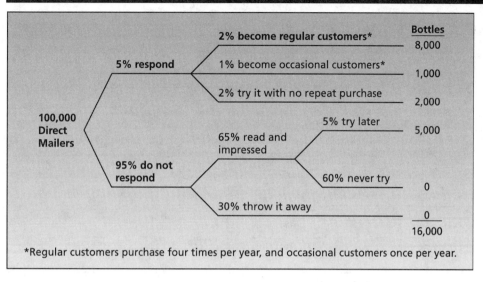

*Regular customers purchase four times per year, and occasional customers once per year.

bottles of the new sparkling wine were purchased as a result of the direct-mail program, even though there was only a 5 percent initial response. [13]

Promotional Price Elasticity

The average price elasticity for consumer nondurable products is –1.76 according to a study of 367 brands.[14] However, the price promotion price elasticities for the three product categories shown in Figure 10-11 are considerably higher.[15]

Assume the market demand for sparkling wine is ten million bottles per year and that a particular brand has a 4 percent market share resulting in a unit volume of 400,000 bottles. Without advertising, this brand should experience a promotional price elasticity of –10. Thus, a 5 percent price promotion should yield a 50 percent increase in unit volume, from 400,000 to 600,000, as shown below:

$$
\begin{aligned}
\text{Unit Volume} &= (10 \text{ million} \times .04) \times [1 + (-10 \times -.05)] \\
&= 400,000 \times 1.5 \\
&= 600,000 \text{ bottles}
\end{aligned}
$$

By combining a price promotion with advertising, the promotional price elasticity can be further increased, as shown in Figure 10-10. For example, the promotion price elasticity of sparkling wine increases to approximately –14 with the support of an advertising campaign. This would produce additional unit sales of 80,000 with a 5 percent price promotion.

$$
\begin{aligned}
\text{Unit Volume} &= (10 \text{ million} \times .04) \times [1 + (-14 \times -.05)] \\
&= 400,000 \times 1.7 \\
&= 680,000 \text{ bottles}
\end{aligned}
$$

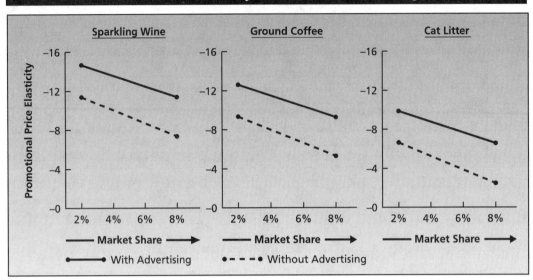

FIGURE 10-11 Promotional Price Elasticity with and without Advertising

In all three cases shown in Figure 10-11, the promotional price elasticity increased significantly with the use of advertising. For cat litter, this effect was very dramatic, doubling promotional elasticities. It is also important to note that the promotional elasticities decreased with the increase in market share.

Recognizing the high level of price sensitivity to promotions and the tremendous short-run revenue gain that can be achieved from a price promotion, one can understand why many companies have increased their use of them. However, a marketing strategy that seeks profitable growth must also produce a higher net marketing contribution. Thus, it is important in market-based management to also assess the profit impact of a marketing communications effort.

PUSH COMMUNICATIONS AND CUSTOMER RESPONSE

Marketing communications directed at intermediaries are designed as push communications; they stimulate intermediaries to engage in aggressive customer promotion efforts. As seen in Figure 10-8, the objective of push communications is to build greater product availability and marketing effort. Businesses that are aggressive in rewarding and supporting channel intermediaries are able to obtain more market coverage (number of desired distributors) than are nonaggressive businesses. This support provides several mechanisms to deliver effective in-store merchandising and marketing efforts of a business's products.

Trade Promotions and Customer Response

Trade promotions designed to stimulate purchase are common among businesses who sell their products through intermediaries. Quite often, trade promotions involve price reductions to distributors or retailers. The idea is that the price incentive will motivate the intermediary to push the product.

For example, assume that a normal can of orange juice concentrate costs $1.49 and the manufacturer offers a $0.20 discount to encourage the retail trade to push the sale of frozen concentrate. Assume also that the normal sales level is one million cans per month; the retailer margin is normally $0.19 per can; the manufacturer's sales and distribution costs are $0.15 per can; and each unit costs $0.50 to produce. In nonpromotion months, the manufacturer would expect to make $650,000 in total contribution, as is shown below:

$$
\begin{aligned}
\text{Total Contribution (current)} &= \text{Current Volume} \times \left(\text{Retail Price} - \text{Retailer Margin} - \text{Sales and Distribution Cost} - \text{Unit Cost} \right) \\
&= 1,000,000 \times (\$1.49 - \$0.19 - \$0.15 - \$0.50) \\
&= 1,000,000 \times \$0.65 \\
&= \$650,000
\end{aligned}
$$

An important question for the manufacturer should be how much volume a trade promotion would have to produce to make a promotional period as profitable as a typical nonpromotion period. With the discount, the manufacturer's net promotional margin per unit drops to $0.45 per can. As shown below, the business would have to increase sales by 44 percent to 1.44 million cans in order to produce the same level of profitability.

$$
\$650,000 = \text{Promotion Volume} \times (\$1.49 - \$0.19 - \$0.15 - \$0.50 - \$0.20 \text{ discount})
$$

$$
\$650,000 = \text{Promotion Volume} \times \$.045
$$

$$
\text{Promotion Volume} = 1.44 \text{ million units}
$$

Forward Buying and Customer Response

Trade promotions such as the one just described often result in forward buying by both customers and retailers. If the product is promoted effectively, customers will buy more during the promotion and will not have the same level of need in the following nonpromotion period. The impact of customer forward buying was presented in Chapter 8 with the discussion of price promotions.

Retailer forward buying involves less buying before the trade promotion as well as buying more than is needed during the promotion to take full advantage of the discounted price. These aspects of retailer trade promotion forward buying are illustrated in Figure 10-12, and the profit impact is presented in Chapter 8 with the discussion of price promotions.

The net effect of forward buying is that retailers are able to buy at lower prices for a period much longer than the promotion. One study found that 80 percent of the products purchased by retailers were purchased at promotional prices. Buying at promotional prices, of course, greatly affects the manufacturer's profitability. This combination

FIGURE 10-12   Retailer Inventories and Forward Buying on a Trade Promotion

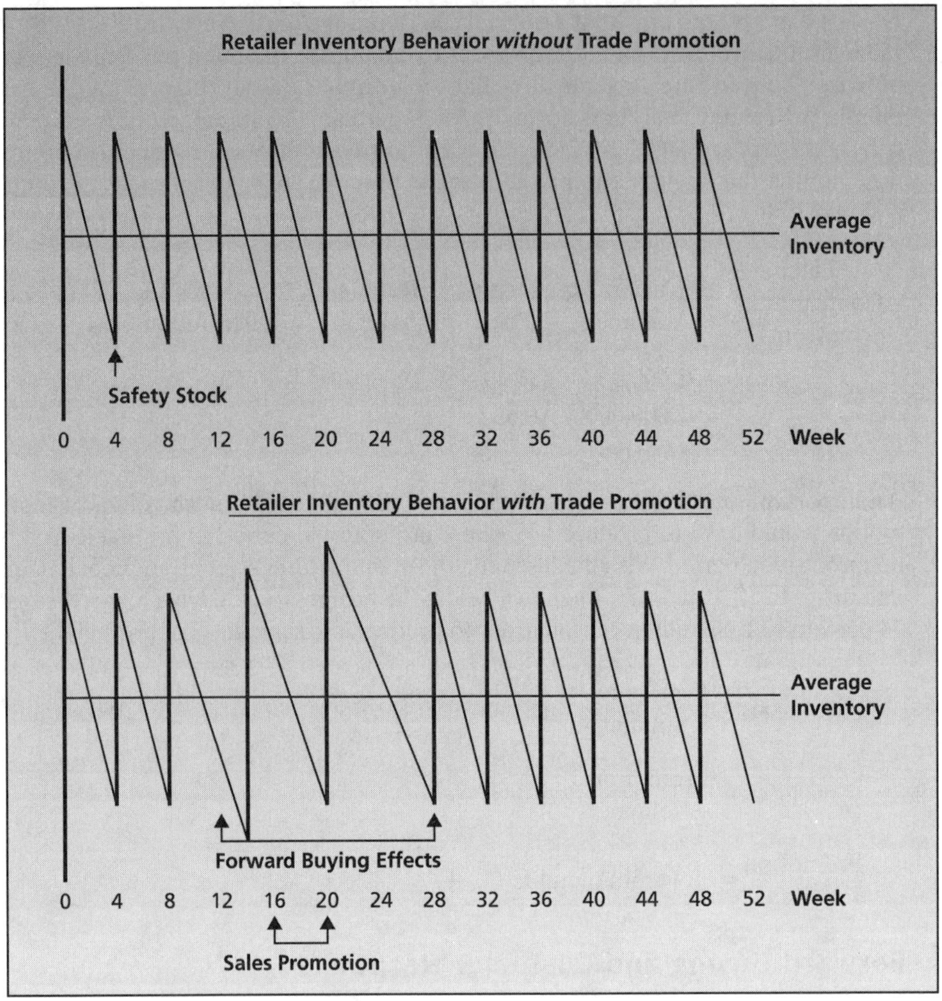

Retailer Inventory Behavior *without* Trade Promotion

Average Inventory

Safety Stock

0   4   8   12   16   20   24   28   32   36   40   44   48   52   Week

Retailer Inventory Behavior *with* Trade Promotion

Average Inventory

Forward Buying Effects

0   4   8   12   16   20   24   28   32   36   40   44   48   52   Week

Sales Promotion

of customer stockpiling (customer forward buying) and deal-prone shopping (switching from one deal to another) makes it very difficult for manufacturers to make a profit on push sale promotions.[16]

Market Infrastructure and Push Communications

Figure 10-13 illustrates a communications market infrastructure that includes both end customers and intermediaries and nonmarket sources that influence them.[17] For example, marketing communications targeted at industry gurus, consultants, and financial analysts create secondary marketing communications that, in turn, influence the trade press, business press, and the general press. These nonmarket sources of influence, in turn, provide information to channel intermediaries and customers.

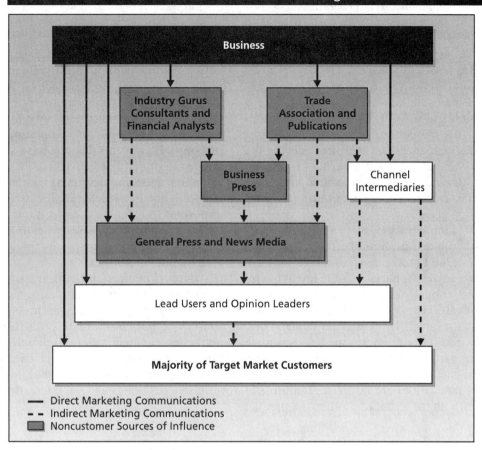

FIGURE 10-13 Market Infrastructure and Push Marketing Communications

The solid lines in Figure 10-13 represent normal marketing communications targeted at customers or intermediaries. The dashed lines represent public relations–type communications targeted at individuals and institutions that influence customers and channel intermediaries. Some of these public relations communications are *primary* communications (from the company to the source of the influence), and others are *secondary* communications (from one source of influence to another). Of course, one of the most important sources of secondary market communications is from lead users and opinion leaders who communicate by word of mouth to the larger market of target customers.

Summary

Without an effective marketing communications program, a marketing strategy will fail. Target customers must be made aware of the product and its benefits, be continually reminded of these benefits, and be stimulated to take action. Building awareness, message comprehension, and interest are essential phases in building a high level of customer response. The customer response index is a diagnostic tool to help a management team determine the sources of weakness in its marketing communications program.

To be effective and cost-efficient, a business's marketing communications must reach target customers and deliver an adequate level of message frequency to maintain desired levels of awareness, comprehension, and interest. Pulsing enables a business to use alternate exposure periods to more economically maintain customer awareness and interest while reducing the problem of ad copy wearout. Heavy-up efforts enable a business to build awareness and interest to higher levels during seasonal buying periods.

To build market share, a business needs both pull and push marketing communications. Pull marketing communications are targeted at customers with the intent of creating enough awareness and interest to motivate customers to demand the business's product. This customer demand creates market pull on intermediaries who, in turn, want the business's products to satisfy this customer demand. Push marketing communications are directed at intermediaries, with the intent of pushing the product through the channel. The objective of push communications is to create greater availability of, interest in, and access to the business's products.

Although the sales response to a marketing communication is difficult to estimate, the customer response index, advertising elasticity, advertising carryover effects, and promotional price elasticity provide systematic methods for estimating this response. However, sales response should not be the primary objective of a marketing communication. For marketing communications designed to increase sales, it is more important to estimate the profit impact of that promotion. Many sales promotions are not profitable, but businesses are forced into them to minimize losses.

In most markets, there is a marketing communications infrastructure that includes customers, intermediaries, and nonmarket sources of influence. Some push-through marketing communications are public relations–type communications directed at nonmarket sources of influence that, in turn, influence customers and intermediaries.

APPLICATION PROBLEM: GARDENBURGER

Gardenburger is a leading producer of meatless burgers with distribution in over 50,000 food service outlets and over 30,000 retail grocery stores, natural food outlets and club store locations. Although widely distributed, Gardenburger felt it had to improve its awareness and interest beyond the "healthy" niche market to the average consumer. To accomplish that goal the company spent $1.5 million on one commercial that was aired during the final episode of *Seinfeld*. A story-board of the television ad is shown in Figure 10-14.

This single ad was approximately 9 percent of the entire annual advertising budget for Gardenburger.

The ad reached 76 million people. Store sales in the following week were 350 percent higher than sales in the same week a year earlier after being adjusted for market growth. The same store sales for the entire meatless market went up 80 percent after being adjusted for market growth. The average weekly ad expenditure by Gardenburger was approximately $350,000. The $1.5 million spent on the

FIGURE 10-14   Gardenburger Television Ad Story Board

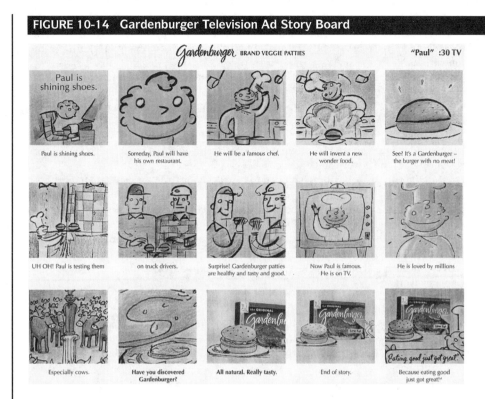

Seinfeld ad was 429 percent of the company's normal weekly ad budget.

For access to interactive software to answer the questions below go to www.rogerjbest.com or www.prenhall.com/best.

Questions

1. What was Gardenburger's cost per exposure assuming all 76 million viewers saw the ad?

2. If average weekly sales for the entire market were approximately $6 million,

how much did the market grow in the week following the Gardenburger ad on the *Seinfeld* show?

3. If average weekly sales were approximately $2 million, how much did the sales of Gardenburger grow in the week following the *Seinfeld* television ad?

4. What was the advertising elasticity for the Gardenburger *Seinfeld* TV ad? (Percent change in sales volume over percent change in advertising budget.) How would you recommend evaluating the overall effectiveness of this ad?

Market-Based Logic and Strategic Thinking

1. Why are customer awareness and message comprehension critical to the success of a marketing strategy?

2. How can interest in ad copy affect interest in a product and, subsequently, customer response?

3. When a business has an excellent marketing communications program and high intention to purchase, but a very low customer response, what kind of a marketing problem does it face?
4. When should a business use a combination of pulsing and heavy-up marketing communications?
5. Why is the message frequency for a marketing communication considerably lower than the number of messages sent?
6. Why will a business's market share be lower if it is not effective in both pull-through and push-through marketing communications?
7. At what stage of a product's life cycle is advertising elasticity likely to be highest?
8. How should the carryover sales effect of an advertising effort be used in evaluating the profit impact of the advertising effort?
9. What are the various behaviors that need to be tracked in order to evaluate the profit impact of a trade promotion?
10. How does the promotional price elasticity for a product change with advertising support? What effect does market share have on promotional price elasticity?
11. Why are the marketing communications infrastructure and public relations–type marketing communications important to the overall success of a marketing communications effort?
12. If advertising elasticity is so much smaller than promotional price elasticity, why should a business advertise?
13. How should a business use the advertising carryover effect in evaluating the sales response and profitability of a marketing communication?
14. Why are indirect sales promotions rarely profitable? If they are not profitable, why do manufacturers continue to offer them?
15. How does retailer forward buying affect trade promotion profitability?

Notes

1. "The 100 Top Brands," *BusinessWeek,* (August 5, 2002), 95–99.
2. Betty Arndt, "Johnson Controls' 'Classic Buildings' Marketing Campaign—A Pre- and Post-Campaign Evaluation," in *Drive Marketing Excellence* (New York, Institute for International Research, 1994).
3. Peter Danaher and Roland Rust, "Determining the Optimal Level of Media Spending," *Journal of Advertising Research* (January–February 1994): 28–34.
4. David Bender, Peter Farquhar, and Sanford Schulert, "Growing from the Top," *Marketing Management* (Winter/Spring 1996):10–19.
5. H. Zielske, "The Remembering and Forgetting of Advertising," *Journal of Marketing* (January 1959): 140; and J. Simon, "What Do Zielske's Real Data Really Show about Pulsing," *Journal of Marketing Research* (August 1979): 415–20.
6. Brian Wansink and Michael Ray, "Advertising Strategies to Increase Usage

Frequency," *Journal of Marketing* (January 1996):31–46.
7. Vijay Mahajan, Eitan Muller, John E. Little, and Hugh Zielske, "Advertising Pulsing Policies for Generating Awareness of New Products," *Marketing Science* (Spring 1986): 86–106.
8. Cliff Havener and Margaret Thorpe, "Customers Can Tell You What They Want," *Management Review* (December 1994): 42–45.
9. David Reibstein, "Making the Most of Your Marketing Dollars," in *Drive Marketing Excellence* (New York: Institute for International Research, 1994).
10. Gary Lilien, Philip Kotler, and K. Moorthy, *Marketing Models* (Upper Saddle River, NJ: Prentice Hall, 1992): 329–56.
11. Gert Assmus, John Farley, and Donald Lehmann, "How Advertising Affects Sales: Meta Analysis of Econometric Results," *Journal of Marketing Research* (February 1984): 65–74.

12. Ron Schultz and Martin Block, "Empirical Estimates of Advertising Response Factors," *Journal of Media Planning* (Fall 1986): 17–24.

13. Stan Rapp and Tom Collins, *Maximarketing* (New York: McGraw-Hill, 1987).

14. Robert Blattberg and Scott Neslin, *Sales Promotion Concepts, Methods and Strategies* (Upper Saddle River, NJ: Prentice Hall, 1990): 356.

15. Albert Bemmaor and Dominique Mouchoux, "Measuring the Short-Term Effect of In-Store Promotion and Retail Advertising on Brand Sales," *Journal of Marketing Research* (May 1991): 202–14.

16. Robert Blattberg and Alan Levin, "Modeling the Effectiveness and Profitability of Trade Promotions," *Marketing Science* (Spring 1987): 124–46.

17. Regis McKenna, *The Regis Touch: New Marketing Strategies for Uncertain Times* (Reading, MA: Addison-Wesley, 1985).

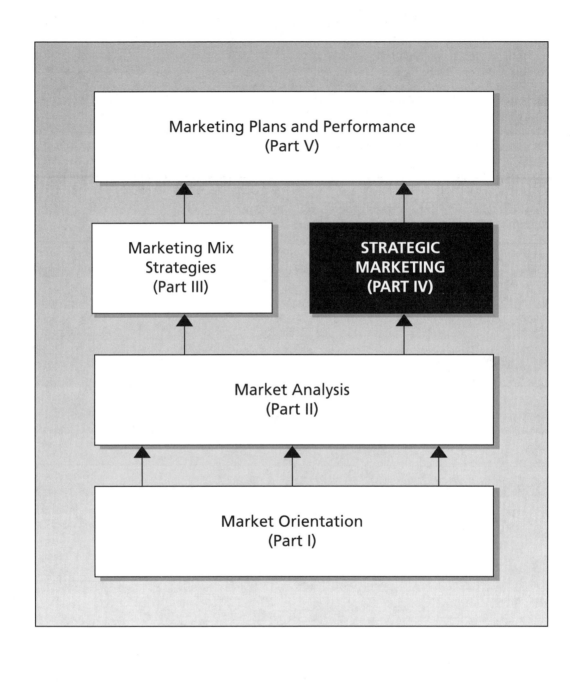

PART IV | STRATEGIC MARKETING

The concept is interesting and well-formed,
but in order to earn better than a "C" grade,
the idea must be feasible.

—YALE UNIVERSITY PROFESSOR'S COMMENTS ON FRED SMITH'S THESIS
PROPOSING THE OVERNIGHT DELIVERY SERVICE KNOWN TODAY AS FEDEX

S trategic market planning sets the strategic direction for a business and plays a critical part in achieving a business's long-run objectives of sales growth, profit performance, and share position. Tactical marketing strategies (covered in Part III) are more short-run, but essential to establishing desired target market positions and producing short-run growth and profit performance. Both impact growth, profitability, and share position—long-run marketing strategies set the strategic direction, while short-run target market positioning strategies provide the tactical marketing strategies needed to incrementally work toward long-run goals.

To facilitate the strategic market planning process, each product–market of interest is strategically assessed with respect to market attractiveness and position of competitive advantage. Using these two dimensions of strategic opportunity and position, in Chapter 11 we present a method of building a strategic market planning portfolio that includes all existing and potential product–markets.

The strategic market plans generated by the portfolio analysis can be either offensive or defensive. Offensive strategic market plans, presented in Chapter 12, are growth-oriented plans built around share penetration or market growth of existing markets or plans to enter new, existing, or emerging markets. Offensive strategic market plans are critical to business growth and future market position and profitability.

Defensive strategic market plans, presented in Chapter 13, are designed to protect market positions and profitability. Defensive strategic market plans can include protecting profitable market positions, reducing market focus to improve profitability, and harvesting and divestment strategies which will terminate with market exit. Defensive strategic market plans are critical to current share, sales, and profit performance.

11 | STRATEGIC MARKET PLANNING

The General Electric Company has evolved from having a relatively concentrated focus on electrical products to having a diverse portfolio of product–markets, as shown in Figure 11-1. Today, the GE portfolio includes light bulbs, household appliances, medical systems, plastics, transformers, jet engines, financial services, transportation equipment, steam turbines, and broadcasting. However, each product–market in the GE portfolio is under continuous review with respect to *share position*, *sales growth*, and *profit performance* in an effort to meet shareholder performance expectations. By the late 1990s, General Electric had created a market value (shares times price per share) of $360 billion, the largest of any U.S. company.

Successful companies such as General Electric, Coca-Cola, and Hewlett-Packard achieve year-after-year success with a great deal of strategic market planning.[1] These businesses are committed to serving shareholders, and this requires continuous review of current performance, new opportunities, and funding and investment decisions that contribute to a balance of short- and long-run performance. Product–market diversification is one aspect of portfolio analysis and strategic market planning.

FIGURE 11-1 Product–Market Diversification

Company	Sales	Market Value
General Electric	$40.7	$360
Coca-Cola	18.7	151
Procter & Gamble	37.2	112
Hewlett-Packard	40.1	73
Compaq Computer	24.6	67
DuPont	45.1	63
Campbell Soup	6.7	19

Note: Sales are in billions and market value is 1998 shares times price per share in billions.

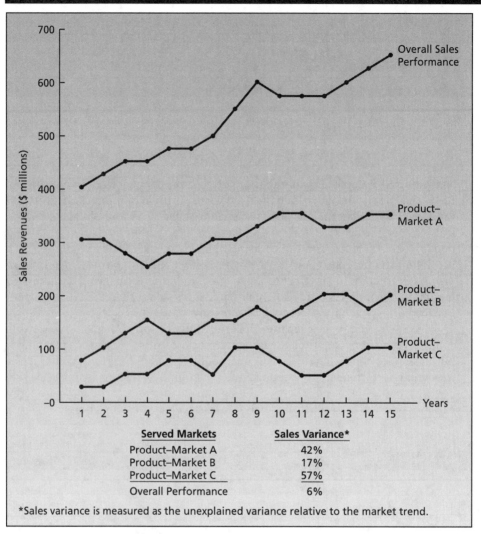

FIGURE 11-2   Product–Market Diversification and Sales Performance

Served Markets	Sales Variance*
Product–Market A	42%
Product–Market B	17%
Product–Market C	57%
Overall Performance	6%

*Sales variance is measured as the unexplained variance relative to the market trend.

PRODUCT–MARKET DIVERSIFICATION

Diversification across product–markets adds two important advantages to the overall performance of a business. First, it reduces dependence on any single product–market. And second, by diversifying, a business can smooth overall performance with offsetting conditions created by the competitive conditions and product life cycles in different product–markets.

For example, Figure 11-2 illustrates the overall sales of a business that is diversified across different product–markets. In product–market A, its core market, sales are growing at an average rate of 1.5 percent per year, but this growth varies from year to year because of economic conditions and competitive forces. Because the business is also positioned in two other, diversified product–markets, it is able to take advantage of offsetting product life cycles and competitive forces. Product–market B is growing at 4 percent per year and product–market C at almost 15 percent per year. Although sales in each of these two markets are much less than in the company's core market, product–market A, each contributes to overall sales growth and stabilizes performance.

The unexplained sales variance over the time period shown for product–market A is 42 percent, and for product–markets B and C, 17 and 57 percent, respectively. When the sales performances of all three markets are combined, the offsetting effects created by different competitive conditions and product life cycles produce more consistent growth, with only a 6 percent unexplained variance in the sales trend for the time period shown.

Product diversification provides one level of diversification. Obviously, the less dependent a business is on a single product, the less vulnerable it is to a major change in performance. For instance, Coca-Cola has a very broad line of beverage products that serves virtually all world markets. For Procter & Gamble, diversification goes further, as P&G has developed product positions in widely diversified consumer household product–markets. And General Electric, as discussed earlier, has expanded into a wide range of product–markets unrelated to its original electrical products.

Market diversification provides another way to achieve growth and risk reduction. DuPont, for example, has diversified across many markets that range from carpets to swimsuits and cookware with products such as Nylon, Dacron, Teflon, Lycra, Kevlar, and many others. This diversification has enabled DuPont to grow to a $50 billion company and yet not be dependent on any one product or market. In the early 1990s, US West split its company in two to better serve diverse markets. US West Communications remained in charge of the more mature core telecommunications businesses, while MediaOne Group was created to grow in high-technology markets. In the late 1990s, Hewlett-Packard did the same thing when it split its company into two companies, one an $8 billion test and measurement business and the other a $39 billion computer and imaging business. This split enabled HP to move faster in emerging computer and imaging markets without abandoning its core product–markets in test and measurement.

Although each product–market is going to experience periods of economic recession and growth, it is unlikely that *all* product–markets will experience the same conditions at the same time. Thus, participation in several diversified product–markets has the effect of offsetting economic conditions and product life cycle influences, thereby reducing the overall variability of business performance.

STRATEGIC MARKET PLANNING PROCESS

Each product–market in a business's portfolio in some way contributes to both the short-run and the long-run performance of the business. And, depending on current and future share position and performance, some product–markets will receive additional investment to grow or defend an important strategic market position. Other product–markets will be required to reduce focus in order to achieve a stronger competitive position and profit contribution with available resources. Still others may have resources withdrawn from them as a business begins to exit these product–markets. Because resources in any business are limited, a business needs a strategic market plan to carefully map out its future share position, sales growth, and profit performance. A strategic market plan sets the direction and provides guidelines for resource allocation.[2]

FIGURE 11-3 Strategic Market Planning Process

In order to specify a strategic direction for a product–market and to allocate resources to obtain desired short- and long-run performance, a business needs a *strategic market planning process*,[3] as outlined in Figure 11-3. The first step in this process is a careful assessment of current *business performance*, *market attractiveness*, and *competitive advantage* for each product–market a business wishes to consider over a three- to five-year strategic market planning horizon. With this information, the business can perform a *portfolio analysis* to better understand the current position of each product–market and its performance. On the basis of the portfolio position of each product–market, a *strategic market plan* can then be specified with respect to a desired set of performance objectives.

However, to make the strategic market plan actionable, the business has to develop a *tactical marketing strategy* in accordance with the strategic market plan and resources allocated. As the strategic market plan and a corresponding tactical marketing strategy are rolled out over a planning horizon, a *performance plan* outlines the short-run and long-run share position, sales growth, and profitability.[4] This chapter reviews the strategic market planning process and how it maps the short- and long-run performance of a business.

BUSINESS PERFORMANCE

Because each product–market can vary in attractiveness and competitive advantage, there can be a wide range of performance outcomes. The primary objective of a strategic market plan is to create a strategic direction and set of objectives for any product–market that affect three critical areas of business performance:

- **Share Position:** How will the strategic market plan contribute to the product–market's share and competitive advantage?
- **Sales Growth:** How much will the strategic market plan contribute to the business's sales revenue growth?

- **Profit Performance:** How will the strategic market plan affect short- and long-run profitability and contribute to shareholder value?

The strategic market plan for any given product–market is intended to produce results in all three areas of business performance. One of the primary objectives of a strategic market plan is to make explicit how share position, sales revenue, and profit performance will change over time. For instance, a strategic market plan to *grow* share in a growing market will produce drastically different levels of performance than will a strategic market plan to *protect* market share in an increasingly competitive mature market.

MARKET ATTRACTIVENESS

The primary purpose of a strategic market plan is to provide a *strategic direction* from which to set performance objectives and guide the development of a tactical marketing strategy. This is an important step in the strategic market planning process, because it requires a careful examination of market attractiveness. This step allows us to compare the relative attractiveness of different product–markets using a common set of attractiveness criteria. To facilitate this step in the strategic market planning process, we need a systematic way to assess market attractiveness.

To assess and index the attractiveness of a product–market, a business must ask itself, "What factors make a market attractive or unattractive?" Factors that typically shape market attractiveness include market size, market growth, competition, margin potential, market access, and fit with the company's core capabilities. These factors can be meaningfully grouped into three dimensions of market attractiveness: *market forces*, *competitive intensity*, and *market access*, as shown in Figure 11-4.

Each of these three dimensions of market attractiveness can be weighted to reflect its importance in relation to the others. In the example presented in Figure 11-5, market forces and market access are each weighted as 30 percent of total importance, whereas competitive intensity is weighted a little more heavily at 40 percent. Each of the dimensions of market attractiveness is further broken down into factors that contribute to a particular aspect of market attractiveness. These factors are also weighted to represent their relative importance within a dimension.

FIGURE 11-4   Factors That Shape Market Attractiveness

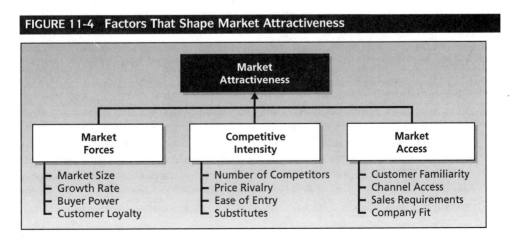

FIGURE 11-5 Indexing the Market Attractiveness of a Market

Market Attractiveness Factor	Relative Importance	Not 0	1	Attractive 2	3	4	Very 5	6	Overall Score
Market Forces									
Market Size	40%							X	240
Growth Rate	30%			X					60
Buyer Power	20%			X					40
Customer Loyalty	10%				X				30
	100%								370
Competitive Intensity									
Number of Competitors	30%				X				90
Price Rivalry	30%			X					60
Ease of Entry	20%						X		100
Substitutes	20%					X			80
	100%								330
Market Access									
Customer Familiarity	20%							X	120
Channel	40%						X		200
Sales Requirements	30%					X			120
Company Fit	10%							X	60
	100%								500

Market Attractiveness	Relative Weight	Factor Score	Overall Score	Maximum Score	Percent of Max.
Market Forces	0.30	370	111	180	62%
Competitive Intensity	0.40	330	132	240	55%
Market Access	0.30	500	150	180	83%
	1.00	1200	393	600	66%

When these and other factors that are considered to be important are weighted by their relative importance, an overall index for market attractiveness can be created, as illustrated in Figure 11-5. Special care should be taken to ensure that all the underlying forces that shape market attractiveness are adequately represented, on the basis of market and profit performance.[5]

In the example shown, each individual factor is also indexed from "very unattractive" to "very attractive" for a given product–market. This score (from 0 to 6) is multiplied by the factor weight to obtain a weighted individual factor attractiveness score. The sum of these individual scores for each dimension is computed and multiplied by the importance given that dimension. For example, market size is assigned 40 percent of relative importance within the market forces dimension and is given a rating of 6: very attractive. This results in a score of 240 (40 × 6) for this factor. This score is added to the scores of the other factors in this dimension to arrive at a total factor-weighted score of 370. This is multiplied by 0.30, the relative importance (weight) assigned to market forces, to produce a weighted overall score of 111 (62 percent of maximum), as shown in Figure 11-5.

When this process is completed for each of the market attractiveness factors and dimensions, an overall score of 393 is obtained. But, because different markets may have fewer or more factors and different dimension weights, the maximum score for different product–markets can vary. Therefore, to maintain comparability, the maximum possible score is derived, and the overall market attractiveness score is determined, as a percent of the maximum. In this example, the maximum score is 600, and the overall index market attractiveness score is 66 percent.

COMPETITIVE ADVANTAGE

The process of developing a multifactor index of competitive advantage follows the same procedure. The first question is, "What makes one business strong, with respect to competitive advantage, and another weak?" In answering this question, many businesses will arrive at a list of factors that determine competitive advantage that can be categorized into three dimensions of competitive advantage: *cost advantage*, *differentiation advantage*, and *marketing advantage*. Each of these drivers of competitive advantage also has underlying forces that shape the business's competitive advantage,[6] as shown in Figure 11-6.

Each of the three dimensions of competitive advantage is assigned a relative weight, just as was done in determining market attractiveness. And, as with market attractiveness, for each of the underlying factors, the relative importance within the dimension must be determined, as illustrated in Figure 11-7. Each factor must be assessed with respect to the competitive advantage of the business in its existing market or the potential position in new markets under consideration.

As shown in Figure 11-7, the competitive forces that shape a differentiation advantage for this business are relatively strong at 68 percent of maximum, while its competitive advantage with respect to marketing advantage is weak at 23 percent of maximum. Overall, the business is midrange in terms of competitive advantage, with a score of 52 percent.

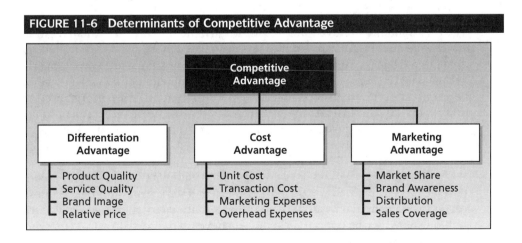

FIGURE 11-6 Determinants of Competitive Advantage

FIGURE 11-7 Indexing a Business's Competitive Advantage

Competitive Advantage Factors	Relative Importance	Way Behind 0	1	Equal 2	3	4	Way Ahead 5	6	Overall Score
Differentiation									
Advantage									
Product Quality	50%						X		250
Service Quality	30%			X					60
Brand Image	10%						X		50
Relative Price	<u>10%</u>						X		<u>50</u>
	100%								410
Cost Advantage									
Unit Cost	40%					X			160
Transaction Cost	10%		X						10
Marketing Expenses	30%				X				90
Overhead Expenses	<u>20%</u>			X					<u>40</u>
	100%								300
Marketing Advantage									
Market Share	30%		X						30
Brand Awareness	10%			X					20
Distribution	30%			X					60
Sales Coverage	<u>30%</u>		X						<u>30</u>
	100%								140

Source of Competitive Advantage	Relative Weight	Factor Score	Overall Score	Maximum Score	Percent of Max.
Cost Advantage	0.40	300	120	240	50%
Differentiation Advantage	0.40	410	164	240	68%
Marketing Advantage	<u>0.20</u>	<u>140</u>	<u>28</u>	<u>120</u>	<u>23%</u>
	1.00	850	312	600	53%

PORTFOLIO ANALYSIS AND STRATEGIC MARKET PLANS

When we combine the overall competitive advantage score with the overall market attractiveness score, we can create a product–market portfolio. Each product–market served by a business can be placed in a portfolio such as the one shown in Figure 11-8. Product–markets strong in market attractiveness and competitive advantage present the strongest portfolio position and best opportunity for profit performance.[7] Having product–markets in this position usually leads to a strategic market plan to *invest to protect* this attractive position of advantage. For each combination of market attractiveness and competitive advantage, there is at least one strategic market plan to be considered,[8] as shown in Figure 11-8.

As shown in Figure 11-8, attractive product–markets usually warrant an *offensive* strategic market plan. Strategic market plans can vary from improving a business's competitive advantage in attractive market situations to entering a new market. In addition, there may be opportunities to help develop or grow attractive emerging markets in which the business has the potential for a strong competitive advantage.

FIGURE 11-8   Portfolio Analysis and Strategic Market Plans

	Very Weak		Very Strong
Very Attractive **Offensive (Entry)** →	Offensive (Grow)	Offensive (Grow) Defensive (Protect)	Defensive (Protect)
	Offensive (Grow) Defensive (Protect/Harvest)	Offensive (Grow) Defensive (Protect/Focus)	Offensive (Grow) Defensive (Protect/Focus)
Very Unattractive	Defensive (Divest or Harvest)	Defensive (Divest or Harvest)	Defensive (Protect or Harvest)

Market Attractiveness (vertical axis)
Competitive Advantage (horizontal axis)

Protect	Invest to protect or hold a competitive advantage. Businesses often fail to invest in hold strategies, and the result is an erosion of competitive advantage.
Grow	Invest to improve or grow competitive advantage. In an underdeveloped or emerging market, this can also mean to invest in order to grow the market, and hence, its attractiveness.
Focus	Narrow market focus to profitable segments or niches within a segment in order to capture profits while limiting the resources committed to this market.
Harvest	Adjust prices and marketing expenses to gradually exit the market while attempting to maximize profits during this gradual exit.
Entry	Invest to enter an attractive market to establish a desired competitive advantage. This strategy could also require investment to accelerate the growth of a new or underdeveloped market.
Divest	Quick divestment from a market. When there are no short-term profits to be gained with a harvest strategy, an immediate exit strategy is appropriate.

On the basis of a portfolio analysis and performance objectives, a business selects either an offensive or a defensive strategic market plan. First, with respect to performance objectives, offensive strategic market plans are geared to deliver above-average performance in the areas of sales growth, share position, and long-run profit performance. Defensive strategic market plans are important in producing short-run profit performance and protecting important share positions, while also contributing to long-run profit. Strategic market planning requires a careful balance of offensive and defensive strategic market plans in order to meet short-run profit objectives and investor expectations while investing in the business to protect important strategic positions, as well as developing stronger share positions in existing or new markets.

Offensive Strategic Market Plans and Performance Impact

Because offensive strategic market plans are more growth-oriented than are defensive plans, they are more likely to occur in attractive markets.[9] For example, consider

Compaq Computer in the late 1990s. In 1997, Compaq was the share leader, with a 12.5 percent share in an 80 million unit personal computer market that was growing at a rate of 15 percent per year. Compaq's average selling price was $2,500, but market prices were eroding at a rate of 6 percent per year. Compaq's margins were holding at 25 percent of sales, and marketing expenses were 8 percent of sales. The combination of these factors produced the following level of performance:

$$\frac{\text{Sales}}{\text{Revenue}} = \frac{\text{Market}}{\text{Demand}} \times \frac{\text{Market}}{\text{Share}} \times \frac{\text{Price}}{\text{per Unit}}$$
$$\text{\$25 billion} = 80 \text{ million} \times 0.125 \times \text{\$2,500}$$

$$\frac{\text{Marketing}}{\text{Expenses}} = \frac{\text{Sales}}{\text{Revenue}} \times \frac{\text{Percent Marketing}}{\text{Expenses}}$$
$$\text{\$2 billion} = \text{\$25 million} \times 0.08$$

$$\frac{\text{Net Marketing}}{\text{Contribution}} = \left(\frac{\text{Market}}{\text{Demand}} \times \frac{\text{Market}}{\text{Share}} \times \frac{\text{Price}}{\text{per Unit}} \times \frac{\text{Percent}}{\text{Margin}} \right) - \frac{\text{Marketing}}{\text{Expenses}}$$
$$\text{\$4.25 billion} = 80 \text{ million} \times 0.125 \times \text{\$2,500} \times 0.25 - \text{\$2 billion}$$

An offensive strategy to grow market share to 14 percent in a growing market presents a bigger strategic challenge. This strategic market plan would require more resources. Assuming resources are available and the same assumptions hold, we can estimate the following year's performance impact of this strategy as shown below:

$$\frac{\text{Sales}}{\text{Revenue}} = \frac{\text{Market}}{\text{Demand}} \times \frac{\text{Market}}{\text{Share}} \times \frac{\text{Price}}{\text{per Unit}}$$
$$\text{\$30.3 billion} = 92 \text{ million} \times 0.14 \times \text{\$2,350}$$

$$\frac{\text{Marketing}}{\text{Expenses}} = \frac{\text{Sales}}{\text{Revenue}} \times \frac{\text{Percent Marketing}}{\text{Expenses}}$$
$$\text{\$2.4 billion} = \text{\$30.3 billion} \times 0.08$$

$$\frac{\text{Net Marketing}}{\text{Contribution}} = \left(\frac{\text{Market}}{\text{Demand}} \times \frac{\text{Market}}{\text{Share}} \times \frac{\text{Price}}{\text{per Unit}} \times \frac{\text{Percent}}{\text{Margin}} \right) - \frac{\text{Marketing}}{\text{Expenses}}$$
$$\text{\$5.2 billion} = (92 \text{ million} \times 0.14 \times \text{\$2,350} \times 0.25) - \text{\$2.4 billion}$$

If an offensive strategic market plan to grow share to 14 percent were successfully implemented, sales revenues in 1998 would have grown by $5 billion to $30.3 billion. More important, net marketing contribution would have increased by $950 million. Overall, this strategy would have contributed to an increased share position, sales growth, and growth in profits.

Defensive Strategic Market Plans and Performance Impact

Defensive strategic market plans are designed to protect important strategic market positions and to be large contributors to short-run cash flow and profit performance. As shown in Figure 11-8, defensive strategic market plans are most likely to occur in attractive markets with strong competitive advantage or in unattractive markets with weak levels of competitive advantage.

FIGURE 11-9 Offensive and Defensive Strategic Market Plans

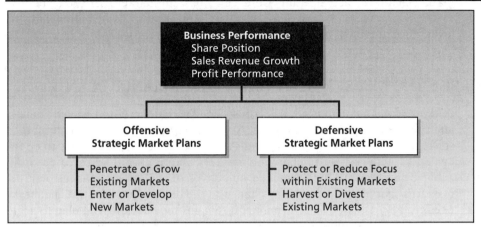

Defensive strategic market plans involve protecting or reducing the market scope within existing markets,[10] as shown in Figure 11-9. Defensive strategic market plans can also involve harvesting or divesting market share positions in existing markets.[11] As such, defensive strategic market plans are less likely to generate significant sales revenue growth except for a defensive strategy to protect (hold) share in a growing market. However, defensive strategic market plans are critical sources of short-run cash flow and profit performance and, in many ways, define the business's current level of share, sales, and profit performance.

A great number of other factors may come into play in selecting one strategic market plan over the other, but let's look at an estimate of Compaq Computer's 1998 performance while using a defensive strategic market plan to protect market share in a growing market. Using the same assumptions already made for market growth, price erosion, margin, and marketing expenses, a defensive Compaq Computer strategic market plan to protect market share would produce the following estimate of 1998's performance:

$$\frac{\text{Sales}}{\text{Revenue}} = \frac{\text{Market}}{\text{Demand}} \times \frac{\text{Market}}{\text{Share}} \times \frac{\text{Price}}{\text{per Unit}}$$

$$\$27 \text{ billion} = 92 \text{ million} \times 0.125 \times \$2,350$$

$$\frac{\text{Marketing}}{\text{Expenses}} = \frac{\text{Sales}}{\text{Revenue}} \times \frac{\text{Percent Marketing}}{\text{Expenses}}$$

$$\$2.2 \text{ billion} = \$27 \text{ billion} \times 0.08$$

$$\frac{\text{Net Marketing}}{\text{Contribution}} = \left(\frac{\text{Market}}{\text{Demand}} \times \frac{\text{Market}}{\text{Share}} \times \frac{\text{Price}}{\text{per Unit}} \times \frac{\text{Percent}}{\text{Margin}} \right) - \frac{\text{Marketing}}{\text{Expenses}}$$

$$\$4.6 \text{ billion} = (92 \text{ million} \times 0.125 \times \$2,350 \times 0.25) - \$2.2 \text{ billion}$$

As the preceding shows, a defensive strategic market plan to protect market share would yield an estimated $2 billion increase in sales revenue and a $350 million increase in net marketing contribution. Although many factors could keep these goals from being met, this strategy, if successfully implemented, would also succeed in protecting a share position, growing sales revenue, and increasing net marketing contribution.

During 1998, Compaq elected to pursue an offensive strategic market plan to grow market share. The actual results were a 14.5 percent market share, $31 billion in sales revenues, and an increase of $1.16 billion in net marketing contribution. However, this level of share growth in a growing market did not occur without a carefully designed and successfully implemented tactical marketing strategy.

MARKETING MIX STRATEGY AND PERFORMANCE PLAN

A *strategic market plan* is a long-term strategy with a three- to five-year time horizon and specific performance objectives. A *market mix strategy* is a short-term marketing strategy with a one-year time horizon. A marketing mix strategy needs to be reviewed each year with respect to changing market conditions and adjusted accordingly to achieve the long-run performance objectives of a strategic market plan. In some instances, market conditions may change to the degree that the strategic market plan needs to be reassessed to determine if it remains the best long-run plan to achieve the business's performance objectives in a particular product–market.

Marketing Mix Strategy

Given a specific strategic market plan, a detailed tactical marketing strategy needs to be developed. This means the development of a marketing mix strategy with respect to product positioning, price, promotion, and place. The degree to which the performance objectives of a strategic market plan are achieved is dependent on the effectiveness of the tactical marketing strategy designed to support this strategic market plan.

For example, Intel's strategic market plan to enter the low-end personal computer market required a different tactical marketing strategy from Intel's strategic market plan to defend its high share position in more expensive microprocessors. Each required different types of products and pricing to achieve a position that would be attractive to target customers relative to competitors' product-price positions.

The strategic market plan sets the strategic direction and provides broad guidelines for resource allocation. However, the tactical marketing strategy is the workhorse that has to succeed for the strategic market plan to achieve both short- and long-run performance objectives. The right strategic market plan with the wrong tactical marketing strategy will not normally produce desired levels of performance.

Performance Plan

The performance objectives and conditions under which a business would use either an offensive or a defensive strategic market plan are very different. As outlined in Figure 11-10, offensive strategic marketing plans are geared to deliver above-average performance in the areas of sales growth, improved share position, and long-run profit performance. Defensive strategic market plans are important in producing short-run profit performance and protecting important share positions while also contributing to long-run profit performance and strategic position.

Offensive strategic market plans require investment for growth, which limits short-run profit performance while building sales revenue and improving share position. In the long run, a growth-oriented marketing strategy will shift from an offensive strategic market plan to a defensive strategic market plan. As shown, defensive strategic market

FIGURE 11-10 Performance Objectives and Strategic Market Plan

Performance Objective	Impact on Business Performance			
	Some	*Moderate*	*Considerable*	*Substantial*
Offensive Strategic Market Plans				
Short-run Profit Performance	X	X		
Short-run Share Position	X	X		
Long-run Profit Performance			X	X
Long-run Share Position			X	X
Long-run Sales Revenue Growth			X	X
Defensive Strategic Market Plans				
Short-run Profit Performance			X	X
Short-run Share Position			X	X
Long-run Profit Performance		X	X	
Long-run Share Position	X	X		
Long-run Sales Revenue Growth	X	X		

plans are key sources of short-run profit performance but are not major contributors to sales revenue growth or long-run share and profit performance.

For example, consider Zi-Tech Acoustics, a $250 million engineering acoustics business. It manufactures and markets a variety of acoustic products to four distinct markets. Figure 11-11 illustrates the market share, sales revenues, and net marketing contribution for the company and in each of the four product–markets it serves. A portfolio analysis based on market attractiveness and competitive advantage produced the product–market portfolio illustrated in Figure 11-12. Also shown in Figure 11-12 is a new market opportunity (M5) uncovered in the strategic market planning process. This analysis, along with the current performance with regard to share position, sales

FIGURE 11-11   Zi-Tech Acoustics' Current Performance: Share, Sales, and Net Marketing Contribution

Market-Based Performance	Market 1	Market 2	Market 3	Market 4	Overall Company
Market Growth	3%	0%	17%	−5%	7%
Market Demand (000 customers)	800	1000	1200	1500	4500
Market Share	23%	13%	7%	12%	13%
Customer Volume	184	130	84	180	578
Revenue per Customer	$ 420	$ 450	$ 660	$ 325	$ 432
Sales Revenue (millions)	$ 77.3	$ 58.5	$55.4	$58.5	$ 250
Variable Cost per Customer	$ 250	$ 300	$ 440	$ 300	$ 305
Margin per Customer	$ 170	$ 150	$ 220	$ 25	$ 127
Total Contribution (millions)	$ 31	$ 19.5	$18.5	$ 4.5	$73.5
Marketing and Sales (millions)	$ 9	$ 7	$ 6.5	$ 7.5	$ 30
Net Marketing Contribution	$ 22	$ 12.5	$12.0	−$ 3	$43.5

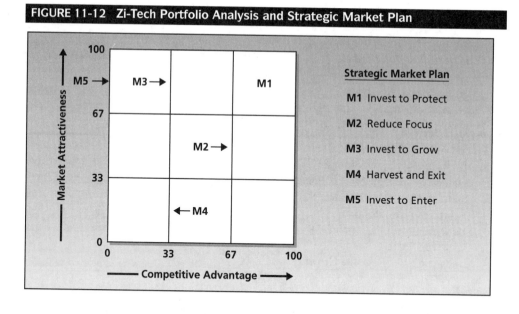

FIGURE 11-12   Zi-Tech Portfolio Analysis and Strategic Market Plan

revenue, and net marketing contribution, led to the strategic market plans outlined in Figure 11-12 and described in the following:

- **Market 1** is a mature market in which Zi-Tech will strive to *protect share* to protect a net marketing contribution that produces over 50 percent of the overall net marketing contribution.
- **Market 2** is mature, and management feels that a strategy to *reduce Zi-Tech's market focus* on more profitable segments would yield greater profits.
- **Market 3** is attractive and growing. These conditions led to a strategic market plan to invest to *grow market share*.
- **Market 4** is unattractive and declining; its competitive advantage is average. A *harvest strategy* would be designed to make a positive net marketing contribution in the short run but to be completely out of the market in five years.
- **Market 5** is a new market opportunity uncovered by the strategic market planning process. Zi-Tech would like to *enter this market*. It will involve losses for the first couple of years, but by year five, Zi-Tech hopes to produce a positive net marketing contribution in market 5.

For each market plan, a set of performance objectives was created, as outlined in Figure 11-13. As shown, in the current year, Zi-Tech produced sales of $250 million in four product–markets. Three of the four product–markets were profitable, and the overall net marketing contribution was $43.5 million. On the basis of the strategic market plans and performance objectives created for each product–market, Zi-Tech hopes to grow overall sales by $100 million to $350 million in four to five years. More important, the Zi-Tech performance plan projects net marketing contribution to grow from $43.5 to $65 million in four to five years.

If this strategic market plan is successful, Zi-Tech will have improved its strategic position in served markets while growing sales and profits over a five-year period. In

FIGURE 11-13   Strategic Market Plan and Performance Objectives

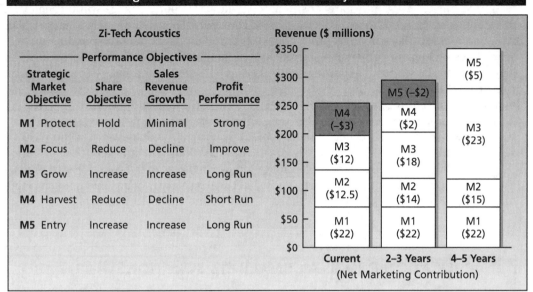

Zi-Tech Acoustics

——————— Performance Objectives ———————

Strategic Market Objective	Share Objective	Sales Revenue Growth	Profit Performance
M1 Protect	Hold	Minimal	Strong
M2 Focus	Reduce	Decline	Improve
M3 Grow	Increase	Increase	Long Run
M4 Harvest	Reduce	Decline	Short Run
M5 Entry	Increase	Increase	Long Run

Revenue ($ millions)

	Current	2–3 Years	4–5 Years
			M5 ($5)
		M5 (–$2)	
	M4 (–$3)	M4 ($2)	M3 ($23)
	M3 ($12)	M3 ($18)	
	M2 ($12.5)	M2 ($14)	M2 ($15)
	M1 ($22)	M1 ($22)	M1 ($22)

(Net Marketing Contribution)

Chapter 16 we will look more closely at how this plan translates into shareholder value. However, a 40 percent increase in sales revenues and a 49 percent increase in net marketing contribution should contribute positively to the net profit and shareholder value.

Summary

Strategic market planning is a process. It is a process that involves assessing the current situation with respect to market attractiveness and competitive advantage along with business performance with respect to share position, sales revenues, and profitability. This type of assessment is made for each product–market served by the business and for new market opportunities the business may want to consider.

From this assessment, a portfolio analysis is created based on two dimensions of performance: market attractiveness and competitive advantage. Each dimension is created with an index based on several underlying forces that shape it. Market attractiveness is indexed with respect to market forces (market size, growth, buyer power, etc.), competitive intensity (number of competitors, substitutes, price rivalry,

etc.), and market access (customer familiarity, channel access, sales force requirements, etc.). Competitive advantage is indexed with respect to cost advantage (unit cost, transaction costs, marketing expenses, etc.), differentiation advantage (product quality, service quality, brand image, etc.), and marketing advantage (market share, brand awareness, channel control, etc.). A strategic market plan is specified for each product–market the business serves or would like to consider entering in the future, based on the product–market's position in the portfolio.

The strategic market plan is a long-run, three- to five-year, strategic market objective that involves share position but has corresponding implications for short- and long-run sales revenue growth and profit performance. Strategic market plans can be "offensive" or "defensive." Offensive strategic market plans involve market penetration strategies to grow share position, sales, and long-run profitability. Defensive strategic market plans involve protecting share, sales, and profits or harvesting strategies to exit markets while maximizing short-run profits. The combination of strategic market plans (one for each product–market) results in an overall view of how the business will grow with respect to share, sales, and profits.

Although the strategic market plan for a given product–market sets short- and long-run goals with respect to market share, sales revenues, and profits, it does not specify how this performance will be achieved. Therefore, for each strategic market plan there needs to be a corresponding tactical marketing plan. The tactical marketing plan is a marketing mix strategy (product, price, place, and promotion) and resource allocation (marketing budget) that specifies the tactical details of how a given strategic market plan will be achieved. On the basis of these marketing tactics and the marketing budget, a three- to five-year forecast of market share, sales revenues, and net marketing contribution, a performance plan is created.

APPLICATION PROBLEM: SMALL BIZ SOLUTIONS

Small Biz Solutions (SBS) is focused on the small business telecommunications market. This is a very large market with many new small businesses entering and exiting each year. Most new businesses fail but many survive. But, in all cases, today's small businesses need phone, fax, and Internet telecom capabilities.

The small business communications market is divided into three distinct segments:

- **Growers (1)**—Existing businesses that are looking for ways to grow and/or become more productive. These small businesses will spend money on technology if it is profitable and serves their need for growth.

- **Maintainers (2)**—Survivors that are generally not managing the business for growth. These small businesses are cost-conscious and want basic services at a low price.

- **New Comers (S3)**—These are the brand new businesses full of aspirations and energy but generally short on cash. Most of these small businesses will fail but in the process buy a telecom capability. Some will also survive and succeed. These businesses will then migrate to either of the two other segments described.

Shown in Figure 1 is a portfolio analysis of the three segments based on market attractiveness and competitive position criteria described in the chapter. As shown, the "growers" segment is both attractive and one in which SBS has a strong competitive position. The "maintainers" segment is average in market attractiveness and slightly below average in competitive position while the "new comers" segment is weaker in market attractiveness but stronger in competitive position.

Shown in Figure 2 is the potential and profit performance of each segment. Clearly, the "grower" segment is where SBS generates its profits. "Maintainers" are the largest segment but have a lower profit margin and overall profit. "New Comers" represent the future but they are expensive to serve, buy less, produce a low percent margin and lose money in the end.

For access to interactive software to answer the questions below go to www.RogerJBest.com or www.prenhall.com/best.

Questions:

1. What would be the profit impact of an "offensive" strategy to increase market share from 5 to 8 percent in the "growers" segment by increasing the marketing expense per customer from 1,333 to $2,000?

2. What would be the profit impact of an "offensive" strategy to increase market share from 7 to 10 percent in the "maintainers" segment by decreasing prices such that revenue per customer in this segment decreased from $12,000 to $11,000?

3. What would be the profit impact of a "defensive" strategy to increase prices in the "newcomers" segment to achieve a revenue per customer of $12,000 while expecting market share to decline from 13 percent to 5 percent?

FIGURE 1   SBS Portfolio Analysis

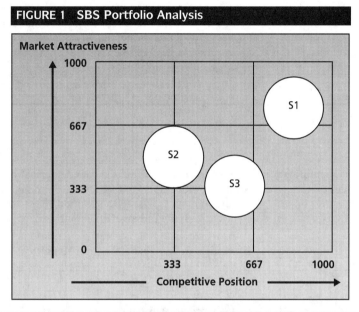

FIGURE 2   Segment Performance

Area of Performance (annual)	Growers	Maintainers	New Comers	Total
Market Demand (customers 000)	300	500	200	1000
Market Share	5%	7%	13%	8%
Customer Volume (000)	15	35	26	76
Revenue per Customer	$20,000	$12,000	$10,000	$12,895
Sales Revenues (millions)	$300.00	$420.00	$260.00	$ 980
Percent Margin	60%	30%	20%	37%
Gross Profit (millions)	$ 180	$ 126	$ 52	$ 358
Marketing Expenses (millions)	$ 20	$ 28	$ 39	$ 87
Marketing Expenses per Customer	$ 1,333	$ 800	$ 1,500	$1,145
Net Marketing Contribution (millions)	$ 160	$ 98	$ 13	$ 271
Operating Expense (millions)	$ 60	$ 84	$ 52	$ 196
Operating Income (millions)	$ 100	$ 14	($ 39)	$ 75

Market-Based Logic and Strategic Thinking

1. How does the level of product–market diversification affect sales growth and performance consistency?
2. Why would the overall variation in sales revenues over a 10-year period be different when comparing General Electric and Compaq Computer?
3. What is meant by the "strategic market planning process"?
4. How is a strategic market plan different from a strategic market planning process?
5. How would you assess the attractiveness of a new consumer product–market for Procter & Gamble? Be specific as to what factors you would include in building an index of market attractiveness for a Procter & Gamble consumer market.
6. How would you assess the competitive advantage Procter & Gamble would have in a new consumer product–market? Be specific as to what factors you would include in building an index of competitive advantage for a Procter & Gamble consumer market.
7. Using the following information, create a portfolio analysis and specify a strategic market plan for a business that serves three product–markets.

Product–Market	Share	Sales (millions)	Market Attractiveness	Competitive Advantage
A	10%	$20	20	40
B	33%	$50	75	80
C	5%	$10	85	15

8. Using the information presented in question 7 and the added information that follows, create a three-year performance plan with respect to market share and sales revenues for each product–market, given the strategic market plan specified below. Also create a projection of overall sales for each year of the three-year planning horizon.

Product–Market	Strategic Market Plan	Share Objective	Market Demand (mil)	Market Growth
A	Reduced Focus	5%	$200	5%
B	Protect Share	33%	$150	7%
C	Grow Share	10%	$200	20%

9. Under what conditions would a business specify an offensive strategic market plan?
10. Under what conditions would a business specify a defensive strategic market plan?
11. What role do offensive and defensive strategic market plans play in the short- and long-run performance of a business?
12. How would the sales and profit performance over a three-year period differ between a business with only defensive strategic market plans and a business that has only offensive strategic market plans? Why is it important to have a balance of offensive and defensive plans?
13. Why is a tactical marketing plan for each strategic market plan an important part of the strategic market planning process?
14. How does a manager develop a tactical marketing plan and marketing budget to achieve a specific strategic market plan?
15. How would the tactical marketing plan and marketing budget for a strategic market plan to grow market share (offensive) differ from those of a reduced focus strategic market plan to reduce share?
16. How does a business create a forecast of its future performance based on the strategic market plans for each product–market it intends to serve over a given planning horizon?

Notes

1. Michael Treacy and Fred Wiersama, *The Discipline of Market Leaders* (Reading, MA: Addison-Wesley, 1995).

2. Some analysts believe the guidelines of the market plan may lead to a strategic advantage. See David A. Garvin, "Leveraging Processes for Strategic Advantage," *Harvard Business Review* (September–October 1995):77.

3. Roger A. Kerin, Vijay Mahajan, and P. Rajan Varadarajan, *Strategic Market Planning* (Boston: Allyn and Bacon, 1990).

4. Frances V. McCrory and Peter G. Gerstberger, "The New Math of Performance Measurements," *Journal of Business Strategy* (March–April 1992):33–38.

5. Kasturi Rangan, Melvyn Menezes, and E. P. Maier, "Channel Selection for New Industrial Products: A Framework, Method and Application," *Journal of Marketing* (July 1992):69–82.

6. L. W. Phillips, D. R. Chang, and R. D. Bussell, "Product Quality, Cost Position, and Business Performance: A Test of Some Key Hypotheses," *Journal of Marketing* 47 (January 1983):26–43.

7. Michael E. Porter, *Competitive Advantage* (New York: Free Press, 1986).

8. David Aaker, "Formal Planning System," in *Strategic Market Management* (New York: Wiley, 1995):341–53.

9. Thomas Powell, "Strategic Planning As Competitive Advantage," *Strategic Management Journal* 13 (1992):551–58; Scott Armstrong, "The Value of Formal Planning for Strategic Decisions: Reply," *Strategic Management Journal* 7 (1986):183–85; and Deepak Sinha, "The Contribution of Formal Planning to Decisions," Strategic Management Journal (October 1990):479–92.

10. William K. Hall, "Survival Strategies in a Hostile Environment," *Harvard Business Review* (September–October 1980):75–85.

11. Kathryn Rudie Harrigan, *Strategies for Declining Businesses* (Lexington, MA: Lexington Books, 1980); and Kathryn Rudie Harrigan and Michael E. Porter, "End-Game Strategies for Declining Industries," *Harvard Business Review* (July–August 1983): 111–20. Also see Katheryn Rudie Harrigan, *Managing Maturing Businesses* (New York: Lexington Books, 1988).

12 OFFENSIVE STRATEGIC MARKET PLANS

Coca-Cola has been described as the "perfect growth company" despite holding a commanding 50 percent market share of the worldwide carbonated soft drink market. From their point of view Coca-Cola represents only a 2 percent *share of stomach* on a worldwide basis. This point is further driven home in Coca-Cola's annual report, which features forty-seven empty Coke bottles and one full one. This way of thinking has enabled Coca-Cola to grow its volume at the rate of 7 to 8 percent, while PepsiCo, its chief rival, is growing unit volume at the rate of 1 percent per year.

Clearly, Coca-Cola is challenging its marketing managers to think *offensively* and find ways to grow Coca-Cola's share of the beverage market. Many businesses, such as Coca-Cola, Microsoft, America Online, Dell Computer, and Intel, experienced considerable growth in the 1990s. To grow, these businesses have had to utilize a variety of strategic market plans that range from market share penetration to development of completely new products and markets. In every case, their strategic market plans have addressed three basic performance objectives:

- **Share Position:** How will the strategic market plan contribute to the business's share position in served markets?
- **Sales Growth:** To what degree will the strategic market plan contribute to sales growth?
- **Profit Performance:** How will the strategic market plan impact short-run and long-run profit performance?

Because resources are limited, a business needs a strategic market plan to carefully map out its future growth and profit performance.[1] Every strategic market plan a business develops will in some way affect both short-run and long-run business performance in each of the three areas of performance identified. And, depending on the situation, some will be *offensive* and some will be *defensive* strategic market plans.

Offensive strategic market plans are more often growth-oriented and, therefore, more likely to occur in the growth stage of a product–market life cycle,[2] as shown in Figure 12-1. Offensive strategic market plans are designed to produce sales growth and improve share position and future profit performance. Defensive strategic market plans are more likely to occur in the latter stages of a product–market life cycle and are often designed to protect important share positions and be large contributors to short-run sales revenues and profits. This chapter examines various offensive strategic market plans, and Chapter 13 will present various defensive strategic market plans.

FIGURE 12-1   Product Life Cycle and Offensive and Defensive Marketing Strategies

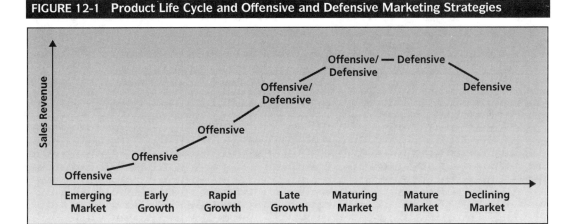

OFFENSIVE STRATEGIC MARKET PLANS

The combination of market attractiveness and competitive advantage creates a portfolio position for any given product–market.[3] As shown in Figure 12-2, attractive markets are most likely to warrant an offensive strategic market plan to improve competitive advantage and share position when the business's competitive advantage is average or below. These offensive strategic market plans can range from entering a new market with no established share position to growing the competitive advantage and market share in existing product–markets. In addition, there may be the opportunity to use an offensive strategic market plan to help grow (make more attractive) an emerging or underdeveloped market in which the business has established a strong position of advantage.

Of the five cells in which an offensive strategic market plan could be used, three (with average market attractiveness) could also use a defensive strategic market plan. In these portfolio positions, more information would be needed before one could select between an offensive or defensive strategic market plan. For example, an offensive strategic market plan may be warranted, given the business's sources of relative advantage. On the other hand, a defensive strategic market plan to protect the current position may be the best alternative in achieving desired performance objectives. Or perhaps the business should narrow its market focus and attempt to minimize investment and capture more profits.

Fundamentally, offensive strategic market plans are geared for growth and inherently involve strategies to penetrate or grow existing markets or to enter or develop new markets, as summarized in Figure 12-3. There is a wide range of potential offensive strategic market plans.[4]

However, a logical place to start is with offensive strategies within *existing markets*. Because the business has already established a working knowledge of customers and competitors and has resources in place to serve existing markets, it should seek to leverage its existing market position with an offensive strategic market plan to further penetrate and develop the product–markets it already serves.

FIGURE 12-2   Selecting Offensive and Defensive Marketing Strategies

MARKET PENETRATION STRATEGIES

As shown in Figure 12-3, there are four fundamental offensive strategic market plans that can be used to grow a business's penetration of an existing market. These strategic market plans range from share penetration to growing market demand in markets served by the business.

Strategies to Grow Market Share

There are many factors that affect a business's ability to grow market share and profitability.[5] One consideration is share potential. To what degree has the business achieved its share potential? And what factors need to be managed to grow share in a given product–market? Each is an important consideration in developing an offensive strategic market plan to grow market share.

FIGURE 12-3   Offensive Strategic Market Plans

Market Share Penetration

In Chapter 3, we introduced the idea of a Share Development Index (SDI). This is the ratio of actual market share to share potential. The share potential of a business is based on what that business believes it should be able to achieve with a successful tactical marketing strategy, given the strength of its competitive advantage and marketing effectiveness in a given product–market. For example, in the following case, a business estimates that it should perform at a 90 percent level in product awareness, 50 percent in product preference, 80 percent in intentions to purchase, 80 percent in product availability, and 70 percent in rate of purchase. Performing at these levels would produce a potential market share index of approximately 20 percent.

$$\begin{aligned} \text{Market Share Potential} &= \frac{\text{Product}}{\text{Awareness}} \times \frac{\text{Product}}{\text{Preference}} \times \frac{\text{Purchase}}{\text{Intentions}} \times \frac{\text{Product}}{\text{Availability}} \times \frac{\text{Purchase}}{\text{Rate}} \\ &= 0.90 \times 0.50 \times 0.80 \times 0.80 \times 0.70 \\ &= 20.2\% \end{aligned}$$

If a business's actual market share were 8 percent, the business would be underperforming and, hence, would have a Share Development Index of 40.

$$\text{Share Development Index} = \frac{\text{Current Market Share}}{\text{Market Share Potential}} = \frac{8\%}{20\%} \times 100 = 40$$

This means that the business has achieved only 40 percent of its potential market share. Therefore, there is an opportunity to grow market share with a market penetration strategy.

To grow share, a business has to examine each of the areas of performance with respect to its expected versus its actual market performance. For instance, the business in the example expects to achieve a 90 percent target market product awareness. If its actual target market awareness were only 67 percent, this performance gap would prevent this business from reaching its full market share potential. Thus, to grow share when it is at less than its full potential, this business would need to examine key performance gaps in its market share response.

There is also the possibility that a business has reached its share potential but feels it can still expand its market share position with a new strategic market plan. For example, product improvements that are able to shift product preference from 50 percent to 70 percent would raise the market share potential (index) from 20.2 percent to 28.2 percent in the example presented. Of course, to achieve this level of share penetration, the business would have to adequately communicate and deliver these product improvements to the full satisfaction of target customers.

Market Share Change

Market shares change as a result of market forces, a business's competitive position, and marketing effort, as illustrated in Figure 12-4. Although there is a wide range of market share change forces occurring in any given market, the net result is some rate of market share change based on the collective influences of these forces that shape market share change.

FIGURE 12-4   Fundamental Forces That Affect Market Share Change

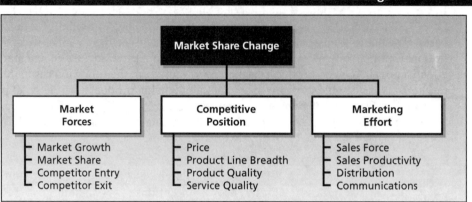

Market forces that shape market share change are generally beyond the control of a business. Market growth, size of shares, and competitor entry all create market forces that tend to lower market share, whereas competitor exit contributes to market share gains.[6] As a result, a silent strategic market plan with respect to either improved competitive position or marketing effort is likely to result in share loss. To grow share, a business needs to more than offset share erosion forces with changes in competitive position or marketing effort, or both.

One way to offset market forces that tend to erode share is for a business to improve its competitive position. Each of the factors that affects a business's competitive position also indirectly affects market share. However, in order to *gain* share with the use of any of these positioning variables, a business needs to increase its *relative* advantage: its position relative to key competitors.

For example, if a business were to improve its product quality, we would assume that this change would contribute to a market share gain. However, if the business's competitors were improving their product quality at a faster rate, then the business's *relative* product quality would actually go down and its market share would be expected to go down as well. Thus, to gain market share, a business has to improve its *relative* competitive advantage on one or more of the positioning variables shown in Figure 12-4 and discussed in Chapters 7 and 8.

Marketing effort also affects market share change, as discussed in Chapters 9 and 10. In a growing market with more customers and competitors entering the market, a business needs to expand its marketing effort in order to protect or gain share. For example, a business with $150 million in sales and fifty salespeople would have a sales productivity of $3 million per salesperson. If total market demand were $600 million, the business would have a 25 percent market share. Let's assume that as more customers enter the market, demand grows to $750 million in three years. To *protect* share, the business would need to increase its sales force to at least sixty-two salespeople or increase the sales productivity of its present fifty salespeople. To *grow* share with a sales force effort, the business would need more than sixty-two salespeople at the current sales productivity of $3 million per salesperson.

Strategies to Grow Customer Purchase

As a business approaches 100 percent of its Share Development Index, additional growth, based on market share gains, becomes increasingly difficult. Up to this point, share gains have been based on correcting ineffective tactical marketing strategies, improving competitive position, or adding to a business's marketing effort. However, there is also the opportunity to grow revenues with existing customers by growing revenue *per* customer. For example, McDonald's once sold a limited product line of hamburgers, french fries, and drinks. With product line extensions in hamburgers, chicken, and fish sandwiches, and a line of breakfast products, McDonald's has been able to grow the average dollars spent at McDonald's by customers who already were McDonald's customers. Of course, these line extensions also attracted new customers to the fast-food industry and drew new customers from competing fast-food businesses.

Businesses with well-known names, such as Kodak, Nike, Honda, IBM, and Disney, are able to introduce line extensions that leverage the awareness and image already created by their company reputation.[7] When Honda entered the lawn mower market in the early 1990s, the Honda lawn mower was immediately perceived by many customers as reliable and of high quality. These perceptions were created by Honda's success in automobiles, motorcycles, and other motorized products. The high level of name awareness also greatly assisted the company's quick penetration of this market. Many lawn mower customers were already owners of other Honda products. This level of awareness led Honda to build a growth strategy around the volume of Honda products purchased by existing Honda customers. This strategy is aptly expressed in Honda's marketing objective: "Our goal is to have five Hondas in every garage."

Obviously, few, if any, Honda customers would purchase five Honda automobiles. But the Honda offensive strategic market plan is to capture the Honda car owner's purchase of lawn mowers, recreational vehicles (motorcycles, snowmobiles, jet skis, all-terrain vehicles, outboard motors), and portable motors and generators. In this way, Honda is growing its business by building the total ownership of Honda products among existing customers. A business's existing customer pool is a customer franchise that offers considerable opportunity for within-market sales growth.

Revenue per customer can also be built with a strategy to build price premiums. Businesses that enhance their products by adding value-added services or building a superior reputation for quality can charge higher prices than competing businesses and still maintain a superior customer value. General Electric's turbines command a price premium relative to competing turbines around the world. This premium is based on superior product quality, engineering and installation services, and a reputation for innovation and technology in the area of turbine design and development. In this way, GE is able to attain a higher revenue per customer than many competing turbine manufacturers.

Strategies to Enter New Customer Segments

Another offensive growth strategy within existing markets is to develop a strategic market plan to enter a new customer segment within an existing market.[8] For example, as the personal computer market has grown, the under $1,000 personal computer segment has emerged. Intel, which did not have a product suitable for this segment, saw competitors such as Advanced Micro Devices take the lead in the under $1,000 segment. With demand in this segment growing faster than in any other segment, Intel

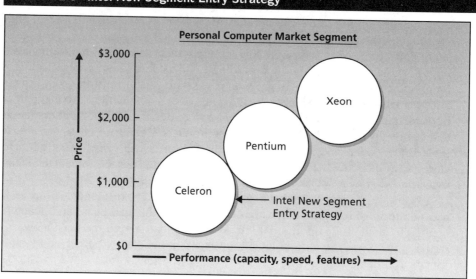

FIGURE 12-5   Intel New Segment Entry Strategy

responded with a new product designed for the price-performance needs of the segment. As shown in Figure 12-5, the Celeron chip provided PC manufacturers a low-cost Intel microprocessor for this segment. This offensive strategic market plan provided a new source of sales revenues and profitability for Intel.

Strategies to Grow Market Demand

At any given point in time, the number of customers in a market is finite. New customer growth strategies can focus on growing market demand by bringing new customers into a market. In Chapter 3, we introduced the concept of a Market Development Index. This index is simply a ratio of current market demand to market potential, the maximum number of customers possible for a particular geographic market scope. For example, the Market Development Index for the wireless phone market in the United States is approximately 33. This means that there are many potential customers who have not entered the market for various reasons. And, since market share battles often lead to price erosion, a strategy to grow market demand may offer an offensive strategic market plan to grow share, sales, and profits.

$$\begin{aligned} \text{Market} \\ \text{Development} \\ \text{Index} \end{aligned} = \frac{\text{Current Market Demand for Wireless Phones}}{\text{Market Potential for Wireless Phones}} \times 100$$

$$= \frac{60 \text{ million customers}}{180 \text{ million customers}} \times 100$$

$$= 33.3$$

But how does a business actually attract new customers and grow market demand? As shown in Figure 12-6, there are basically five market forces that limit market demand from reaching its full potential. Each of these forces must be addressed in

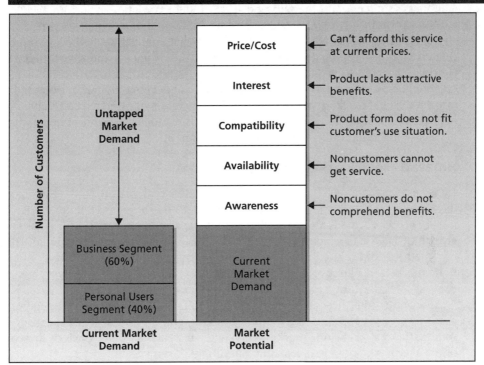

FIGURE 12-6   Factors That Need to Be Addressed in Growing the Market Demand for Wireless Phones

strategic market plans to grow either the entire market or a specific segment within the market. Marketing communications efforts can be used to address awareness and comprehension of benefits for the wireless phone market.

Improving availability is a matter of adding more cell sites in geographic areas where potential demand justifies the investment. On the other hand, compatibility is more likely to be a product issue. To improve use compatibility, wireless providers have to better understand how customers use wireless phones and design products to better serve those use situations. For example, a contractor on a construction site may need a more durable phone, whereas a salesperson may need more features to enhance sales productivity. Finally, because the cost of service, and not the initial cost of a phone, prevents many potential customers from entering the market, some wireless phone service providers have developed special usage rate pricing programs that make the price of service adjustable, based on level of usage. The net effect of these efforts is a new market demand of over 25,000 new customers per week.

NEW MARKET ENTRY STRATEGIES

At some point, every business needs to examine growth opportunities outside the existing markets it serves.[9] This need can occur for three fundamental reasons: (1) the number of attractive market opportunities within existing markets may be limited; (2) new market opportunities outside existing markets are simply more attractive in terms of meeting the business's overall performance objectives; and (3) a move to new markets helps diversify a business's sources of profitability and, hence, reduces variation in performance.[10]

As shown in Figure 12-3, there are four fundamental *new market entry* offensive strategic market plans. New market entry strategies can include entry into established related markets (similar to markets served by the business) and diversified markets (unrelated to markets served by the business), or entry into less established new emerging markets or markets with considerable undeveloped market potential. Entry into established markets (related or diversified) offers existing market demand along with existing competitors. Entry into less established markets requires development of market demand but often in the absence of competition.

Related New Market Entry Strategies

K2 is best known as a ski manufacturer. Over a ten-year period, K2 steadily increased its share of the American ski market until it became the market share leader by the mid-1990s. The American ski market is mature, and opportunities for sales revenue growth through either market growth or increased market share are limited. This situation led K2 to a related new market entry strategy, into the snowboard and in-line skate markets. K2 hopes to achieve significant sales revenue growth over the next ten years as a result of the new market entry strategy.

K2's entry into these two related customer markets enables it to leverage its brand name awareness, reputation for quality, manufacturing and design expertise, and, in some instances, its existing marketing channel and sales systems. Each of these factors offers a variety of potential cost and marketing efficiencies.

There are instances in which entry into a new market can be blocked. Market entry can be very difficult because of the cost of entry, technology requirements, or a lack of market access. In the telecommunications industry, these difficulties have led to many mergers, joint ventures, and strategic alliances among telecommunications, computer, and cable TV companies. In each case, partner companies provide related market expertise and leverage. By blending the strengths of businesses from two related markets, these new entities become potentially more complete businesses from which to build and market products that more completely serve and fulfill customer needs.

Diversified New Market Entry Growth Strategies

Westinghouse acquired CBS in the mid-1990s. The week before, Disney acquired ABC. The Disney acquisition was a *related* new market entry strategy in which Disney could leverage its name, reputation for quality, and creative and production expertise. The Westinghouse acquisition was an *unrelated* new market entry strategy that moved Westinghouse into the increasingly attractive communications market. Disney was leveraging its strength along with new market access. Westinghouse was redefining itself by acquiring CBS in the hope of reshaping its competitive advantage in an increasingly attractive market. However, both of these businesses were pursuing new sources of market share, sales growth, and profit performance.

One of the primary advantages of a diversified new market entry strategy is reduced market dependency, because most markets go through temporary periods of expansion and contraction. For example, the residential construction market is a slow-growth market that fluctuates considerably with economic conditions. A manufacturer of earth-moving equipment for this market could reduce the magnitude of swings in performance by entering a diversified market, such as mining or agriculture, unrelated to the residential construction market. In this way the performance of the business could be subject to smaller variations in overall business performance.

An additional advantage of market diversification is reduced vulnerability. If a business derives the bulk of its performance from one type of market, a major change in that market could threaten the company's performance, and, potentially, its survival. In the mid-1970s, the National Cash Register Corporation (NCR) was focused primarily on the cash register market and had over an 80 percent share of this market. When competitors entered with a new cash register technology, NCR's market share began to decline rapidly. In less than six years, its share had shrunk to less than 25 percent, and the company's survival was threatened.

Thus, there are three good reasons a business might pursue a diversified new market entry strategy:

- **New Source of Growth:** New market diversification offers the potential of adding to the business's sales growth and profit performance.
- **Smoother Performance:** New market diversification offers customer diversification, which can reduce the magnitude of swings in sales and profit performance.
- **Reduced Vulnerability:** New market diversification reduces market dependence and vulnerability, which better protects the business's performance and, in some instances, its survival.

Although these are important benefits, many businesses have failed to perform effectively in diversified markets and have retreated to their core markets. Mobil's acquisition of Montgomery Ward, Coca-Cola's acquisition of Columbia Pictures, and General Motors' acquisition of Data Information Services were each unsuccessful diversified new market strategies. In each case, the new market opportunities went too far from the marketing and business expertise and experience of the acquiring company. On the other hand, Phillip Morris's acquisition of the Miller Brewing Company, Pepsi's acquisition of Kentucky Fried Chicken, and Motorola's move into wireless communication products provided the advantages identified above while still leveraging their marketing and business expertise.

Strategies to Enter New Emerging Markets

As depicted in Figure 12-3, a business can grow by entering new emerging markets into which customers have not yet entered. Although considerably risky with respect to profit performance, this strategy can enable a business to establish an early leadership position in the market. From this position, a business can influence product positioning and market growth.

High-technology markets have rapidly emerging market demand and relatively short product and market life cycles. Businesses in these markets need to move quickly to capitalize on emerging new market opportunities or they will completely miss this opportunity for growth.[11] The pioneer in these emerging new markets has the potential to achieve a competitive advantage if it can sustain its advantage in these early stages of market development.[12] When pioneers can establish a *dominant design*, a standard emerges that followers must follow in order to compete.[13] For example, VHS prevailed over Beta as the design standard in the early evolution of the VCR market.

As the market emerges, *"early followers"* enter the market. Early followers emulate the dominant design and enter the market after letting the pioneer invest in developing the technology, establishing the design standard, and initiating market development. Many Japanese companies use an early follower strategy. Microsoft's entry into the Internet market was as an early follower. CompuServe, Prodigy, and America Online established a dominant position, but as the market developed, Microsoft entered the market and capitalized on emerging new market demand.

With rapid market growth, many customers are attracted to the market, and customer use and experience grow. It is during this phase of market development and growth that segments begin to form as customer needs become more salient and numerous. This growth attracts more competitors, many of whom will fill niche markets to serve the unique needs of a subset of customers.[14] This is a critical point for market leaders in emerging markets to develop multisegment solutions. Businesses that remain narrowly focused will see their market shares erode as new competitors deliver more attractive value propositions. Market pioneers who can sustain a market leadership position through this phase of market development are in the best position to achieve high levels of performance.[15]

Strategies to Develop New Market Potential

Apple Computer's initial entry into the personal computer market was a market growth strategy that focused on the enormous *untapped market potential* of the personal computer market. Apple's philosophy was to bring computing power to the masses. The company's original positioning strategy for Macintosh was: "Only a few have the expertise to operate computers. . . . Introducing Macintosh, for the rest of the world."

In the beginning, they had very few competitors because they were addressing a market ignored by the major computer manufacturers. Only after Apple legitimized this market did competitors begin to flow to this untapped market.

Global markets such as China, India, and Africa make up over half the world population, yet many of the products manufactured for the United States, Western Europe, and more affluent Asian countries have not been formulated for these markets. Constraints due to price, use compatibility, and availability create a large untapped new market potential for many products.

For example, many products need electricity, yet rural areas of underdeveloped countries cannot use electrical products because they do not have electricity. A company such as General Electric, which makes gas turbines for jet engines, has already adapted that expertise to enable a business (called a co-generator) to produce its own electricity and sell any excess to local utilities during periods of excess supply. GE has the capability of building electricity production on a small scale, thereby bringing many of its electrical products to consumers in remote locations around the world.

A growth strategy to develop an untapped new market potential has both high risk and the potential for high return.[16] Because the market is undeveloped, the cost of development can be significant even with a very good customer solution. On the other hand, with few competitors, if any, a business has the opportunity to pioneer a portion of the market largely ignored by competitors. With a "first-mover" advantage, there is the potential to own the market until other competitors venture to enter.

FIGURE 12-7 Alternative Offensive Strategic Market Plans

Area of Performance	Share Penetration Strategy		Market Development Strategy	
	First Year	In 5 Years	First Year	In 5 Years
Market Demand	600,000	600,000	20,000	200,000
Market Share	15%	20%	80%	50%
Market Growth Rate	3%	3%	158%	158%
Target Volume	90,000	120,000	16,000	100,000
Revenue per Customer	$ 450	$ 450	$ 950	$ 450
Total Revenue (millions)	$40.5	$54.0	$15.2	$45.0
Variable Cost per Customer	$ 250	$ 250	$ 650	$ 200
Total Variable Costs (millions)	$22.5	$30.0	$10.4	$20.0
Margin per Customer	$ 200	$ 200	$ 300	$ 250
Total Contribution (millions)	$18.0	$24.0	$ 4.8	$25.0
Marketing Expenses (millions)	$ 7.0	$10.0	$ 6.0	$12.0
Net Marketing Contribution (millions)	$11.0	$14.0	−$ 1.2	$13.0

EVALUATING OFFENSIVE STRATEGIC MARKET PLANS

A market-based business will often find that it has more market opportunities than it has resources to fund. In that case, the business will have to prioritize strategic market opportunities on the basis of its performance objectives. A business with a short-run need for better profit performance would be inclined to select the share penetration strategy, shown in Figure 12-7, rather than a long-run market development strategy. The share penetration strategy is expected to produce $14 million in net marketing contribution in five years. The share penetration strategy offers immediate profit performance and a reasonable level of sales revenue and profit growth.

On the other hand, a business with a good cash position, but facing stagnant growth in maturing markets, might pursue the market development strategy presented in Figure 12-7. This offensive strategy would produce a $1.2 million negative net marketing contribution in the first year of a new market development strategy. However, in five years, this strategy would be expected to produce $13 million in net marketing contribution. Although riskier, this new market development strategy could provide this business needed growth and market diversification in an attractive market. Thus, the selection of one offensive strategic market plan over another depends on the business's short-run profit needs, strategic position and resources, and opportunities for growth.

Summary

Businesses have a short-term obligation to investors to meet their financial promises of growth and performance. At the same time, they have an obligation to investors and employees to carve out a set of marketing strategies that will improve the position of the business in the long run. The purpose of strategic market planning is to examine the market attractiveness and competitive advantage of each market served by a business. On the basis of an assessment of this position, a strategic market objective is developed and resources are allocated accordingly. To accomplish these performance objectives, a business generally needs a combination of offensive and defensive strategic market plans.

Offensive strategic market plans are more growth-oriented and can be broken down into four strategies that address existing markets and four that focus on new market opportunities. Existing markets and current customers offer the most logical place to initiate growth-oriented offensive strategies. When market share is underdeveloped, share penetration offers a very good growth opportunity. Likewise, product line extensions that can be marketed to existing customers provide growth without substantial additions to marketing expenses. New customer opportunities within existing markets

can be addressed with strategies to enter new segments within existing markets or to grow segment or market demand.

New market offensive strategies center around markets with market entry opportunities as well as emerging and undeveloped markets. New market entry into related markets is often pursued as a way of leveraging brand name recognition, channel systems, or manufacturing synergies. Related new market entry offers the least risk, whereas diversified new market entry offers a better opportunity to reduce vulnerability due to changing market conditions. Early entry into emerging markets and development of untapped new market opportunities offer tremendous growth potential but are high risk in terms of profit performance and the time it takes to achieve a high level of profit performance.

APPLICATION PROBLEM: BLOCKBUSTER

The video rental market grew at a rate of 7.6 percent per year from 1997 to 2000. At the same time, Blockbuster continued with an offensive strategy to grow market share and grew their share from 21.8 percent to 30.7 percent. This was largely due to the addition of 2665 new Blockbuster outlets. This increased their outlet share from 18 percent in 1997 to 26.8 percent in 2000. Sales growth was also enhanced with a higher revenue per store. As shown in Figure 1, the sales per Blockbuster outlet grew from $562,264 per outlet to $644,026, a 14.6 percent increase.

As shown in Figure 2, the percent margin per store is 59 percent. The marketing expense is $310,000 per store which includes advertising ($27,662 per store) and general administration ($282,338 per

store). This results in an average net marketing contribution per store of roughly $70,000 and operating income of roughly $10,000 per store.

For access to interactive software to answer the questions below go to www.RogerJBest.com or www.prenhall.com/best.

Questions:

1. What is the profit impact of an "offensive" strategy to grow outlet share to 30 percent share by 2005 with no change in the total number of market outlets, sales per outlet, percent margin, or marketing expenses as a percent of sales?

2. What would be the profit impact of an "offensive" strategy to grow sales per outlet from its current level to $750,000

FIGURE 1   US Market Video Sales, Market Share, and Outlet Performance: 1997–2000

US Market 2000	Outlets	Outlet Share	Sales	Share ($)	Sales/Outlet
Blockbuster	7,700	26.8%	$4,959	30.7%	$644,026
Hollywood Video	1615	5.6%	$1,296	8.0%	$802,477
Movie Gallery	1040	3.6%	$319	2.0%	$306,731
Video Update	652	2.3%	$221	1.4%	$338,957
West Coast	312	1.1%	$104	0.6%	$333,333
All others	17,454	60.7%	$9,228	57.2%	$528,704
US Market	**28,773**	**100.0%**	**$16,127**	**100.0%**	**$560,491**

US Market 1997	Outlets	Outlet Share	Sales	Share ($)	Sales /Outlet
Blockbuster	5,035	18.0%	$2,831	21.8%	$562,264
Hollywood Video	851	3.1%	$287	2.2%	$337,250
Movie Gallery	972	3.5%	$254	2.0%	$261,317
Video Update	308	1.1%	$84	0.6%	$272,727
West Coast	531	1.9%	$230	1.8%	$433,145
All others	20,303	74.1%	$9,314	71.6%	$458,750
US Market	**28,000**	**101.8%**	**$13,000**	**100.0%**	**$464,286**

FIGURE 2   Blockbuster Financial Performance–2000

Blockbuster 2000	($ millions)	Outlet Average
Sales Revenues	$4,959	$644,026
Percent Margin	59%	59%
Gross Profit	$2,926	$379,975
Marketing Expenses	$2,387	$310,000
Net Marketing Contribution	**$ 539**	**$ 69,975**
Operating Expenses	$ 463	$ 60,130
Operating Income	**$ 76**	**$ 9,845**

per outlet in five years? Assume no change in outlet market share or total number of outlets.

3. What would be the profit impact of an "offiensive" marketing strategy to double marketing expenses in order to grow outlet share to 30 percent while the market grows at 6.5 percent a year (in sales per outlet)? Note: Adjust the Marketing Expense (% sales) until you achieve a marketing expense in 2005 roughly double that of 2000.

Market-Based Logic and Strategic Thinking

1. What is the difference between offensive strategic market plans and defensive strategic market plans?
2. Explain why a business might shift from an offensive strategic market plan to a defensive strategic market plan over the life cycle of a particular product.

3. How can a business meet short-run growth and profit performance targets and still invest in strategic market plans that are focused on long-run objectives with respect to share position, sales growth, and profit performance?

4. How would a Nike offensive strategy to grow market penetration differ from a strategy to grow customer purchases (revenue per customer) in the under-18 female athlete market?

5. Hewlett-Packard entered the low-priced printer market with a new brand name (Apollo). Explain the logic of this offensive strategic market plan and how it is likely to affect HP performance.

6. Microsoft has developed a product called *Meeting Pro* to help facilitate the running of small business meetings. Although this is a value-added software product, Microsoft offers this product at no cost to Windows users. Explain how this is an offensive market penetration strategy.

7. Why are offensive strategic market plans crucial for the long-run success of a business? What kind of offensive strategies could McDonald's use to ensure future growth in sales and profits?

8. Microsoft has developed a joint venture with Sony to develop an online alternative to the telephone. What type of offensive marketing strategy best describes this joint venture, and what would the expected short- and long-run performance objectives be?

9. How does a market penetration strategy to grow market share differ from a strategy to enter a new segment in the same market?

10. Why is a marketing strategy to grow customer purchases (revenue per customer) potentially more profitable than many other offensive marketing strategies?

11. Why would a business first pursue offensive marketing strategies to increase market share or grow revenue per customer rather than other offensive marketing strategies?

12. What forces limit new customer growth within existing markets? How could a business grow market demand by addressing these forces?

13. What are the important differences between a related new marketing strategy and a diversified new marketing strategy?

14. When would a business pursue a diversified new market entry strategy?

15. What is the advantage of growing market demand in a new, emerging market?

Notes

1. David Aaker, "Portfolio Analysis," *Strategic Market Management*, (New York: Wiley, 1995):155–69.

2. Bernard Catry and Michel Chevalier, "Market Share Strategy and the Product Life Cycle," *Journal of Marketing* (October 1974):29–34.

3. Philippe Haspeslagh, "Portfolio Planning: Uses and Limits," *Harvard Business Review* (January–February 1982):58–73; and S. Robinson, R. Hichens, and D. Wade, "The Directional Policy Matrix Tool for Strategic Planning," *Long-Range Planning* (June 1978):8–15.

4. David Aaker, "Growth Strategies," *Strategic Market Management* (New York: Wiley, 1995):238–59.

5. David Szymanski, Sundar Bharadwaj, and Rajan Varadarajan, "An Analysis of the Market Share-Profitability Relationship," *Journal of Marketing* (July 1993):1–18; and C. Davis Fogg, "Planning Gains in Market Share," *Journal of Marketing* (July 1994):30–38.

6. Charles Lillis, James Cook, Roger Best, and Del Hawkins, "Marketing Strategies to Achieve Market Share Goals," in *Strategic Marketing Management*, ed. H. Thomas and D. Gardner (New York: Wiley, 1985).

7. Daniel Sheinen and Bernd Schmitt, "Extending Brands with New Product Concepts: The Role of Category Attribute Congruity, Brand Affect and Brand Breadth," *Journal of Business Research* (September 1994):1–10.

8. Gary Hamel and C. K. Prahalad, "Seeing the Future First," *Fortune* (September 5, 1994):64–70.

9. Edward Roberts and Charles Berry, "Entering New Business: Selecting Strategies for Success," *Sloan Management Review* (Spring 1985):3–17.

10. Richard Rumelt, "Diversification, Strategy and Profitability," *Strategic Management Journal* 3 (1982):359–69.

11. G. Stalk Jr., "Time: The Next Source of Competitive Advantage," *Harvard Business Review* (July–August 1988):41–51; and Thomas Robertson, "How to Reduce Market Penetration Cycle Times," *Sloan Management Review* (Fall 1993):87–96.

12. William Robinson and Claes Fornell, "Sources of Market Pioneer Advantage in Consumer Goods Industries," *Journal of Marketing Research* (August 1985):305–17; and William Robinson, "Sources of Market Pioneer Advantages: The Case for Industrial Goods Industries," *Journal of Marketing Research*, 25 (1988):87–94.

13. Roger Best and Reinhard Angelmar, "Strategies for Leveraging Technology Advantage," in *Handbook on Business Strategy* (New York: Warren, Gorham and Lamont, 1989):2.1–2.10.

14. Vijay Mahajan, Subhash Sharma, and Robert Buzzell, "Assessing the Impact of Competitive Entry on Market Expansion and Incumbent Sales," *Journal of Marketing* (July 1993):39–52.

15. Glen Urban, T. Carter, S. Gaskin, and Z. Mucha, "Marketing Share Rewards to Pioneering Brands: An Empirical Analysis and Strategic Implications," *Management Science* 32 (1986):635–59.

16. Igal Ayal and Jehiel Zif, "Market Expansion Strategies in Multinational Markets," *Journal of Marketing* (Spring 1979):84–94.

13 DEFENSIVE STRATEGIC MARKET PLANS

Historical share leaders such as General Motors, AT&T, IBM, and others have been under attack in their core markets for some time. For each, a loss on one share point is considerable in terms of sales revenues, net profits, and cash flow. Relatively new share leaders such as Intel, Cisco Systems, and Microsoft face the same challenge. These businesses, like other *share defenders* are engaged in a battle to protect their share in the markets they serve.[1]

Intel is the worldwide market leader in the microprocessor market. Over the past several years Intel has maintained an 85 percent share of a market growing at 15 to 20 percent per year. A strategic market plan to *protect market share* would provide continued growth in sales revenues despite anticipated price erosion. As shown in Figure 13-1, a *protect share strategy,* along with a strategy to improve margins, yields an increase in total contribution over the five-year planning horizon. Intel's cost of marketing, sales, and administration has historically been 12 percent of sales. Taking this into account yields a projected net marketing contribution that will increase by $4.9 billion from 1997 to 2002. This increase will, in turn, contribute to increased earnings and shareholder value over the same time horizon.

Businesses in less attractive markets or businesses with fewer resources may be forced to *reduce share* in an effort to find a more profitable combination of market share and profitability. Others may be forced to exit markets slowly, with a *harvest* strategy, or quickly, with a *divestment strategy.* Each *defensive strategy* is intended to

---

FIGURE 13-1 Intel Strategy to Protect Microprocessor Market Share

Area of Performance	1997	1998	1999	2000	2001	2002
Market Demand (millions)	83	109	133	155	183	214
Market Share	85%	85%	85%	85%	85%	85%
Unit Volume (millions)	71	93	113	132	155	182
Average Selling Price	$ 240	$ 210	$ 190	$ 182	$ 175	$ 168
Sales Revenues (billions)	$17.1	$19.5	$21.5	$24.0	$27.1	$30.6
Percent Margin	60%	57%	50%	52%	55%	55%
Total Contribution (billions)	$10.3	$11.1	$10.8	$12.5	$14.9	$16.8
Marketing Expenses (billions)	$ 2.1	$ 2.3	$ 2.6	$ 2.9	$ 3.3	$ 3.7
Net Marketing Contribution (billions)	**$ 8.2**	**$ 8.8**	**$ 8.2**	**$ 9.6**	**$11.6**	**$13.1**

maximize or protect short-run profits or to minimize short-run losses. This chapter examines defensive strategic market plans and the role they play in achieving the short- and long-run performance objectives of a business.

DEFENSIVE STRATEGIC MARKET PLANS

A key part of Intel's long-run performance has been its ability to successfully implement a *protect share* strategy in the microprocessor market. Any degree of share erosion will lower unit volume, sales revenues, and net marketing contribution. However, a defensive strategy to protect share should not be misinterpreted to mean a *hold resources constant* strategy. To protect share in a market growing at 15 to 20 percent a year, Intel will have to continue its roll-out of new products and add to its marketing budget. Not doing either would almost guarantee erosion of Intel's market share position in the microprocessor market.

In general, businesses in high share positions in growing or mature markets will use defensive strategic market plans to maintain cash flow that supports short-run profit performance and shareholder value. Without these defensive strategic market plans and their profitability, businesses would face a difficult short-run situation in terms of profit performance and would lack the resources to invest in growth-oriented offensive market opportunities.

For example, consider the business situation presented in Figure 13-2. Currently, the business is in four markets, one of which is losing money. The first market (M1) is a

FIGURE 13-2 Strategic Market Planning and Performance

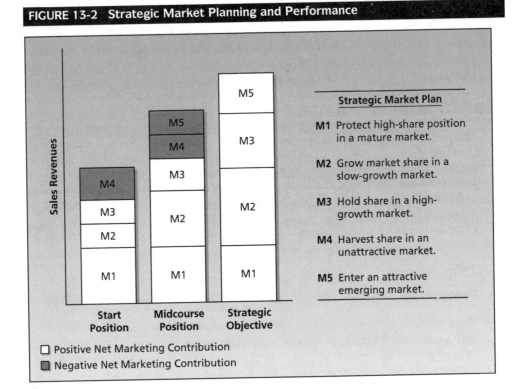

Strategic Market Plan	
M1	Protect high-share position in a mature market.
M2	Grow market share in a slow-growth market.
M3	Hold share in a high-growth market.
M4	Harvest share in an unattractive market.
M5	Enter an attractive emerging market.

□ Positive Net Marketing Contribution
■ Negative Net Marketing Contribution

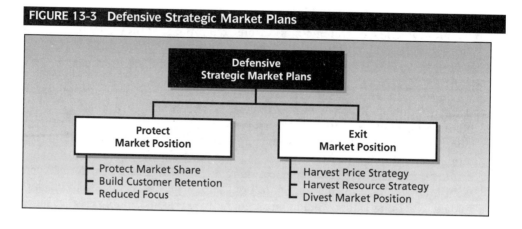

FIGURE 13-3   Defensive Strategic Market Plans

maturing market in which the business holds a high-share position. The business's strategic market plan for this market is to protect this high-share position. The second market (M2) is a slow-growth market in which this business's strategic market plan is to grow share. The third market (M3) is a high-growth market in which the business's strategic market plan is to protect its share position. Market four (M4) is losing money and has been determined to be unattractive. The strategic market plan for this market is to harvest share and maximize short-run profits as the business systematically exits the market. A fifth strategic market plan is to enter an attractive emerging market (M5) in which the business will lose money initially but which will be a good source of future growth, improved share position, and long-run cash flow.

With these five market-based management strategies, this business hopes to grow revenue and profits with a series of strategic moves to *protect, grow,* or *harvest* market share.[2] Each strategic market plan plays an important role in the business's short- and long-run sales and profitability. Figure 13-3 summarizes defensive strategic market plans.

PROTECT MARKET STRATEGIES

The primary goal of a defensive strategic market plan is to protect profitability and key strategic share positions. This goal translates into a combination of defensive strategic market plans. As shown in Figure 13-4, certain portfolio positions based on market attractiveness and competitive advantage lead to more than one defensive strategic market plan. A defensive strategic market plan designed to protect a desired share position can lead to a *protect share, reduced focus, harvest,* or *divest* defensive strategic market plan. In all cases, these defensive marketing strategies are focused on maximizing short-run profits and protecting or improving the overall strategic position of a business.

Protect Market Share

Many share leaders have market shares in excess of 50 percent. However, the conditions under which they have to defend their share position can be drastically different. For example, Campbell Soup has a 60 percent share position in a mature American soup market; Gillette has a 70 percent share and is the share leader in the razor and

FIGURE 13-4   Portfolio Positions and Defensive Strategic Market Plans

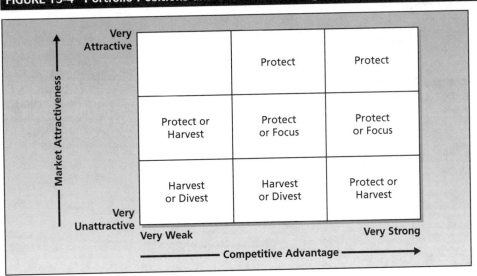

blade market, which is also mature; and Kodak has more than a 60 percent share of the American film market. Their defensive strategies in slow-growth mature markets will be very different from those of businesses with high shares in fast-growth markets. Intel, with an 85 percent share in the fast-growing computer market, and Microsoft, with a 90 percent share in the rapidly developing software market, will each have to exert greater marketing efforts to protect high-share positions while their markets are still experiencing rapid growth. However, each has the same fundamental objective: *protect market share.*

Protecting Share in Growth Markets

Growth markets require a much greater marketing effort and more investment in new products to protect a share leadership position than do mature markets. The faster the market grows, the more marketing resources needed to protect share. If a business does not invest to protect share in a growth market, its market share is almost certain to decline. Thus, growing markets create a much greater potential for share loss than do slow-growth markets. Hence, the resources needed to offset the effects of growth with a defensive strategic market plan to protect share must be much greater.

In the Profit Impact of Marketing Strategies (PIMS) database, the average business will experience approximately a -0.4 percent annual rate of market share change per 1 percent of market growth rate. This means that a business in a market growing at 10 percent a year will experience a 4 percent rate of share erosion if the effects of market growth are not offset by a defensive strategic market plan. Using this average, a business with a 20 percent market share in a market growing at a rate of 10 percent per year would experience an estimated share loss of almost 4 share points in five years if it did nothing to offset the negative impact of market growth. Of course, if the market were growing at 15 percent per year, the business would experience a much faster rate of share erosion, as shown in Figure 13-5.

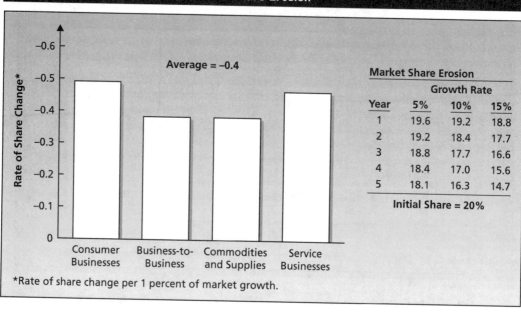

FIGURE 13-5   Market Growth Rate and Share Erosion

| Market Share Erosion | | | |
Year	5%	10%	15%
1	19.6	19.2	18.8
2	19.2	18.4	17.7
3	18.8	17.7	16.6
4	18.4	17.0	15.6
5	18.1	16.3	14.7

Initial Share = 20%

*Rate of share change per 1 percent of market growth.

Although the effects of market growth on market share change are likely to be different among industries, these differences are relatively small in reasonably diverse areas of business, as also shown in Figure 13-5. Thus, the impact of market growth on market share erosion is fairly uniform among different areas of business.

Protecting a High-Share Position

Market share leaders such as Eastman Kodak, Campbell Soup, and Cisco Systems have strong share positions that generate considerable sales revenues and profits that directly affect the financial performance of these businesses. Hence, defensive marketing strategies to protect these high-share positions are critical to short-run profit performance and provide a major source of cash for investment in offensive marketing strategies for future growth and profit performance.

It is hard to imagine how having a large market share could be a handicap with respect to protecting market share. However, in the PIMS database, we consistently find an inverse relationship between market share change and size of market share. As shown in Figure 13-6, the average PIMS business would experience approximately a -0.08 percent rate of market share change per 1 percent of current market share.

This means that a business with a 30 percent market share would experience a -2.4 percent annual rate of share loss, which would lead to a 26.5 percent share loss in five years. A business with a 10 percent market share would never really feel this effect, because the size of its market share is much smaller, and its share would erode only to an estimated 9.6 percent in five years.

Thus, high-share businesses have to invest considerably more to protect share independently of other share-eroding market forces such as market growth, competitor entry, or competitor strategies. As one begins to comprehend the impact that high

FIGURE 13-6   Market Share Erosion and Current Share Position

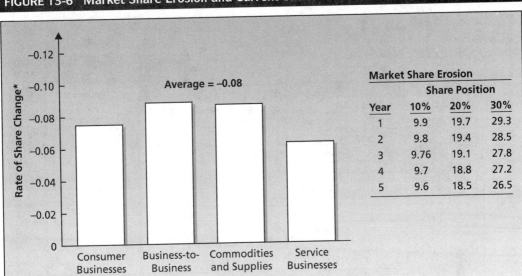

	Market Share Erosion		
	Share Position		
Year	**10%**	**20%**	**30%**
1	9.9	19.7	29.3
2	9.8	19.4	28.5
3	9.76	19.1	27.8
4	9.7	18.8	27.2
5	9.6	18.5	26.5

*Rate of share change per 1 percent of current market share.

share and high market growth rate have on eroding market share, one can better understand the market share losses experienced by Eastman Kodak, IBM, AT&T, General Motors, and other high-share businesses. And, as it is on market growth, the impact of size of market share on the rate of market share change is fairly consistent among diverse areas of business in the PIMS database, as illustrated in Figure 13-6.

To successfully defend high-share positions, businesses need to continuously improve their competitive advantage and marketing effort. Share leaders that make temporary cuts in marketing to improve short-run profit only hurt next year's profits with a reduced market share. Thus, share leaders must remain committed to (1) new product development, (2) efforts to improve product and service quality at a rate faster than the competition, and (3) fully supporting the marketing budgets needed to protect a high-share position.[3]

Protecting a Follower Share Position

Of course, not everyone can be a market share leader. Illustrated in Figure 13-7 are four market structures, each presenting *followers* in a different market share position. A business that is second in market share, but a close follower (Market II in Figure 13-7), has an interesting strategic market decision to consider. Does this follower challenge the leader with an offensive share penetration strategy? Or does it protect its share position and maximize the profits that can be extracted from that share position? Depending on the strength of the share leader, the share leader's commitment to defending its share position, and the follower business's resources and short-run profit needs, either strategic market plan could be pursued. But what does a successful defensive follower strategy look like?[4]

FIGURE 13-7   Market Structure and Share Position

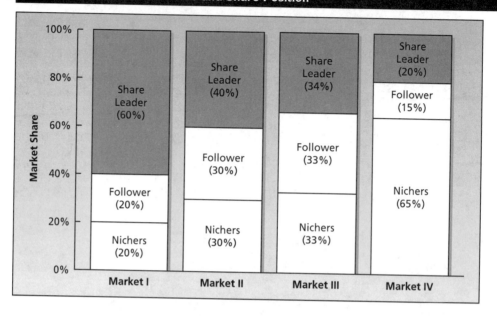

FIGURE 13-8   Successful vs. Unsuccessful Follower Share Strategies

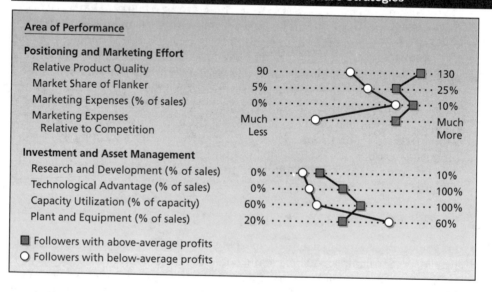

Figure 13-8 profiles the average follower (number two share) business in the PIMS database that has achieved above-average profitability and the average follower business with below-average profit performance. With respect to competitive advantage, profitable share followers have higher relative product quality, which helps support higher levels of customer value, price, and unit margin. However, they also invest more aggressively in marketing as a percentage of sales as well as on a relative basis when

FIGURE 13-9   Marketing Strategies for Profitable Share Leaders and Profitable Low-Share Niche Businesses

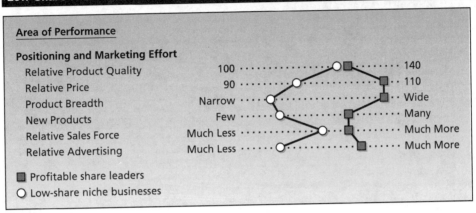

compared with competitors. These effects produce a slightly higher share, which contributes to a higher level of capacity utilization.

These businesses also invest more in research and development as a percentage of sales. This investment translates into a higher level of technological advantage that most likely can be traced back to higher relative product quality. Thus, profitable followers protect their number two share position with investments in both R&D and marketing. As pointed out earlier, without these types of investments, a business could not protect a share position, even in relatively slow-growth markets.

Protecting a Niche Share Position

The strategic decision to engage in a long-run offensive or defensive strategic market plan has to also be made by *niche* share businesses. For example, niche share businesses depicted in Figure 13-7 may elect to pursue offensive strategic market plans to challenge share leaders. Or, perhaps the market situation would lead a business to pursue a defensive strategy to protect a profitable niche market. In many ways, a niche business is simply the share leader in a more narrowly defined market. Thus, share leaders, followers, and niche businesses could each pursue defensive strategies to protect their market share positions.

A business that pursues a niche strategic market plan could be a small business with limited resources or a large business that has pursued a reduced focus strategy within a larger market and still achieves high levels of profitability.[5] For whatever reason, the business could develop a dominant position in a niche market but still have an overall share of the market that is relatively small when compared with the share leader. However, within its market niche, it is the share leader and has the same needs as share leaders in defending its share position.

Shown in Figure 13-9 are average profiles for profitable high-share and profitable low-share businesses. If you examine these two profiles closely, you will notice that there are only two areas of commonality: relative product quality and relative sales force expense.

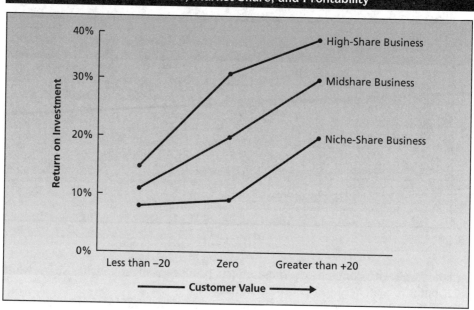

FIGURE 13-10   Customer Value, Market Share, and Profitability

Having above-average product quality and above-average customer contact and market coverage are key success factors for both profitable high-share businesses and profitable low-share businesses.

However, to achieve above-average levels of profitability, low-share niche businesses need to focus in order to keep expenses low.[6] Their niche focus is most evident in their narrow product line, limited new product effort, and limited advertising effort relative to competitors. In addition, relative prices are slightly below the average relative price index of 100. With an average relative price near 96, and relative product quality close to 123, these successful niche businesses create an attractive customer value as shown in the following:

$$\text{Customer Value} = \text{Relative Benefits} - \text{Relative Price}$$
$$+ 27 = 123 - 97$$

As shown in Figure 13-10, low-share niche businesses with above-average customer value are more profitable. As a matter of fact, a low-share business with above-average customer value is more profitable than a high-share business with below-average customer value. Thus, an important component of success for niche share businesses is above-average customer value and sales coverage with a careful product focus.

Building Customer Retention

Protecting a valued share position is certainly a defensive strategy that is at the core of many successful businesses. However, the profit impact of holding a 30 percent market share can be quite different for high and low levels of customer retention.

For example, assume that two businesses each produce $400 of margin per customer the first year, but this margin grows by $25 per year for each year the customer is retained. Further assume that each business spends $500 to acquire a new customer

FIGURE 13-11   Profit Impact of Customer Retention Strategy

| | 75% Customer Retention* | | | | 80% Customer Retention* | | |
Year	Net Cash	Discount Factor	Value	Year	Net Cash	Discount Factor	Present Value
0	−$500	1.000	−$500	0	−$500	1.000	−$500
1	+$300	0.870	+$261	1	+$300	0.870	+$261
2	+$325	0.756	+$246	2	+$325	0.756	+$246
3	+$350	0.658	+$230	3	+$350	0.658	+$230
4	+$375	0.572	+$215	4	+$375	0.572	+$215
5	0	0.497	0	5	+$400	0.497	+$199
Net Present Value @ 15% = +$452				Net Present Value @ 15% = +$651			

*Customer Life = 1 / (1 − Customer Retention)

and $100 per year to retain a customer. As shown in Figure 13-11, the business with a 75 percent customer retention will retain the average customer for four years, whereas an 80 percent customer retention will keep the average customer for five years. That's an extra $199 in discounted net cash flow.

This analysis demonstrates how a business that is able to build a higher level of customer retention can be more profitable than another business, both with the same market share. Whether a high-share market leader, a share follower, or a low-share niche business, a business can build profits with a defensive strategy to protect share while building customer retention.

Reduced Market Focus

As shown earlier in Figure 13-4, a business may find itself in a portfolio position that can lead to more than one defensive strategic market plan. Should the business invest to strengthen its competitive advantage, allocate resources to protect its share position, or reduce its focus position within a market to maximize profitability? All can be viable strategic market plans depending upon different market and business conditions.

A decision to pursue a *reduced focus* defensive strategy would be most appropriate when:

> there are not sufficient resources to invest to protect the current share position or when greater levels of profitability can be derived from a narrower, more selective choice of target customers.

Thus, a reduced market focus prescribes a defensive strategic market plan that involves narrowing market focus and trimming market share in an effort to improve profit performance. This approach may produce a reduction in revenue and marketing budget but higher levels of profitability as a percentage of sales.[7] As shown in Figure 13-12, the whole idea of a reduced focus is to become more efficient. In this illustration, a mass market approach is less efficient than a reduced market focus in terms of marketing productivity. Although sales and profits are reduced, a reduced focus is able to improve marketing productivity from $2 of net contribution per $1 of marketing budget to $3. Thus, this business had to get smaller to become more efficient in producing profits.

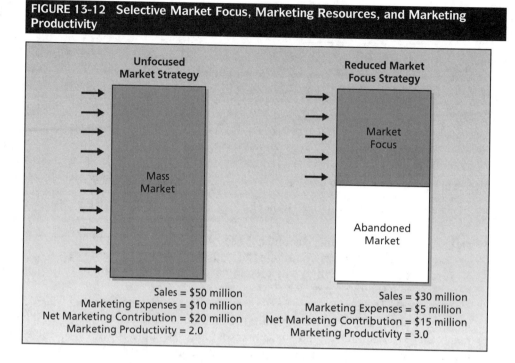

FIGURE 13-12 Selective Market Focus, Marketing Resources, and Marketing Productivity

Unfocused Market Strategy

Mass Market

Sales = $50 million
Marketing Expenses = $10 million
Net Marketing Contribution = $20 million
Marketing Productivity = 2.0

Reduced Market Focus Strategy

Market Focus

Abandoned Market

Sales = $30 million
Marketing Expenses = $5 million
Net Marketing Contribution = $15 million
Marketing Productivity = 3.0

EXIT MARKET STRATEGIES

Portfolio positions that warrant a defensive strategic market plan to exit from a market can lead to a harvest (slow exit) marketing strategy or to a divestment (fast exit) strategic market plan, as depicted in the portfolio model shown in Figure 13-4. When there are additional profits to be made with a slow exit, a harvest strategy can be a good source of short-run profits. If a business were losing money in a given market, it might be more inclined to pursue a quick market exit strategy and divest its share position as quickly as possible. In this case, a divestment strategy also improves short-run profits by eliminating a source of negative cash flow. Each of these defensive strategic market plans involves some aspect of market share management. However, unlike offensive strategic market plans, many of which are focused on growing market share, defensive strategic market plans are focused on protecting or pruning market share.

Harvest Price Strategy

The combination of unattractive markets and weak competitive advantage translates into both weak strategic position and potentially weak profit performance.[8] When a reduced focus strategy cannot produce desired levels of performance, an exit strategic market plan warrants consideration. However, rather than divest a share position and exit quickly, there are often good short-run performance opportunities offered by systematically raising prices and reducing marketing expenses.[9]

FIGURE 13-13   Chemical Business Product Line Performance

Area of Performance	Silicon Pigments	Primary Products	Special Products	Basic Colors	Color Enhancers	Overall Total
Market Demand (millions)	100	167	154	96	556	
Market Share	10%	12%	13%	26%	9%	
Unit Volume (millions)	10	20	20	25	50	125
Unit Price	$4.50	$2.80	$1.60	$0.80	$0.60	
Sales Revenue (millions)	$ 45	$ 56	$ 32	$ 20	$ 30	$ 183
Unit Variable Cost	$3.50	$2.00	$1.30	$0.70	$0.54	
Unit Margin	$1.00	$0.80	$0.30	$0.10	$0.06	
Total Contribution (millions)	$10.0	$16.0	$ 6.0	$ 2.5	$ 3.0	$37.5
Marketing Expenses (millions)	2.0	7.0	5.0	3.0	4.5	21.5
Net Marketing Contribution (millions)	$ 8.0	$ 9.0	$ 1.0	–$ .5	–$ 1.5	$16.0

For example, consider the business situation, outlined in Figure 13-13, that faced a chemical business.[10] Two of five product lines were not covering their marketing expenses. With respect to portfolio position, the business had an average competitive advantage in an increasingly unattractive market. Senior management felt the best strategy would be to divest the business by selling it. However, they could not find a buyer, so they pursued a *harvest price* strategy.

The prices of silicon pigments, primary products, and special products were immediately raised 10 to 19 percent. At the same time, the prices of basic colors and color enhancers were raised 10 percent and then another 10 percent in six months. These changes resulted in an overall price increase of 22.5 percent for basic colors and 25 percent for color enhancers. In addition, marketing expenses were modestly reduced. The initial customer reaction was what was expected. There was an immediate reduction of 14 to 18 percent in the volume of silicon pigments, primary products, and special products. The customer exit for basic colors and color enhancers, with more aggressive price increases, was even greater, as the volume for these two product lines decreased by 33 and 35 percent, respectively.

However, after 18 months, customer defection subsided. And, as shown in Figure 13-14, the increased prices offset some of the lost volume, as sales revenues decreased from $183 million to $170 million. More important, however, each of the product lines now produced a positive net marketing contribution. The overall net marketing contribution more than doubled, from $16 million to $36.1 million.

After attaining this level of performance, the business was successful in finding a buyer. One might wonder why the company would not retain the business after it became profitable. First, this level of profitability was still below the company average and, hence, a drain on overall profits and shareholder value. But more important, this was an unattractive market, and the business wanted to redirect these resources into a better strategic market opportunity.

FIGURE 13-14   Chemical Business Product Line Performance

Area of Performance	Silicon Pigments	Primary Products	Special Products	Basic Colors	Color Enhancers	Overall Total
Market Demand (millions)	100	167	154	96	556	
Market Share	8.6%	10.3%	10.7%	17.1%	6.0%	
Unit Volume (millions)	8.6	17.2	16.5	16.4	33.3	92
Unit Price	$4.95	$3.20	$1.90	$0.98	$0.75	
Sales Revenue (millions)	$42.6	$55.0	$31.4	$16.1	$25.0	$ 170
Unit Variable Cost	$3.50	$2.00	$1.30	$0.70	$0.54	
Unit Margin	$1.45	$1.20	$0.60	$0.28	$0.21	
Total Contribution (millions)	$12.5	$20.6	$ 9.9	$ 4.6	$ 7.0	$54.6
Marketing Expenses (millions)	2.0	7.0	4.5	2.0	3.0	18.5
Net Marketing Contribution (millions)	**$10.5**	**$13.6**	**$ 5.4**	**$ 2.6**	**$ 4.0**	**$36.1**

Harvest Resource Strategy

In many instances, a business may not be able to raise prices as a strategy to harvest share while maximizing short-run profits. A soft drink manufacturer's prices are difficult to alter in the end market. In such a case, a business can reduce the marketing resources it devotes to that product and its market share position. For example, Slice is a low-share soft drink with minimal marketing support. Its market share is less than 5 percent of the lemon-lime soft drink segment and well behind Sprite, which has a 56 percent segment share. While Pepsi has examined different ways to either revitalize the brand or reposition it, its market share remains relatively stagnant. By not supporting Slice, the company is maximizing what profits it can take as Slice slowly exits the market.

In heavily advertised consumer goods markets, share erosion can be rather dramatic with major reductions in advertising budget. From the PIMS database, one learns that the rate of share change is affected by the rate of change in advertising budget. For example, the following shows the rate of share loss for a consumer product that experienced a 25 percent reduction in advertising budget for each of three consecutive years. In this case, a 10 percent market share would erode to 9.6 percent in three years.

$$\text{Market Share (3 years)} = \text{Market Share } (1.00 + [0.05 \times \text{Change in Advertising Budget}])^3$$
$$= 10\% \times (1.00 = [0.05 \times -0.25])^3$$
$$= 10\% \times (1.00 - 0.0125)^3$$
$$= 10\% \times .96$$
$$= 9.6\%$$

When advertising budgets are very large, this can be a significant savings. As long as the product has an adequate profit margin, a business could improve short-run profits as it reduces marketing expenses and slowly loses market share. The profits taken in the short run from the harvested product would normally be reallocated to a more attractive product–market in which the business hopes to build a stronger share position and desired levels of profit.

FIGURE 13-15 General Electric Divestment Strategy for Unattractive Product–Markets

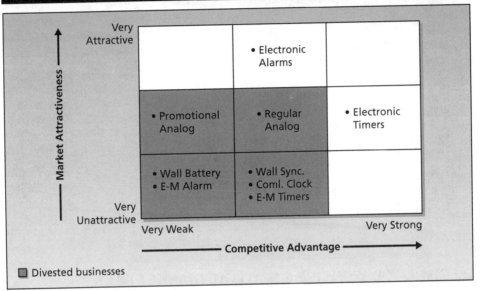

Divest Market Strategies

One of the most difficult decisions any business faces is the decision to quickly sell off (divest) an unattractive product. In some instances, these are products that the company was built on, and it is difficult to let them go. In other cases, they are major investments that are hard to kill because of the money spent and the commitment made to make them successful ventures. As a result, businesses hang on to unattractive market positions with weak or average competitive advantage for far too long.

Figure 13-15 shows the portfolio of General Electric's clock and timer products as it existed in the late 1970s. Many of the products were in unattractive markets or had a weak competitive advantage, or both. GE divested the businesses shown and invested in the two that were in more attractive market positions. Eventually, these product–markets were also divested because they did not match the overall performance objectives of the company.

To divest a share position, a business can either find a buyer for the business or simply close down the operation and sell its assets. The desired choice, in most instances, is to find a buyer. Selling generally yields a greater return and preserves the employment of those working in the business.

A divestment strategy, although desired, may sometimes not be feasible. For example, a business that has a twenty year commitment to produce a critical component for a government missile cannot easily exit the product–market; it has a responsibility to supply that product for the duration of the contract. Likewise, producers of pharmaceuticals or other life-supporting products may have a difficult time divesting a share position for either legal or ethical reasons. Also, a simple divest share position when no buyer is available can be difficult.

FIGURE 13-16   Selecting between Two Defensive Marketing Strategies

	Estimated Performance in Three Years	
Area of Performance	Protect Share Strategy	Reduced Focus Strategy
Market Demand (000)	2,000	2,000
Market Share	30%	20%
Unit Volume (000)	600	400
Unit Price	$400	$450
Sales Revenues (millions)	$240	$180
Unit Variable Cost	$300	$300
Unit Margin	$100	$150
Total Contribution (millions)	$ 60	$ 60
Marketing Expenses (millions)	30	20
Net Marketing Contribution (millions)	**$ 30**	**$ 40**

SELECTING A DEFENSIVE STRATEGIC MARKET PLAN

Consider a business in a market with below-average market attractiveness and average competitive advantage that is making $25 million in net marketing contribution, as shown in Figure 13-16. This is a reasonably good profit performance, but an average competitive advantage in an unattractive market does not warrant an offensive strategic market plan to grow share. However, the share position is profitable enough to keep and, hence, a harvest market defensive strategy may not be appropriate. The choices left for this business are a *protect share* strategy and a *reduced focus* strategy.

If the business elected to pursue a protect share strategy, it would have to invest in marketing and other business activities such as research and development to maintain its 30 percent share. Given these assumptions, it is estimated that the business could maintain sales revenues of $240 million over the next three years. A protect share strategy would produce $30 million in net marketing contribution. With marketing expenses also equal to $30 million, a protect share strategy would yield a marketing productivity equal to 1.0.

The alternative defensive strategic market plan would be to reduce focus. This strategy would purposefully reduce the business's market share from 30 percent to 20 percent. However, the selective market focus strategy would yield a higher average price and unit margin and would require less in marketing expenses. The net result would be a $60 million reduction in sales revenue but an increase in net marketing contribution from $30, to $40 million. With marketing expenses of $20, this strategy also resulted in a market productivity of 2.0, twice that of the protect share strategy.

Overall, a business faces many market situations and a well-defined set of business objectives. Some performance objectives are short-run, others are long-run. Recognizing its performance objectives and its positioning in each of its markets, the business must put together a set of strategic market plans that will meet its performance objectives. Businesses will generally need a combination of offensive and defensive strategic market plans. Whereas offensive strategic market plans are geared for growth and improving share position, defensive strategic market plans are important sources of short-run profits and important in defending strategic share positions. Hence, both are needed and play key roles in meeting a business's performance objectives.

Summary

Businesses have a short-term obligation to investors to meet their financial promises of growth and profit performance. At the same time, they have an obligation to investors and employees to carve out a set of strategic market plans that will improve the position of the business in the long run. The primary purpose of a defensive strategic market plan is to protect key strategic share positions while managing defensive positions to produce short-run growth and profits to meet the business's performance objectives.

Defensive strategic market plans play a critical role in the short-run profit performance of a business and in the protection of key strategic share positions that will support future profit performance. Strategically important share positions require a defensive strategic market plan to protect share position. This can include a protect share position in attractive markets in which a business has an average to strong competitive advantage. A protect market position defensive strategy can also include a strategy to improve customer retention, which, while maintaining a share position, can have a dramatic impact on profits with little or no change in sales revenue. A business may also use a reduced market focus strategy to more narrowly focus its resources in an effort to better defend a desired share position and improve the profits derived from this market.

To protect market share requires much more than a business-as-usual marketing effort. Market forces such as market growth rate, market share size, and competitor entry each create share-eroding forces that can cause share to decrease if not offset with improved competitive advantage or increased marketing effort. Declines in relative competitive advantage in the areas of new product sales, product quality, and service quality can also contribute to market share erosion. And decreases in marketing effort in the areas of sales force and marketing communications will adversely affect defensive strategic market plans designed to protect an important share position.

In situations in which a business is in either an unattractive market or has weak competitive advantage, it may elect to use an exit strategic market plan. If the business is profitable and capable of producing good short-run profits, a harvest strategy would be used. A harvest strategy could involve raising prices or reducing marketing resources or both. This type of defensive strategic market plan enables a business to slowly exit a market while maximizing short-run profits.

On the other hand, if a business is losing money or would like to free up resources at a faster rate, a divest strategy would be more appropriate. A divest strategy would normally seek to sell the business in order to maximize the value derived from the assets and goodwill created by the business. If there are no buyers, a business may simply have to use an accelerated harvest strategy. In some instances, a business may be prevented from exiting a share position because of legal or ethical considerations. Finally, companies tend to hold on far too long to businesses that should be divested. Holding on too long restricts the resources available to invest in offensive marketing strategies designed to improve sales revenue growth, share position, and future profit performance.

APPLICATION PROBLEM: AMAZON.COM

In 2001 Amazon.com was the largest Internet retailer and the top online reseller of books, videos, and music with annual sales of $3.12 billion. Despite losing money each of the last three years, Amazon.com successfully defended its market leadership position while growing net marketing contribution from $114 million in 1999 to $651 million in 2001, as shown in Figure 1. In the fourth quarter of 2001 Amazon.com made its first profit of $5 million.

FIGURE 1 Amazon.com Sales and Marketing Performance: 1999–2001			
Area of Performance	*1999*	*2000*	*2001*
Sales Revenues (millions)	$1,642	$ 2,713	$3,120
Revenue per Customer	$ 117	$ 136	$ 125
Percent Margin	17.7%	23.7%	25.3%
Margin per Customer	$ 20.76	$ 32.15	$ 31.57
Gross Profit (millions)	$290.6	$643.0	$789.4
Marketing Expense per Customer	$ 12.56	$ 9.00	$ 5.52
Marketing Expenses (millions)	$175.80	$180	$138
Customers (millions)	14	20	25
Marketing Expenses (% Sales)	10.7%	6.6%	4.4%
Acquisition Cost (millions)	$152	$ 78	$ 70
Retention Cost (millions)	$ 23.80	$102.00	$ 68.00
Net Marketing Contribution (millions)	**$114.83**	**$462.98**	**$651.36**

Amazon.com's success in defending its leadership position can be traced to the following strategic moves put in place over the past three years:

- **Expanding the product mix** as shown in Figure 2, which bolstered sales but more importantly improved percent margins as shown in Figure 1.

- **Reducing marketing expenses** as a percent of sales, which dropped from 10.7 percent in 1999 to 4.4 percent in 2001. This was due to lower acquisition cost per customer as well as lower retention cost per customer. Repeat business makes up over 73 percent of Amazon.com business up from 67 percent in 1999.

FIGURE 2 Amazon.com Sales and Product Mix			
Product Mix ($ millions)	*1999*	*2000*	*2001*
Books, Music, DVDs & Videos	$1,310	$1,700	$1,690
Electronics, Tools & Kitchen	$ 151	$ 484	$ 547
International	$ 168	$ 318	$ 661
B2B Services	$ 13	$ 198	$ 225
Total Sales	**$1,642**	**$2,700**	**$3,123**

- **Improving customer satisfaction** led to Amazon.com earning the highest customer-satisfaction score of any service company as measured by the American Customer Satisfaction Index for 2001. This made customer retention and attraction easier and hence more cost efficient.

For access to interactive software to answer the questions below go to www.RogerJBest.com or www.prenhall.com/best.

Questions

1. How would net marketing contribution and marketing productivity in 2001 been different if revenue per customer remained at the 1999 level ($117)?

2. How would net marketing contribution and marketing productivity in 2001 been different if percentage margin remained at the 1999 level (17.7%)?

3. How would net marketing contribution and marketing productivity in 2001 been different if marketing expenses as a percentage of sales remained at the 1999 level (10.7%)?

4. If Amazon.com can continue to grow at 5 million customers per year to 2005 (45 million), how will net marketing contribution change if the revenue per customer, percent margin, and marketing expenses (as a % sales) can be maintained to their 2001 levels?

Market-Based Logic and Strategic Thinking

1. How do defensive marketing strategies contribute to a business's performance objectives (sales growth, share position, and profit performance)?
2. What are the differences between defensive marketing strategies and offensive marketing strategies?
3. Why is it more difficult to protect market share in a high-growth market than in a slow- or no-growth market?
4. Why do share leaders have to work harder than share followers to protect share?
5. What are some of the key aspects of performance that would enable a share follower to achieve the same level of profits as share leaders?
6. What aspects of positioning and marketing effort can be managed to achieve a high profit with a reduced focus niche market strategy?
7. Why should a reduced focus niche strategy with above-average customer value deliver above-average profits?
8. How do defensive marketing strategies contribute to the long-run share position and profit performance of a business?
9. Compare defensive marketing strategies to protect a share position with strategies to exit a share position in terms of their contributions to short-run profit performance and the overall share position of the business.
10. Why would a business pursue a reduced market focus strategic market plan?
11. What is the primary objective of a reduced market focus strategic market plan?
12. Under what conditions would a business select an exit marketing strategy over a protect share position strategy?
13. When should a business pursue a harvest marketing strategy, and how could that strategy affect short-run profit performance?
14. When should a business pursue a divest marketing strategy, and how could that strategy affect short-run profit performance?
15. Why would businesses in harvest or divest share portfolio positions continue to support the businesses rather than harvest or divest them?

Notes

1. Donald Potter, "Strategy to Succeed in Hostile Markets," *California Management Review* (Fall 1994):65–82.
2. Sidney Schoeffer, "Market Position: Build, Hold or Harvest," PIMS Letter No. 3 (1978):1–10.
3. Philip Kotler and Paul Bloom, "Strategies for High-Market Share Companies," *Harvard Business Review* (November–December 1975):63–72.
4. Donald Clifford and Richard Cavanagh, *The Winning Performance: How America's High- and Mid-Size Growth Companies Succeed* (New York: Bantam Books, 1985).
5. Carolyn Woo and Arnold Cooper, "The Surprising Case for Low Market Share," *Harvard Business Review* (November–December 1982):106–13.
6. Robert Linneman and John Stanton Jr., "Mining for Niches," *Business Horizons* (May–June 1992):43–51.
7. Robert Hamermesh and Steven Silk, "How to Compete in Stagnant Industries," *Harvard Business Review* (September–October 1979):161–68.
8. V. Cook and R. Rothberg, "The Harvesting of USAUTO?" *Journal of Product Innovation Management* (1980):310–22.
9. Kathryn Rudie Harrigan, "Strategies for Declining Businesses," *Journal of Business Strategy* (Fall 1980):27.
10. George Seiler, "Colorful Chemicals Cuts Its Losses," *Planning Review* (January–February 1987):16–22.

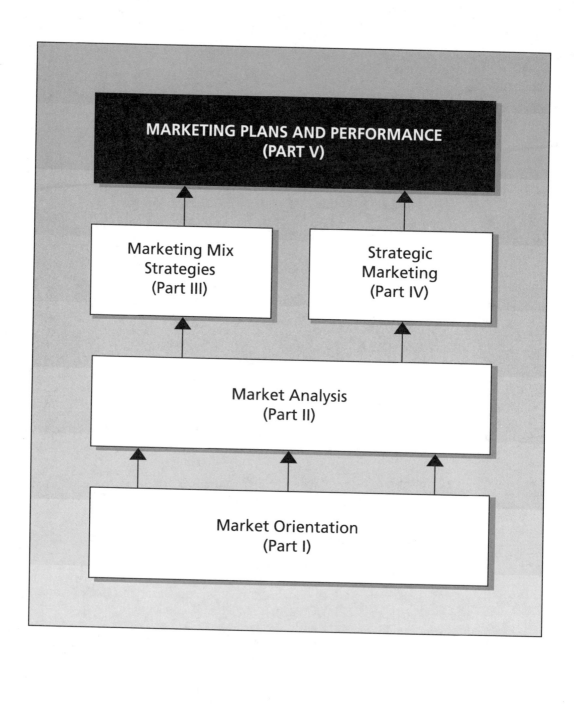

PART

V | MARKETING PLANS AND PERFORMANCE

*It is better to be prepared for an opportunity and not have one
than to have an opportunity and not be prepared.*
—WHITNEY YOUNG JR.

Given a specific strategic market plan and performance objectives, a marketing mix strategy and marketing plan must be developed and successfully implemented in order to move a business toward its planned performance objectives. Chapter 14 presents a process and structure for developing a marketing plan.

Chapter 15 addresses implementation of a marketing plan and the various forces that affect the success or failure of a marketing plan. Ownership, commitment, performance measurement, adaptation, and resource allocation are important aspects of market-based management and successful implementation. Process market metrics such as customer awareness, customer perceptions of performance, trial usage, and customer satisfaction are key market-based performance metrics that are tracked, along with end-result metrics that generally measure profit performance.

Finally, it is important that those in responsible marketing positions understand how marketing strategies individually and collectively affect net profit, cash flow, investment, and, ultimately, shareholder value. Chapter 16 carefully illustrates how each aspect of a marketing strategy ripples through the organizational maze of financial accounting to affect each aspect of profitability and, ultimately, shareholder value. Regardless of a business's assets, technology, and financial leverage, *there is only one source of positive cash flow, and that is the customer; everything else is expense.*

14 BUILDING A MARKETING PLAN

Stericycle, Inc. is in the business of recycling medical waste. It provides a safe, cost-effective, and environmentally friendly method for health care providers to dispose of their medical waste. From 1997 to 2000 Stericycle grew from a 5 percent market share to the market leader with 21.6 percent market share as shown in Figure 14-1.

The market was also growing at a rate of 14.3 percent per year. The combination of market growth and share growth allowed Stericycle to grow sales from $46 million in 1997 to $324 million in 2000. Profit margins also improved from 26.4 percent in 1997 to 39.3 percent in 2000. This allowed gross profits to increase from $12 million to $127 million in three years.

This level of growth also required an investment in marketing. As shown in Figure 14-1 the marketing expenses grew sixfold from $10 million in 1997 to almost $60 million in 2000. Much of this expense could be attributed to growth, as their customer base

FIGURE 14-1 Stericycle Performance: 1997–2000.

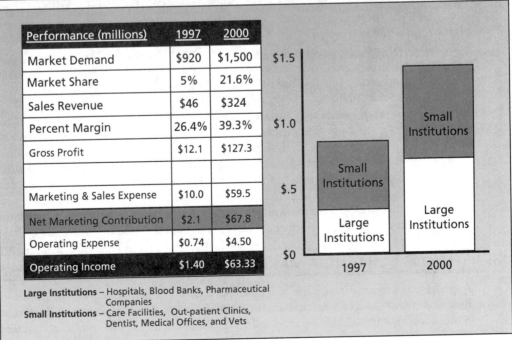

Performance (millions)	1997	2000
Market Demand	$920	$1,500
Market Share	5%	21.6%
Sales Revenue	$46	$324
Percent Margin	26.4%	39.3%
Gross Profit	$12.1	$127.3
Marketing & Sales Expense	$10.0	$59.5
Net Marketing Contribution	$2.1	$67.8
Operating Expense	$0.74	$4.50
Operating Income	$1.40	$63.33

Large Institutions – Hospitals, Blood Banks, Pharmaceutical Companies
Small Institutions – Care Facilities, Out-patient Clinics, Dentist, Medical Offices, and Vets

grew from 43,000 to 242,000 in three years. The net result of this marketing effort was tremendous gain in net marketing contribution from $1.4 million in 1997 to $67.8 million in 2000. This allowed operating income to grow at roughly the same rate.

With limited resources and multiple market opportunities, Stericycle needs to build a marketing plan that will address both these segments in a way that capitalizes on opportunities to grow sales and profits in a growing market. The purpose of this chapter is to do just that. We will first look at the process of building a marketing plan within the context of the market served by Stericycle, and then we will build a sample marketing plan for Stericycle, using publicly available information.

CREATIVITY VERSUS STRUCTURE

The market planning process is a delicate balance of creativity and structure. The opportunity to think creatively and explore market issues outside the realm of day-to-day business is an important part of developing a proactive marketing plan. On the other hand, a marketing plan has to have enough structure to ensure that it is comprehensive and accurate and that marketing strategies, resources, and performance objectives are credibly linked to the market situation.

Developing a marketing plan is similar to painting a picture. The creative use of light and color can make a picture interesting and appealing, but without some degree of form that adds meaning to the composition the picture may be intriguing but confusing. On the other hand, all form and no creative expression yields a sterile picture. The same is true for a marketing plan; both creative insight and structure are necessary to paint a meaningful picture of the market situation, marketing strategy, and logic-based path that leads to desired performance objectives.

Although a marketing plan is intended to help a business systematically understand a market and develop a strategy to achieve a predetermined set of strategic market objectives, there is a paradox between having no marketing plan and having a highly formalized marketing plan.[1] A business with no marketing plan completely forgoes the opportunity to uncover key market insights that are a direct result of the market planning process. At the other extreme, businesses with highly formalized processes often evolve to a level of filling out forms as a basis for a marketing plan.[2]

Both extremes diminish the opportunity to uncover meaningful market insights. What is needed is an *open system* that encourages exploration and creative insight and, at the same time, has a structure that ensures comprehensiveness and completeness. With an open system, marketing planners should act as facilitators in the planning process rather than as developers of a marketing plan.[3] As facilitators, they facilitate acquisition of information, coordinate schedules, manage progress, and ensure that the business's mission, customers, and goals do not get lost in the planning process. Although there are recognizable organizational hurdles, in general, businesses that use a formal planning process are more likely to achieve improved performance than are businesses that have no formal plan.[4]

BENEFITS OF BUILDING A MARKETING PLAN

A good marketing plan is an essential part of a proactive market orientation. Businesses with a strong market orientation are in continuous pursuit of customer, competitor, and market intelligence and work cross-functionally to create value-added customer solutions. While these activities are ongoing, however, there are important benefits that result directly from the process of developing a marketing plan, as well as the successful *implementation* of the marketing plan.

Identifying Opportunities

It is not the plan, but the process, that helps a business uncover new opportunities and recognize important threats. With a systematic evaluation of the market and internal capabilities, there is the opportunity to step back from day-to-day tactical marketing decision making and take a broader, more comprehensive view of the market and business situation.[5] K2, a ski manufacturer, for example, has become the market share leader in the American market for skis. A systematic evaluation of the American ski market showed that it was a mature market and that additional share penetration would be difficult. However, while performing this situation analysis, K2 was led to more fully recognize the emerging markets in snowboards and in-line skates. This discovery, in turn, led to new market entry strategies that are intended to provide new growth, a more diversified strategic position, and new sources of profit.

Leveraging Core Capabilities

As K2 aggressively enters the snowboard and in-line skate markets, it will be able to leverage its brand name and awareness in closely related markets. K2 will also be able to leverage existing manufacturing and engineering expertise, as well as sales and distribution systems that currently serve the American ski market. Thus, an important benefit to a carefully thought-out marketing plan is the greater utilization of existing assets, business and marketing systems, and unique capabilities.

Focused Marketing Strategy

Most markets are complex aggregates of many smaller markets and market *segments*. These segments can be broken down further into smaller market *niches*. Without a good marketing plan, a business could find itself vaguely positioned in a variety of market segments. This position results in going in all directions in the search for customers and not really being able to fully satisfy any of them.

A good marketing plan will delineate target customers such that the positioning strategy can be customized around the needs of the target segment and the marketing effort can be directed at these target customers. In this way, the marketing plan helps bring target customers into clearer focus. Charles M. Lillis, CEO of MediaOne Group, once stated: "I will know when our businesses have done a good job in market segmentation and planning when they can tell me who we should *not* sell to."

Resource Allocation

A well-defined target market focus is also cost-efficient. If you do not know who your customers are, you are going to spend a lot of time and money informing people who are not likely to buy, regardless of your marketing efforts. Or, if they do buy, they will be difficult to retain because your value proposition cannot deliver the customer satisfaction they desire. A good marketing plan will be more productive; it will take fewer dollars to accomplish performance objectives because there are fewer resources wasted on nontarget customers.

PERFORMANCE ROADMAP

A good marketing plan also provides a roadmap for both marketing strategy and expected performance. The marketing plan maps a business's projected market share, sales revenue, and profits over a specified planning horizon. This may sound like a fairly easy task, but the business world is complex, with many factors affecting the situation, strategy, and resources needed. Market conditions are complicated and constantly changing with respect to customer needs, competitor structure and strategies, and the environment within which the market operates. In addition, market information is often incomplete or inaccurate or both.

The environment *within* a business can also make the market planning process difficult. Marketing strategies are often driven internally by short-run profit objectives rather than by market-based performance objectives. Further, resources are often not allocated on the basis of strategy needs and performance objectives, but by organizational needs, political processes, and short-run need for profits. These factors and others make meaningful marketing plans difficult to develop and successfully implement.

BUILDING A MARKETING PLAN: PROCESS AND LOGIC

A good marketing plan is the result of a systematic, creative yet structured process that is designed to uncover market opportunities and threats that need to be addressed in order to achieve performance objectives. As illustrated in Figure 14-2, the development of a marketing plan is a *process,* and each step in the process has a structure that enables the marketing plan to evolve from abstract information and ideas into a tangible document that can easily be understood, evaluated, and implemented. This section is devoted to an in-depth discussion of each step in this process.

Step I: Situation Analysis

The marketing planning process outlined in Figure 14-2 starts with a detailed *situation analysis* of the market and business with respect to current market forces, the business's competitive position, and its current performance. The primary purpose of a detailed situation analysis is to uncover key performance issues that normally might go unnoticed in day-to-day business operations. First, we need to go deeper into the market and business situation with respect to understanding customer needs, competition, and channel systems, as well as business positioning, margins, and profitability, as outlined in Figure 14-3. A thorough situation analysis is required to uncover the key issues that affect performance.

The best place to start the situation analysis is with market demand. After a detailed analysis of market demand, we may find that the market is fully developed or that the total demand is small relative to the business's size and needs for growth. When this is the case, there may be little reason to go further in building a marketing plan for this product–market. Thus, an important place to start the analysis of a particular product–market situation is with an examination of the current market demand, maximum market potential, market growth rate, and factors limiting growth.

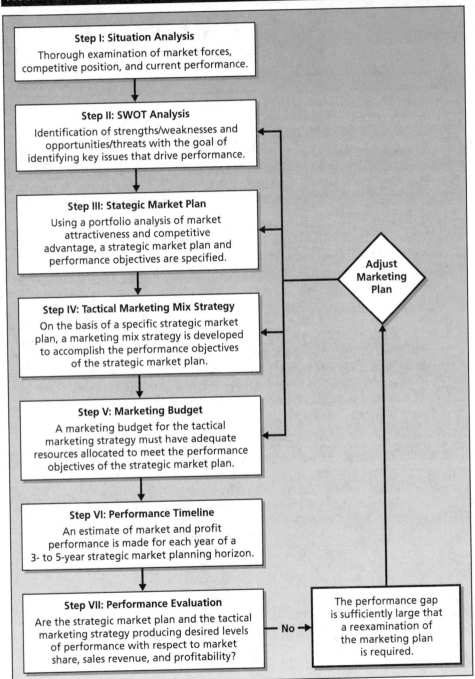

FIGURE 14-2 The Process of Building a Marketing Plan

Step I: Situation Analysis

Thorough examination of market forces, competitive position, and current performance.

Step II: SWOT Analysis

Identification of strengths/weaknesses and opportunities/threats with the goal of identifying key issues that drive performance.

Step III: Stategic Market Plan

Using a portfolio analysis of market attractiveness and competitive advantage, a strategic market plan and performance objectives are specified.

Step IV: Tactical Marketing Mix Strategy

On the basis of a specific strategic market plan, a marketing mix strategy is developed to accomplish the performance objectives of the strategic market plan.

Step V: Marketing Budget

A marketing budget for the tactical marketing strategy must have adequate resources allocated to meet the performance objectives of the strategic market plan.

Step VI: Performance Timeline

An estimate of market and profit performance is made for each year of a 3- to 5-year strategic market planning horizon.

Step VII: Performance Evaluation

Are the strategic market plan and the tactical marketing strategy producing desired levels of performance with respect to market share, sales revenue, and profitability?

Adjust Marketing Plan

— No →

The performance gap is sufficiently large that a reexamination of the marketing plan is required.

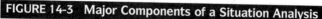

FIGURE 14-3 **Major Components of a Situation Analysis**

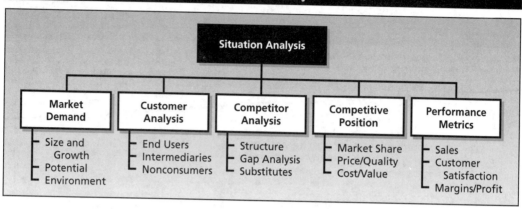

For example, the analysis of the market demand for medical waste recycling shown in Figure 14-4 would provide an excellent opportunity for Stericycle to grow sales revenues over the next five years. Market demand in dollar value was projected to grow by 50 percent. However, just as important in this situation analysis would be how the dollar value of the market demand is projected to shift to the alternate care segment. While the dollar value in the large institution segment is projected to grow, it is projected to grow at a much slower rate in the small institution segment. Both these observations (derived from the situation analysis) would be critical in shaping a strategic market plan and tactical marketing strategies for both segments of the medical waste recycling market.

Recognizing a good opportunity for growth and the segment differences uncovered in this portion of the situation analysis, Stericycle could further examine the needs and buying behavior of each segment to more completely understand the market situation. As shown in Figure 14-5, these segments are quite different in primary needs, price sensitivity, and

FIGURE 14-4 **Situation Analysis: Medical Waste Market Demand**

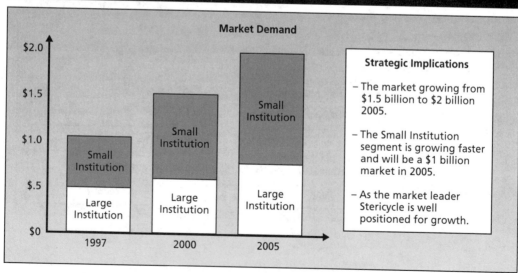

FIGURE 14-5 Situation Analysis: Medical Waste Market Segments

Segment Profile	Large Institution	Small Institution
Value Driver	Low Cost	Value-Added Service
Primary Benefit	Low Price	Easy & Safe Waste Disposal
Price Sensitivity	Very High	Low
Demographics	Hospitals, Blood Banks	Physicians Offices & Clinics
Waste Management Expertise	Above Average	Poor
Market Demand –2000	$500 million	$1000 million
Market Growth (next 5 years)	3.7% per year	7% per year
Number Customer	16,667	1,000,000
Revenue per Customer	$30,000	$1,000
Percent Margin	10%	50%
Margin per Customer	$3,000	$500

Strategic Implications

The "Large Institution" market segment is smaller, growing at a slower rate, more price sensitive, and has much lower margins. This segment is also more concentrated (ie fewer customers). The "Small Institution" market segment is twice as large, growing at twice the rate and is less price sensitive with margins five times greater than those in the Large Institution segment. Also, Stericycle's positioning better matches the needs of the "Small Institution" customer.

experience in managing medical waste. There are also important differences in customer buying and, as a result, significant differences in revenue and margin per customer. These insights are a key part of the situation analysis. Without them, the business is likely to follow an internal strategy based on experience and management perceptions of market needs.

To complete this phase of the market planning process, we must comprehensively examine each of the situational forces outlined in Figure 14-3. When a comprehensive representation of the situation analysis is complete, it is time to move on to identifying and prioritizing *key issues* that affect the business's performance objectives (share position, sales growth, and profit performance).

The "Large Institution" market segment is smaller, growing at a slower rate, more price sensitive, and has much lower margins. This segment is also more concentrated with fewer customers. The "Small Institution" market segment is twice as large, growing at twice the rate, and is less price sensitive with margins five times greater than those in the Large Institution segment. Also, Stericycle's product benefits better match the needs of the "Small Institution" customer.

Step II: SWOT Analysis and Key Performance Issues

The *SWOT analysis* is critical in summarizing key strengths and weaknesses, as well as opportunities and threats. It is important in this process that there be a strong linkage between the situation analysis and the SWOT analysis. These must be interconnected, not separate and distinct, parts of the market planning process. The steps that follow will be only as good as the situation analysis and key performance issues that are uncovered in the situation and SWOT analyses.

Perhaps the most difficult and elusive part of a marketing plan is the identification of key performance issues. A *key performance issue* is a problem or unaddressed opportunity that is an underlying cause that limits market or profit performance or both.

FIGURE 14-6   SWOT Analysis: Stericycle Medical Waste Markets

Strengths
- Market Leader/Well-Known
- Technology Advantage
- Many Locations
- 12 times larger than next largest competitor

Weaknesses
- Not price competitive in Large Institution market
- Low margins in Large Institution market

Opportunities
- Growing medical waste market
- Larger demand and faster growth in small institution market
- Competitor exit should make it easier to grow share

Threats
- Increase in government regulation
- Low margins in the large institution market
- Patent expiration

Strategic Implications

Stericycle is the technology leader and market leader with a market share 12 times larger than the closest competitor. Competitor exit will also aid share grow.

The best opportunity for profitable growth is in the Small Institution market segment.

Stericycle's key weaknesses are primarily associated with the Large Institution market segment.

In the process of sorting out key issues, it is useful to classify them as strengths and weaknesses or opportunities and threats. This is what is called a SWOT analysis. Shown in Figure 14-6 is a SWOT analysis derived from a situation analysis of the medical waste recycling market and Stericycle's position and performance in it. As shown, there are several strengths, weaknesses, opportunities, and threats that Stericycle needs to recognize in building a marketing plan for the medical waste recycling market. It is important that the business also understand the degree to which each of these key issues affects key performance metrics. Because the key issues will be the primary guideline to developing a tactical marketing strategy, it is important that these issues be carefully specified and articulated. This step in the market planning process is critical in terms of the marketing strategy to be developed and the potential impact it has on performance.

Step III: Strategic Market Plan

On the basis of the insights derived from the situation analysis and SWOT analysis, a *strategic market plan* must be developed. The primary purpose of a strategic market plan is to provide a *strategic direction* from which to set performance objectives and guide the development of a tactical marketing strategy.[6] This is an important step in the market planning process because it requires a careful examination of market attractiveness and the business's competitive advantage based on the information provided in the situation analysis.

By analyzing the forces that shape market attractiveness and competitive advantage, the business can create a product–market portfolio. Each product–market opportunity can be placed in the portfolio, as shown in Figure 14-7. On the basis of the relative portfolio position, a long-run market share objective must be specified for each product–market.[7] The alternate care segment is in a very attractive market with an average position of advantage. It represents the stronger strategic position and best opportunity for profit performance. This analysis and current performance indicate that an offensive strategic market plan to grow market share is appropriate.

FIGURE 14-7   Stericycle Strategic Market Plan

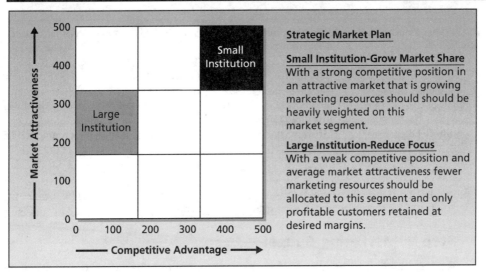

Strategic Market Plan

Small Institution-Grow Market Share
With a strong competitive position in an attractive market that is growing marketing resources should should be heavily weighted on this market segment.

Large Institution-Reduce Focus
With a weak competitive position and average market attractiveness fewer marketing resources should be allocated to this segment and only profitable customers retained at desired margins.

The large institution segment is less attractive but is still above average in overall market attractiveness and competitive advantage. However, in this segment, a defensive reduced focus strategic market plan is more appropriate given limited resources and the profit potential of this segment.

Step IV: Marketing Mix Strategy

The next step in the marketing planning process is the development of a *marketing mix strategy* to put the strategic market plan into effect. Although the overall marketing strategy to protect, grow, reduce-focus, harvest, enter, or exit a market position is set by the strategic market plan, more-specific tactical marketing strategies need to be developed for each of the key performance issues. Each element of a marketing mix strategy is a specific response to a key performance issue that exists within the context of the market situation. Thus, specific marketing strategies developed will be only as good as the key performance issues uncovered as an output of the situation analysis.

For example, given a strategic market plan of reduced focus for the large institution segment, Stericycle would need to develop a specific tactical marketing strategy. Outlined in Figure 14-8 is one approach to the marketing tactics that could be used to implement and achieve the performance objectives specified by the strategic market plan.

Note that the marketing mix strategy presented in Figure 14-8 is in direct response to key performance issues and is not vague. It is clear in its approach to addressing these issues and gives specific details with respect to target share, positioning, pricing, channel system, and the value proposition to be used in target market communications. This level of detail is required in order to evaluate the market and profit impact of this marketing mix strategy. A separate marketing mix strategy will also have to be developed for the large institution segment on the basis of its strategic

FIGURE 14-8   Stericycle Small Institution Segment Strategy

Small Instituion Segment Strategy—Market Penetration

Value Proposition:	*Providing medical offices and clinics with safe and easy disposal of Medical waste.*
Positioning Strategy:	Recognized for outstanding service, unquestionable safety, and customer satisfaction while priced at a premium over lesser competitors.
Channel Strategy:	Direct waste removal and mail-in waste packages will be used to collect medical waste processed at the closest Stericycle medical waste processing location.
Share Objective:	Grow market share from 22 percent in 2000 to 30 percent in 2005.

market plan, key performance issues, and performance objectives. This marketing mix strategy is presented in the complete Stericycle Marketing Plan later in this chapter.

Step V: Marketing Budget

Resources need to be allocated in a *marketing budget* based on the strategic market plan and the marketing mix strategy. Without adequate resources, the marketing mix strategies cannot succeed, and, as a consequence, performance objectives cannot be achieved. One cannot expect to grow share in the growing small institution segment without additions to the marketing budget. A reduced focus in the large institution segment should require fewer resources than a share growth strategy with respect to the marketing budget.

Specifying a marketing budget is perhaps the most difficult part of the market planning process. Although specifying the budget is not a precise process, there must be a logical connection between the strategy and performance objectives and the marketing budget.

There are three ways to build a marketing budget that is based on a specific strategic market plan and the tactical marketing strategy designed to achieve the target level of performance. Each is briefly described with respect to Stericycle:

- **Top-Down Budget:** A new marketing budget based on projected sales objectives is determined, using past marketing expenses as a percentage of sales.
- **Customer Mix Budget:** The cost of customer acquisition and retention and the combination of new and retained customers are used to derive a new marketing budget.
- **Bottom-Up Budget:** Each element of the marketing effort is budgeted for specific tasks identified in the marketing plan.

Sytericycle's marketing expenses in 2000 were $59.5 million and total sales were $324 million. Thus, the marketing budget was 18.4 percent of sales. This is a relatively high marketing budget as a percentage of sales but Stericycle is in a rapid-growth phase. If Stericycle's sales objective were $370 million in 2001, then a "top down" approach would yield a marketing budget of $68 million in 2001 using 18.4 percent of sales for estimating the marketing budget.

Because the rate of new customer acquisition can change the marketing budget required the "customer mix" approach to funding the marketing budget is probably a better approach. Based on new customer growth and assuming the acquisition cost per customer is five times the retention cost per customer, we estimate their acquisition cost to be $800 per customer and the retention cost $160 per customer. With these estimates we can reconcile the marketing budget for 2000 as shown:

$$\text{Marketing Budget} = \left(\begin{array}{ccc} \text{Acquisition} & & \text{Number} \\ \text{Cost per} & \times & \text{of New} \\ \text{Customer} & & \text{Customers} \end{array} \right) + \left(\begin{array}{ccc} \text{Retention} & & \text{Number} \\ \text{Cost per} & \times & \text{of Retained} \\ \text{Customer} & & \text{Customers} \end{array} \right)$$

$$\begin{aligned} \text{Marketing Budget 2000} &= (\$800 \times 32{,}500) + (\$160 \times 209{,}500) \\ &= \$26 \text{ million} + 33.5 \text{ million} \\ &= \$59.5 \text{ million} \end{aligned}$$

If Stericylce wanted to grow by 30,000 new customers in 2001, then the marketing budget needed would be $62.5 million as shown:

$$\begin{aligned} \text{Marketing Budget 2001} &= (\$800 \times 30{,}000) + (\$160 \times 242{,}000) \\ &= \$24 \text{ million} + \$38.7 \text{ million} \\ &= \$62.7 \text{ million} \end{aligned}$$

If Stericycle planned grow by only 20,000 new customers, obviously less marketing budget is needed for new customer acquisition. If this were the case, the 2001 marketing budget would be $54.7. This is $8 million less than the marketing budget needed in 2000. Thus, one can image how the marketing budget as a percentage of sales will decrease as new customer acquisition slows. When this occurs Stericycle's marketing expenses will be based primarily on customer retention.

$$\begin{aligned} \text{Marketing Budget 2001} &= (\$800 \times 20{,}000) + (\$160 \times 242{,}000) \\ &= \$16 \text{ million} + \$38.7 \text{ million} \\ &= \$54.7 \text{ million} \end{aligned}$$

A "bottom-up" approach would require specifying each marketing task and the amount needed to accomplish it given a particular strategic market plan and tactical marketing strategy. For example, we can estimate the bottom-up 2001 marketing budget for a strategy to grow by 30,000 customers as follows:

$8 million	Marketing Management (Marketing strategy, planning and administration
$30 million	Sales Force (customer account managers)
$2 million	Technical Support (customer problem solving and technical training)
$10 million	Customer Service (inside sales and customer administration)
$2 million	Customer Safety Literature(how to handle medical waste)
$5 million	Promotion (free sample and trial programs)
$10 million	Marketing Communications (print ads, direct mail and trade shows)

$67 million   Overall Marketing Budget

As shown, a bottom-up marketing budget provides for a break down of specific expenses for marketing management, sales force, technical support, customer service, customer safety literature, promotional samples, and marketing communications. Each item in the marketing budget has a specific objective and cost based on the strategy to grow customer volume by 30,000 customers. In this case for 2001 this is an estimated marlketing budget of $67 million.

When the new resources required are added to the existing base, a total budget for the marketing plan can be systematically derived. This bottom-up approach to setting the marketing budget is directly tied to a specific marketing strategy and performance objectives. Deviation from the resources required should be reconciled with the tactical marketing strategy and the intended impact on performance. If insufficient resources are available to fund a proposed tactical marketing strategy, then the strategy must be revised to reflect how the available resources will be used to achieve a desired, though reduced, level of performance in share, sales, and profitability.

Step VI: Performance Timeline

Given an adequate allocation of resources, a *performance timeline,* is critical in depicting performance levels for external market metrics and internal operating metrics over the planning horizon. This step must make explicit the timing of specific performance objectives (share position, sales revenue, and profit performance) so that the success or failure of the marketing plan can be evaluated. Performance metrics include external market metrics, such as customer awareness, customer satisfaction, product availability, perceptions of product and service quality, and market share, as well as internal profit performance metrics, such as sales revenues, contribution margins, total contribution, and net marketing contribution.

A Stericycle marketing plan to grow market share to 30 percent in a growing market will require additional marketing resources. Shown in Figure 14-9 is a five-year marketing plan which outlines how share growth is planned in conjunction with assumed rates of market growth. If successful, the marketing plan will grow sales revenues from $324 million in 2000 to $600 million in 2005. The marketing plan also outlines a priceplan which will grow the revenue per average customer from $1336 in 2000 to $1450 in 2005. However, without an adequate marketing budget there is no way a business can grow share in a growing market. The plan also projects new customer growth and customer retention. Using the average acquisition cost of $800 per customer and retention cost of $160 per customer a marketing expense budget is constructed for each year. As shown in Figure 14-9, marketing expenses will grow from $59.5 million in 2000 to $83.6 million in 2005. This results in a projected growth of net marketing contribution from $67.8 million in 2000 to $156.4 million in 2005.

The degree to which these estimates of projected performance are credible is directly related to the credibility of the key performance issues, strategic market plans, marketing strategies, and marketing budgets made to support specific tactical marketing strategies. If these linkages are not credible, then the numbers presented in the performance impact assessment are open to question.

Step VII: Performance Evaluation

Step VII, *performance evaluation,* involves the ongoing monitoring of market and profit performance, and comparisons with the performance timeline. If the marketing plan fails to meet the desired performance objectives specified as part of the strategic

FIGURE 14-9 Stericycle Marketing Performance Plan

Area of Performance	2000	2001	2002	2003	2004	2005
Market Demand ($million)	$1,500	$1,600	$1,700	$1,800	$1,900	$2,000
Market Share	21.6%	23.0%	25%	27%	29%	30%
Sales Revenues (millions)	$ 324	$ 368	$ 425	$ 486	$ 551	$ 600
Number of Customers	242,000	272,593	309,091	347,143	386,667	413,793
New Customers	32,500	30,593	36,498	38,052	39,524	27,126
Retained Customers	209,500	242,000	272,593	309,091	347,143	386,667
Revenue per Customer	$1,336	$1,350	$1,375	$1,400	$1,425	$1,450
Percent Margin	39.30%	39.50%	39.75%	40%	40%	40%
Margin per Customer	$ 525	$ 533	$ 547	$ 560	$ 570	$ 580
Gross Profit (millions)	$ 127	$ 145	$ 169	$ 194	$ 220	$ 240
Marketing Budget						
New Customer Acquisition (millions)	$ 26.0	$ 24.5	$ 29.2	$ 30.4	$ 31.6	$ 21.7
Customer Retention Cost (millions)	$ 33.5	$ 38.7	$ 43.6	$ 49.5	$ 55.5	$ 61.9
Marketing Expenses (millions)	$ 59.5	$ 63.2	$ 72.8	$ 79.9	$ 87.2	$ 83.6
Net Marketing Contribution (millions)	$ 67.5	$ 82.2	$ 96.1	$114.5	$133.2	$156.4

market plan, then the marketing plan has to be reevaluated with respect to all inputs used in the market planning process, as shown in Figure 14-2. These performance gaps require the business to consider several options. One is to reexamine the pricing, customer and channel discounts, unit costs, and the marketing budget to determine if, in fact, there are opportunities to improve performance.

A second alternative is to reexamine the entire marketing plan. Both the situation and the key performance issues would be reviewed to see if there are alternative tactical marketing strategies that would work better in achieving the desired performance objectives. Whichever the case, a credible marketing strategy must be linked to the market situation, key performance issues, and available resources, and then linked to projections of external market metrics and internal profit metrics.

And of course, a final option may be to refrain from pursuing this market opportunity further. It may be that none of the alternative marketing strategies considered can deliver, with credibility and confidence, the desired level of performance. When this is the case, the business is better off abandoning this market opportunity and allocating its resources and management time to other market opportunities.

SAMPLE MARKETING PLAN

To facilitate a better understanding of a marketing plan and the benefits of building one, a sample marketing plan for Stericycle is presented at the end of this chapter. The information used to construct the sample marketing plan shown here was taken from information publicly available in 1997 and 1998. All assumptions, inferences, analyses, and recommendations are mine, not Stericycle's.

Because of space limitations, not all of the supporting assumptions, analyses, and interpretations of the information are presented.

Step I: Situation Analysis

As shown in Figure 14-2, the first step in building a marketing plan is a situation analysis, which encompasses external and internal forces that shape market attractiveness, competitive position, and current performance with respect to share position, sales revenues, and profitability. Described below are the various situational forces I used in building the situation analysis. As shown in the sample marketing plan, each important aspect of the current situation is presented in one page and the implications it has for strategy development are discussed. Outlined below is a brief summary of the situation analysis, the first seven pages of the sample marketing plan.

- **Market Demand:** Presents the current and future level of market demand as well as Stericycle segment sales.
- **Market Segmentation:** Outlines a profile of each segment served by Stericycle with respect to segment needs, size, and growth rates, as well as revenue and margin per customer.
- **Industry Analysis:** Summarizes the industry forces that shape segment attractiveness and profit potential and presents an overall index of industry attractiveness for each.
- **Market Share and Customer Retention:** Presents Stericycle's current level of market share penetration and identifies the major forces that shape Stericycle penetration of this market.
- **Competition and Market Restructuring:** Presents a summary of the current competition and how the competitive landscape of this market will be restructured over the next five years.
- **Channel Systems and Marketing Budget:** Illustrates the channel systems used to reach target segments and the breakdown of the marketing budget with respect to the cost of customer acquisition and retention.
- **Market and Profit Performance:** Presents the market share, customer retention, and lifetime value of each segment as well as sales, margins, and profits currently obtained from each segment.

Although more aspects of the situation and greater detail could have been developed and presented, these situational forces and their respective strategy implications provide us the basis from which to identify key issues that affect performance, which is the next step in the process of building a marketing plan.

Step II: SWOT Analysis

The SWOT analysis is a summary of the key strategy implications uncovered in the situation analysis. The various strategy implications are categorized as a strengths, weaknesses, opportunities, or threats so they can be more fully comprehended. Then, from this SWOT analysis, the most important issues need to be identified and described more completely. Among the strategy implications presented in the SWOT analysis, these are the issues determined to have the greatest impact on future performance. Thus, it is important that these strategic issues be highlighted and become a central focus of the strategy to be developed. For the Stericycle sample marketing plan, the following is a brief description of the SWOT analysis that is presented on page 8 of the sample marketing plan.

- **SWOT Analysis and Key Issues:** Summarizes the strategic implications uncovered in the Stericycle situation analysis and identifies key issues to be addressed in the strategies to be developed.

Recognizing both the information presented in the situation analysis and the strategy implications derived in the SWOT analysis, we next must develop a strategic market plan for each segment.

Step III: Strategic Market Plan

Stericycle faces two market opportunities, one in the large institution segment and the other in the small institution segment. Because the resources in most businesses are limited and market opportunities vary in market attractiveness and potential for competitive advantage, a strategic market plan needs to be specified for each market segment. This process follows and is presented on pages 9 and 10 of the sample Stericycle marketing plan.

- **Strategic Market Assessment:** Market attractiveness and competitive advantage criteria are specified and weighted with respect to importance. On the basis of these criteria, each market segment is assessed and indexed with respect to market attractiveness and competitive advantage.
- **Portfolio Analysis:** A product–market portfolio is created based on the market attractiveness and competitive advantage for each market segment.
- **Strategic Market Plan:** On the basis of the portfolio position, situation analysis, SWOT analysis, and resources, a strategic market plan is specified for each segment.

The strategic market plan for each segment sets a strategic direction and implicitly specifies the short- and long-run performance expectations for each segment. The next step in building a marketing plan is to develop a marketing mix strategy for each target market.

Step IV: Marketing Mix Strategy

The strategic market plan for each segment and the situation forces presented in the situation analysis were used to develop the marketing mix strategy for each market segment, presented on pages 11 and 12 of the sample Stericycle marketing plan.

- **Large Institution Segment Strategy: Reduced Focus:** The marketing mix strategy (product, price, promotion, and place) recommended for this segment is a defensive strategy that is consistent with the strategic market plan specified for this segment and the situational forces presented in the situation analysis.
- **Small Institution Segment Strategy: Share Penetration:** The tactical marketing mix strategy recommended for this segment is an offensive strategy to aggressively build market share. As such, the marketing mix is quite different from the one specified for the large institution segment.

Marketing mix strategies provide the level of detail required to allow resource allocations in the marketing budget and to subsequently build a performance plan.

Step V: Marketing Budget

Producing a marketing budget is a critical step in building a marketing plan and one most businesses do not do a very good job on. Up to now the process of building a marketing plan was relatively free of risk and economic consequences. Now, it is time to resource each strategic market plan and supporting marketing mix strategy with a marketing budget. If this is not done correctly, the whole effort is subject to a higher probability of failure. The "customer mix" approach was used to develop the marketing budget that is summarized and presented on page 13 of the sample Stericycle marketing plan.

- **Resource Allocation and Marketing Budget:** On the basis of the market share objectives of each segment strategy and the respective cost of new customer acquisition and retention of existing customers, a marketing budget was created for each market segment over a five-year planning horizon.

The marketing budget for each segment is consistent with the market share objective for each segment over the next five years. Naturally, the large institution segment, with a reduced focus strategy, will require less marketing budget than the small institution segment, which hopes to more than triple its market share over the next five years.

Step VI: Performance Timeline

The last page of the sample Stericycle marketing plan is a performance timeline. The plan outlines for each segment how market share, sales revenues, margins, marketing expenses, and profitability will evolve over the five-year planning horizon. A brief description follows and is shown on page 14 of the sample marketing plan.

- **Performance Timeline:** The current performance with respect to market share, sales, margin, marketing expense, and net marketing contribution is reported for each segment. Then, on the basis of the strategic market plan and tactical marketing strategy for each segment, a five-year performance timeline is projected.

The performance timeline represents a close reconciliation between situation, strategy, and resource allocation. To the degree that this reconciliation is done accurately, the performance timeline provides a legitimate roadmap from which actual performance can be evaluated as the marketing plan is implemented over time.

Step VII: Performance Evaluation

The sample marketing plan built for Stericycle represents a strategic roadmap for navigation of two specific segment strategic market plans and tactical marketing strategies. As shown in Figure 14-2, after the marketing plan has been implemented, performance gaps are likely to emerge because of changing market conditions and the effectiveness of proposed marketing tactics. Addressing these performance gaps as they occur is a critical part of the marketing planning process. Modifying, adapting, and even abandoning the strategy for a segment are all part of the process of building and implementing a marketing plan. The next chapter is devoted specifically to successful implementation of a marketing plan.

Summary

A marketing plan is a roadmap. It carefully outlines where a business is, its desired destination (objectives), and the conditions it will face in its efforts to reach that destination. Understanding the market situation reveals a set of key issues that need to be addressed in order to reach the desired destination. Situation analysis and identification of key performance issues are key inputs to the marketing plan designed to accomplish a business's objectives.

The strategies developed in a marketing plan will not necessarily succeed just because they have been laid out. Resources in the form of people and money need to be allocated to implement strategies. If adequate resources are not available, attainment of a business's objectives may not be possible, and marketing strategies will have to be revised or abandoned. Thus, the process of developing a marketing plan is not that much different from planning an extensive vacation; it is just much more complex.

There are many benefits to a good marketing plan. The process of market planning can lead a business to discovery of new market opportunities, to better utilization of assets and capabilities, to a well-defined market focus, to improved marketing productivity, and to a baseline from which to evaluate progress toward goals. There is a planning paradox, however. It goes without saying that those with no marketing plans severely restrict themselves in achieving benefits, but it is also true that those with too highly formalized marketing plans may also minimize their potential of achieving benefits. The business with no marketing plan will not see the market around them and the opportunities and threats that need to be addressed while pursuing a market objective. Businesses with highly formalized plans can evolve to merely filling in forms and can thereby miss the opportunity to understand the subtler aspects of the market.

The development of a marketing plan involves process and structure, creativity and form. The process begins with a broad view of market opportunities that encourages a wider consideration of many market opportunities. For each market opportunity, a strategic market objective is set, based on market attractiveness and competitive advantage attained or attainable in the market. For each market to be pursued, a separate situation analysis and marketing plan is required. The situation analysis enables the business to uncover key issues that limit performance. These key performance issues are the basic guidelines from which marketing strategies are developed. Each aspect of the strategy must be scrutinized with respect to the market situation, key issues, strategies to address those issues, and the resources needed to achieve specific performance objectives. With the marketing strategy and budget set, an estimate of market and financial performance metrics must be projected over a specified time frame. If the marketing plan fails to produce desired levels of performance, the marketing strategy needs to be reexamined.

Market-Based Logic and Strategic Thinking

1. Why is a roadmap for a family vacation a good metaphor for the process of developing a marketing plan? What are the similarities and differences?
2. How would the process of developing a marketing plan help Stericycle achieve a higher level of sales growth and profitability?
3. Why would a business with a strong market orientation do a better job in situation analysis than a business with a poor market orientation?

APPLICATION PROBLEM: STERICYCLE, INC.

The marketing plan presented in this chapter is just one way to accomplish a specific strategic market plan. The proposed marketing plan is built around the goal of a 30 percent market share and certain assumptions about market growth and growth in revenue per customer. As a contingency, it would be useful to examine how alternative strategies and different market planning assumptions would impact net marketing contribution over the five-year planning period.

For access to interactive software to answer the questions below go to www.RogerJBest.com or www.prenhall.com/best.

Questions

1. What would be the profit impact (net marketing contribution) of a more conservative share penetration target of 25 percent by 2005? How would marketing expenses change as a percentage of sales with a more modest five-year share objective?

2. How would net marketing contribution change if the market did not grow and remained at $1.5 billion from 2000 to 2005 (assume a 30 percent share objective and all other assumptions remain the same)?

3. What would a "hold share" strategy look like? While retaining all other marketing plan assumptions, how would the sales, marketing expenses (as percent of sales), and net marketing contribution change if the market share was held at 21.6 percent over the five-year planning period?

4. How could businesses engaged in no market planning or in highly formalized market planning both miss meaningful market insights?

5. How would a business with a sound market planning process differ from a business with no marketing plan in the following:

   Discovering opportunities
   Leveraging existing systems, assets, and core capabilities
   Implementing a market-focused strategy
   Allocating resources
   Planning performance

6. Why does the first step in the market planning process involve a situation analysis?

7. What is the role of a SWOT analysis in the market planning process? What is the role of key issues in the SWOT analysis?

8. For each product–market opportunity, how is a strategic market plan determined?

9. How does the strategic marketing plan for a given product–market influence the marketing mix strategy for that product–market?

10. How are key performance issues identified in the SWOT analysis used in selecting a strategic market plan and building a marketing mix strategy?

11. Why is the development of a marketing budget so important to the success of the marketing plan?

12. What are the various ways one could develop a marketing budget for a given strategic market plan and supporting marketing mix strategy?

13. How should the resources needed to support a marketing plan be logically linked to the key issues, marketing strategies, and expected performance?
14. What is the purpose of the performance plan? What role should it play in the successful implementation of a marketing plan?

Notes

1. David Aaker, "Formal Planning System," *Strategic Market Management* (New York: Wiley, 1995), 341–53.
2. Arie Rijvnis and Graham Sharman, "New Life for Formal Planning Systems," *Journal of Business Strategy* (Spring 1982):103.
3. Henry Mintzberg, "The Fall and Rise of Strategic Planning," *Harvard Business Review* (January– February 1994):107–14; and Benjamin Tregoe and Peter Tobia, "Strategy versus Planning: Bridging the Gap," *Journal of Business Strategy* (December 1991):14–19.
4. Thomas Powell, "Strategic Planning As Competitive Advantage," *Strategic Management Journal* 13 (1992):551–58; Scott Armstrong, "The Value of Formal Planning for Strategic Decisions: Reply," *Strategic Management Journal* 7 (1986):183–85; and Deepak Sinha, "The Contribution of Formal Planning to Decisions," *Strategic Management Journal* (October 1990):479–92.
5. Philip Kotler, *Marketing Management: Analysis, Planning, Implementation and Control,* 7th ed. (Upper Saddle River, NJ: Prentice Hall, 1991), 62–72.
6. Gary Hamel and C. K. Prahalad, "Strategic Intent," *Harvard Business Review* (May–June 1989):63–75; and Michael Treacy, and Frederic Wiersema, "Customer Intimacy and Other Value Disciplines," *Harvard Business Review* (January–February 1993):84–93.
7. Rajan Varadarajan, "Product Portfolio Analysis and Market Share Objectives: An Exposition of Certain Underlying Assumptions," *Journal of the Academy of Marketing Science* (Winter 1990): 17–29.

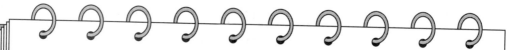

STERICYCLE MARKETING PLAN
2000-2005

Stericycle is the market leader in a growing market in which Stericycle is strategically positioned to dominate competition in the Small Institution Medical Waste Market. This marketing plan reconciles important assumptions with strategic market objectives and a marketing budget needed to grow market share from 21.6 percent to 30 percent and more than double marketing profits over the next five years.

Roger J. Best
Marketing Consultant

CONTENTS

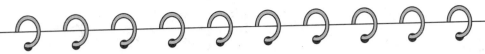

MARKET DEMAND

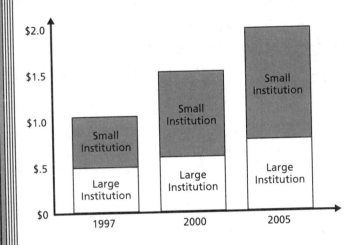

Strategic Implications

– The market growing from $1.5 billion to $2 billion 2005.

– The Small Institution segment is growing faster and will be a $1 billion market in 2005.

– As the market leader Stericycle is well positioned for growth.

MARKET SEGMENTATION

Segment Profile	Large Institution	Small Institutions
Value Driver	Low Cost	Value-Added Service
Primary Benefit	Low Price	Easy & Safe Waste Disposal
Price Sensitivity	Very High	Low
Demographics	Hospitals, Blood Banks	Physicians Offices & Clinics
Waste Management Expertise	Above Average	Poor
Market Demand-2000	$500 million	$1000 million
Market Growth (next 5 years)	3.7% per year	7% per year
Number of Customers	16,667	1,000,000
Revenue per Customer	$30,000	$1,000
Percent Margin	10%	50%
Margin per Customer	$3,000	$500

Strategic Implications

The "Large Institution" market segment is smaller, growing at a slower rate, more price sensitive, and has much lower margins. This segment is also more concentrated (i.e. fewer customers). The "Small Institution" market segment is twice as large, growing at twice the rate, and is less price sensitive with margins five times grater than those in the Large Institution segment. Also, Stericycle's positioning better matches the needs of the "Small Institution" customer.

MARKET SHARE

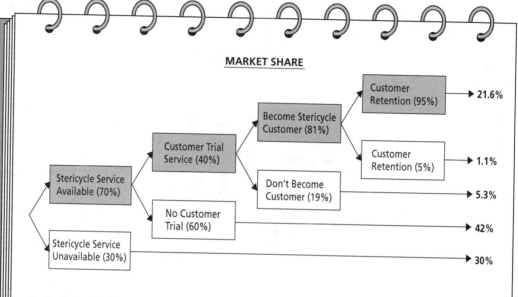

Strategic Implications

The biggest constraint to Stericycle's share growth is customer trial. Expanding locations will improve availability of Stericycle's service. However, a higher rate of customer trial where Stericycle is available will enable Stericycle to grow market share.

MARKETING CHANNELS

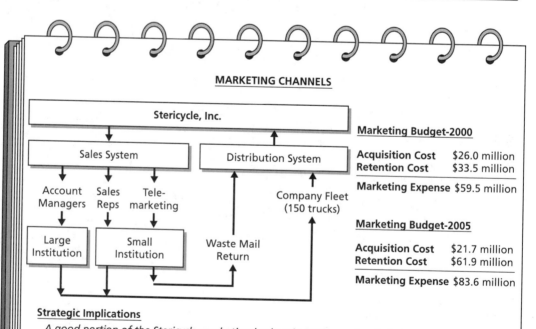

Marketing Budget-2000

Acquisition Cost	$26.0 million
Retention Cost	$33.5 million
Marketing Expense	$59.5 million

Marketing Budget-2005

Acquisition Cost	$21.7 million
Retention Cost	$61.9 million
Marketing Expense	$83.6 million

Strategic Implications

A good portion of the Stericycle marketing budget in 2000 was devoted to new customer acquisition. This will continue over the five-year planning period but diminish to a lower level of the overall marketing budget by 2005. The channel used to acquire new "Small Institution" customers is critical in gaining customer trial and delivering high level customer service and managing customer relationships.

SWOT ANALYSIS

KEY ISSUES

Stericycle is the technology leader and market leader with a market share 12 times larger than the closest competitor.

The best opportunity for profitable growth is in the Small Institution market segment.

Stericycle's key weaknesses are primarily associated with the Large Institution market segment.

Strengths
- Market Leader/Well-Known
- Technology Advantage
- Many Locations
- 12 times larger than the next largest competitor

Weaknesses
- Not price competitive in Large Institution market
- Low margins in Large Institution market

Opportunities
- Growing medical waste market
- Larger demand and faster growth Small Institution market
- Competitor exit should make it easier to grow share

Threats
- Increase in government regulation
- Low margins in the Large Institution market
- Patent expiration

Strategic Implications

The key issues can be directly linked to current positioning and performance. To the degree these issues are addressed in the marketing plan, Stericycle has the potential to achieve above average levels of profitable growth.

STRATEGIC MARKET PLAN

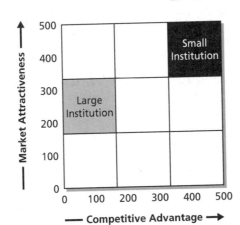

Strategic Market Plan

Small Institution – Grow Market Share
With a strong competitive position in an attractive market that is growing, marketing resources should be heavily weighted on this market segment.

Large Institution – Reduce Focus
With a weak competitive position and average market attractiveness, fewer marketing resources should be allocated to this segment and only profitable customers retained at desired margins.

Strategic Implications

The portfolio analysis yields two strategic market plans. In the Large Institution segment, Stericycle should focus on high margin customers and give up share to do so. In the Small Institution segment, Stericycle should invest to achieve market share penetration.

MARKETING BUDGET

Marketing Budget Items	2000	2001	2002	2003	2004	2005
Number of Customers	242,000	272,593	309,091	347,143	386,667	413,793
New Customers	32,500	30,593	36,498	38,052	39,524	27,126
Retained Customers	209,500	242,000	272,593	309.091	347,143	386,667

Marketing Budget	2000	2001	2002	2003	2004	2005
New Customer Acquisition (millions)	$26.0	$24.5	$29.2	$30.4	$31.6	$21.7
Customer Retention Cost (millions)	$33.5	$38.7	$43.6	$49.5	$55.5	$61.9
Marketing Expenses (millions)	$59.5	$63.2	$72.8	$79.9	$87.2	$83.6

Strategic Implications

Using a new customer acquisition cost of $800 per customer and the customer growth needed to achieve a 30 percent share in 2005 acquisition costs will continue to be a major portion of the Stericycle marketing budget over this planning period. Given this market share and the customer growth the marketing budget will grow from $59.5 million to $83.6 million in 2005.

PERFORMANCE PLAN

Area of Performance	2000	2001	2002	2003	2004	2005
Market Demand (millions)	$1,500	$1,600	$1,700	$1,800	$1,900	$2,000
Market Share	21.6%	23.0%	25%	27%	29%	30%
Sales Revenues (millions)	$324	$368	$425	$486	$551	$600
Number of Customers	242,000	272,593	309,091	347,143	386,667	413,793
Revenue per Customer	$1,336	$1,350	$1,375	$1,400	$1,425	$1,450
Percent Margin	39.30%	39.50%	39.75%	40%	40%	40%
Margin per Customer	$525	$533	$547	$560	$570	$580
Gross Profit (millions)	$127	$145	$169	$194	$220	$240
Marketing Expenses (millions)	$59.5	$63.2	$72.8	$79.9	$87.2	$83.6
Net Marketing Contribution	$67.81	$82.17	$96.12	$114.50	$133.24	$156.43

Strategic Implications

The proposed marketing plan is built around a 30 percent market share in 2005. To achieve this goal in a growing market will require the marketing budget to increase from $59.5 in 2000 to $83.6 million in 2005. The overall profit impact is net marketing contribution of $156.4 million by 2005.

CHAPTER

15

PERFORMANCE METRICS AND STRATEGY IMPLEMENTATION

A successful marketing plan provides a business with the roadmap it needs to pursue a specific strategic direction and set of performance objectives. However, this is just a plan; it does not guarantee that the desired performance objectives will be reached any more than having a roadmap guarantees the traveler will arrive at the desired destination. The marketing plan must now be successfully implemented.

A manufacturer of electric utility equipment engaged in an extensive market segmentation project in an effort to revitalize its sales and profitability. The effort revealed several market segments, all of which were reachable and judged to be attractive. A multi-segment strategy was developed with separate segment strategies for each market segment. However, the sales force was divided into three sales regions and had not been part of the segmentation study and strategy development. The marketing manager knew that without their support and commitment this marketing strategy would fail.

To successfully implement this strategy, the marketing manager had to sell the strategy to three regional sales vice presidents. Two of the VPs agreed to implement the strategy, but one elected not to become involved. The results, shown in Figure 15-1, illustrate the importance of effective strategy implementation. In the two sales regions

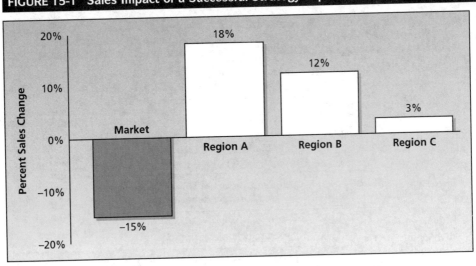

FIGURE 15-1   Sales Impact of a Successful Strategy Implementation

in which the marketing strategy was implemented, sales increased by 18 percent and 12 percent, in a market in which total demand declined by 15 percent. By contrast, there was only a 3 percent sales gain in the sales region that did not implement the marketing strategy.[1]

To achieve marketing success and reach target performance objectives, a business needs a good marketing plan and a well-executed implementation of the plan. A good marketing plan without a dedicated implementation effort will fail. This chapter will cover the forces that affect implementation of a strategy and a marketing plan, the importance of performance metrics, and the mechanics of a marketing plan variance analysis.

MARKETING PERFORMANCE METRICS

No matter how efficient a business's production operations, how expert its R&D, or how wise its financial management, if the customer doesn't buy or rebuy a business's products or services, marketing strategy will fail. As shown in Figure 15-2, market-based marketing strategies are designed to deliver customer satisfaction and retention. The degree to which a marketing strategy is successful will be detected first by market metrics that track customer satisfaction, retention, and perceptions of value; only subsequently will success or failure be observed in financial performance in the form of gains in revenue, total contribution, net profit, and cash flow. And, as shown in Figure 15-2, ultimately the results of a marketing strategy will affect shareholders in the form of earnings growth and expectations of improved future earnings.

The best the investment community can do is to report financial performance and expectations based on what the business says future performance will be. However, a business managed by a market-based management system is better able to detect and

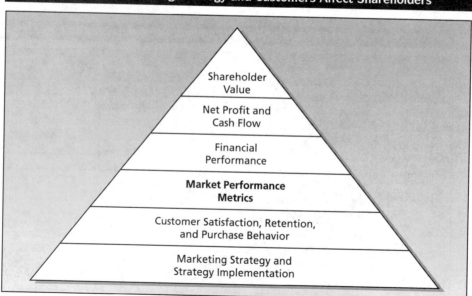

FIGURE 15-2 How Marketing Strategy and Customers Affect Shareholders

Shareholder Value

Net Profit and Cash Flow

Financial Performance

Market Performance Metrics

Customer Satisfaction, Retention, and Purchase Behavior

Marketing Strategy and Strategy Implementation

report future success by tracking market metrics, many of which *lead* changes in financial performance.

For example, an increase in the percentage of dissatisfied customers may not result in an immediate decrease in sales or net profits. First, dissatisfied customers often give a business a chance to correct the source of their dissatisfaction. Remedying problems quickly and meaningfully can often translate into improved customer loyalty. Second, it often takes time for customers to make a change in product or supplier. Thus, there is often a time lag between customer dissatisfaction (a market metric) and sales decline (a financial metric).

To illustrate the importance of market metrics in market-based management and its profit impact, consider the example in Figure 15-3. In period I, the business had no customer dissatisfaction and net profits of $5 million on sales of $50 million. The total variable cost was $25 million and fixed expenses were $20 million. In period II, 10 percent of the business's customers became dissatisfied. In this example, however, the business did not have a market-based metric that tracked customer dissatisfaction. Thus, there would be no reason for concern because sales and profits were at a normal and expected level.

In period III, dissatisfied customers began to leave the business, and sales slowly declined. During this period, all fixed expenses remained the same, but there was less profit margin produced, and, hence, both sales and profits were down. The business took action in period IV by cutting marketing expenses in proportion to lost net income with the goal of returning net profits to their previous level. But sales were still

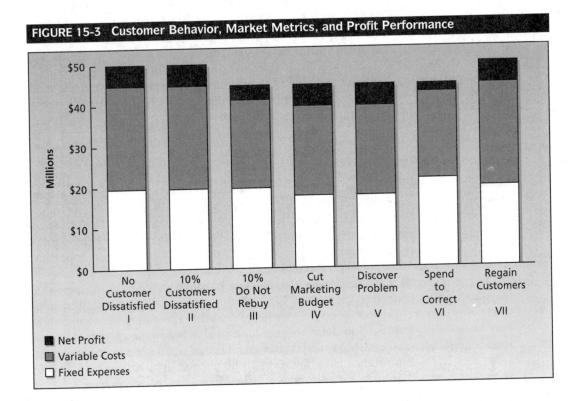

FIGURE 15-3　Customer Behavior, Market Metrics, and Profit Performance

down, and, in period V, the business created a task force to investigate the problem. The task force found that the customers that had been lost had left because of a particular source of dissatisfaction.

In period VI, the business restored the marketing budget and added budget to correct the problem and to replace lost customers. There were no immediate sales gains, and net profit decreased because of the increased expenses. However, finally, in period VII the business was back to where it had been in period I; no customer dissatisfaction, sales of $50 million, and net profits of $5 million.

That sequence of events could easily have occurred over three to five years. But a market-based business would have detected the problem in period II and would have immediately made corrections to restore customer satisfaction and retain its customer base. If the problem had been detected and corrected in period II, net profits over the seven periods would have totaled $35 million. The total in Figure 15-3 is $25 million. In other words, there were $10 million less in profit to reinvest in the business and contribute to earnings. In this way, stockholder value was diminished.

The purpose of this example is twofold: First, it points out the importance of market metrics that track customer behavior (remember, customers are the only source of positive cash flow). Second, it demonstrates that many market metrics are leading indicators of financial performance and an important market-based management tool that should contribute to better financial performance.

PROCESS VERSUS END-RESULT MARKET METRICS

Primarily, market metrics are ongoing measures of market performance. And, because many market metrics precede financial performance, using them is critical to strategy implementation and financial performance. However, not all market metrics are leading indicators of business performance. There are *process market metrics* and *end-result market metrics.*[2] Both are important, but process market metrics are particularly important because they are also leading indicators of financial performance.[3] End-result market metrics correspond more closely to internal financial performance metrics.

Process Market Metrics

Customer awareness, interest, product trial, customer satisfaction and dissatisfaction, along with perceptions of relative product quality, service quality, and customer value, all serve as process market metrics and leading indicators of end-result performance. Changes in each, positive or negative, precede actual changes in customer behavior. As a result, these in-process measures of customer thinking and attitude are important leading indicators of financial performance.

For example, perhaps customers are satisfied, but their perceptions of the value they derive from your product, relative to competing alternatives, are steadily diminishing. You may well have done nothing wrong to dissatisfy customers; the competition may have simply improved in delivering customer value based on a combination of total benefits and total cost. However, the net effect is that customer perceptions of the value created by your product have diminished. This change, in turn, opens the door to competitors' products that your customers may be inclined to try or purchase.

FIGURE 15-4   Customer Dissatisfaction and Customer Exit

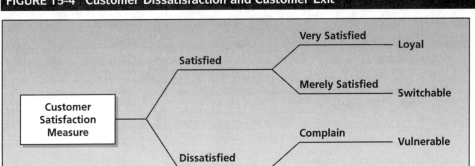

The whole purpose of process market metrics is to track customer perceptions and attitudes that precede changes in customer behavior and financial performance. For example, customer satisfaction is a process metric of considerable importance with many alternative measures.[4] As shown in Figure 15-4, measures of customer satisfaction can be broken down into different classifications. Very satisfied customers are loyal and buy in considerable amounts.[5] Merely satisfied customers are less loyal and more easily switch to competitors' products. Dissatisfied customers, of course, are likely to leave, although those who complain can be retained but remain vulnerable until the source of their dissatisfaction is adequately addressed. However, very few (less than 10 percent) dissatisfied customers complain,[6] and of those who do not complain, the majority stop buying from the business. And, because most dissatisfied customers do not complain, a business may not know it has a problem. Eventually, these customers leave, and to maintain sales and profits, the business has to attract new customers. Businesses that use measures of customer satisfaction effectively have a process metric that enables them to take corrective action in order to avoid adverse effects on financial performance.

Thus, a market-based business with several process market metrics will detect early adverse changes in customer attitudes and perceptions. With an early warning signal, the market-based business can take corrective action before customers alter their purchase behavior. Without process market metrics, this problem may go undetected and unresolved until after declines in financial performance, as was illustrated in Figure 15-3.

End-Result Market Metrics

End-result market metrics include market share, customer retention, and revenue per customer. Each of these metrics occurs simultaneously with financial performance metrics. However, each provides a different set of performance diagnostic insights. For example, let's assume sales revenues are increasing and ahead of forecast, and financial performance is also better than expected. Most businesses would feel pretty good about their performance. However, if end-result performance metrics show that the business is losing market share in a growing market, and poor customer retention is

FIGURE 15-5 Customer Retention is a Key End-Result Market Metric

Business Performance	80% Retention	90% Retention	Performance Gain
Customer Demand	1,000,000	1,000,000	None
Market Share	20%	20%	None
Customer Volume	200,000	200,000	None
Revenue per Customer	$460	$480	+$ 20
Total Revenue (millions)	**$ 92**	**$ 96**	+$4 Million
Retained Customers	160,000	180,000	+20,000
Revenue per Customer	$500	$500	None
Cost per Customer	$200	$200	None
Margin per Customer	$300	$300	None
Total Contribution (millions)	**$ 48**	**$ 54**	+$6 Million
New Customers	40,000	20,000	−20,000
Revenue per Customer	$300	$300	None
Cost per Customer	$400	$400	None
Margin per Customer	−$100	−$100	None
Total Contribution (millions)	**−$ 4**	**−$ 2**	+$2 Million
Overall Total Contribution	$ 44	$ 52	+$8 Million
Marketing Expenses	$ 15	$ 16	+$1 Million
Net Marketing Contribution	**$ 29**	**$ 36**	+$7 Million

masked by new customer growth, there should be concern. Without end-result market metrics, the business has only an internal measure of performance.

Even for a business that is not losing market share, poor customer retention has a powerful impact on financial performance, as illustrated in Figure 15-5. In this example, a business with a 20 percent market share and a 90 percent level of customer retention, produces 24 percent more net marketing contribution than the same business with an 80 percent customer retention.

Because existing customers generally spend more than new customers and the cost of serving an existing customer is less than that of acquiring and serving a new customer, the margin per customer is generally different. In this example, an existing customer produces $300 of margin per year, whereas a new customer results in a net loss of $100 per year. Retaining a larger percentage of existing customers improves total contribution and net marketing contribution even when an additional $1 million is added to marketing expenses for a customer retention program. Overall, the assets increase a little because higher revenues result in proportionately higher accounts receivable. However, return on assets still increases from 18 percent to over 30 percent.

Thus, the combination of market share, customer retention, and revenue per customer provides a totally different picture of performance than financial performance metrics. Both financial and market metrics are important, and each provides a different insight into business performance and successful implementation of a marketing plan.

FIGURE 15-6 Successful Implementation of a Marketing Plan

SUCCESSFUL STRATEGY IMPLEMENTATION

Even if a flawless marketing plan could be developed, there would still be no guarantee that the marketing strategy and marketing plan would succeed in meeting the desired performance metrics. The marketing plan must still be successfully implemented. It is very difficult to implement a poor marketing plan; but it is still possible to fail to implement a good marketing plan. Shown in Figure 15-6 are three major forces that contribute to success or failure in implementing a marketing plan. As shown, each of these major forces has specific factors that contribute to the degree to which that force either positively or negatively affects the implementation of the marketing plan. Collectively, these factors will shape the behavior and organizational structure in a way that facilitates successful implementation.[7]

Owning the Marketing Plan

Perhaps the most common reason a marketing plan fails is a lack of *ownership*. If people do not have an ownership stake and responsibility in the marketing plan, it will be business as usual for all but a frustrated few. As shown in Figure 15-6, the ownership of a market plan can be enhanced with *detailed action plans, a champion and ownership team, compensation based on performance metrics,* and *top management involvement.*

Detailed Action Plans

The development and use of detailed action plans may be the single most effective market management practice in determining the success of a marketing plan. A detailed action plan involves each aspect of the marketing strategy, but in greater detail with respect to specific actions that have to occur for the marketing plan to be implemented. Figure 15-7 outlines how a particular tactical marketing strategy within a marketing plan will be implemented. In this case, the strategy is broken down into five important action items, each of which must occur for this aspect of the marketing plan to succeed. As shown, for each of the five action items specified, an individual is assigned a specific responsibility, a measure or goal is delineated, and a time frame within which the action item should be completed is agreed upon.

FIGURE 15-7 Detailed Action Plan for a Channel Strategy

Marketing Strategy To create adequate end user product availability, 80 manufacturers' reps and five missionary salespeople will be used to sell and distribute our product to 5,000 industrial supply houses.

No.	Action Item	Responsibility	Measure	Time Frame*
1.	Identify target supply houses and establish contracts.	P. Elliot	5,000 Dealers	12 months
2.	Contact manufacturer reps.	T. Smith	80 Reps	6 months
3.	Hire missionary sales force.	P. Wilson	5 People	3 months
4.	Develop rep training program.	S. Bradley	Program Pilot	6 months
5.	Develop dealer training program.	R. Otto	Program Pilot	6 months

*From time of implementation.

Any number of action items could be added to this action plan, but the important point is that significant elements of this strategy have specific ownership. In this way, individuals have ownership and are accountable for implementing a portion of the marketing plan. Assigning responsibility enables a business to break the "business as usual" routine and fosters successful implementation of the marketing plan.

Champion and Ownership Team

Whereas laying out individual responsibilities in the detailed action plan is a way to get a wide range of people involved in implementation, every successful marketing strategy has a *champion:* a person who is devoted to the successful implementation of the marketing strategy and marketing plan. And, although there is nothing wrong with having a single owner or champion, the creation of an *ownership team* can leverage the unique talents of multiple people and exert more organizational leverage than a single individual.[8] With a champion and an ownership team in place, the implementation process can stay on track even when some members of the team are gone for extended periods of time because of business trips, training programs, sickness, or vacations.

Compensation

Most people respond to financial rewards. Tying the compensation of those principally responsible for implementation of the marketing plan to performance metrics increases the incentive to successfully implement the marketing plan. Compensation can be tied to both external market metrics and internal financial metrics, which will be discussed later in this chapter. Market metrics are most important in the early stages of marketing plan implementation. Market metrics such as end-customer awareness and interest, product availability, and trial are market behaviors that must occur before financial metrics such as sales revenue, total contribution, net marketing contribution, and net profit can occur. The overall goal of compensation tied to market metrics is to create motivation and responsibility.

Management Involvement

Senior managers must stay committed to their involvement with the marketing plan and to their review of its progress. When top managers lessen the time available to review the marketing plan and performance, they send an implicit signal of lack of interest and support. This signal weakens the motivation of the ownership team and the chance for successful implementation.

Supporting the Marketing Plan

Though there are potentially many factors that could affect the degree to which a business is committed to a marketing plan, *time to succeed, resource allocation, communication,* and *skills to succeed* are critical[9].

Time to Succeed

In many instances, commitment to a marketing plan weakens when financial performance is not on track. Without meaningful market metrics, a business may pull support for a marketing plan without knowing why it is not working. It may be that the marketing strategy and plan are very good, but implementation has been poor. It may also be that the market metrics are on target but that it simply may take more time for financial metrics to respond to desired or target levels.

Time to succeed will, in part, depend on the marketing strategy and the nature of the market opportunity. A share penetration strategy in an existing market should take less time to succeed than a strategy to enter a new market that is undeveloped. In either case, the time to succeed, along with market metrics that signal progress, are important aspects of commitment to the marketing plan and successful implementation.

Resource Allocation

If the process and structure of marketing planning are followed as described in chapter 14, the marketing plan should be allocated sufficient resources with respect to personnel and funding. If less than the required resources are reserved for the marketing plan, the chances for success are greatly reduced. Of course, if the resources needed are not systematically determined in the marketing planning process, it is even more likely that the marketing plan will be underresourced. (It is rare that marketing plans are overresourced.) Thus, an important step in successful implementation is to ensure that the resources needed are fully committed to support implementation of the marketing plan.

Communication

It is difficult to get support either *internally,* within the company, or *externally,* from the market, if the marketing plan and its strategic intent are not aggressively communicated. Although senior management and the market management team are likely to fully understand the logic and tactics of the marketing plan, others—in sales, customer support, manufacturing, and finance—may not understand the strategic objectives and marketing strategy being implemented. As a result, these employees, who may play key roles in successful implementation, will continue in a business-as-usual mode of operation. To facilitate communication and understanding, some businesses have created videos for employees describing strategic market objectives and the marketing strategy.

Internal communication of a marketing plan, including the specific role individuals within the business play with respect to the market plan, is critical. To the degree possible, these job functions should be integrated into detailed action plans, as described earlier. In this way, key individuals understand their roles and responsibilities in the successful implementation of the market plan.

External communication of the marketing plan is also critical. Each of the following groups must be made aware of different aspects of the marketing plan:

- **Target Customers:** Need to be made aware of the benefits of the product, the value proposition, and where the product can be acquired.
- **Channel Intermediaries:** Need to understand target customers, their profit potential, and inventory, sales, and service requirements.
- **The Trade Press:** Needs to be informed as to product benefits and availability of the product.
- **Market Influencers:** Must be informed. These could include consultants, financial analysts, or others who influence customers and channel intermediaries.
- **The General and Business Press:** Must receive news releases that can further communicate the market plan to potential customers, distributors, and investors.

Of course, the extent to which external market communications are engaged depends on the nature of the marketing strategy and product. A new product made to more effectively treat metal-working fluids in small machine shops would not interest most consumers, the general press, or even the business press. However, trade press publishers, consultants, the EPA (Environmental Protection Agency), and others may be interested in promoting awareness of a new product that greatly reduces the problems of disposal of hazardous waste, lowers the cost of disposal, and improves working conditions.

Required Skills

Do those implementing the marketing plan have the required skills to effectively implement the marketing plan?[10] For example, a bank wanting to improve customer satisfaction and retention may have to do some training to communicate new policies and customer-oriented employee attitudes. Two of the five action items detailed in Figure 15-7 involved training. For that marketing strategy to succeed, it was essential that manufacturers' reps and distributors were trained with respect to product knowledge, service requirements, how to sell the product, and how to explain the value derived from this product. Without a training effort, this strategy would likely not succeed.

In many instances, even members of the management team may need additional training to successfully implement the marketing plan. A business implementing a program to get more new product sales may need to provide some management training on the new product. Without the necessary skills, the management team might produce a meaningful objective but have no way of successfully accomplishing it.

Adapting the Marketing Plan

The marketing planning process does not stop when marketing plan implementation begins; it continues through strategy implementation. As do all systems, a marketing plan needs to be adapted to survive changing or unanticipated conditions. To survive, as well as to succeed, the marketing plan needs to be *adaptive*. Four factors that contribute to the adaptive nature of a marketing plan are *continuous improvement, feedback measurements, persistence,* and *adaptive roll-out* of the marketing plan.

Continuous Improvement

A marketing plan that is not adapted to unexpected or changing market conditions will fail. Because market conditions are complex and changing, a business must be flexible in modifying its marketing plan to adapt to the changing market conditions. In many instances, these may be small changes, made in order to more finely tune the business's marketing strategy and value proposition. However, in some cases, a major shift in marketing strategy may be required.

The term *adaptive persistence* has been attributed to the success of many Japanese marketing strategies. One of Japanese management's greatest assets is their ability to adapt when a marketing plan is not working and to stick with it—to *persist*. The whole concept of continuous improvement is implicit in Japanese marketing plan implementation. While the marketing plan sets the direction and provides the initial roadmap, once it is in place, the flexibility to adapt is an important aspect of continuous improvement.

Feedback Measurements

An essential element of any adaptive system, whether mechanical, electrical, or human, is feedback. Mechanical, electrical, and human systems have built-in sensors and feedback systems. Management systems also require measurements to provide a mechanism for feedback. Measurements of process-oriented market metrics play the role of a sensor in a marketing plan feedback system. These measurements signal the status of the marketing plan with respect to progress toward end-result metrics such as sales, market share, total contribution, and net profit.

Key process metrics that provide leading signals as to the success of the marketing plan and implementation include:

- Customer awareness, interest, intentions to buy, trial, and repeat purchase.
- Intermediary market coverage, interest, support, and motivation.
- Business responsiveness to customer inquiries and problems.

Each of these market metrics has to reach an effective level of performance before financial metrics can begin to perform. The importance of market metrics is twofold. First, they provide an early signal as to the progress of the marketing plan. If market metrics are behind target performance levels specified in the marketing plan, then financial metrics and profit performance will be slower to materialize than projected. Second, the market metrics provide a signal as to which aspect of the marketing plan is not working. Is it the channel system, the communications strategy, or the product-price positioning strategy that is the cause of poor market performance? Each of these could trigger different strategies designed to better adapt the marketing plan to market conditions.

Persistence

One of the great traits of Japanese managers is their inherent ability to adapt and persist throughout the implementation of the marketing plan. Rarely have Japanese marketing strategies worked initially. However, Japanese marketing managers remain committed to the strategic market objective and persist by adapting their market plans. Quite often, their marketing strategies need to be modified, but it is their determination to make them work that underlies the secret of their market success.

On the other hand, American managers are often quick to drop a marketing strategy and plan when it meets the first bit of resistance. Perhaps expectations of performance have been overstated—or time to succeed misspecified. Whichever the case, marketing strategies developed in a corporate office often lack the realism of the marketplace and may need to be adapted during implementation. Without a high degree of management persistence, there is little chance of successful implementation, particularly when aspects of the marketing plan need to be modified.

Adaptive Roll-Out

There are many benefits to a regional roll-out as opposed to a nationwide launch, and it signals a business's marketing strategy to competitors as effectively. First, fewer resources are required in a small-scale regional launch of a marketing plan than in a nationwide launch. Second, problems with distributors, marketing communications, and product positioning can more readily be addressed and corrected on a small scale. Third, if the marketing plan is more effective than planned, additions can be made to production capacity without the potential of stockout and the loss of opportunities to capture customers when they want to buy. Fourth, even for a marketing plan that is tracking as planned on a regional basis, additional marketing insights will result that can be opportunistically integrated into the marketing plan as full marketing plan implementation is pursued. And fifth, the financial metrics generated from a successful roll-out signal long-run profit potential and can be used to help fund the full introduction. Because of these benefits, many foreign competitors have used regional roll-outs upon entering the American market.

Many American businesses, however, do not want to take the time to engage in a corrective roll-out of a marketing plan. However, it is rare that a marketing plan will succeed as conceived on paper. At risk are customers and distributors who might lose interest in the business's value proposition when it is ineffectively presented. In addition, the cost of a full market introduction when things go wrong is enormous, even when customers and distributors are retained through the repositioning period.

Assessing Marketing Plan Implementation

No single factor presented in Figure 15-8 will make or break the successful implementation of a marketing plan. However, when the sum of these factors is adequately addressed, the chances for successful marketing plan implementation are greatly improved. Shown in Figure 15-8 is a summary of these factors and a profile of a business that worked to improve its marketing plan implementation. Although this business did not perform well on every factor, it performed much better than it had in past efforts. This level of implementation effort, along with a good marketing strategy and marketing plan, will enable the business to achieve a market success well beyond planned performance, and in a much shorter time than expected.

At the heart of successful implementation of a marketing plan is a business's market orientation. The greater the degree to which the business has built a market-based organization, the more likely is successful marketing plan implementation.[11] A market-based business with a strong customer focus and competitor orientation that works well across functions has a greater level of market sensitivity and urgency from which to both develop and implement a marketing plan.

FIGURE 15-8   An Assessment of Marketing Plan Implementation

Owning the Plan
- Detailed Action Plan — None ▪ _ _ _ _ _ □ Extensive
- Ownership — None _ ▪ _ _ _ _ _ □ Champion
- Compensation — None _ ▪ □ _ _ _ _ Performance-based
- Management Involvement — None _ _ _ ▪ _ □ _ High

Supporting the Plan
- Time to Succeed — Inadequate _ ▪ _ □ _ _ _ Sufficient
- Resource Allocation — Insufficient _ ▪ _ □ _ _ _ Sufficient
- Communication Effort — None _ ▪ _ _ □ _ _ Thorough
- Required Skills — Poor _ _ ▪ _ □ _ _ Exceptional

Adapting the Plan
- Continuous Improvement — None _ ▪ _ _ _ □ _ Ongoing
- Feedback Metrics — None ▪ _ _ □ _ _ _ Extensive
- Persistence — None _ _ ▪ _ □ _ _ Relentless
- Roll-out — Full Launch _ ▪ _ □ _ _ _ Roll-out

▪ Past Efforts
□ Current Efforts

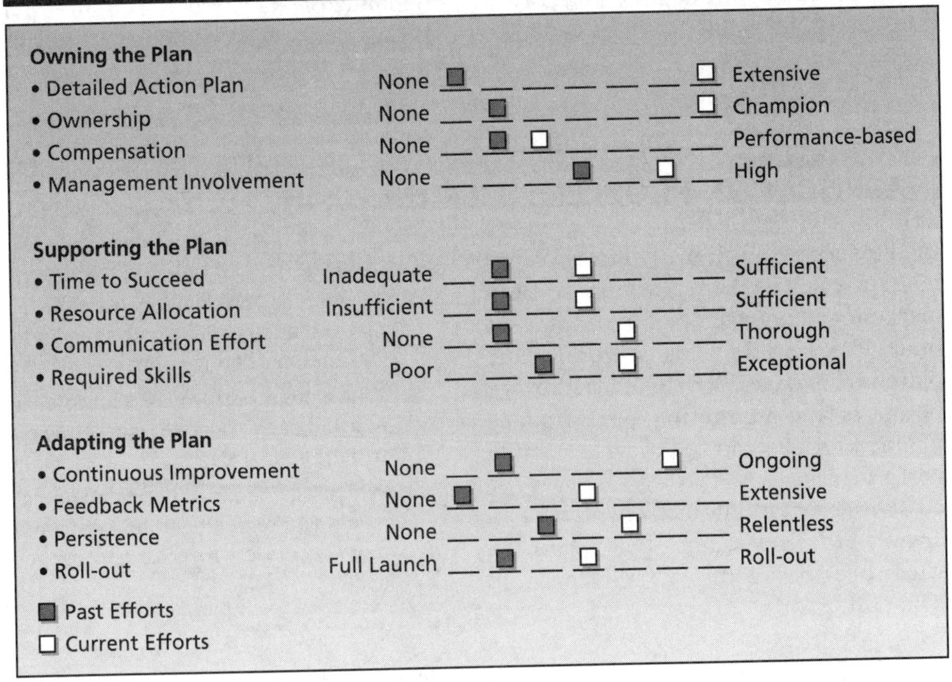

Summary

Developing a sound marketing plan is only the first half of achieving market success. The marketing plan must be successfully implemented. Without ownership, support, and adaptation, the marketing plan will fail. Detailed action plans, a market plan champion or ownership team, performance-based compensation plans, and top management involvement contribute to ownership of the marketing plan and provide a better chance for successful implementation.

Successful marketing plan implementation also requires time to succeed, sufficient resources, communication, and skills. In addition, numerous unanticipated problems and obstacles will arise during implementation. These require that marketing plans be adaptive. Continuous efforts to improve the marketing plan, based on feedback measures, are an important part of successful implementation. In addition, businesses that are persistent in adapting their marketing plan have a greater chance for success. And a regional roll-out of the marketing plan provides a less expensive venue for adapting the marketing plan.

Performance metrics play a key role in marketing plan implementation. There are market performance metrics and financial performance metrics. Market metrics are external measures of market performance, such as awareness, customer satisfaction, and market share. Financial performance metrics are internal measures of performance such as unit margin, net profit, and return on investment. Market performance metrics, however, include both process metrics and end-result metrics. Customer awareness, perceived performance, and customer satisfaction are process performance metrics that occur ahead of end-result performance metrics such as sales, market share, net profit, and return on investment. Process market metrics play an important role in the early signaling of the success or failure of a marketing plan and its implementation effort.

APPLICATION PROBLEM: STERICYCLE, INC.

In the second edition of this book we made a year 2000 forecast based on a marketing plan developed in chapter 14, much like we did in this edition for the planning period 2000 to 2005. Shown below is the marketing performance planned for 2000 and Stericycle's actual performance.

For access to interactive software to answer the questions below go to www.rogerjbest.com or www.prehall. com/best.

Questions

1. What areas performed better than planned and how did each contribute to 2000 net marketing contribution?

2. Which areas performed below plan and how did each affect net marketing contribution in 2000?

3. Which aspect of marketing planning would you recommend be improved to more accurately forecast performance in 2005?

Area of Performance	2000 Plan	2000 Actual	Performance Gap
Market Demand (millions)	$1,300	$1,500	$200
Market Share	16%	21.6%	5.6%
Sales Revenues (millions)	$208	$324	$116
Customer Volume	208,000	242,515	34,515
Revenue per Customer	$1,000	$1,336	$336
Percent Margin	41.00%	39.30%	−1.7%
Margin per Customer	$ 410	$ 525	$115
Gross Profit (millions)	$ 85	$ 127	$ 42
Marketing Expenses (millions)	$ 52	$ 59	$ 7
Marketing Expenses per Customer	$ 250	$ 245	($ 5)
Net Marketing Contribution (millions)	**$ 33.3**	**$ 67.9**	**$34.6**

Market-Based Logic and Strategic Thinking

1. Why is implementation as important as marketing plan development in achieving market success?
2. How do detailed action plans contribute to individual ownership of a marketing plan?
3. Why does a marketing plan need a champion or an ownership team?
4. How should a business tie compensation to successful implementation of a marketing plan?
5. Why is time to succeed an important element of commitment to a marketing plan?
6. What kind of signal is management sending when it does not have time to review a marketing plan and its performance?

7. What is meant by persistence in terms of commitment? What is meant by the term *adaptive persistence* as it is often used to describe the Japanese style of marketing plan implementation?
8. Why are continuous improvement and feedback measures important aspects of successful marketing plan implementation?
9. What are the advantages and disadvantages of a regional roll-out of a marketing plan?
10. What role do resources, organizational communications, and training play in the support and successful implementation of a marketing plan?
11. Why are performance metrics important?
12. What is the difference between a market performance metric and a financial performance metric?
13. Why are process metrics an important part of the implementation process? What is the relationship between process metrics and end-result metrics?

Notes

1. Dennis Gensch, "Targeting the Swithcable Industrial Customer," *Marketing Science* (Winter 1984):41-54.
2. George Cressman, "Choosing the Right Metric," *Drive Marketing Excellence* (November 1994), Institute for International Research, New York.
3. Robert Kaplan and David Norton, "The Balanced Scorecard—Measures That Drive Performance," *Harvard Business Review* (January–February 1982):71–79.
4. Robert Peterson and William Wilson, "Measuring Customer Satisfaction: Fact or Artifact," *Journal of the Academy of Marketing Science* 20 (1992):61–71.
5. Thomas Jones and Earl Sasser Jr., "Why Satisfied Customers Defect," *Harvard Business Review* (November–December 1995):88–99; Frederick F. Reichheld and W. Earl Sasser Jr., "Zero Defections: Quality Comes to Services," *Harvard Business Review* (September–October 1990): 106–11; and Frederick F. Reichheld, "Loyalty-Based Management," *Harvard Business Review* (March–April 1993):64–73.
6. Patrick Byrne, "Global Logistics: Only 10% of Companies Satisfy Customers," *Transportation and Distribution* (December 1993); and Tom Eck, "Are Customers Happy? Don't Assume," *Positive Impact* (July 1992):3.
7. Nigel Piercy and Neil Morgan, "The Marketing Planning Process: Behavioral Problems Compared to Analytical Techniques in Explaining Marketing Plan Credibility," *Journal of Business Research* 29 (1994):167–78; and Nigel Piercy, *Marketing Organization: An Analysis of Information Processing, Power and Politics* (Chicago: George Allen & Unwin, 1985).
8. Robert Ruekert and Orville Walker Jr., "Marketing's Interaction with Other Functional Units: A Conceptual Framework and Empirical Evidence," *Journal of Marketing* (January 1987):1–19.
9. William Egelhoff, "Great Strategies or Great Strategy Implementation—Two Ways of Competing in Global Markets," *Sloan Management Review* (Winter 1993):37–50.
10. Thomas Bonoma, *The Marketing Edge: Making Strategies Work* (New York: Free Press, 1985).
11. George Day, "Building a Market-Driven Organization," *Market-Driven Strategy* (New York: Free Press, 1990), 356–76.

16 PROFIT IMPACT OF MARKET-BASED MANAGEMENT

Businesses such as Disney, IBM, MBNA, Nordstrom, Ritz-Carlton, and Lexus have one thing in common, a passion for customer satisfaction. It is the core value that drives their business cultures and the marketing strategies that evolve. These businesses are also highly profitable, and for some time they have created value for customers, employees, and shareholders.

HOW TO OVERWHELM CUSTOMERS AND SHAREHOLDERS

The process starts with a strong market orientation and a passion for customer satisfaction, as illustrated in Figure 16-1. Although there are many ways to better serve customers in a effort to improve customer satisfaction, a business with a passion for customer satisfaction will start with its dissatisfied customers by encouraging them to complain.

Encouraging customer complaints is easier said than done. Most customers don't complain for a variety of good reasons. A market-based business will develop proactive customer satisfaction programs and systems to encourage customer complaint and will measure its success with the rate at which they hear from dissatisfied customers. Capturing customer complaints provides a wonderful opportunity to discover and address sources of dissatisfaction. The most effective and lowest-cost customer research any business will ever engage in is hearing from dissatisfied customers.

However, a business with a passion for customer satisfaction will go further to understand customer needs, frustrations, and opportunities to create customer solutions that build higher levels of customer satisfaction. A *day in the life of a customer* is one way to further discover ways to build customer satisfaction. A day in the life of a customer is a *process-focused,* not *product-focused,* effort to understand how customers acquire, use, and replace products, and the sources of frustration that occur in these processes. The outputs of this effort are customer solutions designed to enhance customer satisfaction and improve customer retention, as shown in Figure 16-1.

With higher customer retention, a business can lower its cost of customer acquisition and improve marketing productivity. Recall, a common rule of thumb is that it is five times more expensive to replace a customer than to retain one. Thus, higher customer retention means that fewer dollars of marketing budget are needed to maintain a certain level of market share. These gains drop to the bottom line, which contributes directly to improved net profits and shareholder value. In this last chapter we make

FIGURE 16-1   How to Overwhelm Customers and Shareholders

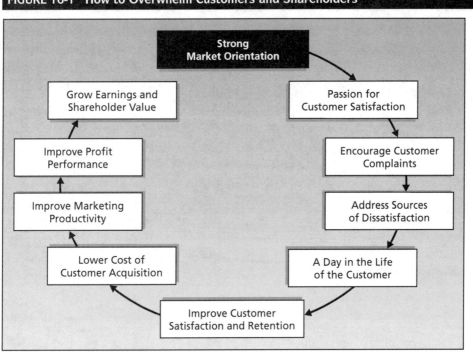

explicit the relationship between customer satisfaction and profitability and share-holder value, but also, in a broader sense, we demonstrate how every marketing strategy affects profits, and shareholders.

CUSTOMER SATISFACTION AND PROFITABILITY

The American Customer Satisfaction Index (ACSI) was developed by Claus Fornell[1] at the University of Michigan Business School and is used to measure customer satisfaction with goods and services available to household consumers in the United States. Using their measures of customer satisfaction they have found that businesses scoring in the top 50 percent produced over 2.4 times greater shareholder value than businesses in the bottom 50 percent in customer satisfaction. Fornell explains the importance of the relationship between customer satisfaction and shareholder value in the following way:

> "With few exceptions cash flows accrued from two sources: current customers and new customers. For most companies, the flow is much greater from the current customers. It is as simple as that. The satisfaction of current customers has a great deal of impact on shareholder value."

To manage this process, a business must first understand its levels of customer satisfaction, dissatisfaction, complaint recovery, and customer retention, as well as the cost of

FIGURE 16-2 AirComm Customer Satisfaction and 80 Percent Customer Retention

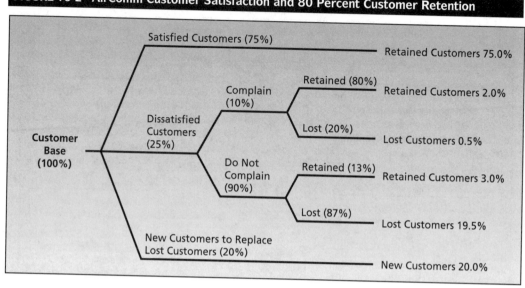

customer acquisition. Figure 16-2 presents the current customer situation for AirComm, a wireless telecommunications business.

As shown in Figure 16-2, AirComm has achieved a 75 percent level of customer satisfaction, which here translates into an 80 percent customer retention, given the rate at which AirComm recovers customer complaints and resolves dissatisfaction. At current levels of performance, 25 percent of AirComm's customer base is dissatisfied, but the business hears from only 10 percent of these dissatisfied customers. When AirComm *does* recover a customer complaint, it is able to retain 80 percent of these dissatisfied customers. The business loses 87 percent of those dissatisfied customers it *does not* hear from. Of course, this level of customer complaint recovery contributes to AirComm's overall level of customer retention.

At this level of customer satisfaction and retention, AirComm produces a net profit of $50 million on sales of $500 million, a 10 percent return on sales. As shown in Figure 16-3, the major driver of profitability is percentage of retained customers. At an 80 percent level of customer retention, AirComm's retained customers produce $120 million in net marketing contribution, while customers who are lost and those who replace them produce a combined net marketing contribution of –$30 million.

Improving customer retention to 90 percent would improve overall net profits by $20 million, with no change in sales revenue. Retained customer profitability would improve modestly, but the greatest gain in profitability would be due to a lower cost of new customer acquisition. As shown in Figure 16-4, the return on sales is 14 percent with 90 percent retention, a healthy increase over the 10 percent return at the 80 percent level of customer retention.

FIGURE 16-3   AirComm Profitability at 80 Percent Customer Retention

Area of Performance	Retained Customers	Lost Customers	New Customers	Overall Performance
Number of Customers	800,000	200,000	200,000	1,200,000
Revenue per Customer	$500	$300	$200	
Total Revenue (millions)	$400	$ 60	$ 40	$500
Variable Cost per Customer	$300	$200	$150	
Margin per Customer	$200	$100	$ 50	
Total Contribution (millions)	$160	$ 20	$ 10	$190
Marketing Expenses (millions)	$ 40	$ 10	$ 50	$100
Market Exp. per Customer	$ 50	$ 50	$250	
Net Marketing Contribution (mil)	**$120**	**$ 10**	**−$ 40**	**$ 90**
Operating Expense (millions)				$ 40
Net Profit (before taxes) (millions)				$ 50
Return on Sales				**10.0%**

Retention Cost = $50 per Customer; Acquisition Cost = $250 per Customer.

FIGURE 16-4   AirComm Profitability at 90 Percent Customer Retention

Area of Performance	Retained Customers	Lost Customers	New Customers	Overall Performance
Number of Customers	900,000	100,000	100,000	1,100,000
Revenue per Customer	$500	$300	$200	
Total Revenue (millions)	$450	$ 30	$ 20	$500
Variable Cost per Customer	$300	$200	$150	
Margin per Customer	$200	$100	$ 50	
Total Contribution (millions)	$180	$ 10	$ 5	$195
Marketing Expenses (millions)	$ 54	$ 6	$ 25	$ 85
Marketing Exp. per Customer*	$ 60	$ 60	$250	
Net Marketing Contribution (mil)	**$126**	**$ 4**	**−$ 20**	**$110**
Operating Expense (millions)				$ 40
Pretax Net Profit (before taxes) (millions)				$ 70
Return on Sales				**14.0%**

*Marketing expenses focused on customer retention were increased by 20% (from $50 to $60 per customer) in an effort to improve customer satisfaction and achieve 90% retention.

HOW MARKETING STRATEGIES AFFECT PROFITABILITY

A passion for customer satisfaction is one way a market-oriented business builds superior profits. Businesses with a strong market-orientation see current and potential customers as key sources of profitability, cash flow, and earnings. Customers, products, and assets are all important parts of business and business success, but only one produces money. Each is an important aspect of a business, and each needs to be managed on a day-to-day basis for a business to be efficient and profitable. However, financial reports and product-line income statements often dominate the thinking of a business that lacks a market orientation. Products will come and go; assets will be purchased and consumed; but *the customer is the only enduring asset a business has.* Keeping in mind that the customer is the only source of positive cash flow, it is the responsibility of those in marketing to understand how customers affect a business and its profitability.[2] This section addresses these issues in an attempt to bring into greater focus customers and the importance of their role in contributing to the profits of a business.

Customer Volume

Recognizing the *customer* as the primary unit of focus, a market-based business will expand its focus to customers and markets, not just products or units sold.[3] This is an important strategic distinction because there is a finite number of potential customers, but a large range of products and services can be sold to each customer. And, as shown below, a business's volume is its customer share in a market with a finite number of customers at any point in time, not the number of units sold.

$$\begin{array}{c} \text{Customer} \\ \text{Volume} \end{array} = \begin{array}{c} \text{Market Demand} \\ \text{(customers)} \end{array} \times \begin{array}{c} \text{Market Share} \\ \text{(percentage)} \end{array}$$

Figure 16-5 presents an overall flow chart of how market-based net profits are derived. Customer volume, at the top of this diagram, is derived from a certain level of customer

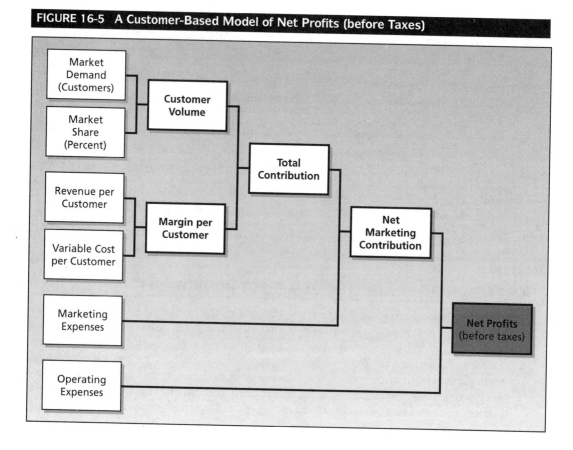

FIGURE 16-5 A Customer-Based Model of Net Profits (before Taxes)

market demand and a business's share of that customer demand. Without a sufficient volume of customers, net profit will be impossible to obtain. Marketing strategies that affect customer volume include marketing strategies that:

- Attract new customers to grow market share
- Grow the market demand by bringing more customers into a market
- Enter new markets to create new sources of customer volume

Each of these customer-focused marketing strategies affects net profits, invested assets, cash flow, and, as we will show later, shareholder value. Thus, a key component of profitability and financial performance is customer purchases and the collective customer volume produced. Without customer purchases, there is no positive cash flow or potential for net profits or shareholder value.

Margin per Customer

When customers decide to purchase an assortment of products and services from a business, the result is a certain revenue per customer. And, of course, a corresponding set of variable costs that go into each purchase and sales transaction must be taken into account to determine margin per customer:

$$\frac{\text{Customer}}{\text{Margin}} = \frac{\text{Revenue}}{\text{per Customer}} \times \frac{\text{Variable Cost}}{\text{per Customer}}$$

This measure of customer profitability, as shown in the preceding and in Figure 16-5, could be computed on a transaction basis, monthly or annually. The bottom line is that a business has to make a positive margin per customer or it will produce no profits and, therefore, no shareholder value. In many instances, new customers may produce a small or negative customer margin. Over time, we would expect a business to manage its marketing strategies so as to increase customer margin. If it does not, it has several alternatives to consider, one of which is to not continue to serve that customer as part of the business's marketing strategy. In general, marketing strategies designed to improve margin per customer include marketing strategies that:

- Grow revenue per customer by product line extensions
- Grow revenue per customer by adding services that enhance customer value
- Improve margin per customer with improved products and services for which the customer is willing to pay a premium price
- Develop more cost-efficient marketing systems that lower variable sales and transaction costs
- Eliminate customers that are not able to produce an acceptable level of customer margin

As shown in Figure 16-5, *revenue per customer* and *variable cost per customer* come together to produce a certain level of *margin per customer*. Because the customer is the primary unit of focus of market-based management, it is the business's responsibility to develop marketing strategies that systematically build customer volume and customer margin.

Total Contribution

Ultimately, whether tracking product revenues and variable product costs or tracking customer volume and margin per customer, the end result will be a total contribution produced by the marketing strategies that have been developed and implemented. Once again, *both approaches* are needed in managing different aspects of a business. However, those in marketing should be more concerned with a customer perspective and how to develop marketing strategies that affect both customers and the total contribution of the business.

$$\frac{\text{Total}}{\text{Contribution}} = \frac{\text{Customer}}{\text{Volume}} \times \frac{\text{Customer}}{\text{Margin}}$$

As shown in Figure 16-5, the total contribution produced by a marketing strategy is the product of the customer volume it produces and customer margin derived from customer purchases. The total contribution produced by a marketing strategy is an important component in the profitability equation because from this point forward only expenses are introduced. Hence, building market-based strategies that increase total contribution is an important priority in developing marketing strategies that deliver profitable growth.

Net Marketing Contribution

All marketing strategies require *some* level of marketing effort to achieve a certain level of market share. Expenses associated with sales effort, market communications, customer service, and market management are required to implement a marketing strategy designed to obtain a certain customer volume. The cost of this marketing effort is shown in Figure 16-5 as *marketing expenses* and must be deducted from the total contribution to produce a *net marketing contribution*. This is the net contribution or dollars produced after the marketing expenses are deducted from the total contribution produced.

$$\frac{\text{Net Marketing}}{\text{Contribution}} = \frac{\text{Total}}{\text{Contribution}} - \frac{\text{Marketing}}{\text{Expenses}}$$

In effect, this is how the marketing function contributes to the business's profits. If the marketing team develops a marketing strategy that fails and, therefore, lowers net marketing contribution, then that marketing strategy has, in effect, lowered the net profits of the business.

Marketing strategies are generally designed to affect total contribution, whether by increasing market demand, market share, or revenue per customer, or by decreasing variable cost per customer. The net marketing contribution equation should make it clear that such strategies are profitable only if the increase in total contribution exceeds the increase in marketing expenses required to produce that increase in total contribution. That is, for a marketing strategy to improve profits for the business, it has to improve net marketing contribution.

Net Profit (Before Taxes)

Although marketing strategies contribute to net profits through net marketing contribution, net profits (before taxes) of a business are generally beyond the control of the marketing function or the marketing management team. Marketing strategies produce a certain level of net marketing contribution from which all other business expenses must be deducted before a net profit is realized, as illustrated in Figure 16-5. These operating expenses include fixed expenses, such as human resources management, research and development, and administrative expenses, and other operating expenses, such as utilities, rent, and fees. In most instances, there would also be allocated corporate overhead, which includes company expenses such as legal fees, corporate advertising, and executive salaries.

$$\begin{matrix} \text{Net Profit} \\ \text{(before taxes)} \end{matrix} = \begin{matrix} \text{Net Marketing} \\ \text{Contribution} \end{matrix} - \begin{matrix} \text{Operating} \\ \text{Expenses} \end{matrix}$$

However, there are instances when a marketing strategy can affect operating expenses. For example, a strategy to improve a product to attract more customers and build market share could involve research and development expenses to develop the new product.

HOW MARKETING STRATEGIES AFFECT ASSETS

Most businesses do not consider the impact marketing strategies have on a business's investment in assets. As will be demonstrated, the assets of a business are indirectly affected by marketing strategies. We will limit our discussion to accounts receivable, inventory, and fixed assets. These assets normally account for the majority of a business's investment in assets.

Investment in Accounts Receivable

We frequently do not think about the effect a marketing strategy can have on accounts receivable. Accounts receivable is the money owed a business and varies in proportion to sales revenues and customer payment behavior. As sales revenues increase or decrease, there will be a corresponding change in accounts receivable. In addition, customer payment behavior will determine the time customers take to pay for what they have purchased. For example, if customers take an average of 45 days to pay their bills, for approximately 12.5 percent of a year (45 divided by 365) customers are holding the business's money. If annual sales were $100 million, the accounts receivable would be approximately $12.5 million at any point in time.

$$\begin{matrix} \text{Accounts} \\ \text{Receivable} \end{matrix} = \begin{matrix} \text{Sales} \\ \text{Revenues} \end{matrix} \times \begin{matrix} \text{Percent Days} \\ \text{Outstanding} \end{matrix}$$
$$= \$100 \text{ million} \times 0.125 \ (12.5\%)$$
$$= \$12.5 \text{ million}$$

To put this in marketing terms, accounts receivable is a function of customer volume, revenue per customer, and customer payment behavior. When we state this relation in terms of marketing strategy, we can express accounts receivable in the following way:

$$\begin{matrix} \text{Accounts} \\ \text{Receivable} \end{matrix} = \begin{matrix} \text{Customer} \\ \text{Volume} \end{matrix} \times \begin{matrix} \text{Revenue per} \\ \text{Customer} \end{matrix} \times \begin{matrix} \text{Percent Days} \\ \text{Outstanding} \end{matrix}$$
$$= 20,000 \times \$5,000 \times 0.125 \ (12.5\%)$$
$$= \$12.5 \text{ million}$$

In this form, one can readily see how strategies that affect customer volume and revenue per customer also affect accounts receivable. In addition, the selection of target customers could be based partly upon their bill-paying behavior. Thus, a business may avoid customers who are slow payers, thereby lowering the level invested in accounts receivable. For example, about 3 percent of residential phone customers are labeled "movers and shakers." These are customers who run up large telephone bills but move on and shake loose before paying their bills. If these customers could be identified early, it would be wise to avoid them when possible.

In addition, a business's service quality also affects how fast customers pay their bills (and, hence, the level of accounts receivable). For example, consider how customer service affects the following customer payment behavior:[4]

- Eight out of 10 Fortune 500 companies report that the level of customer service they receive affects their decision to pay a bill on time.
- More than half of the Fortune 500 companies withhold payment from suppliers when they are dissatisfied with the level of service they have received.

Thus, a business with a strong market orientation and commitment to service quality and customer satisfaction is likely to be paid faster than businesses that deliver lower levels of service quality or customer satisfaction. In this way, the market orientation of a business affects the business's investment in accounts receivable.

Investment in Inventory

Many businesses are required to carry large inventories to adequately serve target customers. Long production runs and uncertain market demand often require a business to maintain a certain level of finished goods inventory. There are also work-in-process inventories (partially finished goods) and raw materials inventories. All these inventories are assets with market values.

As with accounts receivable, the size and value of inventories vary with sales revenues and target customer purchase behavior. As such, inventory at any time is roughly equal to total cost of goods sold times a percentage of days of inventory on hand. The need to have inventory on hand to cover an average of 30 days of sales would equate to 8.2 percent days of inventory (30 days divided by 365 days in a year). If the manufactured cost of goods sold for a year is $40 million, the average investment in inventory would be $3.28 million, as shown here:

$$\frac{\text{Inventory}}{\text{Investment}} = \frac{\text{Total Cost}}{\text{of Inventory}} \times \frac{\text{Percent Days}}{\text{of Inventory}}$$
$$= \$40 \text{ million} \times 0.082 \ (8.2\%)$$
$$= \$3.28 \text{ million}$$

In terms of marketing strategy, the investment in inventory can be expressed as:

$$\frac{\text{Inventory}}{\text{Investment}} = \frac{\text{Customer}}{\text{Volume}} \times \frac{\text{Unit Cost}}{\text{per Customer}} \times \frac{\text{Percent Days}}{\text{of Inventory}}$$
$$= 200,000 \times \$200 \times 0.082 \ (8.2\%)$$
$$= \$3.28 \text{ million}$$

Once again, marketing strategies that affect market demand, market share, and the unit manufacturing cost will affect investment in inventory. Likewise, channel marketing strategies will affect investment in inventory. A shift from a direct sales and distribution system to a distributor channel system could lead to lower inventories as a business is able to shift inventory requirements to distributors and, hence, lower the business's investment in assets.

Investment in Fixed Assets

Fixed assets include investments in buildings, land, equipment, office furniture, and so on. Most of these assets are depreciated each year as business expenses, and, therefore, at least from a financial accounting point of view, lose value over time. However, the amount and value of fixed assets at any point in time is relative to sales volume. A marketing strategy to grow sales volume substantially in a growing market would typically require additional fixed assets to accommodate that volume increase.

Thus, fixed assets are a function of sales volume which, in turn, is a function of marketing strategies to grow customer volume or volume per customer or both. Most businesses have excess manufacturing capacity, which is a large component of fixed assets. A marketing strategy to grow volume, by growing customer demand or increasing customer market share, will increase capacity utilization. If the increased volume produced increases net profits, this marketing strategy will result in an overall increase in the business's return on assets, because no addition to assets was necessary. Naturally, in situations where fixed assets have to be added to accommodate growth, the investment in assets would be greater. A business that derives profits from an increase in volume has to have profits sufficiently large to produce a higher return on assets.

In general, most managers do not consider the impact of a marketing strategy on assets or return on assets. Although not scrutinized at this level, every marketing decision affects one or more of the return-on-asset components shown in Figure 16-6.

For example, consider a scanner manufacturer's marketing strategy to capture a significant share of the retail scanner market. The business knew that a major customer was price-sensitive and that competitors would price aggressively to get this customer's volume. Recognizing the importance of price, the scanner manufacturer offered a price lower than competing offers but required full payment within 10 days, with no cash discount. Unit margins were lower, but the large volume captured produced a large total contribution, and, with a very minimal investment in accounts receivable, the business produced a much higher return on assets. The net result was a marketing strategy that produced higher net profits and a lower level of investment, each of which contributed to an increase in return on investment.

RETURN MEASURES OF PROFITABILITY

Accounting and financial measures of profitability include net profit, return on sales (ROS), return on assets (ROA), and return on equity (ROE). As the following shows, net marketing contribution is a key driver of net profits. To grow net profits in any given year, a business has two fundamental options: lower operating expenses or grow net marketing contribution.

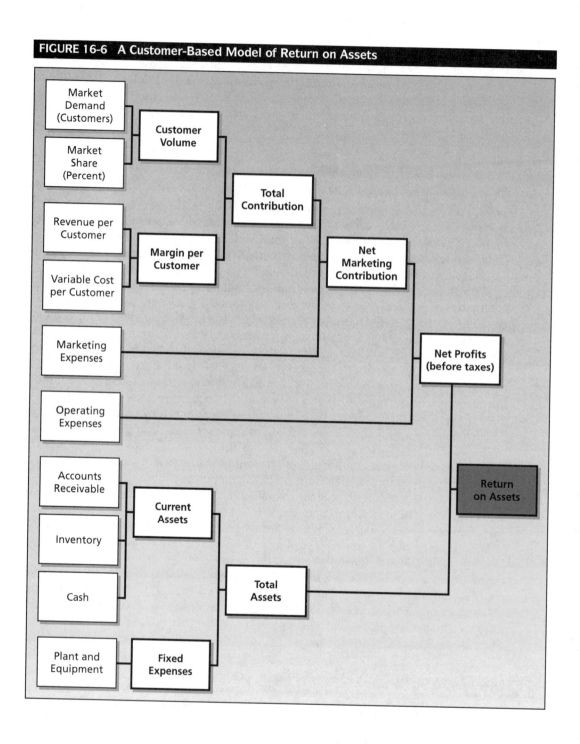

FIGURE 16-6 A Customer-Based Model of Return on Assets

$$\text{Net Profit (after taxes)} = \underbrace{\left[\left(\begin{array}{c}\text{Customer}\\\text{(new)}\\\text{Volume}\end{array} \times \begin{array}{c}\text{Margin per}\\\text{Customer}\\\text{(new)}\end{array}\right) - \begin{array}{c}\text{Marketing}\\\text{Expenses}\end{array}\right]}_{\text{Net Marketing Contribution}} - \begin{array}{c}\text{Operating}\\\text{Expenses}\end{array} - \begin{array}{c}\text{Interest}\\\text{and}\\\text{Taxes}\end{array}$$

The three fundamental measures of profit performance—return on sales (ROS), return on assests (ROA), and return on equity (ROE)—are based on the net profit produced in any given period:

$$\text{Return on Sales (ROS)} = \frac{\text{Net Profit (after taxes)}}{\text{Sales}}$$

$$\text{Return on Assets (ROA)} = \frac{\text{Net Profit (after taxes)}}{\text{Assets}}$$

$$\text{Return on Equity (ROE)} = \frac{\text{Net Profit (after taxes)}}{\text{Equity}}$$

For example, as shown in Figure 16-7, the sales of Stericycle in 1997 were $46 million and net income was $1.44 million. This resulted in a return on sales of 3.14 percent. In 1997 Stericycle had assets of $61.2 million which resulted in a ROA (return on

FIGURE 16-7   Stericycle, Inc. Financial Performance, 1997–2000

Area of Performance	1997	2000
Market Demand (millions)	1,000	1,500
Market Share	4.6%	22%
Sales Revenue (millions)	$46	$324
Revenue per Customer	$1,075	$1,336
Percent Margin	26.40%	39.30%
Gross Profit (millions)	$12.1	$127.3
Marketing Expenses (millions)	$10.70	$59.50
Marketing Expenses per Customer	$251	$245
Net Marketing Contribution (millions)	**$1.44**	**$67.83**
Operating Expenses (millions)	0	$45.73
Operating Income (millions)	$1.44	$22.1
Interest & Taxes (millions)	0	$7.60
Net Income (millions)	**$1.44**	**$14.50**
Balance Sheet Information		
Total Assets (millions)	$61.20	$597.90
Total Liabilties (millions)	$16.20	$463.20
Owners Equity (millions)	$45.00	$134.70
Return Measures of Performance		
Return on Sales	3.14%	4.48%
Return on Assets	2.36%	2.43%
Return on Equity	3.21%	10.76%

assets) of 2.36 percent. With owner's equity of $45 million, ROE (return on equity) was 3.21 percent.

The growth plan introduced in 1997 produced tremendous gains in sales and profits by 2000, as shown in Figure 16-7. Net marketing contribution grew from $1.44 million to $67.8 million, which played a significant role in the growth of net income. While the return on sales and return on assets made very modest improvements, return on equity grew from 3.21 percent in 1997 to 10.75 percent in 2000.

MEASURES OF SHAREHOLDER VALUE

Having demonstrated the importance of the customer and market-based management with respect to net profits, assets, and return measures of profit performance, we need to extend our discussion of how market-based management affects shareholder value.[5] To do so, we need to first develop a way of linking market-based management and net marketing contribution to profit performance and shareholder value.

Return measures of performance such as ROS, ROA, and ROE, present an aspect of profit performance. Although these are important, shareholder value is more closely associated with earnings per share, economic value-added, [6] and price-earnings ratio. Each of these is briefly described below, and illustrated in Figure 16-8, for AirComm at the 80 percent level of customer retention.

- **Earnings per Share (EPS):** Net profit (after taxes) divided by the number of shares. For AirComm, a net profit (after taxes) of $3 million and 6 million shares translates to $0.50 per share.
- **Economic Value-Added (EVA):** Net profit (after taxes) minus the business's capital investment times the cost of capital yields a measure of how much value it created by that level of net profit (earnings). For AirComm, a net profit (after taxes) of $30 million minus capital investment ($150 million) times the cost of capital (12 percent), yields an EVA of $12 million.
- **Price-Earnings (PE) Ratio:** The price of a share of stock divided by the earnings per share. For AirComm, the share price of $15 divided by its earnings per share of 0.50 yields a price-earnings (PE) ratio of 30.

A market-based strategy to improve customer retention from 80 to 90 percent would yield improved profit performance, as shown in Figure 16-9. Earnings per share would increase from $0.50 to $0.70, EVA would improve from $12 million to $24 million, and the price-earnings ratio would drop from 30 to approximately 21. Or, to maintain a price-earnings ratio of 30, share price would have to increase from $15 per share to $21 per share. As shown in Figure 16-10 net marketing contribution is the only positive source of earning per share. When the AirComm net marketing contribution based on 80 percent retention ($110 million) is divided by 60 million shares the net marketing contribution per share is $1.83. When operating expenses, per share ($.47) and interest and taxes per share ($.46) are deducted from the net marketing contribution per share the result is $.70 per share.

Thus, businesses with a strong market orientation and passion for customer satisfaction and retention should deliver higher levels of profitability and shareholder value, even with no change in sales revenues.

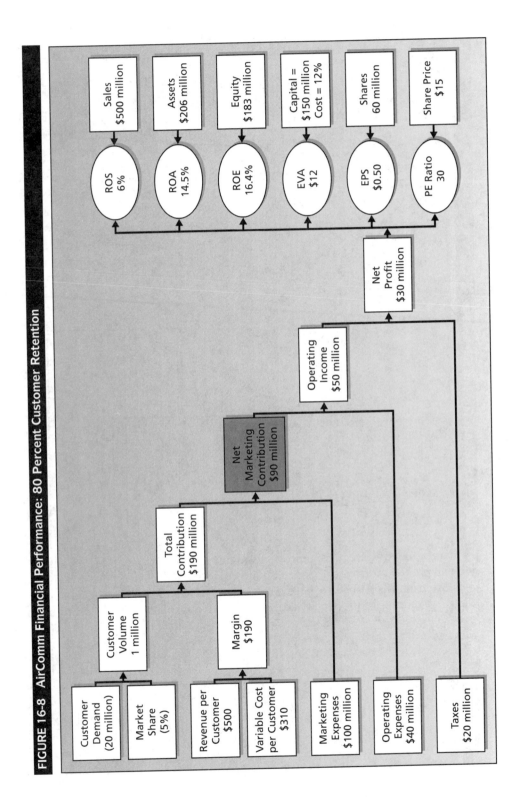

FIGURE 16-8 AirComm Financial Performance: 80 Percent Customer Retention

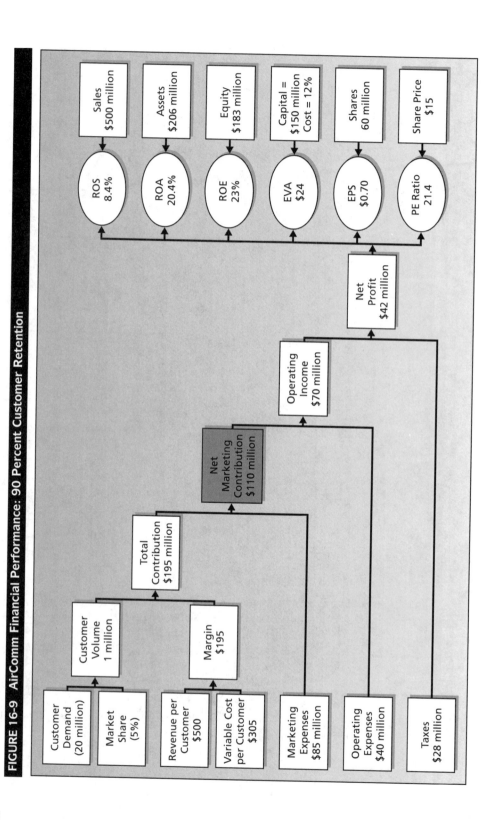

FIGURE 16-9   AirComm Financial Performance: 90 Percent Customer Retention

FIGURE 16-10 Net Marketing Contribution per Share

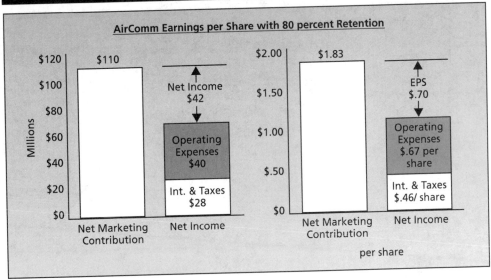

MARKET-BASED MANAGEMENT

To be profitable, a business needs to achieve above-average market performance and operational performance.[7] In fact, market and operational performance are interrelated, as illustrated in Figure 16-10. A business with poor levels of customer satisfaction can expect sales to these customers to decline and the speed with which they pay their invoices to decrease. These businesses have to spend more marketing dollars in an effort to maintain a certain level of sales. The combination of these effects influences all aspects of financial performance shown in market and operational performance metrics.

The central theme of this book has been how a business can develop and deliver marketing strategies that:

- Deliver high levels of customer satisfaction and superior customer value.
- Improve market position, sales, and profitability.
- Improve earnings and shareholder value.

Market-based management, as shown in Figure 16-11, is at the base of a business with a strong market orientation. A strong market orientation translates into a strong customer focus, competitor orientation, and a team approach that cuts across organizational functions. The result is a market-based business that is in a strong position to develop and deliver market-based strategies designed to attract, satisfy, and retain customers. Implemented successfully across a wide range of market situations, a market-based approach to market management will deliver higher levels of profitability, cash flow, and shareholder value than will a cost-based approach.

One should never forget that the only source of positive cash flow is the customer. Without customers, technology, assets, and management are of little value. The job of a market-based business is to understand customers, competition, and the market environment within the context of the business's technology, assets, and management capabilities and to render a market-based strategy that delivers superior levels of customer satisfaction, profitability, and shareholder value.

FIGURE 16-11 Market-Based Management and Shareholder Value

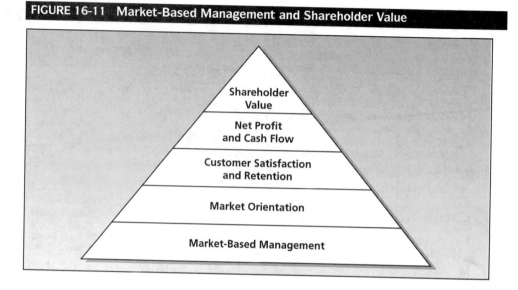

Summary

Marketing strategies directly affect customers and sales revenues. However, they also affect margins, total contribution, and marketing expenses. These effects, in turn, lead to a net marketing contribution. Because operating and overhead expenses are beyond the control of marketing managers, net marketing contribution plays an important role in evaluating the profit impact of marketing strategies. Thus, throughout this book we have sought to determine the profit impact of a marketing strategy based on the level of net marketing contribution produced.

Marketing strategies also directly impact assets. Changes in sales produce corresponding changes in accounts receivable and inventory. Likewise, a major increase in volume based on a particular marketing strategy may require additional operating expenses and investment in fixed assets. Marketing strategies impact both the numerator of the ROA (return on assets) equation as well as the denominator. This presents a much broader view of the impact a marketing strategy has on a business's profitability.

The net marketing contribution for each product–market strategy contributes to both profit performance and shareholder value. Return measures of profit performance (ROS, ROA, and ROE) are driven by market performance and net marketing contribution. Shareholder measures of performance (earnings per share, EVA, and price-earnings ratio) are directly influenced by product–market performance and profitability.

Finally, it is the market orientation that is at the heart of market-based management. With a strong market orientation, a business will develop marketing strategies that are intended to attract, satisfy, and retain target customers. A market-based managed business should at the same time be evaluating alternative marketing strategies that contribute to the business's growth, short- and long-run profit performance, and strategic position. If successful, a market-driven business should deliver high levels of customer satisfaction, profitability, and shareholder value.

APPLICATION PROBLEM: STERICYCLE, INC.

Shown below is Stericycle's actual performance from 1997 to 2000. As shown, the market grew and their market share grew, both of which contributed to a 704 percent gain in sales over this three-year period. Percent margins also improved from 26.4 percent to 39.3 percent which helped boost gross profits more than 10 fold.

Marketing expenses were increased by almost 100 percent per year. The combination of these results produced growth in net marketing contribution from $1.44 million to $67.83 million. After other expenses, interest, and taxes were deducted, Stericycle produced $14.5 million in net income. Divided by the number of shares held by shareholders, this produced earnings per share of $.72.

The stock price over this period grew from $14.60 per share to $38.10 per share while the price-earnings ratio (PE ratio) dropped from 109 to 53.

Area of Performance	1997	2000	% Change
Market Demand (millions)	1,000	1,500	150%
Market Share	4.6%	22%	478%
Sales Revenue (millions)	$46	$324	704%
Revenue per Customer	$1,075	$1,336	124%
Percent Margin	26.40%	39.30%	149%
Gross Profit (millions)	$12.1	$127.3	1049%
Marketing Expenses (millions)	$10.70	$59.50	556%
Marketing Expenses per Customer	$251	$245	98%
Net Marketing Contribution (millions)	**$1.44**	**$67.83**	4698%
Operating Expenses (millions)	0	$45.73	Na
Operating Income (millions)	$1.44	$22.1	1530%
Interest & Taxes (millions)	0	$7.60	Na
Net Income (millions)	**$1.44**	**$14.50**	1004%
Shares (millions)	10.77	20.14	187%
Earnings per Share	**$0.13**	**$0.72**	537%
Price per Share	**$14.60**	**$38.10**	261%
PE Ratio	109	53	49%

For access to interactive software to answer the questions below to to www.rogerjbest.com or www.prenhall.com/best.

Questions

1. What were the key factors driving the increase in net income from 1997 to 2000?

2. What was the net marketing contribution per share in 1997 and 2000?

3. For 2000, estimate the net marketing contribution per share and explain how net marketing contribution per share will contribute to earnings per share.

Market-Based Logic and Strategic Thinking

1. Why is it important for those in responsible marketing positions to understand the profit impact of marketing strategies?
2. What should be the role of net marketing contribution in the development of a marketing strategy? Why is net profit often a misleading indicator of the profit impact of a marketing strategy?
3. How does a marketing strategy affect the assets of a business? Why should the accounts receivable and inventory change with a change in marketing strategy? When will the fixed assets change?
4. How does the net marketing contribution of a marketing strategy affect return on assets (ROA)?
5. How do investments in customer retention contribute to higher levels of profit performance?
6. Explain how the net marketing contribution of a marketing strategy affects return measures of profit performance.
7. How do changes in customer retention affect shareholder measures of performance such as earnings per share?
8. Explain how Stericycle's market share gain affected net marketing contribution, net profits, and return measures of performance.
9. Why should shareholders and Wall Street analysts be interested in a business's customer retention?
10. Why would two businesses with the same sales have different shareholder value if one had a 60 percent level of customer retention and the other 80 percent?
11. How would you use the net marketing contribution for each product–market to forecast earnings and earnings per share?
12. What role does net marketing contribution play in understanding the earnings level of a business?
13. How does the market orientation of a business affect customers, business performance, and shareholders?
14. Why should a market-oriented business with a passion for customer satisfaction produce higher levels of earnings per share and, therefore, have greater shareholder value than a business which is not market-oriented?

Notes

1. "Customer Satisfaction: The Fundamental Basis for Business Survival," *Siebel Magazine* (Vol. 50, No. 1):19-25.
2. Robert Kaplan and David Norton, "The Balanced Score Card—Measures That Drive Performance," *Harvard Business Review* (January–February 1992):71–79.
3. Eric Hardy, "The Forbes 500's Annual Directory," *Forbes* (April 22, 1996):232–78.
4. "Customer Service Impacts Cash Flow," *Positive Impact* (August 1993):5–6.
5. Sidney Schoeffler, "Impacts of Business Strategy on Stock Prices," PIMS Letter No. 20 (1980):1–9.
6. "Valuing Companies," *The Economist* (August 2, 1997):53–55; Eric Olsen and Thomas Rawley, "Stock Prices Performance: Corporate Agenda for the 1980s," *Journal of Accounting and Corporate Finance* (Spring 1987):3–15; Bill Birchard, "Mastering the New Metrics," *CFO: The Magazine for Senior Financial Executives* (October 1994); and Bill Barmhardt, "Chicago's Top 100 Companies," *Chicago Tribune* (May 15, 1995); Thomas Rawley and L. Edwards, "How Holt Methods Work for Good Decisions, Determine Business Value More Accurately," *Corporate Cashflow Magazine* (September 1993); and Bernard Reimann, "Stock Price and Business Success: What Is the Relationship?" *Journal of Business Strategy* (Summer 1987):38–50.
7. Robert Hayes, "Strategic Planning: Forward in Reverse," *Harvard Business Review* (November– December 1985):111–19.

Glossary

acquisition cost The marketing expense to acquire one new customer.

advertising carryover effects Sales occurring after the period in which an advertisement was run.

advertising elasticity The percent change in volume per 1 percent change in advertising expenditures.

agents, brokers, and reps Salespeople who work for a business on a commission basis.

assets Cash, accounts receivable, inventory, plant and equipment, and other assets.

bottom-up marketing budget A budget based on the cost of each specific marketing task needed to implement a tactical marketing strategy.

brand assets Assets a brand can attain based on market leadership, awareness, brand relevance, reputation for quality, and brand loyalty.

brand encoding The process of branding products within a business based on a combination of company name, name, sub-brand name, number, letter, product name, or key benefit.

brand equity The attractiveness of a brand based entirely on its name and image.

brand image The perceived image of what a brand stands for in the mind of a target customer.

brand liabilities Liabilities a brand can incur based on customer dissatisfaction, environmental problems, product failures/recall, lawsuits/consumer boycotts, and questionable business practices.

brand management The process of naming products, managing brands, and brand-line extensions to fully attain maximum brand equity and a brand's full profit potential.

brand personality The personality a brand takes on based on human personality characteristics.

break-even volume The unit volume at which total sales equals total cost.

break-even market share The market share needed to reach break-even volume.

channel partners Companies within a business's marketing channels that distribute, resell, or add value to a business's products and participate in the process of connecting businesses with end-users.

channel system A particular combination of distribution and sales.

co-branding Combining two brand names to create a new brand, like the Eddie Bauer Ford Explorer.

capital Owner's equity plus long-term debt add up to the capital a business has invested in their business.

company benefits The level of perceived benefit a customer attaches to a company or brand name.

competitive advantage A relative advantage one business has over another that is sustainable and translates into a benefit that is important to target customers.

competitive benchmarking Benchmarking a company outside your industry on a certain business practice in which the benchmark company is known for excellence.

competitive bid pricing Pricing a bid based on the historical success of past price-to-cost bid ratios and the competitive bid situation.

competitive position A business's position relative to a benchmark competitor's position with regard to price, product quality, delivery, new product sales, and so on.

competitor analysis Benchmarking a key competitor with respect to important areas of performance.

competitor orientation The degree to which a business tracks competitors' strategies and benchmarks its performance relative to competitors.

competitor reactive pricing Setting price based on competitors' prices without knowing what customers need or would be willing to pay for a firm product or service.

competitor response price elasticity The percentage change in a competitor's price per 1 percent change in the price of a business's product.

cost advantage A sustainable lower cost relative to competition.

cost-based pricing Pricing that is determined by a business's cost and margin requirements.

cost of capital. The percentage paid (like interest) for capital (money obtained from investors and lenders).

cost-plus pricing Price that is set based on the cost of the product plus a desired profit margin.

cross price elasticity The percent change in volume in one product when the price is changed 1 percent in another product.

customer focus The degree to which business seeks to understand customer needs and use situations, and tracks customer satisfaction.

customer life The number of purchase periods a customer is retained by a business.

customer's lifetime value The net present value of cash flows produced over a customer's life.

customer mix marketing budget A marketing budget based on the cost of new customer acquisition and retention.

customer reactive pricing Setting price based on a thorough understanding of customer needs and price sensitivity but without taking into account competitors' prices and positioning.

customer relationship management A process devoted to developing and managing one-on-one relationships with target customers.

customer retention The percentage of customers retained from one purchase period to another.

customer satisfaction The degree to which customers are satisfied or dissatisfied with a business, product, or specific aspect of a product or service provided by a business.

customer value Total benefits minus the cost of acquiring those benefits.

day in the life of a customer The process a customer goes through in acquiring, using, and disposing of a product.

defensive strategic market plan A long-run plan to protect or exit a market position.

differentiation advantage A sustainable product or service advantage that translates into a benefit important to target customers.

direct channel system A channel system that retains ownership of the product and requires management of its sales, distribution, and customer service.

discount rate A business's cost of capital.

discount factor The net present value of $1.00 when discounted from a particular point in time and at a particular discount rate.

distributors Intermediaries who take title (ownership) of a product and are responsible for its sale, distribution, and customer service.

divest market strategy A defensive strategic market plan to exit a market by selling or closing down a business.

earnings per share Net profits (after taxes) divided by the number of shares held by shareholders.

economic value-added Net profits (after taxes) minus the product of a business's investment in capital assets times its cost of capital.

e-marketing Electronic marketing using the Internet as a marketing channel.

empathic design process An observational approach to discovering customer problems, frustrations, and inconveniences in using your product.

end-result performance metrics Performance metrics that occur at the end of a normal accounting period.

external performance metrics Market performance metrics that track external performance with respect to market penetration, competitive position, and customer satisfaction.

exit market strategies Defensive strategic market plans that specify a market exit strategy that can range from immediate exit with a divestment strategy to a slow exit with harvesting strategy.

firmagraphics Characteristics used to describe a business such as size, financial position, years in business, type of business, number of locations, etc.

flagship brand The highest priced and quality brand in a business's product line.

flanker brand A product extension of a business's core brand.

floor pricing A price that is set on a financial requirement like gross margin or return on investment.

forward buying The practice of buying a greater volume of a product when it is on sale.

grow market share strategy A long-run offensive strategic market plan to grow market share.

harvest market strategy A defensive strategic market plan to slowly exit a market while maximizing profits.

harvest pricing Raising price in a series of steps in an effort to improve margins and maximize total contribution until the product exits the market.

heavy-up message frequency A period when a business increases its advertising effort.

horizontal brand-line extension Extending the brand to a line of related products.

horizontal market opportunity Market with closely related substitute products.

indirect channel systems Channels in which intermediaries take ownership of a business's product and the responsibility for its sale, distribution, and customer service.

industry analysis A structural analysis of a competitive environment based on competitor entry/exit, buyer/supplier power, substitutes, and competitive rivalry.

ingredient co-branding Adding a brand name to another product's brand like "Intel inside" on Dell and Compaq computers.

in-process performance metrics Performance metrics that occur during a reporting period and precede end-result performance metrics.

internal performance metrics Performance metrics that are internal measures of a business's operations.

inventory turnover The number of times an inventory is sold per year.

lead user solutions A process of studying how lead users (highly involved users) use a product to gain insights into how a product can be improved or a new product developed.

low cost leader pricing The low cost producer sets price based on cost in an effort to have the lowest market prices.

margin per unit The selling price of a product minus all the variable costs associated with producing, distributing, and selling the product.

market analysis An external analysis of market demand, customer needs, competition, distributors, and environmental forces that influence market demand and customer behavior.

market attractiveness The relative attractiveness of a market based on market forces, competitive environment, and market access.

market-based management The commitment of a strong market orientation and management

of markets that strives to deliver superior customer value and profitability.

market-based organization A business organized around markets with market units as profit centers.

market-based pricing Pricing based on target customer need, competitors' product position, and the strength of a business's product, service, or brand advantage.

market definition A specification of market scope that makes clear current and potential customers.

market development index The ratio of current market demand to market potential (maximum market demand).

market infrastructure Channel intermediaries and channel influencers that shape opinions and communicate information about a business and its products.

market orientation The degree to which a business has a strong customer-focus and competitor orientation and works as a team across functions to develop and deliver a market-based strategy.

market penetration strategies Offensive strategic market plans designed to further penetrate existing markets or enter new markets.

market potential The maximum market demand that should occur when all potential customers have entered a market.

market segmentation Grouping customers into segments on the basis of similar needs and differentiating demographic characteristics.

market share The percentage of current market demand obtained by a business.

market share index A hierarchy of market share factors (such as awareness, availability, interest, intention to buy, and purchase) that results in an estimate of market share.

market vision A broad view of the market based on a fundamental customer need that goes beyond existing product solutions.

marketing advantage A sustainable advantage over competitors in either channels of distribution, sales force, or marketing communications.

marketing expenses All fixed expenses associated with selling, marketing, and managing of a marketing strategy targeted at a particular market.

marketing mix A combination of the 4Ps (product, price, promotion, and place) designed for a specific target market.

marketing planning process A process that starts with a situation analysis, which leads to a specific strategic market plan, tactical marketing strategy, and marketing budget, and results in a performance plan.

marketing productivity Dollars of net marketing contributions produced by a strategy per dollar of fixed marketing expenses.

mass customization An individualized marketing mix in which products, prices, promotion, and place are customized to the individual needs of a niche market or individual customers.

mass market A market which is not segmented and all customers and potential customers are treated as one.

message frequency The average number of times a target customer recalls seeing an advertisement in a given period of time.

mixed channel systems A combination of direct and indirect channel systems in which a business and intermediary perform different functions with respect to sales, distribution, and customer service.

multisegment strategy Two or more separate and distinct marketing mix strategies (4Ps) that are created for different needs-based market segments.

needs-based segmentation Market segmentation based on customer needs and/or the benefits they seek in satisfying a particular problem or buying situation.

net marketing contribution The total contribution produced by a marketing strategy minus marketing expenses needed to produce it.

net present value The value in today's dollars of a cash flow that occurs over time and is evaluated with a particular discount rate.

net profit Sales revenues minus all expenses including taxes and interest.

new market entry strategies Offensive strategic market plans designed to enter new markets.

niche market A small segment of a market which is often overlooked or ignored by large competitors.

offensive strategic market plans Long-run plans (3 to 5 years) to penetrate markets or enter new markets.

one-on-one marketing Building one-on-one relationships with key customers a business wants to retain.

operating expenses Overhead expenses that are not the direct result of marketing activities.

operating income Sales minus all expenses before taxes and interest.

penetration pricing A low price strategy to achieve a high market share/high volume position.

perceived value pricing Pricing to create a greater customer value based on customer perceptions of product, service, company benefits, and the perceived cost of acquiring those benefits.

perceptual mapping A display of competing products based on their relative substitutability and customer ideal products based on their strength of preference for each competing product.

performance timeline A 3- to 5-year forecast of market and profit performance metrics.

plus-one pricing Adding at least one differentiating feature that allows a product to price slightly above competing products that lack this product or service feature.

portfolio analysis An evaluation of a product, market, or business with respect to market attractiveness and competitive advantage.

price-earnings ratio The price of a share of stock in a business divided by the business's earnings per share.

price elasticity The percentage change in unit volume for a product per 1 percent change in price.

price per unit The selling price of a product or service.

price premium The dollar amount, or percentage, by which the price of a product exceeds competing products.

prisoner's dilemma A price situation in which businesses are forced to follow downward price moves by competitors to remain competitive.

product benefits The overall benefit a customer derives from the product performance and features.

product bundling Combining for sale two or more products at a total price that would be lower than the price paid if each product were purchased separately.

product differentiation The degree to which a business's product is meaningfully different and superior when compared by customers to competing products.

product-focused A business that is focused internally on product development and utilizes marketing primarily as an advertising and sales function.

product life cycle The life of a product as it progresses from introduction through growth, maturity, and decline.

product line extensions Products that are added to a product line under an umbrella brand which is well known and has an established reputation for quality.

product line positioning A planned sequence of alternative product offerings that differ in product performance and price.

product-market diversification The degree to which a business has different products across different markets.

product positioning The manner in which customers perceive a business's product features and price in comparison to competitors' product features and prices.

product unbundling Offering for sale an individual product that is normally sold as a product bundle.

promotional price elasticity The percent volume increase per 1 percent price decrease during a price promotion.

protect market share strategy A defensive strategic market plan in which a business develops a marketing strategy to protect/defend its competitive position and market share.

pull communications Marketing communications directed at end-user customers in an attempt to motivate target customers to seek a business's products (i.e., pull the products through the channel).

push communications Marketing communications directed at intermediaries in an attempt to motivate them to push a business's product through the channel in an effort to reach target customers.

reduced market focus A planned reduction in market share by reducing focus to a smaller number of customers.

reference price A price point used by customers to evaluate the price of competing products.

relative cost A business's cost per unit relative to a competitor's cost per unit.

relative market share A business's market share divided by the share of the market share leader competitor or next largest share competitor.

relative new product sales The sales of new products introduced over the last three years divided by the new product sales produced by a competitor over the same time period.

relative price A business's price divided by the price of a competitor or the average price of several competitors.

relative product quality An overall relative index based on customer perceptions when comparing a business's product against a competitor's product on each aspect of product quality.

relative service quality An overall relative index based on customer perceptions when comparing a business's service against a competitor's service on each aspect of service quality.

return on capital Net income after taxes divided by a business's investment in capital

retention cost The cost of retaining one customer over a given period of time.

return on assets The net profit produced by a business divided by its total assets.

return on equity The net profit produced by a business divided by its owner's equity.

return on sales The net profit produced by a business divided by its total sales.

sales revenue The price times the volume sold for each of the products sold by a company.

segment pricing Pricing based on segment price sensitivity and customer need for additional product features and/or services.

service benefits The overall benefit a customer derives from the various components of service a business provides.

share development index The percentage of current market demand obtained by a business.

served market The target market to be served by the business.

service differentiation The degree to which a business's service is meaningfully different and superior when compared by customers to competing products.

share follower The business with the second largest market share in a given market.

situation analysis An external analysis of market forces and internal analysis of business performance that are used to identify key performance issues and guide strategic market planning and development of tactical marketing strategies.

skim pricing A high price position that attracts a limited number of customers but is sustainable because competitors cannot match the business's competitive advantage and value proposition.

strategic account pricing A customer price that is negotiated and managed over several years with the intent of maintaining a close supplier-customer relationship.

strategic market definition A broad definition of market demand that includes the business's served market and relevant substitute product–markets.

strategic market planning The specification of a long-run (3- to 5-year) strategic market plan that will result in specific performance objectives with respect to market share, sales revenues, and profitability over the planning horizon.

strategy implementation The actions taken to implement, track, and adapt a tactical marketing plan derived from a specific strategic market plan.

supply chain management Involves the management of the flow of physical materials, information, and money to and from a business and its suppliers and channel partners.

SWOT analysis A summary of strengths/weaknesses and opportunities/threats that are uncovered in a situation analysis.

tactical marketing strategy A one-year marketing mix strategy (4Ps) for a particular target market and specific strategic market plan.

target market A collection of customers that the business has decided to focus on in building a marketing mix strategy.

team approach The degree to which a business works across functions as a team in creating and delivering market-based customer solutions and implementation strategies.

top-down marketing budget A marketing budget based on a certain percentage of sales.

total contribution Total sales minus total variable cost of sales.

trade-off analysis Customer preferences for different combinations of price, product, service, and company benefits.

transaction value The economic value a channel partner can obtain from transactions with a company based on margin per square foot inventory (square feet), inventory turnover, and marketing expenses.

two-tier marketing channel A channel and sales system that involves two or more intermediaries.

umbrella brand A core brand that is well known and under which brand extensions can be easily introduced.

unit volume vector A projection of volume sold in 3 to 5 years based on different combinations of market growth and market share.

untapped market opportunities The gap between current market demand and market potential.

value-added resellers Intermediaries that buy products from several manufacturers and customize them for certain market applications.

value in-use pricing Pricing to create a dollar savings for a customer based on a lower total life cycle cost when compared to a competitor's total life cycle cost.

value map A graph of relative performance and relative price.

variable cost per unit All of the variable costs associated with one unit sold.

vertical brand-line extensions Variations in the brand that add more variety and options for customers.

vertical market opportunities Forward or backward integration along the supply chain that starts with raw materials and moves vertically through different stages of production, distribution, sales, and service.

volume The number of units sold for a particular product in a given period of time.

Photo Credits

CHAPTER 1

page 17, Figure 1.10: Adapted and reprinted by permission *Harvard Business Review* from "Zero Defections: Quality Comes to Services," by F.F. Reichheld and W. Earl Sasser, Jr. (September–October, 1990). Copyright © 1990 by the President and Fellows of Harvard College; all rights reserved.

CHAPTER 4

page 83, Figure 4.2: Ad courtesy of the Weyerhaeuser Corporation. page 87, Figure 4.5: Adapted from Forbis, John, and Nitin, Mehta. "Value-Based Strategies for Industrial Products," *Business Horizons* (May–June, 1981) 32–42. page 88, Figure 4.6: Ad courtesy of Sealed Air Corporation. page 90, Figure 4.7: Ad courtesy of Rohm and Haas Company.

CHAPTER 5

page 122, Figure 5.10: Advertising and photo courtesy of DuPont.

CHAPTER 6

page 149, Figure 6.11: *Source:* PIMS Database, Strategic Planning Institute, Cambridge, MA. page 149, Figure 6.12: Used with permission of US West Media Group. page 152, Figure 6.15: *Source:* PIMS Database, Strategic Planning Institute, Cambridge, MA. page 153, Figure 6.16: *Source:* Best, Roger J., Del I. Hawkins, and Charles M. Lillis, "Building a Value-Based Pricing Strategy," Working Paper (1994), University of Oregon. page 154, Figure 6.17: *Source (left side): Marketing Models* by Kotler & Lilien, © 1992. Adapted by permission of Prentice-Hall, Inc., Upper Saddle River, NJ. *Source (right side):* PIMS Database, Strategic Planning Institute, Cambridge, MA.

CHAPTER 7

page 166, Figure 7.1: Ads courtesy of Loctite. page 170, Figure 7.6: *Source:* Garvin, David. "Competing on Eight Dimensions of Quality," *Harvard Business Review* (November–December, 1987):101–105. page 182, Figure 7.13: *Source:* PIMS Database, Strategic Planning Institute, Cambridge, MA.

CHAPTER 9

page 237, Figure 9.15: *Marketing Models* by Kotler & Lilien, © 1992. Adapted by permission of Prentice-Hall, Inc., Upper Saddle River, NJ.

CHAPTER 10

page 263, Figure 10.14: Ad courtesy of Gardenburger. page 247, Figure 10.4: Ad courtesy of Johnson Controls, Inc. page 249, Figure 10.5: Adapted from Bender, David, Peter Farquhar, and Sanford Schulert. "Growing from the Top," *Marketing Management* (Winter/Spring, 1996):10–19. page 250, Figure 10.6: *Source:* Zielske, H. "The Remembering and Forgetting of Advertising," *Journal of Marketing* (January, 1959):140. page 254, Figure 10.8: Adapted from Reibstein, David. "Making the Most of Your Marketing Dollars," Drive Marketing Excellence, Institute for International Research, New York, NY, 1994. page 258, Figure 10.11: *Source:* Bemmaor, Albert, and Dominique Mouchoux. "Measuring the Short-Term Effect of In-Store Promotion and Retail Advertising on Brand Sales," *Journal of Marketing Research* (May, 1991):202–214.

CHAPTER 13

page 308, Figure 13.5: *Source:* PIMS Database, Strategic Planning Institute, Cambridge, MA. page 309, Figure 13.6: *Source:* PIMS Database, Strategic Planning Institute, Cambridge, MA. pages 310–311, Figures 13.8 and 13.9: *Source:* PIMS Database, Strategic Planning Institute, Cambridge, MA. page 312, Figure 13.10: *Source:* PIMS Database, Strategic Planning Institute, Cambridge, MA.

Index